NO
CRYSTAL
STAIR

CONTRIBUTIONS IN AFRO-AMERICAN AND AFRICAN STUDIES

NO CRYSTAL STAIR

Black Life and the *Messenger*, 1917-1928

Theodore Kornweibel, Jr.

Contributions in Afro-American and African Studies,
Number 20

GREENWOOD PRESS
Westport, Connecticut
London, England

To the Memory of my Father

Library of Congress Cataloging in Publication Data

Kornweibel, Theodore.
  No crystal stair.

  (Contributions in Afro-American and African studies ; no. 20)
  Bibliography: p.
  Includes index.
  1. The Messenger (New York, 1917-1928). 2. Negroes—Social
conditions—To 1964. 3. Brotherhood of Sleeping Car Porters. I. Title.
II. Series.
E185.5.M582K67   301.45'19'6073   75-16967
ISBN 0-8371-8284-0

Library of Congress Catalog Card Number: 75-16967
ISBN: 0-8371-8284-0

First published in 1975

Greenwood Press, a division of Williamhouse-Regency Inc.
51 Riverside Avenue, Westport, Connecticut 06880

Printed in the United States of America

Well, son, I'll tell you:
Life for me ain't been no crystal stair.
It's had tacks in it,
And splinters,
And boards torn up,
And places with no carpet on the floor—
Bare.
But all the time
I'se been a-climbin' on,
And reachin' landin's,
And turnin' corners,
And sometimes goin' in the dark
Where there ain't been no light.
So, boy, don't you turn back.
Don't you set down on the steps
'Cause you finds it's kinder hard.
Don't you fall now—
For I'se still goin', honey,
I'se still climbin',
And life for me ain't been no crystal stair.

"Mother to Son," Langston Hughes, 1926

Contents

Acknowledgments

I owe many debts of gratitude for assistance in the preparation of
this book. Thomas C. Holt, Marilyn Leonard, A. Philip Randolph, C.
Duncan Rice, and the late Arna Bontemps and James W. Ivy all read
portions of the manuscript in its dissertation form. Thanks go to those
participants in the events described here who graciously allowed me interviews; they are listed in the bibliography. The following individuals
responded to various inquiries: Harold Anthony, Jr.; Herbert Aptheker;
Thomas L. Dabney; Archibald J. Carey, Jr.; Kenneth Kusmer; Claude
Murphy; Allan Spear; Perry C. Thompson; Theodore Vincent; Fred P.
Wall; Carl S. Matthews; Bernice Wilds. The staffs of the following were
helpful: James Weldon Johnson Collection, Yale University; Manuscript
Division, Library of Congress; Chicago Historical Society; Tamiment
Institute; National Archives; Moorland Foundation Library, Howard
University; Schomburg Collection, New York Public Library; A. Philip
Randolph Institute; Easton (Pa.) Public Library. I would also like to
add appreciation to Ronald Robbins and Daniel Evans for their cheer-
ful and expert reference services. Grants from the Ford Foundation

and Lafayette College provided financial aid, the latter paying my research assistant, Cornell Wright. Thanks for secretarial labors go to Mrs. Arlene Ahles, Hilda Cooper, Claudette Dahlinger, Betty French, Faith Shireman, Bernice Turner, and especially Marilyn Kastenhuber. Finally, members of my family have furnished sustenance, cheer, and encouragement throughout the entire project.

Preface

Times of true opportunity have been few for the black community in the United States. While more favored segments of the population have enjoyed frequent periods of mobility and progress, only rarely before the present has such a period come to blacks, and then only embryonically. One such time was the Reconstruction era, another the period between 1915 and 1929, the era of World War I. In this latter span new opportunities opened as they had not since the years of flux and change following the Civil War. For the first time in two generations there was renewed hope, based on some measure of reality, coursing through the bloodstream of black America. Whether permanent gains could be won from these times of change remained to be seen.

This era of new prospects was due largely, directly and indirectly, to the Great Migration, the movement of one and a half million peasants out of the South and into the urban centers of the North and Midwest. The possibilities for change were enormous. Perhaps the most immediate, most easily recognized prospect was for a new economic life, as thousands entered, for the first time, a money economy. What would the consequences of expanded job opportunities mean? Perhaps, if foreign immigration were to slow down or cease, a labor shortage would provide leverage whereby the race might extract new concessions or rights from the country at large. Perhaps the coming of black workers to the North in large numbers, sometimes working side by side with whites, would encourage the already powerful white labor movement to take a serious interest in their aspirations and problems. Perhaps black laborers who for years had worked as helpers, silently learning the skills of those they aided, would now begin to mount the ladder of upward mobility in industry and gain increasingly skilled positions.

There was also the prospect that a freer, healthier, more stimulating social atmosphere might be found in the North. What would be the effect on the self-esteem of masses of people who had lived so long under the yoke of physical oppression and psychological repression? Some perceived the advent of a new racial militancy, of new manners of speaking and new avenues of protest. These possibilities, certainly, were only real in the North, at least at the beginning; but might not changes and progress come to the South, if only by indirection? As the migrations increased, as the human flood in some years became an exodus, and as the agricultural labor supply of the South in consequence decreased, might there be changes in the Southern social structure? What cracks might develop in the racial status quo as its economic base was threatened? There were those who professed to believe that every North-bound migrant was, ultimately, striking a blow for the brother or sister left behind. And indeed for a time it seemed that the South, recognizing the danger, might attempt to reexamine its traditional treatment of black people and move to retain them, not by oppression, but by improvement, through liberalization.

One of the greatest hopes in this period of expansion and change was that new political bargains might be struck, that a new degree of participation in national political life might be won by the race. War was looming on the horizon; might black loyalty and full participation in whatever role the country chose rebound to its benefit? If the record was not entirely clear on this hope—the Civil War example was ambiguous at best—black leadership nonetheless acted as if new rights would be won and with few exceptions joined the colors with enthusiasm when war finally came. Another aspect of the possible political bargains had to do with the Republican party, the only party of consequence to all

but a handful of the race. The GOP was out of power. Could black votes
concentrated in city wards rectify this? If so, if blacks could help restore
the Party of Lincoln to power, what would be the rewards? The race
had a long list of possibilities: antilynching legislation, enforcement of
the War Amendments and protection of voting rights in particular, and
an end to degrading segregation. On the other hand, if the party system
was itself in flux, was there some leverage to be utilized through third
party activity? Perhaps the Socialist Party might be mobilized for an
assault on racism if it were given the prospect of a million new urban
voters. Alternatively, the threat of defections to a third party might
impel the two major parties to tend their own fences and offer meaningful concessions to the race as the price of loyalty or conservatism.

Race leadership too was in flux and ferment after 1915. Booker T.
Washington was dead, and all the conflicting views and perspectives so
long pent up were now released, free to seek their own high ground.
Much depended on the anti-Bookerite school, unfortunately middle
aged and too inured to negativism in opposing the Tuskegee viewpoint.
But perhaps new ideas and strategies would be born out of a more open
atmosphere. And with the heavy hand of the Tuskegee Machine about
gone, there emerged fresh opportunities for journalism to enter and
spark debate. New periodicals would be started with encouraging fre-
quency, and if many did not survive infancy, a few did. Could a youthful, independent press, not tied dogmatically to the past of either Washington or W. E. B. DuBois, become a new beacon of progress, a lantern
of hope, even a bellweather of rapid and radical change?

Finally there were prospects for a renewal of racial nationalism. With
old leaders dead or obsolete, with old ideologies no longer "official"
ideologies, with a newly concentrated urban population that might form
the basis for a mass movement or mass action, there were possibilities
aplenty. In the realm of culture the previous twenty years had witnessed
a slow but steady building, and if successful writers had often been fet-
tered by the strictures and stereotypes of white taste, the likes of James
Weldon Johnson and Paul Lawrence Dunbar nonetheless proved as much
to their own race as they did to whites. Might not this foundation be
built upon to develop a new black culture, or at least a distinctive black
culture? As for political or economic nationalism, the field was wide
open. Again, owing in good part to the death or moribundity of older

leadership, the air was clearing for the sounding of new ideas, new strategies, new goals and visions. The war would help here, giving blacks a fresh perspective on themselves and on the rest of the colored world. Were there possibilities for, was there merit in, ties with Africa? If so, should they be cultural, spiritual, economic, or even, as some said, military?

It was a wide-open world for black Americans in the late teens and early twenties, or so it might appear. Change was a matter of course. The theoretical possibilities seemed almost endless. There was, initially at least, cause for considerable optimism. But matters did not turn out as hoped; prospects dimmed rapidly. New ideas and new strategies found the traditional barriers of racism not significantly weakened by the wartime changes and upheavals. And the hoped-for unanimity of purpose within the race proved disappointingly illusory.

The country at large did not turn out to be "thankful" for blacks' participation in World War I. Black civilians and soldiers alike expected that the victorious doughboys would be greeted with open arms, symbolically and in actuality. But whites made it all too clear, as soon as the victory parades had passed, that the racial status quo had changed not a whit and that the "social equality" enjoyed in Europe was a horrible aberration not to be repeated at home. If this was not sobering enough, the ensuing Red Scare and its violations of personal liberty, so lustily applauded by the majority of the population, showed clearly that the country was in no mood for radical thought and radical talk, whether by Bolsheviks or by militant black people. Repression became the course of the day, and no minority viewpoint was exempted.

What was perhaps even more important in betraying the promise the race had perceived was the fact that no significant part of the white Establishment was interested in or willing to take responsibility for the social consequences of the migrations and war service. Neither capital, labor, nor government took it upon itself to integrate the black population into the mainstream of life—not to integrate in the narrow sense, but to provide the openings and tools whereby the ex-peasants could meld into the body politic and contribute along with all other groups without being singled out by race. But government was indifferent to social distress among all groups. Capital freely, often happily, made use of the thousands of nonunionized black workers but took precious few steps to encourage healthy race relations between black and white laborers and did not, with a handful of exceptions, use its influence in the larger community to work for better housing, better education, an overall improved social atmosphere for its new employees.

Organized labor was equally shortsighted, preferring to shut its eyes to any commonality of interest between black and white proletarians, and instead treated black labor as alternately a pariah and a scab class. The labor movement was on the defensive anyway and in no mood to battle its own membership for the principle of unionizing Negroes. In fact it was little interested in any unskilled workers, of whatever color. The Republican party, too, was not motivated to sponsor any amelioration or beneficial change. Blacks were cruelly disappointed when the return of the GOP to national power did not result in "recognition" but rather a continuation of the erosion of the race's "influence." Not even all the traditional "Negro positions" were handed back to party hacks. Those who did cash in again on party largess were as venal or ineffective, sometimes both, as before the war. Their power was nil, their only privilege being that of distributing minor patronage and holding honorary but powerless offices. As for remedial legislation, the Republican party, not the Democratic, earned the larger share of blame for sabotaging enactment of an antilynching statute.

The nonpolitical black leadership class proved unable to cope with the modern world and singularly uninspired in finding solutions to the new problems facing the race. Much of the leadership continued the twin emphases of moderate civil rights in the North and racial conciliation with slow economic improvement in the South. But the times demanded something different, and whatever it was, the well-known figures—men like DuBois, Kelly Miller, Robert R. Moton, Emmett Scott, George E. Haynes, T. Thomas Fortune, and William Monroe Trotter—could provide no imaginative solutions. The leadership still reflected the Talented Tenth—that small minority of the race possessing educations, professions, and relative financial security—and only dimly understood the changes that were coming to black life in this open period. Leaders did not, above all, comprehend the need for new economic organization, for getting the race on a secure economic basis *first*, before an assault on segregation and disfranchisement could be mobilized. The old leaders, too, did not feel an urgency for all-black organization—black-led, black in goals, black in strategy—if the race was to bring itself to a position of demanding power and influence in pluralist America. But how could men like Moton and Haynes and DuBois, themselves so much the creations of white opinion or bound up in white-influenced activities, understand that the day must soon come when blacks and blacks alone would choose their own leaders and disregard white opinion and wishes, when blacks would similarly choose their own ideologies? Unfortunately the unique opportunity that arose in this period, the Garvey movement, was the victim largely of its own mistakes. Racial-political nationalism, which was on one level as promising as any alternative in the postwar world, disintegrated through a failure to concoct an American program to go along with its international goals. Internecine warfare—between Garveyites, the communistic African Blood Brotherhood, noncommunist black radicals, and the bourgeois leadership establishment—in the end killed all possibilities for a real mass movement for a decade. Only cultural nationalism began to fulfill the promise of the new era. The Harlem Renaissance was and is a glowing event in black history, but it had essentially no meaning for the masses. Cultural nationalism alone, at least that modeled along "formal" lines, could not begin to solve the race's problems.

Such, then, were the race's possibilities and disappointments in the teens and twenties. One offspring of this period was a singular magazine called the *Messenger,* edited by two young ex-Southerners, Chandler Owen and A. Philip Randolph. Their monthly, founded in 1917 and lasting to 1928, is not only an important voice but a particularly useful eye in examining these years. It was both participant and mirror. It involved itself in debate and action on all the issues and opportunities important to the race in the wartime and postwar years. Since the magazine unabashedly took sides on all questions, it provides a convenient starting point from which to examine the prospects for change and the reasons for the black community's failure to compel such transformation from the white community. Through the eyes of the *Messenger* one sees, with depressing clarity, that whatever the promise, whatever the optimism, life for the black population in the teens and twenties, as even the youthful Langston Hughes knew, was "no crystal stair." But like that mother speaking to her son, the magazine never quite lost its optimism. Life had not fulfilled its promise. But was there not a better prospect in the future?

1 | World War I and Black Dissent

One summer night in 1918 two young black men were speaking to a crowd in Cleveland as they had in several other cities. While one inveighed against the World War and pointed to the hypocrisy of "making the world safe for democracy," the other circulated through the audience hawking copies of their periodical, the *Messenger*. As always, Justice Department agents were in the crowd, and this night they did more than take notes. One agent approached the podium and placed the speaker under arrest while his companion was similarly apprehended in the audience. The charge against the two was treason.

Neither the arrest nor the charge was unexpected. The two radicals, Chandler Owen and A. Philip Randolph, knew that America's involvement in the war had voided personal liberties and given license to a xenophobic superpatriotism. They must have known that conscientious objectors to the war, as they themselves were, were being tortured and hung from their wrists at Fort Leavenworth; that vigilante action was being visited on all manner of radicals and ethnic and racial minorities; that Eugene Debs had been similarly arrested a few days before; that unpopular speakers of all persuasions were subject to mob suppression

3

and police brutality. The arrest was no surprise. The fact that bail was refused until a high-powered Socialist party lawyer, Seymour Stedman, arrived to handle the defense, was also not particularly shocking. Owen and Randolph got off easily, ludicrously: the judge before whom they were brought refused to believe that the two twenty-nine-year-old "boys" could possess the knowledge and intelligence to write the inflammatory editorials presented as evidence by the prosecutor, and preferred to think that unscrupulous persons had used the names of the two to cover their real identity. Showing both judicial and racial paternalism, the judge dismissed the charges and, so he thought, sent the two home to their parents. Safely out of the courtroom, they proceeded instead to their next speaking engagement, by then minor martyrs in the antiwar movement.[1]

Why was there such concern about two young hotheads mounting soapboxes here and there, agitators who, as the New York *Age* complained, "for months have stood on the street corners in Harlem and vilified those with whom they differed politically." The *Age* gleefully detailed the pair's arrest and the subsequent order for Owen to report for army service. (Randolph was spared induction because he was married; had the war lasted much longer, he too would probably have been called.) Relief over the government's attention to the two men must have run deep, as one newspaper soon after Randolph's arrest labeled him the "most dangerous Negro in America."[2] That an obscure young man should suddenly be catapulted to such notoriety indicates the depth of the country's concern, in the middle of a war to ensure a more democratic world, that somehow black Americans could not be counted on for unequivocal patriotism. Were blacks less than totally loyal, asked whites, both professional jingoes as well as more thoughtful citizens. The news coming out of the Black Belt and the northern ghettos was not altogether comforting.

The day before the United States entered World War I the front pages of the nation's dailies told a most disquieting story: German agents were making a particular effort to encourage disloyalty among blacks and even to incite them to rebellion. The New York *Herald Tribune* headlined "German Negro Plots Feared in Six States." Alleged conspiracies had been uncovered by federal agents in Alabama, Georgia, and the Carolinas in which blacks were being taught disloyalty and given encouragement to migrate to the North; in response, local whites were forming Klan units to meet possible uprisings. In Jacksonville, Florida, the citizenry was on edge over rumors of a German plot to arm the blacks. Federal authorities in Louisiana and Mississippi were also said to have uncovered evidence of German plots in which blacks had been promised the vote and complete social equality for their support of the German cause. Nor was the North being spared the efforts of alien agents. The same newspaper solemnly reported that influential Harlemites had told the authorities about a cultured white man, ostensibly a Dutch sociologist, whose real occupation was spreading the pro-German virus. He was said to have mingled freely with the population, made several trips into the South, and had several persons under his direction. In conversation he stressed that "his country" practiced no race distinctions and appeared surprised that blacks could bring themselves to salute America's flag and sing its national anthem.

All this was disquieting enough. But another front page story on the same day must have been even more frightening. This concerned the so-called Plan of San Diego. Rumors had been floating around for some time about a plot to seize Texas and establish an independent republic. The perpetrators—German agents, professional Mexican revolutionists, black agitators, and Japanese agents—were said to have cooked up this scheme two years previously when they met in San Diego, California. The following day, fortunately, brought some relief when the press reported that the Plan of San Diego was not what it appeared to be. First of all, the Germans had nothing to do with it. Second, neither did blacks. It was, in fact, the brainchild of embittered Mexican-Americans in San Diego, Duval County, Texas, who proposed an uprising to effect a return to Mexico. Sensing the need for additional numbers, they included the local black population in the scheme, without, however, bothering to consult that group. The scheme was discovered and the conspirators fled after a brief alarm among whites over a possible massacre.[3] But that reassuring news would not quiet the fears of black disloyalty, for on the same day other reports rekindled the apprehensions of already worried patriots.

This time the scene was set in Birmingham, where the authorities arrested two men, one white, one black, who were posing as Bible salesmen and ministers, but in fact, it was believed, were urging blacks in several Southern states to migrate to Mexico. Special trains would be ready to take them in a week. In that same city, on the same day, another black individual was arrested in the local railroad terminal for having made speeches urging his race to work on behalf of Germany. This news, coming on the day Congress declared war on Germany, could not have been anything but unsettling. Birmingham was apparently a hotbed of unrest, for two days later another dispatch told first of two whites believed to be German agents who were circulating in the nearby mining regions and persuading black laborers to leave for Mexico, as well as two more blacks jailed on charges of treason for allegedly urging blacks to side with Germany in the war. The same day, a Boston African Methodist Episcopal (AME) minister was quoted as saying that he had learned of enemy activity in his own city; a German agent had been telling blacks not to enlist. After urging that the spy be brought to justice, the preacher let it be known that he would enjoy being allowed to shoot the miscreant after he was duly convicted.[4]

And so it went; from time to time throughout the war, the reading public was regaled with rumors that boiled down to German or other subversive activity among a black population that seemed peculiarly vulnerable to such blandishments. In mid-1917 reports from Washington indicated that there was a campaign afoot to send anonymous postcards and letters to blacks urging them to rise against whites and promising that Germany would draw no color line when it won the war. The Green Corn Rebellion in Oklahoma in August 1917 provided more disquieting news. In April of the following year a whole rash of rumors and reports fueled a continuing undercurrent of concern about black loyalty. Early in that month reports out of the South told of the workings of "German money" in Lexington, Mississippi, and Memphis, Tennessee. This was the story of a black preacher who had recently built a $25,000 home in Memphis and whose congregation in Lexington had just erected a $10,000 brick edifice. How else could blacks collect such large sums, if not from German sources? The link here was that the minister, the Reverend C. H. Mason, was alleged to have been preaching pro-German sermons and advising resistance to the draft. And, not by coincidence, a foreigner by the name of Demitrius Giannokulion was said to have conducted meetings for a week in Lexington and to have "received a message in code." Readers were left to draw their own conclusions. When interviewed by the authorities, Mason freely admitted that he preached conscientious objection in his church, but maintained he was not advising unlawful resistance, only encouraging his parishoners to apply for a legal status. To many patriotic Americans, of course, conscientious objection was merely another form of disloyalty. Coming from blacks in the South, was it perhaps even more pernicious? The black New York *Age*, for one, didn't think so; it was of the editorial opinion that charges of German money being used for subversive purposes were ridiculous. The more important thing to investigate was the fact that Southern draft boards seemed to be inducting all black registrants whether they were fit or not, so as to fill their quotas and exempt whites.[5]

In mid-April 1918, white New Yorkers were regaled with unsettling news in their own backyard. Ever-alert federal agents had uncovered the activities of one Max Freudenheim, who claimed he was an Austrian with eighteen years' residence in the United States. The authorities were confident, however, that he would be shown to be a German. Freudenheim worked as an insurance collector in Harlem and the Bronx, where he gathered weekly ten-cent premiums from black policy holders. His *modus operandi,* it was alleged, was to engage clients in conversation about the war and then tell them that Germany was bound to win. He also claimed that Germany had acted benevolently in East Africa and thus could be depended on for honorable intentions if American blacks helped the Central Powers. In fact, a victorious Germany would set up a colony exclusively for blacks in the American South, guarantee social equality for those who wished to remain in New York City, and establish somewhere in the world a great state where Negroes would be supreme. Germany was soon to invade the country, he said, so blacks must quickly choose which side they were on. The authorities suspected that Freudenheim was only one of several agents operating in the metropolitan area, and their successful penetration could be gauged from the fact that more than a few persons had reported pro-German statements in and around Harlem.[6]

The Freudenheim stories were elaborated a few days later when several dailies brought forth new evidence of German subversion, not only in Harlem, but also in the San Juan Hill section on the West Side. Rumors were circulating that black troops in the American Expeditionary Forces in France were being used only as shock or sacrifice troops; that black troops were being abused by white officers; that the Germans had threatened to torture to death any captured blacks. Most alarming to the public was the rumor that in a certain unnamed New York hospital lay two hundred black soldiers whose eyes had been gouged out and their limbs cut off after being captured by the Huns. That such rumors were extremely dangerous was widely acknowledged, and a prominent Harlem politician, the dentist E. P. Roberts, was quoted as saying that the most active rumor centers were the several German-owned saloons in upper Manhattan.[7]

Finally, soon after the Armistice, all the allegations of German subversion among blacks were brought together, if not exactly proved, in the hearings of a subcommittee of the Senate Judiciary Committee, which eventually produced three volumes of testimony on the *Brewing and Liquor Interests and German and Bolshevik Propaganda.* Most of the information on activities to subvert black loyalty was given by Captain George B. Lester of the Army Intelligence Service. Lester gave not one specific as to which black leaders were influenced or what black newspapers received or printed German propaganda. But such picayune details seemed unnecessary. The German propaganda machine, Lester charged, was under the direction of a Dr. Albert; this apparatus had a separate department for Negro matters, which kept records of all lynchings and interracial clashes—anything "which showed the alleged oppression of the colored race." Based on this evidence, the propaganda bureau then produced articles that were sent to both black and white newspapers. In addition to written propaganda, field operations were carried out in 1915 and 1916, although high wages apparently made the German arguments less forceful.

German subversion was carried out, according to Lester, not primarily by Germans, but by specially trained "Mexicans and halfbreeds" who received their instruction in Mexico and were then sent into the Black Belt. Their primary task was to stir up trouble between blacks and whites, although the preaching of pro-German propaganda was not neglected. For this purpose local black leaders, whom Lester never named, were subsidized as well as given the usual propaganda about lynching, discrimination against black soldiers, and Germany's honorable intentions toward colored peoples. Overall control of this effort, it was alleged, was centered in the hands of the German consul in Chicago, and after war broke out, of the minister to Mexico.[8]

What should we make of the allegations, throughout the war, of dangerous German activities among the country's black population?

Concerning Captain Lester's testimony in particular, we have the opinions of two New York newspapers, one the leading white daily, the other the most influential black weekly. The august, Republican *Times* reported that enemy propaganda in the South was so intense that "the Germans not only followed the negroes into the cotton fields and mills, but also into the army." Subversion in the South was relatively unsuccessful, because of high wages and job opportunities in the North, but the effect of propaganda on the army became a very serious matter as stories of atrocities and discriminations spread. The *Times,* then, took all this very seriously, as did much of the rest of the white press. Compare, on the other hand, the analysis of James Weldon Johnson, well-known race figure and columnist for the New York *Age.* Noting that Lester nowhere gave specifics as to names and particular activities, Johnson concluded that there was no evidence to demonstrate a serious German impact on the black population. Rather, the whole scare should probably be chalked up to "a panicky state of mind due to [white] guilty conscience." Blacks never were in any way pro-German, said Johnson.[9] He was, strictly speaking, correct. There is no concrete evidence to show such activities. But there *was* enough antiwar sentiment within the black population to stir fears of treason and subversion. After all, could most Americans, black or white, be expected to differentiate between pro-Germanism and antimilitarism in the course of one of the most stridently xenophobic wars in the country's history?

If ever the "paranoid style" applies to a description of American politics and public expression, the World War I era qualifies.

As in the past, the belief in conspiracy provided an excuse for closing ranks and for renewed dedication to a selfless cause. . . . Over two hundred thousand citizens enlisted in the American Protective League, described by its official historian as "a vast, silent, volunteer army organized with the approval and operated under the direction of the United States Department of Justice, Bureau of Investigation." This meant that anyone who was deprived of shooting Huns in France could at least defend his country by taking secret oaths and becoming a member of a local vigilante society; he could then spy on his neighbors, report "disloyal utterances," and perhaps help send an I.W.W. sympathizer to a concentration camp.[10]

The federal government's concern over disloyalty predated official American entry into the conflict. Before April 1917 the Attorney General instructed all federal attorneys to keep vigilance and enlist the aid of urban police forces in watching known pacifists and German sympathizers. The Secretary of War assigned small contingents of troops to strategic positions near immigrant populations and industrial centers. When the Attorney General asked loyal Americans to become "volunteer detectives" and report any suspicions of disloyalty or subversion, the response was in the thousands, although most of the rumors proved groundless. George Creel's Committee on Public Information published advertisements asking patriots to "report the man who spreads pessimistic stories . . . to the Department of Justice." (To reach blacks in its propaganda efforts, the CPI assigned Ralph W. Tyler, an Ohio journalist and Republican wheelhorse, to its staff.) In sum, the entire country was to be mobilized behind both a total war effort and total conformity to official views on the war.[11]

With this mentality given public sanction, it should come as no surprise that black Americans, too, were sucked into the vortex of popular hysteria, xenophobia, and paranoid suspicion. After all, nativism and intolerance of the foreigner and foreign, subversive ideas were no white Anglo-Saxon monopoly. Booker Washington had several years before warned against the increasing southern European immigration, fearing that it would create new racial problems in the South by setting up job competition with the darker race. To other blacks the European immigrant was prone to lawlessness and ill-equipped to fit into the fabric of American society. Blacks, as well as whites, feared that Europe was dumping its socialistic labor on American shores. When the Russian Revolution made Bolshevism a topic of household discussion, blacks generally disapproved of it as did most whites. It is probable that blacks tended to compensate for their second-class position in America by demonstrating their loyalty to the American system through 100 percent Americanism and nativism. These were time-honored methods of affirming one's citizenship. Black leadership, of both the Bookerite and DuBoisian schools, believed that racial uplift was the key to the country's racial problem—that as blacks improved themselves, displayed intelligence and industriousness and cleanliness and, yes, loyalty—they would eventually gain enough sympathy from the "quality" white folks who counted that true racial equality would be won. In effect this was to be a purchase. Might not black patriotism buy black progress? Many blacks thought so, not only those who took the stories of German subversion seriously, but also those who discounted them as hysteria. And of course the reverse might be true. As Emmett Scott saw it, if the race failed to prove its Americanism totally, to take its part in the fight, then it might lose the momentum of racial progress: "The moment the American Negro failed to perform all of the duties of citizenship, he immediately abdicated the right of claiming the full privileges of citizenship."[12]

The nationally known black figures, as well as the major community institutions like the uplift organizations and the press, backed the war effort, although some of them only took such a position after an initial period of skepticism. But the important generalization here is the near unanimity at the leadership level in backing the war effort to the hilt and countenancing no action or utterance that would impede that effort. For all the criticism he suffered for his "Close Ranks" stance, W. E. B. DuBois spoke for an important segment of the educated and middle-class-oriented population. But he spoke for much less of the total population than he supposed: as will be demonstrated later, a considerable stream of both antiwar sentiment and plain apathy lay not far beneath the surface of black America. But these trends have been overshadowed by the attitudes of the better-known individuals and institutions, concerning which the evidence has always been more accessible.

The protest and uplift organizations lined up behind the war with few qualms. The most hesitation came from the smallest of the national groups, William Monroe Trotter's National Equal Rights League. The Boston (home) branch pointed out that blacks were bitter over the country's discriminations and would likely fight with more enthusiasm if they were promised better treatment, but it firmly rejected any thought of taking up arms against the country. Trotter personally thought that the war would provide opportunities for all subjugated and oppressed groups to gain relief. In addition he saw the war as the chance to redeem the race's military record that had been unjustly sullied in the Brownsville Affair. It should be noted that while Trotter personally supported the war, he was not about to put aside the race's grievances; on the contrary, he called DuBois "a rank quitter of the fight for our rights" after the latter's "Close Ranks" editorial. Trotter

was enough of an independent that he could support the war effort
yet respect and aid pacifists like Randolph and Owen; he was the only
individual in Boston who was willing to preside at one of the *Messenger*
editors' antiwar meetings.[13]

The major protest organization, the National Association for the Advancement of Colored People, had no official qualms about the war, although some members of its top leadership did have reservations. But
officially the organization was worried lest the country come to believe
that German agents were enjoying success in appealing to blacks. If the
white public came to this view, the association warned the black press in
a confidential memorandum, the oppression of blacks under the guise of
martial law was a real possibility. Furthermore, if whites believed that
blacks were disloyal, then blacks would be excluded from the draft and
the right to serve in the army. Nothing should stand in the way of blacks'
making every effort faithfully to serve their country, for this would be
rewarded in the postwar world. So the association urged the black media
to declare their unequivocal loyalty to the country and in the process
downplay any stories about German propaganda among blacks. And despite his reservations before American entry, DuBois's editorials in the
Crisis during the war gave blacks abundant reasons for supporting the
war.[14]

The National Urban League gave the most cooperation of any black
group to the war effort, making no bones about where its loyalty lay.
One of its self-appointed tasks was to sustain black labor morale so as
to ensure production of necessary war materials. This role put the league
dangerously close to apologetics for autocratic management, as in the
case of its cooperation with the Newport News Shipbuilding and Dry
Dock Company. The league was impressed with the sincerity of the
company in hiring blacks and made little protest against its policy of
paying blacks considerably less than the prevailing white wage. In addition to serving as a funnel for black labor, the league also encouraged
war bond drives, aided draft boards in their deliberations, and cooperated with other government agencies.[15]

Perhaps of equal service to the war cause was the loan of the Urban
League's most important black member, social worker George E. Haynes,
to the Department of Labor to serve as director of the Division of Negro
Economics. Haynes's nearly impossible task was somehow to encourage

cooperation between black and white labor and between black workers and white employers, and his office too often proved to be incapable of preventing discrimination by both white unionists and unenlightened elements of the federal bureaucracy. Probably most effectual in allaying workers' discontent by propagandizing their crucial part in the war effort, Haynes was a frequent, if conventional, speaker at patriotic rallies.[16]

Two other figures, more prominent than Haynes, played important roles in sustaining black patriotism and denying allegations of black indifference to the war and its goals. Emmett Scott, an intimate of the Tuskegee circle and longtime official of Howard University, was appointed a special assistant to the Secretary of War. Scott was a fortunate choice, for, in the words of one recent historian, he was "an old hand at dampening Negro dissent." He cooperated with George Creel's Committee on Public Information in arranging conferences for important black figures, cranked out releases for the black press, set up a speakers bureau that included nearly every prominent name associated with black pulpit, press, and politics, and delivered patriotic speeches himself. In addition Scott was the funnel through which black soldiers' complaints of discrimination or other indignities were to be handled. Scott managed to make some minor progress against draft board discrimination, but he found that Secretary of War Newton D. Baker, above all, wanted him to avoid trouble by not tampering with racial folkways in attempting to extend black soldiers' rights. Whether he managed to be more than an apologist for the War Department is an open question. From Scott's perspective, however, blacks could not legitimately demand their full rights unless and until they fully performed their patriotic duties.[17]

If there was a public figure of a reputation to rival DuBois, it was Robert Russa Moton, successor to Booker Washington as principal of Tuskegee Institute. Moton was quoted soon after the declaration of war as saying that "this is our country and it is our flag. We are one people, black and white, North and South. Internal misunderstandings are wholly domestic matters; but when a foreign nation insults the American flag and kills our citizens, white or black, that is an entirely different matter. The negro is patient and forgiving, but a brave and loyal fighter." This was the "Close Ranks" philosophy expressed in Southern conciliatory terms. A little over a year later Moton expressed

the optimism shared by almost the entire black leadership establishment: the war was opening up vast opportunities, and white attitudes
toward the darker race were becoming perceptibly more generous. Given
such changes, "we cannot believe these sincere exponents of world democracy mean that the Negroes . . . should not be given an equal chance
to live, to work, to secure any education, and to ride on public convey-
ances, without embarrassment and under conditions equal in comfort
and safety to that enjoyed by any citizen." It was not a time to agitate,
but to "serve in the great struggle for democracy"—abroad, of course.[18]

Seconding these national figures, taking their examples and exhorta-
tions to the masses, was the black press. A mood of restraint was typical
of black journalism in wartime, even despite the humiliations of the
Houston executions and the tardiness of the federal government in moving toward equal opportunity in the armed forces. A fighting quality
would come to this press in the postwar months, stimulated by all the
unfinished and unfulfilled issues of the war, but during the hostilities
it was overwhelmingly loyal and rarely was real opposition heard. The
influential Chicago *Defender* urged that

> in common with white American citizens let us put our shoulders to
> the wheel and push with might and main to bring this war to a suc-
> cessful conclusion. If we have any grievance at home—and we have
> many of them—we will set about the task of solving these after the
> greater task of winning this war is over. To this end we can afford
> to wait patiently. Every great crisis in the history of this country
> has wrought for our betterment.

Editors were far more willing than their counterparts in World War II
to be idealistic about the effect of the war on the race's future, much
more trustful of the high-sounding slogans and propaganda for a better
future. Even the initially skeptical, like DuBois and James Weldon Johnson, were quickly turned into warm supporters. Johnson wrote shortly
before American entry to ask if blacks should fight if it came to that.
He quickly answered his own question by saying that blacks must never
cease to claim their citizenship rights, which included the right to fight
for one's country. To shirk this duty, to let any rights go by default,
was to weaken the claim to full rights. Johnson acknowledged, however,

that it was doubtful whether blacks would spring to the colors with the eagerness that had characterized past wars. When the declaration of war came, however, he was willing to overlook any personal qualms and line up behind the President, although he could not forget the injustices initiated by the Wilson administration. Emmett Scott wrote proudly soon after the conclusion of hostilities that "our editors were conservative on all current questions, at no sacrifice of courage and absolute frankness in upholding of principles." Conservative, yes; whether they were frank in upholding principles is another matter. The fight for domestic rights had abated. The black press in World War II saw this clearly and from the beginning insisted on a Double Victory effort.[19]

The major organization of businessmen, the National Negro Business League, also registered no opposition to the war. A stand in opposition could hardly come from its membership, composed of those with middle or upper status or pretensions who, perhaps more than any other segment in the black community, placed their hopes for mobility and recognition on loyal and full participation in the mainstream of American life. The leading educational institutions, too, offered no opposition; they also were geared toward placing their graduates in the American mainstream as much as white society would permit, and the success of their financing depended on maintaining the goodwill of "important whites," especially the country's philanthropists. It is probably no accident that, on the day before the country officially entered the war, the principal of Hampton Institute and the chairman of the board of trustees of Tuskegee Institute, both white men, issued statements asserting that blacks could be firmly depended on to be as loyal and patriotic as any white citizen. The black colleges were hardly bastions of dissent, and it is unlikely that any views that seriously challenged the conventional wisdom would have been long tolerated, save in exceptional institutions like Virginia Union University, which had a commendable history of rejecting accommodation and allowing expression of divergent opinions. Finally, no official declarations opposing the war came from the black religious groups. Some individual ministers opposed the war, as will be shown below, but on the denominational level there was no dissent.[20]

The leading institutions and figures of the race did not back the war effort merely out of conventional patriotism. In fact, there was a considerable rise in optimism parallel to that rise in idealism which Woodrow Wilson stimulated through his version of the war's aims. Nearly all black commentators, pro- and antiwar, felt certain that things would not be the same once the war was finished. Soon after hostilities began, DuBois wrote that blacks were bound to benefit. Suppose that blacks were not allowed to fight in the army. Then they would stream north and take the jobs abandoned by the whites going into the armed services. There would certainly be fewer whites returning than had left, DuBois noted with a touch of sarcasm. And in the process thousands of blacks would be learning lucrative trades, so it would not be so easy for white America to rob and exploit the race subsequently. If, on the other hand, the country allowed blacks to fight, and they fought well, then they would get credit for their accomplishments. And in order to be prepared for battle, the black soldiers would have to be taught the arts of war, which would surely make it more difficult for whites to lynch with impunity after the war. Either way the race would gain.

Others agreed, if not in so sanguinary terms. Kelly Miller wrote that "the Negro will emerge from this war with a double portion of privilege and opportunity," in large measure because blacks had always been devoted to good causes, as loyal to the Stars and Stripes as were the black Mammies of yore to their white folks. Robert Russa Moton, ever the Southern conciliator, said that

> there have been so many marvelous and unexpected changes in the mental attitude of stronger groups toward weaker ones, and so many efforts to bring about universal democracy, that the Negro himself has experienced much more of a genuinely friendly attitude toward himself from the white race. He has also found so many more doors open to him than hitherto, until he sometimes wonders what it all means.

The New York *Age* editorialized that great changes and evenhanded justice were soon to come; already, it was rumored, the Secretary of the Interior was considering the idea of guaranteeing every returning soldier, no matter what his race, either his previous job or a farm with forty years to pay for it. A few whites too, it seems, were thinking along similarly optimistic lines; a New York *Herald Tribune* editorial stated that the war would bring a revolution in race relations, for the country would be dishonorable if it did anything less than treat its black doughboy heroes the same as the white ones. Finally, soon after the end of hostilities, as the war histories of Emmett Scott and W. Allison Sweeney rushed into print, the dawn of the bright new day was glimpsed. Optimism among the faithful ran wild, at least until the full fruits of the demobilization and return to normalcy began to be felt.[21]

So many national figures, organizations, and almost the entire black press agreed that the race was fundamentally, almost biologically, patriotic, and that its loyalty and faithfulness would surely be rewarded; many, although not all, also agreed that there was no antiwar sentiment among blacks and that German propaganda efforts, at least on the home front, were futile. The New York *Amsterdam News* proudly stated that blacks were "almost blindly loyal to 'Old Glory,' and devoted to the only country that [they know]." Only the "ignorant and the vicious" would be influenced by German agents or be otherwise less than fully enthusiastic about the war.[22] But the *Amsterdam News* was ignoring an antiwar phenomenon that was significant, if not always fully visible. It was not pro-German sentiment; rather, it was the view either that white Americans' reasons for fighting were irrelevant to blacks, or that the war was being fought with the blood and sacrifice of the oppressed and misled for the benefit of the comfortable and safe few. Put more simply, there *was* black opposition to the war, voiced in two ways: It was either the white man's war, or a capitalists' war. Perhaps both.

It was easy to be ignorant of black apathy or cynicism about the war, for the newspapers spoke infrequently of dissent and instead printed story after story of enthusiastic responses to liberty loan drives, loyalty day parades, and participation in food conservation and Red Cross work. Precisely what proportion of the black population actively supported the war is difficult to gauge, and about all that can be said with certainty is that the image drawn in 1917-1918 and perpetuated ever since, that the whole black population flocked to the colors without hesitation, is a gross distortion. Obviously, most of the leadership needed no convincing. The Wilson administration's propaganda machine coopted much of the rest of the Talented Tenth. That same machine, very much aware of the depth of the stay-out-of-war sentiment in the 1916 election, went to work on those, white and black, who could not be convinced by a war declaration. The heavy hand of government, employed in ferreting out "conspiracies" and otherwise coercing the skeptical or apathetic, drove most dissent into silence or prudent declarations of "support" of the war. So the degree of antiwar sentiment and action that *is* visible, in both the black and white populations, is to a degree only the visible tip of the iceberg.

There are examples aplenty to suggest that genuine antiwar sentiment characterized more than a handful of the black population. George Schuyler claimed to have known many persons who publicly expressed patriotism but privately would not have shed tears had the German armies swooped down on the Black Belt. Schuyler also felt that many who heard the propaganda speeches of a George Haynes or an Emmett Scott must have been skeptical. During the course of the war he talked privately with several persons who said it made no difference to them who won the war: Germans couldn't be worse to blacks than were white Americans, and what the country needed was a good whipping.[23]

What Schuyler was talking about was a heightened political consciousness. This had been building in Harlem, for example, in the years immediately before American entry into the war, when that city was a mecca for radical ideas and questions, for reports and news on the persecutions and progress of colored people throughout the globe. For persons subject to these influences it may well have seemed ridiculous for blacks to fight in a war for democracy when they did not enjoy it at home. It is not surprising, then, that on the day before the declaration of war, recruiting officers in New York reported their concern about the lack of enthusiastic black response to the army's invitation. At other times recruiters were booed in Harlem appearances. Nor was this heightened consciousness confined to New York. The Richmond *Planet,* on at least one occasion during the war, urged blacks not to volunteer for military service and was rewarded by being banned from the mails. Professor Uzziah Miner of the faculty of Howard University Law School published a small book criticizing the hypocrisy of the wartime rhetoric and the use of black troops; naturally such sentiments had to be printed at their author's own expense.[24]

We know of other individuals, scattered throughout the country, who were voicing similar cynicisms. J. C. St. Clair Drake, father of the sociologist, told his friends that he couldn't feel much sympathy for the suffering Belgians after what King Leopold and his gang had done to the Congolese. Horace Cayton remembers that "I wasn't against the war, nor was I very bitter about the many injustices dealt out to Negro soldiers. It seems to me I felt much as all Negroes felt: this was their [white-men's] war, and since they weren't willing to accept us as civilians, then let them fight it. It was something that didn't concern Negroes. It was a white-folks' war." The same sentiment was expressed by a Harlemite who was asked if or when he was going to enlist in the army; he replied that "them Germans ain't done *nuthin'* to me, and if they have I forgive 'em.' " An individual drafted out of the Sea Islands responded to that question in the same way. Young William L. Patterson too was convinced it was a war for the benefit of the other race, and risked his neck in so saying. Impetuously mounting a table at an Elks picnic in Oakland, he urged that blacks take no part in the white-man's war. Unfortunately he was overheard by two black sailors who reported this to the military police, with the result that Patterson was arrested and held incommunicado for five days and only released after an NAACP lawyer came to his rescue. Back east in New York City a solitary figure among the black clergy there, the Reverend George Frazier Miller, who was also an occasional contributor to the *Messenger,* opposed the war from his pulpit and refused to fly the nation's colors outside his church. This activity, as well as the frequent favorable mention of socialism in his sermons, contributed to recurring troubles between Miller and his vestry. In Washington, D.C., the respected Reverend Francis Grimké publicly refused to buy Liberty Bonds because of the country's discrimination. Meanwhile Justice Department agents arrested nine blacks in Chicago— all residents of Greenville, Mississippi—who had fled north to escape registering for the draft. And in Lloyd, Florida, two black farmhands who were among the first men drafted in the county borrowed a shotgun and shot off fingers and an arm to make themselves unsuitable for military service.[25]

Probably the most dramatic instance of black opposition to the war was the Green Corn Rebellion in eastern Oklahoma. The tenant farmers in this cotton area were long ripe for radicalism, and socialist and IWW organizers had crisscrossed the area for several years. By 1917 the terrible poverty of the region had made both black and white croppers ripe for radical action. In the elections of the previous year they had voted against those who favored war, and they now felt betrayed by Wilson's declaration of hostilities and the draft, viewing the latter as an invitation to certain death. Turning to violence, the residents of several counties assembled in early August, cut telegraph lines, attempted to burn railroad bridges, and laid hazy plans for a march to Washington to seize the government and stop the war, planning to subsist along the way on green corn and barbecued beef. Whites, blacks, and a sprinkling of Indians made up the rebel force. The movement never passed the assembly stage, however, and within a few days local sheriff's posses had rounded up several hundred participants and the disturbance came to an end.[26]

As to the patriotism and eagerness to fight of blacks drafted into the army, we must weigh the testimony of those authors who wrote war histories for the general public—Emmett Scott, Kelly Miller, and W. Allison Sweeney—who testify to the undying loyalty of all the black troops, against a few recorded incidents to the contrary. Former lieutenant William N. Colson, writing in the *Messenger*, observed that many black soldiers were soon disillusioned after their induction, even if they had not been before that time. It didn't take them long to see that they were fighting a war for someone else—the white man—and consequently their morale suffered. It slipped so far, in fact, that to generate enthusiasm for bayonet drill the usual picture of the Kaiser was discarded and instead the black recruits were invited to eviscerate the image of a "rabid white southerner." Another commentator noted that black soldiers were often frankly told that they were fighting only for democracy in Europe, and for every one who was thus frankly advised, dozens knew it without being told. Some men became conscientious objectors while in the military, and their fate was to suffer a prison regimen at Alcatraz and Fort Leavenworth. We do not know the precise numbers of such individuals, but their persecution, on account of both their blackness and their scruples, is plainly recorded.[27]

War historian W. Allison Sweeney quotes Emmett Scott, straight from the War Department, to the effect that his bureau heard of only two black conscientious objectors, and that after being examined, it was found, their objections seemed pretty remote from their consciences. There were otherwise no black slackers or pacifists: "Negroes had no such organizations nor leaders." Sweeney was correct only about organizations. There was a considerable number of blacks who evaded the draft—a higher percentage than among whites—and some of these must have been acting on ethical principles. Several black inmates at Fort Leavenworth and Alcatraz were religious objectors. So too was the Reverend Mason of Memphis and Lexington, Mississippi. And then there were A. Philip Randolph and Chandler Owen of the *Messenger.* The two young editors both considered themselves conscientious objectors, and emphasized in their speeches and writings that blacks should not be expected to support a war for a country that continued to lynch, Jim Crow, and disfranchise them. Lying behind this was a basic and orthodox socialist faith that the war was fought by the many for the benefit of the few. Several articles in the *Messenger* railed against the war profiteers, noting that throughout history soldiers have been either chattel slaves or industrial slaves. The victims of war were legion: widows, orphans, maimed soldiers. So too were the victors: the increasing number of war-profit millionaires. The solution was to tax war profits 100 percent; this, it was claimed, would soon end any sentiment in favor of war.[28]

The *Messenger* had to be cautious in what it said about the war and to what extent it was willing to advise noncooperation. It did not take anything more outspoken than an innocuous article entitled "Pro Germanism Among Negroes" to give the postal authorities the excuse to lift the magazine's second-class permit. This article implied that blacks were apathetic to the war because "they are still so absorbed in suppressing American injustices that their minds have not yet been focused on Germany." The zeal of the Post Office Department in attacking the radical press and withholding the second-class privilege was well known. Postal officials had stated that "when in its wisdom and its patriotism the majority has spoken in legal and proper manner, every loyal member of the minority should become one with the majority." Those who would not come around did not deserve the protection of the law. Postmaster General Albert S. Burleson interfered with the mailing of several publications, including the *Nation, New Republic,* Milwaukee *Leader, Masses,* and the *Jeffersonian,* most of whose articles were quite innocuous.[29] It was only prudent, then, that Randolph and Owen confine their more radical sentiments to pamphlets and the public platform. An example of the former was a thirty-page publication entitled *Terms of Peace and the Darker Races.* In it the two argued that Germany could not be beaten

at arms, and so there must be a "peace without victory." But in achieving such a peace, all nations, save Russia, were obstacles. Not until all
governments were democratized, including the United States, could lasting peace come, for democratization would bring referenda on war policies, redistribution of wealth, and universal and compulsory education.
The real bone of contention between the opposing powers was said to
be competition for the cheap labor and rich resources of the darker
people of the world. But having studied current socialism well, the two
noted that exploitation was due to a people's weakness, not its color—
witness the Irish. The two concluded by proposing that several international bodies be set up to guarantee that fair territorial adjustments
be made, that "Africa should exist largely for the Africans," that the
British West Indies should enjoy self-government, and that the yoke of
disfranchisement and discrimination be lifted from American blacks.
The black man's problem, even in the United States, then, was an
international one, which could not be divorced from the root economic causes of the war.[30] How widely such pamphlets circulated is unknown, but it is certain that wherever Randolph and Owen lectured—
in churches, in meeting halls, or more often, on soapboxes—such materials as well as the *Messenger* were peddled.

The most difficult question to resolve is the degree to which the
antiwar utterances of individuals like the *Messenger's* editors and the
Reverend Mason struck a responsive chord in the minds of their black
listeners. Did the black masses see the war as their own fight, or as the
white man's exclusively? Randolph today believes that

> the Negro community basically was friendly to our antiwar position,
> but the leadership was not. . . . The mass of the Negro community . . .
> was against the war, but they had no way of demonstrating it except
> attending meetings that were antiwar. We held meetings all over New
> York, and Philadelphia, and around the country, and the masses of
> people came out; but the leaders were afraid.[31]

Often, he remembers, many people came to their meetings who probably had no firm positions on the war, but who wanted to hear the
discussion. Roi Ottley, similarly assessing the war spirit several decades
after the fact, also concluded that reservations about the war ran deep:

The truth is, Negroes exhibited little enthusiasm for the war—actually, their eyes were fixed on Washington, not London, Paris or Berlin. The sympathy white people felt for the invaded Belgians was not shared by Negroes, who knew too well of Belgian atrocities in the Congo. And they held British imperialism, ruling millions of their African brothers, was no less savage than German conquest of the Cameroons. Nor did they feel the United States was altogether virtuous.[32]

Although it is impossible to quantify, it is probable that a relatively large segment of the black population was simply apathetic about the war. This group might be temporarily drawn into the group enthusiasm of a Liberty Loan parade, but it might just as easily be drawn into the excitement of an antiwar street meeting. Randolph and Owen and others like them were not speaking to empty streets or churches; there was an audience that was willing to listen to their arguments, and at least part of that audience must have been receptive, else it would soon have melted away.

Owen and Randolph were frequenters of the Lenox Avenue-135th Street corner, along with the whole legion of lecturers, propagandists, and bombasts who made up the faculty of Streetcorner University. The Justice Department, as well as the amateur detectives of the American Protective League, noticed and kept tabs on the comings and goings of such orators. The former, to its credit and in contrast to the Post Office Department, recognized that it was responsible not only for law enforcement and some censorship, but also, in the greater sense, for the maintenance of civil liberties. This view was largely due to Attorney General Thomas W. Gregory. But the Justice Department could not adequately control the APL auxiliaries, nor could it, of course, license outright sedition, and it was probably inevitable that Randolph and Owen would be nabbed at some time or another.[33] Certainly the larger public was aware of the presence of radical and antiwar agitation, and it would scarcely have tolerated laxity on the part of the Justice Department. More than a few whites sensed that somehow what went on behind the walls of the country's Dark Ghettos and in its sharecropper cabins was perhaps not dedicated to complete fidelity to the country and its cause. The fundamental error of those whites who held these suspicions

is an important one. They believed that the unrest they could sense was
due to German agents, German money, German anything. Black people
could have told them better, and several did: it was American lynching,
American disfranchisement, American indignities, that made many blacks
less than fully enthusiastic about the war effort. Supporters of the war
like James Weldon Johnson and Emmett Scott knew that black morale
could slip dangerously, and they saw their task as bolstering that morale.[34] To them it was an obvious responsibility, an easily assumed
task. The fact that so many black figures took this choice so easily hardly needs further explanation. But what explains the divergent path of
the A. Philip Randolphs and the Chandler Owens?

It had already been a long journey for the two, from Southern
births to editorship of "The Only Radical Negro Magazine in America"
to persecution by the 100 percent Americanism crowd. They were products of the new social forces of the early twentieth century: the expanding vision of black people that coupled with harassments and humiliations in the Southland, made for waves of migrations northward that
have not yet ceased. Both young men came North, independently, perhaps not knowing precisely what they were seeking, certainly not envisioning the future that was to be theirs. They were unique and they
were not unique; they took a path few others took, and proved brilliant
examples of a style and ideology; yet they were on the same general
highway of hopes and aspirations as the lowliest of migrants who
never found a Promised Land in the North. But they hurried on to
assume leadership, not only of their fellow migrants, but, they hoped,
of all black people in America.

As Chandler Owen put it, both he and his colleague had grown up
in the South, had known its discriminations, ridden its Jim Crow cars,
been disfranchised, attended its segregated schools. But they fought
their way up and out. By the time of their exodus they were already
members of the Talented Tenth, that relatively privileged segment of
the black population that received a decent education and which had
both home and personality factors to propel it upward against the
rigidities of American caste. These Talented Tenth migrants were not
unaware of the significance of the break with their past and homeland.
"To presume to be an actor and creator in the special occurrence of a
people's birth (or rebirth) requires a singular self-consciousness. In the

opening decades of the twentieth century, down into the first years of the Great Depression, black intellectuals in Harlem had just such a self-concept." They called themselves New Negroes, several years before the vogue of that appellation in the mid-1920s. And they were new, in the sense that theirs was the opportunity of a destiny not previously available to large numbers of blacks. Owen and Randolph took that opportunity, shaped it to their own form and uses, and offered it to their race in the fearless journalism of the *Messenger.*[35]

Chandler Owen, "a plump, light brownskinned man," his immaculate dress setting off bright, alert eyes in a full face, was a North Carolinian, born in Warrenton on April 5, 1889. His parents enjoyed sufficient affluence to pay for a high school education at St. Paul's School in Lawrenceville, Virginia, which he left in 1907. From there his next step was again northward, to Richmond and matriculation at Virginia Union University. We may find significance in the family's choice of schools, for Union was no ordinary black college. It had been founded a year before the new century began by the American Baptist Home Mission Society, and its express purpose was to educate its charges as men, not as colored men or as ex-slaves. They were to be given the same quality education, and have as much expected of them, as would white students. Union's predominantly white faculty rejected an emphasis on industrial skills and consciously provided an education for the Talented Tenth. In racial philosophy it abjured Bookerite accommodationism and advocated liberal attitudes. The quality of the institution's education may be gauged from its products: Among the noted graduates of that period, in addition to Owen, were Charles S. Johnson, Eugene Kinkle Jones, Abram L. Harris, T. Arnold Hill, James W. Ivy, and from a slightly earlier period, the Reverend Adam Clayton Powell, Sr. [36]

From Union, Owen completed his northward progression and gained admission to the New York School of Philanthropy, the social work arm of Columbia, and later to the university's law school. He was one of the first beneficiaries of a social work fellowship from the Urban League, as well as one of the first ungrateful recipients to turn on that organization. League Fellows were provided with tuition and a monthly stipend of fifty dollars, course work at Columbia, and accreditation for field work experience. In the case of Owen the fellowship provided access to books and libraries and the company of other young scholars

and potential iconoclasts. Owen did the rest and severed his relationship
with the league, causing some embarrassment for George E. Haynes,
who had sponsored him. In 1915 Owen met A. Philip Randolph, a
part-time student at City College. The two formed a firm friendship
and shared their schoolbooks and developing ideas. Owen had learned
the ideas of Lester Ward at Columbia and exchanged them with Randolph
for his knowledge of Marx. The two spent many hours together at
Randolph's apartment (while his wife was out supporting her husband),
or else roamed the New York Public Library, studying the classics of
political sociology as well as socialism and working class history. Their
education took them as well to radical forums, both at the Rand School,
the New York City worker's university, and to the street corners where
they heard the likes of Elizabeth Gurley Flynn, August Claessens,
Abraham Shiplacoff, Hubert Harrison, Morris Hillquit, and Eugene Debs.
With the last two they would soon strike up close friendships and political relationships.[37]

   Of the sources of the pair's early ideas and outlook, none was more
important than Lester Frank Ward. Ward provided an optimistic alternative to the dreary, deterministic world view of the reigning Sumnerian
and Spencerian laissez-faire schools of sociology: to Ward conscious change
was good, possible, and far superior to unplanned or unconscious evolution.
Scientifically gathered sociological data, precisely what Owen was studying
at the School of Philanthropy, was to be the key tool in the positive
direction of social forces. In *The Psychic Factors of Civilization* Ward
detailed how social problems could be solved through governmental
action and planning. His ideal legislators would be trained sociologists.
Ward, like other thinkers that the two young men would absorb, was a
reformer and addressed himself to an audience of reformers. His proposals
were for wholesale, "structural" reforms, not mere "detailed" changes
that left the basic social order intact. Structural reform clearly meant
class changes, legislation in the interest of all groups of society, a greater sharing of the wealth of society without an absolute leveling. He
stopped short of predictions of a classless or one-class society, believing that both capitalists and laborers needed one another. But he wholeheartedly welcomed the formation of labor unions and other examples
of collective action. Finally, Ward's primary faith was in political democracy, although not formal socialism; while he welcomed the growth of
the Socialist party, he never formally committed himself to it. Socialism

erred in imposing artificial equalities on society—it was the artificiality
to which Ward objected. Socialism was an art, not a science; Ward preferred the latter.[38] All these ideas had profound impact on the lives of
young Randolph and Owen. The *Messenger* warmly supported the march
of socialism but eventually shied away from a purely theoretical doctri-
nalism. The two, like Ward, saw themselves as reformers, seeking structural changes. They shared with Ward the belief that class changes were
both necessary and possible, and that a strengthening of the position
of the laboring man was a key to this progress. If there was any one
concept that united Ward and the early *Messenger,* it was social planning
through scientific, hardnosed analysis of the prevailing social forces.
Randolph and Owen were confident that they, much more so than the
previous generation of black leaders, possessed the new intellectual tools
to understand and mold the twentieth century.

   With Ward, and to a lesser extent Marx, as their intellectual bench-
marks, the two worked out their own personal political synthesis. They
both stopped going to school by the end of 1916, feeling that they had
already gotten all the truth there was to be had from a formal classroom
experience. Joining the legion of soapbox orators and radical speakers,
propagandizing for radical labor unionism and a new political consciousness, they talked themselves into joining the Socialist party. As a team
they must have been striking. Randolph had the better speaking gift, a
trained Shakespearean voice that could reach and hold a crowd's attention. Owen was a brilliant writer and analyst, possessed a phenomenal
memory and, according to a long-time acquaintance, "unusual creativity,"
especially in public relations.[39] With these advantages they were destined
to travel far together.

   Young Phil Randolph came from a background similar to that of his
good friend in that both, from an early age, had the urge to excel and
make something of themselves, which made less significant the fact that
Randolph did not have the collegiate and graduate education that Owen
possessed. Randolph was born ten days later than Owen on April 15,
1889, in Crescent City, Florida, into a household short on material
resources but rich in intellectual and moral depth. His father was a tailor
by vocation, but by avocation a minister to several small and scattered
AME churches in the vicinity of Jacksonville. His mother supplemented
the family income with a small shop for mending and cleaning clothes.
These combined resources were not always adequate to support the

family, and more than once Phil and his older brother James stayed
home from school because they had no serviceable shoes to wear. The
two youngsters aided the family finances by selling newspapers; in their
walks to Jacksonville to pick up their wares, they encountered the region's racial folkways as they battled white newsboys for their place in
the delivery line. But these negative experiences were put into perspective by a father who taught his sons that race was a distinction that
was unimportant to God, who was himself neither black nor white,
and that it was a man's quality that mattered. Color was no determinant of either intelligence or character, he told them. What the
two accomplished in this world would depend on their own abilities
and drive. The cardinal virtues were piety, industry, respect for learning, purity of conduct, and respectability.

The Reverend Randolph had faith that his sons would accomplish
much, and gave them a boost by convincing them that education was
the key that would open up the door to success. Young Phil's intellectual curiosity was encouraged, and he made frequent trips to the
segregated public library in the colored section of Jacksonville. One
of the most inspiring works he read there was W. E. B. DuBois's *Souls
of Black Folk,* which convinced him to aspire to become a member of
the Talented Tenth and an asset to his race. The father also bequeathed
a gift of fine English speech to his younger son. He had absorbed Shakespearean diction from visiting troups, and his son would forever after
speak with an Oxford accent. As for formal schooling, the Randolph
sons were fortunate to live in the neighborhood of Cookman Institute,
a school established by the American Missionary Association after the
Civil War and run and staffed largely by whites. But this high school
did not teach submission; it taught, as well as the materials in its text-
books, that its students must have faith in themselves and that they
could then serve other, less fortunate members of their race.[40]

In addition the father taught the sons two great virtues, one by rote,
the other by example. The elder Randolph drew on his own impoverish-
ment and told young Phil that

someday you will grow up and you will marry, you will have to take
care of your family, you will have to get a job and work at it. And
at the same time you ought to feel that you have the responsibility
to also help the great masses of black people in America to go for-

ward in fighting for and securing their economic security and their
civil rights. You can't have one without the other. Otherwise you'll
simply be a lackey. . . . You must be ready to fight for your rights.

The second lesson from his father described the power of concerted
action and unity; blacks need not be helpless, even in the face of grave
odds. Randolph tells the story:

> I remember when he went out into the night to meet with some
> other Negroes for the purpose of protecting a Negro from being
> lynched. He had a rifle . . . and he gave it to our mother. She sat
> with it on her lap and he said, "Now, you protect the boys until
> I come back. We're going to prevent the lynching of this young
> fellow." And he went and the lynching never occurred. And he
> said that the lynchers came—they were walking up and down one
> side of the street and the jail was on the other side. The Ku Kluxers
> were walking up and down just before the jail and they saw them
> [the armed blacks] on the other side of the street and apparently
> they were there for the purpose of protecting this boy and pretty
> soon they [the whites] disappeared.

Randolph adds that "now there is something that was more revolutionary than sitting down and reading Karl Marx." Both mother and father
possessed spirit and will, and this example was perhaps the young man's
most valuable lesson.[41]

Randolph received his diploma from Cookman Institute (now Bethune-
Cookman College), but the North and wider opportunities beckoned.
Saving money from his work as a railroad section hand, he journeyed to
New York City, where he rented a room in Harlem and found his first
job as an elevator runner in one of the new downtown skyscrapers. He
moved from one low-paying and menial job to another, and in the meantime enrolled in evening classes at City College. Legend has it that there
is a piece of graffiti on a West Side apartment building hallway that
says "Philip Randolph Swept Here." Whether he actually made such an
impression on any particular premises may be fanciful, but he did im-
press, negatively, a succession of employers. Several jobs ended abruptly
when it was discovered that the young laborer, appalled at the working
conditions, was trying to organize his fellow workers to gain satisfaction

of their grievances. One such job, as a waiter on a Fall River Line steamer, ended after the first trip. A similar situation occurred while Randolph
was working as a porter for the Edison Company. All the while he kept
up his studies at CCNY and was especially influenced by the philosopher
Morris R. Cohen, who gave the eager student materials to read that
proved that blacks were biologically the same as whites. Around the
same time, Randolph met Chandler Owen, and in those heady days
when the theories of Marx were receiving a respectable examination
in the nation's university classrooms, the two dug into economics,
politics, and sociology with zeal and earnestness.

Shortly before this Randolph had met and married the former
Lucille E. Green, a Howard graduate and former schoolteacher from
Virginia, who was to be a most fortunate helpmate in the next two
decades, sustaining her husband through her earnings first as a Mme.
Walker's beautician and later as the first black municipal social worker
for the city. She shared, besides the trials of a life of radicalism, his
interests in the theater. For recreation and self-development the budding
thespian hired a voice teacher to perfect his Oxford accent and organized
a Shakespearean society in Harlem, playing Hamlet, Othello, and Romeo
and giving recitals in churches and clubs.[42]

Randolph's study of socialism and his participation in the Socialist
party in the teens represent one of the most important decisions of
his life. He was an intellectual and could conceivably have cultivated
the life of the mind or become an academic. But he had the organizer's
blood in him, the activist itch. Where he worked, he organized. Where
he listened and studied, he planned and took mental notes. Lester
Ward's *Dynamic Sociology* and *The Psychic Factors of Civilization*,
Charles A. Beard's *Economic Interpretation of the Constitution*, Thor-
stein Veblen's *Theory of the Leisure Class*—these and more provided
the meat for future plans of the inseparable pair. Rand School lectures
introduced them to Morris Hillquit, who would soon draw them into
precinct work for the Socialist party. The same platform also gave them
an entrée to Eugene Debs. The attraction between the older radical and
the two young black men was mutual, and they enjoyed lengthy discussions of history, sociology, and economics. While Debs was not a
learned man in the formal sense, he was a natural revolutionist who impressed the two as having great personal strength and power as well as

the skill to show people how to take action and follow it through. Debs was a truly inspirational figure: he had gaps in his theoretical knowledge of socialism, but Randolph knew that such a "literary limitation" was of little consequence. His magnetic quality stemmed from his broad knowledge gained through direct action.[43] This lesson Randolph was later to value, as he rejected first doctrinaire communism and, at one point, orthodox socialism.

All the while Randolph and Owen were sharpening their political ideas and developing an organizational consciousness. Their first contact with socialism had been with a student group at CCNY, in which Randolph soon became a leader and frequent speaker. This led to attendance at Socialist meetings, party membership, sidewalk speaking from Harlem to Wall Street, and eventually the formation of a party branch in Harlem with Randolph and his new wife on the 1917 ticket running, respectively, for secretary of state and the state legislature.

One by-product of this was the formation of the Independent Political Council, whose original purpose was to promote clean, progressive government, but which eventually became an adjunct of Morris Hillquit's campaign organization in late 1917. The council drew together young black students with intellectual aspirations from Columbia, City College, and New York University. The group met on weekends to discuss socialism, Marxism, and to debate any important subject. This eventually proved to be a frustrating experience to Randolph, for his fellow members would not get out of the realm of the abstract into the present and practical. They were content to discuss the race's problems, or the implications of the French Revolution or the Reconstruction period, but they could not be dragged to a Socialist party meeting. Furthermore, they were, in Randolph's view, too preoccupied with race. In vain he tried to show his fellows that they could not fight for blacks alone, that they must fight for mankind, and for the multiracial working class especially. But the group refused to leave its ivory tower, refused even to invite a white speaker whom Randolph recommended. He responded, in frustration, that the struggle for a new world was an integrated struggle, that black workers could not be saved by ignoring white workers, and vice versa. White intellectuals who were committed to the abolition of racism were needed, he said, because blacks could not do the job alone. The matter ended there—Randolph never did get them to

street meetings.[44] But he and Owen learned valuable lessons from the
council about the difficulties of political organization and the pitfalls
of idle theorizing.

Concurrent with the activities of the Independent Political Council,
Randolph and Owen were involved in more down-to-earth affairs involv-
ing black labor. The young Socialists joined a small employment bureau
on Lenox Avenue that bore the prophetic title "The Brotherhood."
Soon recognizing that a major problem for recent Southern migrants
was deficient education in skills in demand in New York, the two incor-
porated a training program on the side. The problem of jobs soon took
them into the question of unionism. While looking for headquarters for
the Independent Political Council, they became acquainted with officers
of the Headwaiters and Sidewaiters Society of Greater New York, who
offered free office space in return for editing the union's journal, to be
called the *Hotel Messenger*. They accepted the offer, but their tenure was
to last only eight months because the pair persisted in editorial honesty.

Once Randolph and Owen began to interview hotel workers, they
discovered that from the common waiter's and pantryman's point of
view the headwaiters were as much an oppressor as were the employers.
The headwaiters lorded it over their "inferiors" and coerced them into
gambling in headwaiter-run crap games and purchasing their uniforms
through the headwaiters. These were in addition to grievances of inadequate wages and poor working conditions. Randolph and Owen wrote
stinging editorials against those who had employed them and quickly
found themselves out of a job. But this eight-month experience had
given them the taste for crusading journalism, and being fired by the
headwaiters did not seem to dampen their enthusiasm, for they quickly
shortened the periodical's title to the *Messenger* and published their
first independent issue in November 1917. They could count on at
least initial financial and moral support from the Socialists, for by then
they were coordinating party activities in Harlem for Morris Hillquit's
mayoralty campaign. And when Randolph and his wife were on the
ballot, the two young men recognized that street meetings and speeches
to Christian Endeavor Leagues could not hope to reach the wide audience
that was potentially theirs. A periodical could fill this gap.[45]

So by the time of the first issue of the new *Messenger* the two were
radical in the definition of the day, involved in both antiwar and Socialist party activities. They had published two booklets in 1917, *Terms of*

Peace and the Darker Races and *The Truth About Lynching*. The latter
was a conventional and occasionally bourgeois analysis of the causes
and possible remedies for mob violence. Randolph wrote on the causes,
showing how capitalism produced peonage and sharecropping; a corrupt
political and judicial system; and a captive, prostituted press, church,
and school. The result was a "social volcano" in the South, and Randolph
predicted a cataclysmic upheaval that would marvelously sweep away
prejudice along with "derelict capitalism" and "false civilization." Chandler Owen detailed more specific preventions for lynching, which included
labor organization in the South and the migration of excess labor from
that section, the political organization of Northern black voters, and
moral education for the poor illiterate Southern masses whose weaknesses for "barrooms, the gambling dens and those cesspools of corruption and ruin" enhanced their candidacy for lynching, although Owen
hastened to add that that was no justification for the horrible crime.[46]
If all this was a stock, and at times positively unenlightened, view of
lynching, it nonetheless could be useful Socialist ammunition, catering
both to the hopes for a better day and to popular prejudices about blacks.

By early 1918, then, the two were valued members of the New York
Socialist group and aspiring leaders in the black community as well. In
the spring of that year they began a coast-to-coast antiwar lecture tour.
Bundles of their magazine were freighted ahead to be sold to captive
and captivated audiences. Detention in Cleveland was only a brief halt
in the spreading of their message. After their release they went on to
Chicago, only to find that the news of their arrest had preceded them
and that the church where they had planned to hold their next meeting
was locked and the minister nowhere to be found. With the doors barred
and a large crowd waiting, some boxes were found and the meeting com-
menced in the streets. They visited other cities and held similar street
assemblies. Invariably federal agents were in the crowds and delivered
orders to tone down the rhetoric, cease attacks on the President, and
never set foot in Washington, D.C. Taking this last warning as an invitation, the two hastened for the capital and proceeded to lambaste Woodrow
Wilson with impunity, in his own backyard. But Owen's time was soon
cut short. Neither man had applied for formal exemption as a conscientious objector, and while Randolph's marital status gained him an exemption, Owen was sent to Camp Upton in September. The New York *Age*
could not conceal its pleasure that the South Carolinian had at last

been forced to "bend his efforts toward helping whip the Hun." That
removed Owen from politics and journalism until his release early in
1919. With one-half of the partnership out of pocket and the other
with speaking commitments to honor, it is no wonder that the magazine
was only fitfully published until March 1919, when a more or less regular schedule was established.[47]

What measure of men were these two, what collective personality did
they form and imprint on their publication and public appearances? They
were men quite different in temperament, but this did not make for un-
congeniality. George Schuyler, who was managing editor of the *Messenger*
in the latter half of the twenties, has painted vivid pen portraits of the
two. Owen "was a facile and acidulous writer, a man of ready wit and
agile tongue endowed with the saving grace of cynicism." He was also
"gifted in hyperbole and his sarcasm was corroding." Of the two he was
less interested in street meetings and the rough and tumble of political
organizing; he preferred instead to deliver well-organized and well-docu-
mented, if undramatic, formal addresses. He would never make a politician, for it was not in him to pander to the masses. Eventually Owen
would tire of overt political activism and end active affiliation with the
magazine about a year after his removal to Chicago in 1923. Theophilus
Lewis, also an acquaintance on the *Messenger,* agrees with Schuyler that
Owen did not have the idealism possessed by Randolph, although the
fact that he had conscientious scruples against the war indicates both
idealism and courage. His forte was in writing and publicity, and he
always considered himself a public relations expert. His mastery of words
found a place on the public platform, and after his death friends still
remembered him as a forceful debater and sought-after orator. During
the later years of his *Messenger* association he was happiest when freed
from the routine of the magazine's office and out on the road speaking
to various groups to bolster the flagging finances of the journal.[48]

Randolph, in Schuyler's words, was "one of the finest, most engaging
men I had ever met. Slender, brown-skinned, handsome, erect and always
immaculately dressed, he was undemanding and easy to get along with. He
was leisurely and undisturbed, remaining affable under all circumstances.
. . . He had a keen sense of humor and laughed easily, even in adversity."
When matters got heated in the *Messenger* office, or when unpaid bills
accumulated alarmingly, he "showed no dismay and his aplomb seemed
impenetrable. With the sonorous voice and the delivery of a Shakespear-

ean actor, he calmed all tension, anger, and insistent creditors." To nearly all his close acquaintances Randolph has represented absolute integrity, even, Bayard Rustin suggests, approaching saintliness. He has struck many as the kind of person who uses no artifices, who hides nothing behind a mask of duplicity. Talking with him has been a moving experience for many; Roi Ottley remembered that "his rumbling voice fairly vibrates the room. . . . What seems to captivate . . . is the impression he gives of being all *soul.*" Young Roy Wilkins's first contact with him as a cub reporter on the Kansas City *Call* likewise made a lasting impression. Randolph possessed as well the executive talent of managing men in difficult situations. The *Messenger* office was not always a model of tranquillity and order, but he could be depended on as a calming influence. Later, during the most difficult days of the Pullman porters' struggle, Randolph proved especially adept in keeping up the spirits and self-worth of his closest and most important subordinates. A reading of his correspondence with Milton Webster reveals a talent for giving orders without ordering, for preserving the self-respect of an individual of rugged character, and a strong sense of certitude. Randolph could manage such tact because he desired no great personal gain, preferring to live his life for causes larger than himself. In the late fifties Chandler Owen suggested to his faithful friend that he, Owen, initiate a testimonial movement to raise a trust fund to ensure Randolph an old age free of poverty. Randolph urged Owen to forget the idea, adding without self-pity that some persons in life were destined to be poor, and he was one, and it made little difference to him. Murray Kempton meant the same thing when he once said that Randolph worked for Henry David Thoreau. This persistent selflessness and idealism, which endured when the Pullman Company made several attempts to buy him off with blank checks, had taken root even before he articulated his objections to World War I. It stemmed, in fact, from his home upbringing and parental example.[49]

What a combination this "saintly" man and his iconoclastic, Mencken-esque friend made. Together the two, one a practical, often cynical man, the other a calm, peaceful, earnest individual, created a magazine that in some respects embodied their dissimilar personalities but in larger respects reflected their common persistence, dedication, and militancy. For the next decade the *Messenger* would explore nearly every alternative and avenue open to black people in the changing postwar world.

NOTES

1. New York *Post,* December 30, 1959, p. 23; Frederick G. Detweiler, *The Negro Press in the United States* (Chicago, 1922), p. 171; Marcus H. Boulware, *The Oratory of Negro Leaders, 1900-1968* (Westport, Conn., 1969), p. 119; William L. Patterson, *The Man Who Cried Genocide: An Autobiography* (New York, 1971), p. 35; *Nation* 110 (December 7, 1918): 704-705; Oswald Garrison Villard, *Fighting Years* (New York, 1939), p. 335n; Norman Thomas, *Conscientious Objectors in America* (New York, 1927); Julian F. Jaffe, *Crusade Against Radicalism: New York During the Red Scare, 1914-1924* (Port Washington, N.Y., 1972), pp. 67-69.

2. New York *Age,* September 7, 1918, p. 1; Arna Bontemps, " 'The Most Dangerous Negro in America,' " *Negro Digest* 10 (September 1961): 238; interview, A. Philip Randolph, July 13, 1972.

3. New York *Herald Tribune,* April 5, 1917, p. 1; New York *Globe,* April 6, 1917.

4. New York *Evening Telegram,* April 6, 1917; New York *Times,* April 7, 1917, p. 3; April 9, 1917, p. 2; Boston *Herald,* April 9, 1917.

5. New York *Times,* August 27, 1917, p. 7; New York *Globe,* April 1, April 2, 1918; New York *Sun,* April 2, 1918; New York *Age,* April 6, 1918, p. 4.

6. New York *Herald Tribune,* April 8, 1918; New York *Herald,* April 8, 1918; New York *Evening Telegram,* April 9, 1918; New York *Sun,* April 9, 1918; New York *Journal,* April 9, 1918; New York *Times,* April 9, 1918, p. 3.

7. New York *Journal,* April 12, 1918; New York *American,* April 12, 1918; New York *Times,* May 10, 1918, p. 8. The existence of similar rumors had been made known to the federal government a month earlier. See Emmett Scott, *Scott's Official History of the American Negro in the World War* (New York, 1969), pp. 352-353.

8. *Brewing and Liquor Interests and German and Bolshevik Propaganda: Report and Hearings of the Subcommittee on the Judiciary* (66th Cong., 1st Sess., Sen. Doc. 62) (Washington, D.C., 1919), 2: 1784-86; Chicago *Evening Post,* December 14, 1918.

9. New York *Times,* December 15, 1918, pp. 1, 10; New York *Age,* December 21, 1918, p. 4.

10. David Brion Davis, ed., *The Fear of Conspiracy: Images of Un-American Subversion From the Revolution to the Present* (Ithaca, N.Y., 1971), pp. 208-209.

11. Jaffe, *Crusade Against Radicalism,* pp. 49-50; William Hard, "Mr. Burleson, Espionagent," *New Republic* 19 (May 10, 1919): 42; Jane Lang Scheiber and Harry N. Scheiber, "The Wilson Administration and the Wartime Mobilization of Black Americans, 1917-1918," in Milton Cantor, ed., *Black Labor in America* (Westport, Conn., 1970), p. 128.

12. John Higham, *Strangers in the Land: Patterns of American Nativism 1860-1925* (New York, 1963), p. 169; Seth M. Scheiner, *Negro Mecca: A History of the Negro in New York City, 1865-1920* (New York, 1965), pp. 134-36; Carl S. Matthews, "After Booker T. Washington: The Search for a New Negro Leadership, 1915-1925" (Ph.D. dissertation, University of Virginia, 1971), pp. 67-69; *Scott's Official History,* p. 413.

13. Stephen R. Fox, *The Guardian of Boston: William Monroe Trotter* (New York, 1970), pp. 215-19.

14. Undated (sometime in April 1917) form letter, NAACP Press Committee, "To the Editors of the Colored Newspapers," Admin. File: Clippings, German Propaganda, NAACP Papers, Library of Congress; Elliott M. Rudwick, "W. E. B. DuBois in the Role of *Crisis* Editor," *Journal of Negro History* 43 (July 1958): 225ff.

15. New York *Age,* July 6, 1918, p. 2; Guichard Parris and Lester Brooks, *Blacks in the City: A History of the National Urban League* (Boston, 1971), pp. 95-96, 110.

16. Parris and Brooks, *Blacks in the City,* p. 105; John D. Finney, Jr., "A Study of Negro Labor During and After World War I" (Ph.D. dissertation, Georgetown University, 1967), pp. 160, 183, 193ff, 209; Scheiber and Scheiber, "The Wilson Administration and the Wartime Mobilization," p. 127.

17. Fox, *The Guardian of Boston,* pp. 219-20; *Scott's Official History,* pp. 346, 355-56, 361, 412, 414; Scheiber and Scheiber, "The Wilson Administration and the Wartime Mobilization," pp. 124-25; New York *Age,* October 25, 1917, p. 2; May 25, 1918, p. 2; July 6, 1918, pp. 1, 7; May 24, 1919, p. 2; Matthews, "After Booker T. Washington," pp. 97-104, 158-60.

18. "German Plots Among Negroes," *Literary Digest* 54 (April 21, 1917): 1153; Robert R. Moton, "The American Negro and the World War," *World's Work* 36 (May 1918): 74-75, 77.

19. Detweiler, *The Negro Press,* pp. 67, 69-70; Lester M. Jones, "The Editorial Policy of the Negro Newspapers of 1917-1918 as Compared with That of 1941-42," *Journal of Negro History* 29 (January 1944):

24-26 (quoting the Chicago *Defender,* May 18, 1918); New York *Age,* February 15, 1917, p. 4; April 5, 1917, p. 4; *Scott's Official History,* p. 361; Arthur E. Barbeau and Florette Henri, *The Unknown Soldiers: Black American Troops in World War I* (Philadelphia, 1974), p. 12.

20. New York *Times,* April 6, 1917, p. 11; Emma Wesley Brown, "A Study of the Philosophies of Accommodation and Protest on Five Colleges Established in Virginia for Negroes, 1865-1940" (Ed.D. dissertation, Teachers College, Columbia University, 1967), pp. 106-40; interview, James W. Ivy, December 11, 1970; W. Allison Sweeney, *History of the American Negro in the Great World War* (New York, 1969), pp. 113-14.

21. *Crisis,* June 1917, pp. 61-62; New York *Age,* December 29, 1917, pp. 1-2; July 13, 1918, p. 4; November 22, 1917, p. 4, quoting the New York *Herald Tribune;* Moton, "The American Negro and the World War," p. 74; Kelly Miller, *An Appeal to Conscience* (New York, 1969), Chapter 4; *Scott's Official History,* p. 354; Sweeney, *American Negro in the Great World War,* pp. 302-305.

22. New York *Amsterdam News,* April 11, 1919.

23. George S. Schuyler, "Our White Folks," *American Mercury* 12 (December 1927): 386.

24. New York *Herald Tribune,* April 5, 1917, p. 1; Theodore G. Vincent, *Black Power and the Garvey Movement* (Berkeley, Calif., n.d.), p. 34; Napoleon B. Marshall, *The Providential Armistice: A Volunteer's Story* (Washington, D.C., 1930), p. 12.

25. Vincent, *Black Power and the Garvey Movement,* p. 34; Horace R. Cayton, *Long Old Road* (Seattle, 1964), p. 98; Elton C. Fax, *Garvey: The Story of a Pioneer Black Nationalist* (New York, 1972), p. 74; Barbeau and Henri, *The Unknown Soldiers,* pp. 14, 204; Patterson, *The Man Who Cried Genocide,* p. 35; William M. Welty, "Black Shepherds: A Study of the Leading Negro Clergymen in New York City, 1900-1940" (Ph.D. dissertation, New York University, 1969), pp. 151-53; New York *Times,* June 8, 1917, p. 3; August 5, 1917, p. 12.

26. David A. Shannon, *The Socialist Party of America: A History* (Chicago, 1967), pp. 106-108; James Weinstein, *The Decline of Socialism in America: 1912-1925* (New York, 1967), pp. 139-40; New York *Times,* August 4, 1917, p. 8; August 5, 1917, p. 15. August 6, 1917, p. 1; Charles C. Bush, "The Green Corn Rebellion" (M.A. thesis, University of Oklahoma, 1932), pp. 1, 22.

27. *Messenger,* August 1919, pp. 23-25; January 1922, pp. 335-36; Herbert J. Seligmann, *The Negro Faces America* (New York, 1920), p.132.

28. Sweeney, *American Negro in the Great World War,* pp. 113-14,

116-17; Barbeau and Henri, *The Unknown Soldiers*, pp. 36-37; *Messenger*, November 1917, pp. 7-8; January 1918, pp. 9, 11; July 1918, pp. 11, 12, 24.

29. Harry N. Scheiber, *The Wilson Administration and Civil Liberties, 1917-1921* (Ithaca, N.Y., 1960), pp. 32-34; Hard, "Mr. Burleson, Espionagent," 42-43; " 'The Nation' and the Post Office," *Nation* 107 (September 28, 1918): 336-37; Detweiler, *The Negro Press*, p. 171; *Messenger*, July 1918, p. 13.

30. A. Philip Randolph and Chandler Owen, *Terms of Peace and the Darker Races* (New York: The Poole Press Association, 1917), pp. 5, 8, 9, 12-13, 15, 17ff.

31. Interview, A. Philip Randolph.

32. Roi Ottley, *The Lonely Warrior: The Life and Times of Robert S. Abbott* (Chicago, 1955), p. 154.

33. Scheiber, *The Wilson Administration*, pp. 42-43.

34. New York *Age*, December 8, 1917, p. 4; May 11, 1918, p. 4; *Scott's Official History*, pp. 347-48.

35. *Messenger*, October 1919, p. 11; Nathan Irvin Huggins, *Harlem Renaissance* (New York, 1971), pp. 3, 18.

36. George S. Schuyler, *Black and Conservative: The Autobiography of George S. Schuyler* (New Rochelle, N.Y., 1966), p. 137; interview, James W. Ivy, December 11, 1970; interview, Perry Thompson, October 22, 1972; interview, Claude Murphy, August 28, 1972; Registrar, Virginia Union University, to James W. Ivy, November 14, 1972, in writer's possession; Brown, "Philosophies of Accommodation and Protest," pp. 106-14; Jervis Anderson, "Early Voice," *New Yorker* 47 (December 2, 1972): 84; Chicago *Defender*, November 7, 1967, p. 5. Owen died penniless, in Chicago on November 2, 1967. For a short biography, see Theodore Kornweibel, Jr., "Chandler Owen," in Rayford Logan, ed., *Dictionary of American Negro Biography* (New York, 1977).

37. Parris and Brooks, *Blacks in the City*, pp. 37-38, 142, 154, 490n; Anderson, "Early Voice," December 2, 1972, p. 86.

38. Lewis A. Coser, *The Functions of Social Conflict* (Glencoe, Ill., 1964), pp. 16-19; Howard Becker and Harry Elmer Barnes, *Social Thought from Lore to Science*, 3rd ed. (New York, 1961), 3: 968-73; Charles Hunt Page, *Class and American Sociology: From Ward to Ross* (New York, 1964), pp. 54-69.

39. Anderson, "Early Voice," December 2, 1972, p. 88; New York *Post*, December 29, 1959, p. 56; interview, Fred P. Wall, August 30, 1972.

40. Anderson, "Early Voice," December 16, 1972, p. 79; James J. Flynn, *Negroes of Achievement in Modern America* (New York, 1970), pp. 236-38; "Biographical Sketch: A. Philip Randolph" (New York: A. Philip Randolph Institute, n.d.); John Henrik Clarke, "A. Philip Randolph: Portrait of an Afro-American Radical," *Negro Digest* 16 (March 1967): 17; Saunders Redding, *The Lonesome Road: The Story of the Negro's Part in America* (Garden City, N.Y., 1958), p. 249; interview, A. Philip Randolph, July 13, 1972; New York *Post,* December 29, 1959, p. 56; Richard Bardolph, *The Negro Vanguard* (New York, 1959), pp. 189-90.

41. Interview, A. Philip Randolph; Phyl Garland, "A. Philip Randolph: Labor's Grand Old Man," *Ebony* 24 (May 1969): 32; Flynn, *Negroes of Achievement,* p. 236; New York *Post,* December 28, 1959, p. 52.

42. "The Reminiscences of Benjamin F. McLaurin," Oral History Research Office, Columbia University, 1962, p. 159; Flynn, *Negroes of Achievement,* pp. 238-39; Clarke, "A. Philip Randolph," p. 17; Bontemps, "The Most Dangerous Negro," p. 237; Redding, *The Lonesome Road,* pp. 249-50; Garland, "A. Philip Randolph," pp. 32, 36; New York *Post,* December 29, 1959, p. 56; Bardolph, *The Negro Vanguard,* p. 190; Murray Kempton, "Medal for a Leader," New York *World-Telegram,* September 16, 1964.

43. Interview, A. Philip Randolph; "The Reminiscences of Benjamin F. McLaurin," p. 220; Anderson, "Early Voice," December 16, 1972, p. 79.

44. Interview, A. Philip Randolph; *Messenger,* November 1917, pp. 16-20, 28, 33; New York *Post,* December 30, 1959, p. 23. The two authored a brief pamphlet under the imprint of the council entitled "Some Reasons Why Negroes Should Vote the Socialist Ticket."

45. *Messenger,* November 1917, p. 20; Anderson, "Early Voice," December 2, 1972, pp. 88-89; Garland, "A. Philip Randolph," pp. 32-33; New York *Post,* December 29, 1959, p. 56; Sterling D. Spero and Abram L. Harris, *The Black Worker: The Negro and the Labor Movement* (New York, 1968), pp. 388-90; interview, A. Philip Randolph.

46. Asa Philip Randolph and Chandler Owen, *The Truth About Lynching* (New York: Cosmo-Advocate Publishing Co., 1917).

47. New York *Post,* December 30, 1959, p. 23; Boulware, *Oratory of Negro Leaders,* p. 119; *Messenger,* April 1922, p. 390; Anderson, "Early Voice," December 2, 1972, p. 104; "Homage to A. Philip Randolph on His 80th Birthday," *The United Teacher* (New York), May 4, 1969; New York *Age,* September 7, 1918, p. 1.

48. Schuyler, *Black and Conservative*, pp. 135-37; "The Reminiscences of George S. Schuyler," Oral History Research Office, Columbia University, 1962, pp. 100-101; interview, Theophilus Lewis, September 28, 1970; interview, Claude Murphy; interview, Senator Lewis A. Caldwell, August 30, 1972; interview, Perry Thompson; Anderson, "Early Voice," December 2, 1972, pp. 115-16.

49. Schuyler, *Black and Conservative*, pp. 135-37; "The Reminiscences of George S. Schuyler," pp. 100-101; interview, Theophilus Lewis; Chandler Owen to A. Philip Randolph, October 25, 1959, and Randolph to Owen, November 2, 1959, in possession of A. Philip Randolph Institute, New York; Roi Ottley, *"New World A-Coming: Inside Black America* (New York, 1969), pp. 248-49; Garland, "A. Philip Randolph," p. 34; *A. Philip Randolph at 80: Tributes and Recollections* (New York: A. Philip Randolph Institute, 1969), p. 25; Kempton, "Medal for a Leader."

2 | Radical Journalism and Radical Journalists

Journalism, for oppressed peoples everywhere in the modern world, has proved a potent weapon. Neither colonizers nor master races have been able totally to snuff out the spark of independence that finds expression in the printed word. The earliest black press in pre-Civil War America, recognizing its precariousness, urged its readers to solidarity, self-development and preservation, and eventually counterattack. Following the blighted hopes of Reconstruction and the long decline to the nadir, a similar expression through the black press began to take place in the opening years of the twentieth century. Again it was a call to regroup, shuffle leadership, find some more viable and hopeful strategy, above all to present a new attitude of impatience to white America. Again it was prompted by threats, if not to continued existence, at least to any promise of autonomy and progress in American life. A "New Journalism" paralleled the birth of a "New Crowd Negro"; often the same individuals were part of both groups. In the late teens this state of newness blossomed in extraordinary vigor as periodicals like the *Messenger,* the *Crusader,* and *Negro World* were born. Their spirit could not be quarantined and isolated by an uneasy white America, and soon after the war's end all black America seemed, to whites at least, to be in ferment, thinking dangerous thoughts and publishing dangerous statements. To many the culprit was the black press. Not surprisingly, the black press took special pride in that accusation.

White Americans had a rare opportunity to learn something factual and relatively unbiased about black life when E. P. Dutton published a small volume in 1920 entitled *The Voice of the Negro: 1919.* Its author was a white academic, Robert T. Kerlin, improbably a professor of English at a small college in Virginia, who was soon to be fired for his too sympathetic interest in the black race. Kerlin's book consisted mainly of quotations from the aroused black press of the latter half of 1919, when newspapers and magazines of all political persuasions reacted with anger and aggressiveness to the wave of race riots that began in the summer. Kerlin noted at the outset that to know anything about black people, one would have to read their press.[1] The implications of this statement must have been startling to many white Americans. First of all, there *was* a black press. Second, it provided a broad forum for the expression of all manner of black thought, from militancy to conciliation. Finally, and most importantly, Kerlin implied that one was not so likely to learn blacks' real thoughts, their most personal reactions, through any of the usual white pipelines; blacks talked most candidly through their own community institutions.

A rise in the tone of complaint, in the scope of complaint, was more rapid than perhaps ever before from about 1917 on, as a result primarily of two social forces: migrations out of the South and the World War. The Great Migration for the first time created a vast urban black population in this country. In the decade and a half up to the Great Depression, nearly 1.5 million Southern blacks, most of them agricultural peasants, left their native section and came north, to settle overwhelmingly, and with little choice, in the industrial and commercial cities. This concentration created a situation ripe for new voices in journalism. For one thing, it concentrated an audience and created a market as never before. Now, with more than 100,000 blacks in some cities, tens of thousands in many others, there existed the population density and diversity on which prospective publishers might count. A corollary to this was the fact that more and more blacks than ever before were now in a money economy, earning actual cash wages, having money to spend not only on the necessities of life but also on luxuries like amusements, recreation, and reading materials. Before the urban migrations, probably a majority of blacks participated in a near-barter economy centered on the sharecropping and crop-lien systems. But there was real money to spend in the Northern cities, and the exercise of this spending power was a liberating experience in itself.

The population concentration in the cities was also responsible for an increase in literacy. Schools were better and more accessible, on the whole, although they were still often "Negro schools" in philosophy if not in name. And they were schools that operated nine months out of the year, in an environment where it was less likely that younger children would be withdrawn from their classrooms to help support the family. The gradual rise in educational background, then, would pay off increasingly for the race's press. Finally, and perhaps of most significance, the move north was an expression of racial consciousness, of self-improvement, an act of defiance against white folkways. Some saw a Promised Land, although not all dreamed so unrealistically. But all saw the chance to better themselves. In a sense the migrations were selective in that the persons who migrated tended to be those most willing to take a chance on a new life and most able to perceive the American racial situation realistically, as well as those who would have a heightened sense of racial awareness. It may well be that the Great Migration siphoned off the more militant members of the race from the South. If so, then this factor alone would predict the appearance of a new tone in the race's journals.

World War I was the second major cause of a new militancy in the press. Black Americans were bombarded as never before with the rhetoric of democracy and freedom. Although segments of the white population were ambivalent about it, the black population's loyalty and active participation in the war effort seemed essential to an American victory. This new attention and participation on a higher level in American public life could not but cause an increase in reflection on the plight of the race in America, an increase in self-analysis both individually and collectively. While by and large the press held itself in restraint through the end of the war, it blossomed into aggressiveness soon thereafter.

Another by-product of the war was a more knowledgeable attitude toward international questions. Eugene Gordon, a black reporter, noticed that during the war "the more enlightened of the editors created for the first time in the history of Negro journalism an appearance of inclining toward internationalism. Russia and her experiment; Hayti and her problems. the League of Nations; France's occupation of the Ruhr; all these came as grist to the mill of Negro editorial opinion." One might add as well discussion of the fate of Germany's African colonies and the future power of Japan. Black Harlem in particular was aware of the war's implications for all peoples of color. The ground was also being prepared, for both new periodicals and for a more strident voice in those already established, by the growing numbers of soapbox speakers. The new radical press of Harlem would do much more to heighten a consciousness of Africa.[2]

The foundation for the militant journalism of the late teens was laid in the first decade of the century. An important step was the founding of the Boston *Guardian* by William Monroe Trotter in 1901. Trotter rejected the etiquette of cloaking protest in the niceties of circumspection and genteel language. Like Garrison, he was determined to be heard, and was not going to so mask his words that he risked being misunderstood. Four years later a more flamboyant newspaper was born, Robert Abbott's Chicago *Defender*. The *Defender* fearlessly exposed every lynching and indignity and still managed to circulate in the South, if sometimes clandestinely. It also pioneered yellow journalism in the black press, featuring bold, provocative headlines and an emphasis on sin and scandal. The *Defender* was above all a "tell it like it is" newspaper, and while not politically radical, it set a new standard for the black press.

A third step in the direction of a more militant press was the founding of the *Crisis,* ostensibly the official organ of the NAACP but in reality the personal fiefdom of W. E. B. DuBois. DuBois has often been called the father of militant race journalism. This unfairly ignores not only Trotter but a score of fearless editors from the nineteenth century. But DuBois was a pathbreaker in the sense that he unabashedly used the *Crisis* as a journal of opinion, often largely *his* opinion. DuBois freed himself from the theoretical restrictions of balance and neutrality and helped establish the respectability of more personal and political expression. Never one to deny his own talents, he assumed the editor's prerogatives of announcing himself the authority on countless subjects, giving vast amounts of advice and counsel and pontificating on anything that amused, interested, or annoyed him. He saw himself as both advocate and theoretician. In truth he transcended the definition of editor and assumed the roles of publicist and philosopher.

A final step in the direction of more aggressive journalism was the death of Booker Washington in 1915, which removed a major moderating influence. The Tuskegee Machine's control over the black press had been seriously eroded in the five years before Washington's death, and his successor, Robert R. Moton, had neither the influence nor the desire to try to repair the damage already done. With Washington receding into the status of a revered memory, the nation's black press began to free itself from the dead weight of racial accommodation.[3]

What has come to be called "New Negro Journalism" had its beginning in late 1917 with the birth of the *Messenger,* and its first full flowering in the space of the next twelve months as 1918 brought Marcus Garvey's weekly *Negro World,* Cyril Briggs's *Crusader,* William Bridges' *Challenge,* and Hubert Harrison's *Negro Voice.* The *Emancipator* and the *Negro Veteran* would briefly appear in the following year. The *Messenger* set the pace by breaking with traditional habits of both aggressive and defensive black journalism, providing a release for that segment of the black population that wanted to speak loudly and clearly on many of the things that had been only privately uttered before.

Aside from the *Messenger* the two most important journals were those of Briggs and Garvey. The *Crusader* was begun in September 1918 by means of a donation by the West Indian shipowner J. Anthony Crawford to Cyril Briggs, also a West Indian, who until then had been editor of the *Amsterdam News.* The donation was to fund an organization to stimulate freedom for Africa and the formation of a Negro state. Briggs was soon to turn the monthly to other interests when he became part of the small black communist nucleus and then a member of the communistic African Blood Brotherhood, which adopted the *Crusader* as its official voice. For a time Briggs and the *Messenger's* editors managed peaceful coexistence, exchanging lists of agents and subscribers, but as the *Messenger* charted increasing opposition to doctrinaire communism this amity disappeared.[4]

Garvey's *Negro World* was soon to become a truly unique black periodical, not really rivaled until the *Black Panther* in the sixties. Of all the publications of the late teens and twenties the *Negro World,* which had sections in Spanish and French, reached the most international audience, circulating not only in the United States but in the Caribbean, Central America, Europe, and in parts of Africa, not always with the permission or pleasure of white officials in these areas. Only the Chicago *Defender* rivaled it in domestic circulation. At a very early time the *Messenger* could tolerate Garvey's paper as another member of the dissenting fourth estate, but it was not long before an intense and personal opposition developed in which each side only mentioned the other to vilify it.

By mid-1919 the new militance had infected nearly the whole black press to one degree or another. "Other periodicals and newspapers began strengthening their policies relative to the questions of interracial relationship, feeling secure in the conviction that what the *Messenger* could dare, so could they." Bitterness over the summer of riots was written large over the front pages of nearly all the press. Only a few journals went to the extreme of approving complete social equality and the Bolshevik revolution, but all types of periodicals—even fraternal, missionary, and Sunday School quarterlies—featured articles on racial violence and were frank to denounce the wrongs visited on the race. Kerlin could hardly find a publication that did not overtly protest unjust conditions. The fear of being stigmatized as radical had, for the time being at least, been lost. The grievances bottled up during the war were released in a floodtide, no matter what the white public's reaction or dismay, and a new tenor was showing in discussions of the race's possibilities for the future. Most of the black newspapers editorialized on the passing of the Old Negro and called for new leadership that would display firmness, courage, aggressiveness. This was not a call for radical leadership; rather, it was a widely voiced opinion that sane, even conservative, leadership must press for the full list of the race's demands. Race traitors, Uncle Toms, and similar tale-bearers were held up to the greatest contempt.[5] There was, as never before, a "voice of the Negro," and that voice was militant, persistent, even strident. The *Messenger,* the *Crusader,* and the *Negro World* were considerably more outspoken than the old-line weekly newspapers, but they all spoke to the same grievances in similar tones of impatience, if not of remedy.

The postwar black press was entering a process of maturation. For the first time large numbers of blacks were going to their own periodicals for news and guidance, in all parts of the country, city and farm. Papers were read, reread, passed from hand to hand. The black press was both a molder of public opinion and a source of news and perspective. There was now a sizable number of competent weekly newspapers, so increasingly persons could read black news and not have to depend on the white dailies, which customarily ignored all but black crime and "humor." In a previous day one would not have encountered black newspapers on newsstands, but this, too, had changed. The Chicago *Defender* could be purchased in New York, Washington, Baltimore, and other large cities, and not merely in the colored sections of town. This expansion of marketing, to meet a new demand, benefited all periodicals, and even small-circulation ones like the *Messenger* could be found in newsshops far from home.[6]

One estimate puts the number of black periodicals in 1921 at nearly 500, a growth of about 50 since 1916. Fifty percent were newspapers (all but two weeklies); 45 percent were the organs of religions, fraternal, and educational groups; and the remaining 5 percent were a miscellany of business, medical, musical, and political publications. New York, with a black population of over 150,000, was the home of 17 publications, including 4 well-known newspapers (the *Age,* the *Amsterdam News,* the *News,* and the *Negro World)* as well as nationally circulating monthlies like the *Crisis,* the *Messenger,* and the *Crusader.* Other large cities had comparable numbers of racially oriented publications. Circulation of a few newspapers was respectable indeed. By 1922 the Chicago *Defender* printed over 200,000 copies weekly, and 6 other papers circulated over 30,000 copies per issue. Each copy of a popular journal like the *Defender* was probably read by several persons, or circulated among the patrons of barbershops and cafes. Total readership of all black publications had leapt at least 100 percent between 1915 and 1920, while advertising grew apace. The existence of a national black press association, an Associated Negro Press Service, and other clipping services, again points to increasing maturity. The ANP, founded in 1918, distributed black news nationwide, so important racial stories could now appear simultaneously all over the country. On the business side more and more capital was being invested, and black publishers and editors were increasingly inclined to see journalism as a profession, something from which to earn one's living, not just a hobby or intellectual pastime. There were still weaknesses—a shortage of investment capital and a great lack of black printing establishments capable of putting up a newspaper—but these could not overshadow the strengths.[7] Black America had found a new voice. Race leadership may have been in disarray, but this mattered less and less as the black press moved increasingly into a leadership and opinion-molding role.

Magazine publication must be considered somewhat separately from the newspapers, since the monthlies encountered particular difficulties. The black public was on the whole more willing to patronize a publication that was superficial, sensational, and current rather than the more analytic, although often more aesthetically pleasing, magazines. The majority of magazines in the World War I era were subsidized by social, religious, or educational organizations, with only a small fraction independent and free of restraints on comment and content. The life of the independent black monthly was a short one; those subsidized by some larger organization obviously stood a better chance of longevity. Several attempts were made to establish family monthlies, but these all had short lives in this period.[8] Yet there was an embryonic family market, for the *Crisis, Opportunity,* and to a lesser extent the *Messenger* maintained their viability in the twenties in part by adding sports and society pages, short stories, and theater reviews.

Although common trends characterized all of the black press in the late teens, it must be stressed that important differences distinguish the various periodicals, and in this respect the *Messenger* stands out as a singular example. From the beginning it was self-consciously ultra-militant; the third issue carried the subtitle "The Only Radical Negro Magazine in America," which gave way to "A Journal of Scientific Radicalism." For roughly the first half of its eleven-year life the magazine identified itself with and propagated the notion of the New Crowd Negro. This had nothing to do, originally, with the "New Negro" ideology of the literary Renaissance; "new" in the *Messenger's* case meant a politically radical perspective on every pressing issue of the day. The *Messenger* was against the war, and after the conclusion of hostilities, against the restoration of the *status quo ante.* The magazine also opposed both major parties and despised all so-called leaders affiliated

with them. Almost every nonpolitical leader from W. E. B. DuBois to
Marcus Garvey was similarly scorned. They were all called Uncle Toms
of one variety or another, and most of them were members of an
obsolete older generation as well.

New Crowd Negro radicalism was not just negative; in its positive
emphases it welcomed the Bolshevik revolution in Russia, hinting that
such an upheaval might be good for America, and wholeheartedly embraced socialism. Radical trade unionism—either the IWW or independent
black groups—was favored. Positive government was demanded to ensure
civil liberties, guarantee absolute social equality including intermarriage,
and protect the right of blacks to arm themselves in their own defense.
In the meantime New Crowd Negroes urged blacks to leave the hated
South even though it was recognized that the North was not a great
deal more progressive. New forms of racial protest should be evolved;
the bourgeois methods of the NAACP and Urban League, it was alleged,
had failed utterly to come to grips with fundamental change. All of
these facets of the New Crowd were expressed in tones of iconoclasm
and provocation.

This brand of militancy could be repeated only so long without
tangible gains; if no positive results were forthcoming, its appeal would
surely lessen. This is what happened in the early twenties as the hopes
for radical change fast diminished. New, militant, nondiscriminatory
unions did not survive; the Socialist party grew weak after unimpres-
sive election returns and the bitter schism with the Communists; the
latter group seemed to be preoccupied with infantile tactics. Continuing months of economic depression proved less than fruitful times for
recruiting blacks to radicalism. Meanwhile the old political parties refused to run scared before the New Crowd; on the contrary, a stodgy
Republicanism joined a racist Southern Democracy to defeat antilynching legislation. Even a new protest group established by the *Messenger*
coterie failed to survive adolescence. As these disappointing realities
became more clear, the magazine was forced to reflect this unwelcome
situation. Ceasing to be "A Journal of Scientific Radicalism," it called
itself "The World's Greatest Negro Monthly." At the same time it became more sympathetic toward previously despised institutions, particularly black business and the AFL, and perforce came to focus on a
somewhat different readership. The original *Messenger* had been aimed

at black and white intellectuals and radical-minded workers. By 1923 it was shifting toward a Talented Tenth and Black Bourgeoisie orientation although still retaining a black-worker perspective. More space was given to "culture" and the literary Renaissance was greeted, if not embraced. Long panegyrics to successful black entrepeneurs and a business and industry page became regular features. Society and sports news plus items of interest to women and children gave the magazine a family orientation.

This evolution was arrested in 1925 by a rechanneling of the energy of the two editors. Chandler Owen left New York for Chicago in 1923, and although still on the masthead, he only occasionally contributed to the magazine thereafter. More importantly, Randolph accepted the call to be chief organizer of a fledgling union of Pullman porters. The *Messenger* now became the official organ of the Brotherhood of Sleeping Car Porters, and while most of the more bourgeois changes that had come to the magazine in the previous two years were retained, much of the remainder was given over to Brotherhood news and exhortation. Political commentary suffered a severe decline, and some issues had no editorials at all. By late 1927 the masthead carried the subtitle "New Opinion of the New Negro." It was no longer the "greatest" black magazine and in fact had to struggle more than ever to survive; it finally succumbed in mid-1928 as the Brotherhood reached its own nadir.

It is astonishing that the magazine survived for eleven years, for from the first it operated on a shoestring. In the most radical years, from 1917 through 1921, revenue trickled in from several sources. Sales alone were never enough to support the magazine. So the editors held benefits, sold five-dollar shares of "stock" (it was alleged by critics that whites bought the largest portion), and drew moral and financial support from the Socialist party, which regarded the magazine as a valuable addition to the radical press. Outright contributions ranging from $1,200 on down, came from labor groups, particularly an IWW local and various needle trade unions in New York. There were, however, no large individual contributors. And available evidence indicates that support from the socialist unions dried up after 1924.

In mid-1925 new revenue appeared as the magazine became the official organ of the Pullman porters. New subscriptions arrived and the general budget of the union subsidized the magazine to some extent.

Later in the same year came the biggest windfall of all: $11,200 from the Garland Fund (American Fund for Public Service). Young Charles Garland, who believed that one had no right to enjoy money unless one earned it, set up a fund to give away his million-dollar inheritance to unpopular causes. With the new monies the magazine paid off some, if not all, of its debts, hired a secretary-treasurer-bookkeeper, and spruced up the publication with new features and colored covers. But the funds were all too soon exhausted, and support from the Brotherhood dwindled as that organization came on hard times.[9]

Revenues from advertising were rarely sufficient to cover the deficits from low sales. Up to 1920 about half the ads were taken by Harlem small businesses and mail-order firms, the other half consisting of announcements for radical groups and periodicals like the Rand School, *Gale's Magazine, The Agnostic,* and the *Crusader.* The years 1921 and 1922 saw a decline in radical-political advertisements. There were a few ads, but the income from this source was certainly insufficient to carry the magazine. By 1923 the radical advertisements had all but disappeared, mirroring the shift away from radicalism of the magazine itself, but the more sympathetic view toward black business ushered in the most flush advertising period of the *Messenger's* history. Big black business—cosmetics, insurance, banking, and publishing—bought full- and double-page ads. These revenues were supplemented in 1923 and 1924 by a large volume of paid labor greetings from sympathetic liberal unions that appeared in the New Year's, May Day, Labor Day, and Christmas issues. But these two types of revenue did not last.

At about the time the *Messenger* became the organ of the Brotherhood, the large business ads ceased, and ironically, the complimentary messages from the unions also ended. Thereafter advertising revenues were meager at best, and had the BSCP not sustained the magazine it would surely have folded much sooner. Keeping the magazine afloat was a continuous and onerous task. The finances of both the *Messenger* and the parent Brotherhood were so precarious in 1926 that when Randolph's mother died while he was organizing in Oakland, there was no money for him to buy a ticket to return east for the funeral. When Chandler Owen was still actively working for the magazine in the early twenties, he spent much of his time "on the road" speaking to audiences and trying to drum up new subscriptions. It was a slow, uncertain process, and sometimes outright donations had to be solicited. This too could be frustrating, even humiliating; Randolph tells the story of writing to Ethel Waters for a contribution and being told to see her at the Cotton Club in Harlem where she was performing. Randolph arrived at the appointed hour, only to be refused admission, as were all blacks not employees or performers. He finally had to pass word to Miss Waters through an obliging employee and meet her outside the club.[10]

The two editors found that, in addition to the exertions involved in securing advertising, their job was filled with petty but time-consuming irritations. The postwar months brought many problems, foremost of which was the continued denial of a second-class mailing permit. This had been revoked by the Post Office Department in mid-1918 and was not returned until mid-1921. For three years the struggling magazine had to pay first-class mailing charges on its subscriptions. A printers' strike in early 1920 did not help matters, and the postwar shortage of newsprint made for several decidedly thin, and particularly expensive, issues. The irregularity of publication during the first three years prompted gossip that the magazine was on the verge of folding, and at one time the editors complained that there was a Justice Department provocateur in their midst spreading these lies. The black press in late 1920 carried rumors that the two editors had taken bribes and misappropriated Socialist party funds, and energy had to be expended fighting these tales. At the same time, a dispute with the former office manager resulted in an adverse court judgment that required the magazine to pay nearly a thousand dollars in back salary. Finally, one eternal task, and a time-consuming one, was that of checking up on newsstands and getting paid by them for the magazines sold.[11]

It is clear that no one connected with the magazine was getting rich from it. Randolph was able to survive because his wife ran a franchised Mme. Walker beauty emporium; when that declined, she became a municipal social worker. Owen supported himself with commissions from the advertisements he sold as well as from his lecture tours. Nearly all of the staff writers were unpaid. The theater critic only got free tickets and the book reviewer the free copies sent by publishers. When George Schuyler was first hired in 1923 as full-time all-duty man, his pay was ten dollars weekly (soon raised to fifteen when he threatened to quit). There was no compensation for short stories or poems published, but this was also true of a more established and prosperous journal like the *Crisis.* The good fortune of the Garland Fund brought some improvement: Schuyler's salary was raised to twenty-five dollars, another office worker was hired, overdue bills were paid off, writers were paid as much as ten dollars for short stories, and new features were added. But flush times quickly ended, and the magazine folded in mid-1928 simply because there was no money with which to bail it out.[12]

If revenue from advertisements could not support the *Messenger,* neither could its circulation. There can be no absolute accuracy about circulation, partly because all business records were destroyed by fire. The most detailed figures given by the editors claimed that in the period from June 1919 to November 1919, certainly the magazine's most flamboyant period, sales rose to a monthly peak of 26,000, which was never again equaled.[13] By the early twenties readership had declined drastically. Subscription drives and special introductory offers to the contrary, sales during the decade probably rarely exceeded 5,000 monthly. A slight increase may have resulted from the enthusiasm for the Brotherhood, but without stirring and frightening events like those of 1919, readership remained pitifully low in comparison with figures during the Red Scare months. The *Messenger* was not alone in this regard, for the *Crisis* also suffered similar declines: from a high of 95,000 monthly in 1919, there was a quick drop to about 65,000 in the following year, and thereafter a steady decline to 30,000 in 1930.[14]

Who read the *Messenger*? The editors estimated in 1921 that readership was approximately two-thirds black and one-third white. The latter were probably liberal and radical intellectuals and members of the socialist trade unions. Roger Baldwin, Clarence Darrow, Mary White Ovington, Heywood Broun, Morris Hillquit, and Carl Van Vechten at one time or another graced the subscription list. Overseas, Ramsay MacDonald and Sidney Webb in England and individuals in Liberia, South Africa, and other parts of that continent were claimed as subscribers, while Claude McKay read the *Messenger* in London. Institutions holding subscriptions included the Library of Congress, the New York Public Library, and the Harvard, Princeton, and Radcliffe libraries.[15]

At the peak of circulation in 1919 the *Messenger* enjoyed a nearly nationwide circulation, certainly only bettered by the *Crisis* in the magazine field. Copies were sold by the thousands through dealers or agents in Los Angeles, Chicago, Philadelphia, Pittsburgh, New York, Washington, D.C., and Seattle and in the hundreds in Detroit, Richmond, Atlanta, and Boston. There was also a fairly large unpaid circulation among prisoners of both races at Fort Leavenworth. The foregoing list covers the major centers of Northern black population but does not include the majority of Southern and border-state urban areas. Credit for the large numbers sold in these cities went to aggressive dealers; where there were no such dealers there was only a small mail and newsstand circulation. Readership in the South was not as large as elsewhere, but George Schuyler remembers that the magazine enjoyed a reputation there as a journal willing to tell the unvarnished truth. In some parts of the South it was unwise to peddle the *Messenger* openly, but in relatively liberal Richmond, copies could be openly marketed, and in fact a radical student at Virginia Union, Thomas L. Dabney, sold it as well as the *Crusader,* the *Emancipator, Negro World,* and the *Challenge.*

Two other sources of distribution should be noted. From the beginning street hawkers peddled not only the *Messenger* but other new or radical periodicals whenever a crowd assembled. The first issue was sold at streetcorners while Owen and Randolph were speaking for Morris Hillquit's mayoralty campaign. After the war's end the victory parades provided large crowds where buyers might be found; the same held true later for the Garvey parades. In the early years copies were occasionally purchased in bulk by white liberal individuals or groups. The Reverend John Haynes Holmes, pastor of a large mid-Manhattan church and espouser of liberal and pacifist causes, made copies of the *Messenger* available to his parishioners on the literature table outside the sanctuary. Sympathetic labor unions similarly distributed copies to their memberships.[16]

What segments of the black population read the *Messenger?* Arna Bontemps recalled that in the twenties those in artistic circles bought the magazine for the theater criticism of Theophilus Lewis. Schuyler believes that some middle-class blacks as well as workers like the IWW dockers in Philadelphia also subscribed. It is likely, however, that the frequent antireligious statements deterred many blacks, of whatever economic status, from appreciating the periodical. It failed, therefore, to cover completely any one social class. But the *Messenger* left an impact on individuals of widely differing backgrounds and degrees of discontent. Witness the case of William L. Patterson, later a prominent figure in the Communist party. As a young law student in San Francisco in the late teens, Patterson came across the magazine in a bookstore:

> I was stirred by its analyses of the source of Black oppression and the attempt to identify it with the international revolution against working-class oppression and colonialism. This was an enriching and exhilarating experience. For the first time I was being made aware that the study of society and the movement to change it constituted a science that had to be grasped if Black America was ever to attain equal rights.

When Patterson found himself in England a few months later and was asked to write articles on the racial situation in his country he realized that nearly all he knew about black America, as well as about the Bolshevik revolution, had come from reading the *Messenger* and the *Masses* and from talks with white radicals. Patterson's tale is not unique—the *Messenger* was singularly important to other individuals as well, including several who wrote for it.[17]

Publishing a magazine, even a very political organ like the *Messenger,* proved to be more than a two-man job. Without the assistance of others, a regular monthly schedule could not have been maintained. Dozens of individuals wandered in and out of the *Messenger's* milieu over its eleven-year history, and although one could not have foretold it at the time, the masthead is a striking list of young men, just at the beginning of their careers, who would later achieve prominence in the black community. Foremost among these, of course, was Randolph. His mind and pen attracted many to the magazine. He and Owen shared the editorial duties into the early twenties, but after 1923, when Owen moved to Chicago, Randolph had to find some assistance. After 1925, when he became general organizer of the Brotherhood of Sleeping Car Porters, he spent relatively little time in the offices although he continued to write nearly all of the editorials as well as most of the Brotherhood articles.[18]

Chandler Owen began to tire of the operation after 1920. He got more enjoyment out of his lecture tours, and by 1923 he appears to have been drifting away from radicalism and socialism, becoming especially embittered at the socialist garment workers' unions because his brother Toussaint, a highly skilled tailor, had been rejected for membership as a cutter. In 1923 Owen relocated in Chicago and became managing editor of Anthony Overton's new paper, the *Bee,* while remaining on the *Messenger* masthead. For several years the *Bee* was the only black newspaper in Chicago that supported the porters' new union and Owen was a valuable asset to his friend Randolph, not only assisting the initial organizing committee of the BSCP in late 1925 but also engaging the rest of the black press in battle over the unionization issue, which resulted in a lengthy lawsuit brought by the Chicago *Whip* against both Owen and Randolph. The two editors won the suit, despite the influence and money of the Pullman Company backing the *Whip.* Meanwhile Owen involved himself in local Republican politics and in early 1928 challenged white incumbent Martin Madden for representative of Chicago's Black Belt. Owen's showing was dismal—he polled last among five candidates in the primary, garnering less than 1 percent of the tally—but he continued his association with the GOP and in later years held several party positions of influence.[19]

After Randolph and Owen, the most important figure on the magazine was George S. Schuyler; he really kept it operating after Randolph became involved in the BSCP. Schuyler, a few years younger than Randolph, grew up in a middle-class home in Syracuse and served as an officer in the army during the war. Returning to Syracuse, he joined the Socialist party, partly because it was the only intellectual group he could find. Indulging his recently discovered interest in writing, he composed press items for the party as its local educational director. Tiring of parochial Syracuse, he made his way downstate, and after floating around for a time as a Bowery bum, met the *Messenger* editors and was offered an office boy's job when Chandler Owen left on a

lecture tour in late 1922. Schuyler's prior editorial experience was
limited, but a fellow staffer remembers him as a very practical man
and a quick learner. He was just what the magazine needed; one of
the first things he did was to bring order to the ramshackle premises.
Schuyler has described its quarters then as an "office" in two tiny
rooms on the third floor of a converted brownstone. "The furnishings
were nondescript, the files were disorganized, back copies of the magazine were scattered about indiscriminately, and finding anything was a
chore." Schuyler showed a multitude of talents in running the office,
answering mail, reading manuscripts and proofs, handling subscriptions,
and distributing the finished product to newsstands. He was in fact
managing editor long before he got that title on the masthead. In addition he wrote occasional articles and a satirical column called "Shafts
and Darts," which Langston Hughes remembered as the most interesting
part of the magazine. This column was purposely iconoclastic and
spared no public figure or stereotype; favorite targets were Garvey,
DuBois, black communists, the Black Bourgeoisie, and the tendency of
successful black men to marry women of lighter complexion.[20] No
slave to consistency, Schuyler would soon marry a young white woman
from Texas whom he met through the *Messenger*.

   A number of other young blacks were attracted to the *Messenger*
who later made reputations in the wider world. Two of them, Abram
L. Harris and James W. Ivy, like Chandler Owen, were graduates of
Virginia Union University. Harris, later a noted economist, was a contributing editor from 1923 to about 1926 while at the same time
teaching and working toward a doctorate in economics and serving with
the Urban League. He wrote occasional articles and gave counsel on
matters pertaining to economics. For his services he received a small
stipend, which was a rarity for the *Messenger*. Years later he described
this period of his life as one of studying Marx and Veblen and, in general, being in "a state of social rebellion." While a student at VUU
he had been involved in an attempt to establish an integrated Socialist
local in Richmond; he was also one of the group of students who read
and distributed radical magazines like the *Messenger* on the campus.[21]

   One of Harris's acquaintances there was James W. Ivy, who one day
would edit the *Crisis*. Impressed as a student by the arguments of the
Messenger, Ivy attended a lecture by Chandler Owen at Union where

the editor invited interested students to visit the magazine's office if they were ever in New York. Upon graduation Ivy availed himself of the offer and worked in the office for a summer before returning to the South to teach. While in New York he met Schuyler and the two became friends, and in 1927 Schuyler appointed him staff book reviewer, without pay. Not only did Schuyler need someone who was dependable; he had come to admire Ivy as an intellectual and knew his passion for books.[22]

Wallace Thurman served a comparatively short time on the *Messenger,* but the fact that he was one of the bright lights of the Harlem Renaissance makes his an important name on the masthead. He took over as managing editor while Schuyler took an extended leave of absence in 1926. An aspiring writer when the Renaissance began to gain public notice, he, like many others in far-flung parts of the country, was irresistibly drawn by the magnet of Harlem. Already in Los Angeles he had tried to publish a magazine, which lasted only six months. In New York he had a series of editorial jobs, including that on the *Messenger.* While he was cynical about the magazine's radical posture, he was nonetheless happy in being able to use his friendship with other young writers, particularly Langston Hughes, to improve the literary quality of the journal. During this time there appeared many poems by the young generation of new poets as well as Hughes's first published short stories. When Schuyler returned, Thurman left the magazine although he continued to write occasional reviews of important new books; the by-line of this important novelist and playwright was undoubtedly an asset.[23] Another budding literary figure on the *Messenger,* although in a different vein altogether, was Joel Augustus Rogers, one of the most persistent students of black history of his generation. Born in Jamaica in near-poverty, with little formal education, a journalist and a Pullman porter, Rogers came to the *Messenger* on the recommendation of his friend George Schuyler. Beginning in early 1923, the magazine published his learned monthly columns on black history, contemporary events, and the colored peoples of the world. His emphases on non-American figures of history gave the magazine a more international flavor and wider audience appeal.[24]

In addition to the above, three other staff writers are of note. These individuals wrote for the magazine in its most militant, early years and added invaluable corroboration to the voices of protest raised by the two editors-in-chief. Wilfred A. Domingo, a Jamaican-born importer of tropical products, was a socialist who later joined the Communist party and handled publicity and propaganda for the African Blood Brotherhood. He wrote pieces for the *Messenger* on the future of socialism and its benefits for blacks, but severed his connection with the magazine in 1923 when he could no longer stomach the anti-West Indianism of its "Garvey Must Go" campaign.[25] Another individual who joined the staff when Domingo did was William N. Colson, a graduate of Virginia Union University and Columbia Law School and, also like Chandler Owen, an early Urban League Fellow. League official Eugene Kinkle Jones described him as "a man of somewhat radical ideas—frank, intelligent, decisive, unbending when it came to demands for opportunity on an equal basis for Negroes." Service in the American Expeditionary Forces in France as a junior officer proved embittering and led him to write a series of angry articles for the *Messenger* detailing the discriminations and indignities suffered by black troops.[26]

A third noteworthy member of the early staff was the Reverend George Frazier Miller, a man a generation older than nearly all the other *Messenger* writers, born in South Carolina in 1864. Miller was the type of person who could mention in his *Who's Who* biography an A.B. and D.D. from Howard as well as the fact that he was a Socialist. Since 1896 he had been pastor of a Brooklyn church and involved in any number of racial and radical causes. An attender at the founding session of the Niagara Movement, and a longtime NAACP member, he also helped organize the silent parade to protest lynching that marched down Fifth Avenue on July 28, 1917. During and immediately after the war black New York knew him for his debates with opponents of socialism and communism, his alleged preaching of socialism from his pulpit, and his refusal to fly the nation's flag in his church. Not unexpectedly, he wrote on socialism for the *Messenger*.[27] Miller, Colson, and Domingo were invaluable to the success of the early years of the periodical; Chandler Owen wrote in 1922 that they, along with the two chief editors, were the real heart of the magazine. It is certain that no two men alone could have put out a journal of the quality of the *Messenger* for four years, and so Owen's compliment to the three is not idle praise.[28]

The *Messenger* was more than a magazine, and its staff more than
individual writers. Together they made up an intellectual circle, a locus
of discussion and debate, of fellowship and fraternization. Saturday
afternoons at the office, particularly after it was moved to more spacious
quarters (a whole first floor!), found many of the leading intellects of
Harlem assembled to discuss any topic on someone's mind—"The Negro
Question," socialism, communism, the West Indies, Shakespeare, Shaw.
Debate was often sharp, vociferous, with many different viewpoints
represented. As Theophilus Lewis remembers the gatherings, people met
"for discussion and straightening out the affairs of the world." The
majority of attendants were of the same generation as Randolph and
Owen, few from the generation of DuBois. But age was no barrier—
even the perennial T. Thomas Fortune, who in early years was a *Messenger* target, frequented the meetings. Nor were Garveyite ties an impediment; "Sir" William Ferris was accepted by the group because it
recognized the quality of his mind and education. Despite *Messenger*
distrust of the NAACP, one would find such Association officials there
as Robert Bagnall and William Pickens. Similar but smaller get-togethers
took place at the Randolphs' every Sunday over a leisurely breakfast.
There one would find, besides the editor, his wife, Lucille, and his
scholarly older brother, James, and two or three other interesting persons. Schuyler remembers that after breakfast, about noon, they might
all emerge and join the promenaders on Seventh Avenue and end up
enjoying the vaudeville at the Alhambra.[29]

The *Messenger* was the magnet that drew these diverse minds together. It dealt, usually honestly if partisanly, with the important issues
of the day—government oppression of radicalism and Establishment
neglect of black rights, the new cultural developments, Garveyism
and the struggle for civil rights in America, black labor and black
capitalism, politics and black leadership. These issues, which form
the outline of the chapters to follow, were the major preoccupations
of the *Messenger* as it evolved from its initial radicalism toward a more
bourgeois center of gravity and ultimately into labor journalism.
Not infrequently the magazine's commentary was the most detailed
and pungent to be found in any black periodical. Bright minds, earnest voices, eloquent words, high ideals—all found a locus in the *Messenger*.

NOTES

1. Robert T. Kerlin, *The Voice of the Negro: 1919* (New York, 1920), p. x; Gunnar Myrdal, *An American Dilemma: The Negro Problem and Modern Democracy* (New York, 1944), 2: 909-10.

2. Eugene Gordon, "The Negro Press," *Annals of the American Academy of Political and Social Science* 140 (November 1928): 252; Frederick G. Detweiler, *The Negro Press in the United States* (Chicago, 1922), pp. 67, 69-70; Rollin Lynde Hartt, "I'd Like to Show You Harlem," *Independent* 105 (April 2, 1921): 335; Theodore G. Vincent, *Black Power and the Garvey Movement* (Berkeley, Cal., n.d.), p. 40; Richard B. Moore, "Africa-Conscious Harlem," *Freedomways* 3 (Summer 1963): 320.

3. Detweiler, *The Negro Press*, pp. 61-62; Elliott M. Rudwick, "W. E. B. DuBois in the Role of *Crisis* Editor," *Journal of Negro History* 43 (July 1958): 214-15, 218.

4. Detweiler, *The Negro Press*, p. 77; Dorothy Deloris Boone, "A Historical Review and a Bibliography of Selected Negro Magazines, 1910-1969" (Ed.D. dissertation, University of Michigan, 1970), pp. 96-97; *Messenger*, December 1919, p. 6; April-May 1920, p. 12.

5. Gordon, "The Negro Press," *Annals*, p. 252; Kerlin, *Voice of the Negro*, pp. ix, 11, 14, 24-27.

6. Eugene Gordon, "The Negro Press," *American Mercury* 8 (June 1926): 208; Kerlin, *Voice of the Negro*, pp. ix-x; Myrdal, *An American Dilemma*, 2: 908-909.

7. Detweiler, *The Negro Press*, pp. 1-7, 13, 28, 77-78; George W. Gore, Jr., *Negro Journalism* (Greencastle, Ind., 1922), pp. 14-19.

8. Gore, *Negro Journalism*, p. 21; Boone, "A Historical Review and a Bibliography," pp. 11-12, 27-30.

9. *Messenger*, January 1918, p. 21; May-June 1919, pp. 18-19; July 1919, p. 33; August 1919, pp. 18-19; April 1922, p. 391; New York (State) Legislature, Joint Legislative Committee Investigating Seditious Activities, *Revolutionary Radicalism: Its History, Purpose and Tactics, with an Exposition and Discussion of the Steps Being Taken and Required to Curb It* (Albany, 1920), 2: 1312, 2007; John H. M. Laslett, *Labor and the Left: A Study of Socialist and Radical Influences in the American Labor Movement, 1881-1924* (New York, 1970), p. 121; *Report and Proceeding of the Seventeenth Convention of the International Ladies' Garment Workers' Union* (Boston, 1924), 250; George S. Schuyler, *Black and Conservative: The Autobiography of*

George S. Schuyler (New Rochelle, N.Y., 1966), pp. 135-36; *Opportunity,* November 1926, p. 335; Walter White, *A Man Called White* (Bloomington, Ind., 1970), pp. 141-42; interview, Theophilus Lewis, September 28, 1970; interview, George S. Schuyler, October 16, 1970; New York *World,* July 19, 1922. A letter to the author from Miriam Allen deFord, April 17, 1971, describes the high opinion in which the Socialist party held the *Messenger.*

10. Jervis Anderson, "Early Voice," *New Yorker* 47 (December 9. 1972): 62; interview, Bernice Wilds, October 16, 1972; Chandler Owen to John Fitzpatrick, April 7, 1922, John Fitzpatrick Papers, Chicago Historical Society.

11. Detweiler, *The Negro Press,* p. 171; *Messenger,* February 1920, pp. 8, 10; August 1920, p. 64; October 1920, p. 102; November 1920, p. 129; December 1920, pp. 179-81; July 1921, pp. 220-21; August 1922, p. 467; Chicago *Defender,* October 30, 1920, p. 3; New York *Age,* October 30, 1920, p. 5; Roy Lancaster to Milton Webster, March 21, 1927, Brotherhood of Sleeping Car Porters Papers, Chicago Hist. Soc.

12. Interview, George S. Schuyler; Schuyler, *Black and Conservative,* pp. 134, 159; interview, Theophilus Lewis; *Messenger,* May 1926, p. 157; Langston Hughes, *The Big Sea* (New York, 1940), pp. 233-34; interview, A. Philip Randolph, July 13, 1972.

13. The 26,000 figure is in Detweiler, *The Negro Press,* p. 171. Circulation was frequently exaggerated in the magazine's claims. The August 1919 issue listed three separate figures: 33,000 blacks and a few thousand whites (page 10); 33,000 total, white and black (page 19); and 22,000, with 5 readers per copy (page 33). Disgruntled business manager Victor R. Daly, in his suit to recover back wages, testified that the largest circulation the magazine ever had was 21,000 in September 1919: see New York *Age,* October 30, 1920, p. 5.

14. Interview, George S. Schuyler; Rudwick, "W. E. B. DuBois in the Role of *Crisis* Editor," p. 234.

15. Detweiler, *The Negro Press,* p. 177; Abram L. Harris, "The Negro Problem as Viewed by Negro Leaders," *Current History* 18 (June 1923): 414; Charles S. Johnson, "Rise of the Negro Magazine," *Journal of Negro History* 13 (January 1928): 17; *Messenger,* April-May 1920, pp. 5-6; April 1922, p. 390; January 1924, p. 5; *Opportunity,* November 1925, back cover; Claude McKay, *A Long Way from Home* (New York, 1937), p. 67.

16. *Messenger,* January 1922, p. 336; April 1922, p. 390; November 1922, p. 529; December 30, 1959, p. 23; interview, George S. Schuyler;

interview, James W. Ivy; Detweiler, *The Negro Press,* pp. 13, 171; Thomas L. Dabney to author, September 11, 1972; interview, Katherine Batley, June 16, 1972.

17. Interview, Arna Bontemps, April 22, 1970; interview, George S. Schuyler; interview, James W. Ivy; William L. Patterson, *The Man Who Cried Genocide* (New York, 1971), pp. 30-31, 49.

18. Schuyler, *Black and Conservative,* pp. 135-36; interview, Theophilus Lewis; interview, George S. Schuyler.

19. "Reminiscences of George S. Schuyler," Oral History Research Office, Columbia University, 1962, pp. 100-101; Schuyler, *Black and Conservative,* p. 138; interview, George S. Schuyler; Brailsford R. Brazeal, *The Brotherhood of Sleeping Car Porters: Its Origin and Development* (New York, 1946), p. 21; *Messenger,* February 1926, p. 37; September 1926, p. 273; February 1928, p. 37; *Blue Book of the State of Illinois: 1929-1930* (Springfield, 1929), p. 945; Anderson, "Early Voice," December 9, 1972, p. 58; interview, Perry Thompson, October 22, 1972; Randolph to Milton Webster, April 18, 1927, and Owen to Chicago Local, BSCP, August 10, 1926, BSCP Papers, Chicago Hist. Soc.; Theodore Kornweibel, Jr., "Chandler Owen," in Rayford Logan, ed., *Dictionary of American Negro Biography* (New York, 1977).

20. Schuyler, *Black and Conservative,* pp. 113ff, 134-36, 142, 147; "Reminiscences of George S. Schuyler," pp. 69-70, 96, 141-42; interview, George S. Schuyler; interview, Theophilus Lewis; Hughes, *The Big Sea,* p. 233; George S. Schuyler, "What Chance for Negroes in Journalism," *Negro Digest* 7 (November 1948): 16; Arna Bontemps, " 'The Most Dangerous Negro in America,' " *Negro Digest* 10 (September 1961): 239.

21. *Messenger,* August 1923, p. 748; *Crisis,* April 1926, p. 272; Abram L. Harris, *Economics and Social Reform* (New York, 1958), p. xiv; James W. Ivy to the author, January 5, 1971.

22. "Reminiscences of George S. Schuyler," p. 111; Schuyler, *Black and Conservative,* p. 144; interview, James W. Ivy.

23. Schuyler, *Black and Conservative,* pp. 158-59; Hughes, *The Big Sea,* pp. 234-35; Mae Gwendolyn Henderson, "Portrait of Wallace Thurman," in Arna Bontemps, ed., *The Harlem Renaissance Remembered* (New York, 1972), pp. 149-50; miscellaneous items in the Wallace Thurman Papers, James Weldon Johnson Collection, Yale University.

24. Roi Ottley, *"New World A-Coming": Inside Black America* (New York, 1968); Schuyler, *Black and Conservative,* p. 143; W. Burghardt Turner, "Joel Augustus Rogers: An Afro-American Historian," *Negro History Bulletin* 35 (February 1972): 35-37.

25. Very little is known of Domingo. See occasional references in Schuyler, *Black and Conservative*, esp. p. 142.

26. *Messenger*, January 1923, p. 564; Arvarh E. Strickland, *History of the Chicago Urban League* (Urbana, Ill., 1966), pp. 20-21; White, *A Man Called White*, pp. 63-64; Guichard Parris and Lester Brooks, *Blacks in the City: A History of the National Urban League* (Boston, 1971), p. 119; E. Franklin Frazier, *The Free Negro Family* (New York, 1968), pp. 53-54.

27. *Crisis*, March 1927, p. 17; James Weldon Johnson, *Along This Way* (New York, 1933), p. 323; William M. Welty, "Black Shepherds: A Study of the Leading Negro Clergymen in New York City, 1900-1940" (Ph.D. dissertation, New York University, 1969), pp. 151-52; Frank Lincoln Mather, ed., *Who's Who of the Colored Race* (Chicago, 1915); Washington *Bee*, July 22, 1905, p. 5; St. Augustine's Protestant Episcopal Church, *Joint Celebration: Fiftieth Anniversary of St. Augustine's P. E. Church and Thirty Year Service of the Rector the Rev. George Frazier Miller, M.A., D.D.* (Brooklyn, 1926); New York *Age*, March 1, 1919, p. 4; March 15, 1919, p. 4; March 29, 1919, p. 4; August 2, 1919, p. 4; November 22, 1919, p. 1; December 6, 1919, p. 1; December 13, 1919, pp. 1, 2.

28. *Messenger*, April 1922, p. 391.

29. Interview, Theophilus Lewis; interview, George S. Schuyler; "Reminiscences of George S. Schuyler," pp. 71-72, 75-76; Schuyler, *Black and Conservative*, pp. 139-40, 142-44.

3 | Black Radicalism and the Red Scare

The year following the Armistice was one of social ferment and unrest, of the "Red Summer" of racial conflict and the nationwide Red Scare. Although the anti-Red hysteria emanating from government, press, and patriotic organizations focused mainly on alien, "Bolshevik," and anarchist activities, the black population was also drawn into the vortex of suspicion and accusation as prejudice increased in all sectors of American life. Since it had been widely broadcast during the war that German propaganda was achieving alarming success among the black population and that enemy agents were ready to incite blacks to attack a defenseless home front, it was not at all inconceivable to many citizens that blacks might be involved in subversive activities in the postwar months. Well-known whites claimed that domestic radicals as well as foreign agitators were attempting to stir up sentiments of race hatred and retaliation among blacks. Not a few thought that there was a significant number of influential blacks, often characterized as race leaders, who were directing their race into subversive activities. Probably the two most important sources arousing popular sentiments against radicals were the Department of Justice under Attorney General A. Mitchell Palmer and the New York State Joint Legislative Committee Investigating Seditious Activities, popularly known as the Lusk Committee, after its chairman, State Senator Clayton R. Lusk. These two agencies, through the public utterances of their chiefs, press releases, and published reports, made it their business to inform the nation of the Red menace.

The Red-hunters created a special definition of radicalism reserved for blacks. Racial radicalism was different from other varieties, not because it seemed to pose more or less of a threat than, for example, socialism, anarchism, or "Bolshevism," but because it attacked folkways as well as systems of government and economics. It was easier to defend the country against socialistic or anarchistic ideologies than it was to justify racial oppression in contradiction to constitutional guarantees and traditional liberties. Furthermore, racial radicalism was an attack from within, from a position where Americans sensed they were vulnerable. External enemies were dangerous enough, but to have to contend with internal disloyalty was especially threatening.

White Americans had good cause to suspect that blacks did not view and respect the racial status quo the same way they did. Blacks were restive, and a New Crowd Negro spirit was abroad. This restiveness derived in part from the migrations to Northern urban centers. In forsaking their rural environments for the long chance of urban life, Southern blacks were beginning to emancipate themselves from ancient folkways that restricted black self-respect and ambition. The war itself had a major influence in the emergence of a New Crowd Negro perspective. White Southerners were right when they warned that allowing blacks to serve in the armed forces would create grave problems for whites after the war, and indeed military service was mind-expanding and ultimately disillusioning for many black troops. Many black soldiers gained their first opportunity to travel outside their native regions. For the first time in American military history they had officers of their own race in appreciable numbers, although almost all were below field grade. Black soldiers quickly learned that the war against Germany was to be fought by a segregated army, although those who served in France sometimes found that white Frenchmen (and women) did not imbibe the social prescriptions underlying Jim Crow. Friendly relations with the French and a pride in the battlefield achievements of black units gave the returning soldier a confidence that he had not had before. And he expected that America, white and black, would be grateful for his service. Instead he returned to find unemployment, Jim Crow veterans' organizations, the lynching of black men daring to wear their uniforms publicly in certain parts of the country, widespread race rioting in mid-1919, and a nation on the march toward a "normalcy" known only too well to blacks. The New Crowd Negro, born in the migrations and christened in the war, reached his majority in the "Red Summer" of 1919.

Fear, anger, and the urge to retaliate stalked many a black community in the middle of 1919. Race clashes tore through both Northern and Southern cities and not a few rural areas as well. Where no actual riots occurred, fears were no less prevalent, and preparation for anticipated violence was widespread. White police in Harlem acknowledged that many of the community's black residents went about their daily business armed; taking away all the guns the police could find would not make any difference, for there were likely thousands more hidden away. Claude McKay recalled that he and other Pullman and dining car employees routinely packed pistols on stopovers in unfamiliar towns.[1]

The black press was almost unanimous by the middle of 1919 in reflecting a mood of aggressive self-defense. The stance of the Washington *Bee* was typical: "The black man is loyal to his country and its flag, and when his country fails to protect him, he means to protect himself." The emphasis here was still on lawfulness, by both races. Most papers stressed this view. The New York *Age* in commenting on the riots said that "it behooves the Negroes of the country, while steadfastly invoking the protection of the law and manfully contending for their rights under the law, to strictly maintain a position within the law. Inflammatory orations urging bloodshed and retaliation should be frowned upon and discouraged." This did not, however, preclude self-defense in the face of violent provocation. Bishop George C. Clement of Knoxville, Tennessee, gave the following advice to students of Morris Brown University in September 1919, in a widely reprinted address:

I would urge all members of my race to obey the law and keep clear of Bolshevism and all incendiary suggestions. We must demand protection of life and property by the government, which is guaranteed as the surest antidote for Bolshevism. I believe my people should defend their homes and families. Certainly this crisis calls for great moderation and self-control. We still have faith in true democracy and expect a righteous race adjustment.

Here self-defense and moderation were equally praised, with no contradiction between the two. The same was expressed by other clergymen. A Washington minister, well known for being "constructive" and an advocate of law and order, nonetheless advised his people to protect themselves when it became necessary. Henry Hugh Proctor, a black Congregationalist minister from Brooklyn and a longstanding accommodationist, nevertheless took pride in the bravery of black veterans who resisted the Huns of America in the Red Summer. W. E. B. DuBois summed up the sentiment of most of the black press and (at least Northern) leadership when he said that "we must tread here with solemn caution. We must never let justifiable self-defense against individuals become blind and lawless offense against white folk. We must not seek reform by violence. We must not seek Vengeance."[2]

The black newspaper press by August 1919 was appreciably more outspoken and militant than it had been six months earlier. But its newly found voice was moderate in tone compared to a small segment of the press that shouted its anger and dissent. There were at least six periodicals published in New York in the postwar months that were easily radical from any Establishment perspective as well as from the viewpoint of most black newspaper editors: these were *Negro World*, the *Veteran*, the *Crusader*, the *Challenge*, the *Emancipator*, and the *Messenger*. (In addition, the *Crisis* was considered by many whites, particularly Southerners, to be a dangerous publication.) It took little deviation from the status quo for whites to label black outspokenness as "radicalism." Most whites simply believed that any advocacy of racial change of which they disapproved constituted radicalism.[3]

The *Messenger* was by nearly any measurement a crusading and militant periodical, and, so James Weldon Johnson believed, the best-known and most influential black radical organ in the country. Whether

it is judged by standards of its day or our own, many of the sentiments it expressed as well as the language it used were certainly radical.
When the Justice Department and the Lusk Committee singled it out
as particularly dangerous, there was indeed some basis for this apprehension. Certainly it was the one that appealed most to, and was most
read by, intellectuals, both white and black. Its alleged sponsorship by
well-heeled white liberals made it seem more dangerous than others.
Attorney General A. Mitchell Palmer called it "by all odds the most
able and the most dangerous of all the Negro publications" and claimed
that it represented the most educated portion of radical black thought.
Both Palmer and Lusk, in their investigations and reports, devoted more
attention to it than to any of the other black journals. Quite simply, the
Messenger was a consistently frightening voice to worried whites, paragraph after paragraph, issue after issue. Moreover, its principle editors,
Chandler Owen and A. Philip Randolph, were instructors at the notorious Rand School, which the Lusk Commitee claimed was a center
for sedition and which the New York *Times*, in a "straight" news story,
accused of spreading "the reddest kind of red propaganda."[4]

The radicalism of the *Messenger* can be gauged from the articles
that the Department of Justice, the Lusk Committee, and members of
Congress considered sufficiently subversive to warrant public scrutiny.
To Lusk and Palmer the rhetoric in which the ideas were clothed was
as dangerous as the ideas themselves. The emotional and psychological
impact of radical language on the worried guardians of the country's
security should not be understated.

An editorial calculated to disturb even moderates was entitled "The
March of Soviet Government," in the May-June 1919 issue:

Still it continues! The cosmic tread of Soviet government with cease-
less step claims another nation. Russia and Germany have yielded
to its human touch and now Hungary joins the people's form of
rule. Italy is standing upon a social volcano. France is seething with
social unrest. The triple alliance of Great Britain—the railroad, transport and mine workers—threaten to overthrow the economic and political bourbonism of "Merry Old England." The red tide of socialism
sweeps on in America. South America is in the throes of revolution.

Soviet government proceeds apace. It bids fair to sweep over the
whole world. The sooner the better. On with the dance!

The same issue had other shocking pieces approving a "Negro Mass Movement," condemning the jailings of Roger Baldwin, Eugene Debs, Kate Richards O'Hare, and Ben Fletcher and criticizing black leadership for a lack of militance. Another editorial proclaimed, "We Want More Bolshevik Patriotism!" in which "the people are more articulate and the profiteers less articulate . . . which surges with turbulent unrest while men—black or white—are lynched in this land. . . . What we really need is a patriotism of liberty, justice and joy. That is Bolshevik patriotism, and we want more of that brand in the United States."[5]

The contents of the July 1919 *Messenger* followed the same general tone. A poem describing in graphic detail the lynching of a black man on a Sunday in a "Christian" country was illustrated with a drawing of the victim, hanging from a telegraph pole, being burned in a fire fueled by an American flag. The lead editorial was entitled "The Hun in America":

To the Negro, the Huns in America, [*sic*] have made the Declaration of Independence and the Constitution of the United States mere "scraps of paper." The agencies of law and order and justice are to the Negro, agencies of lawlessness, disorder and injustice. The flag for which he has fought, mocks and deserts him, while his life and property are taken away. The press and church are stirred more by Bolshevism in Russia than by anarchism and murder in Tennessee. And when the Treaty of Peace is signed, the Huns of Germany will be taken to the bosom of the Huns of America, while the Negro who fought against the Huns of Germany, is lynched.

A new Negro is rising who will not compromise, surrender or retreat a single step—a Negro with an iron will and an inflexible determination to put down the HUN in America. Law or no law, blood or no blood, lynch-law must go.

Another article urged blacks to be informed about American economic and racial imperialism in Mexico. A long analysis unfavorably compared the AFL to the IWW, while W. A. Domingo explained the proposition "Socialism the Negroes' Hope." Former army lieutenant William N. Colson discussed "Propaganda and the American Negro Soldier" and concluded that many blacks were disappointed that the United States had not been more severely chastised by Germany. Because of these statements, Postmaster General Albert S. Burleson held up the July *Messenger* for several days pending a determination whether it was seditious and thus should be denied the privilege of using the mails.[6]

The August *Messenger* began with an IWW cartoon, but what drew particular notice from whites was the suggestion that physical force be used to stop mob violence:

> Whenever you hear talk of a lynching, a few hundred of you must assemble rapidly and let the authorities know that you propose to have them abide by the law and not violate it. Offer your services to the Mayor or the Governor. . . . Ask the Governor or the authorities to supply you with additional arms and under no circumstances should you Southern Negroes surrender your arms for lynching mobs to come in and have sway. To organize your work a little more effectively, get in touch with all the Negroes who were in the draft. Form little voluntary companies which may quickly be assembled. Find Negro officers who will look after their direction. Be perfectly calm, poised, cool and self-contained. Do not get excited but face your work with cold resolution, determined to uphold the law and to protect the lives of your fellows at any cost. When this is done, nobody will have to sacrifice his life or that of anybody else, because nobody is going to be found who will try to overcome that force.

In addition an article by the Reverend George Frazier Miller entitled "Drama of the Bombs" advanced the thesis that the ruling Establishment had carried out the May Day and June 1 bomb scare and bombings in order to discredit the radical movement. Lieutenant William N. Colson continued his story of black soldiers during the World War with "An Analysis of Negro Patriotism," concluding that "intelligent Negroes have all reached the point where their loyalty to the country is conditional. The patriotism of the mass of Negroes may now be called doubtful." The same issue also contained a poem honoring conscientious objectors.[7]

Attorney General Palmer considered the September 1919 *Messenger* "more insolently offensive" than any other issue, and his fellow Red-hunters would have agreed. The lead editorial, authored by W. A. Domingo, was entitled "If We Must Die," and besides including the text of Claude McKay's poem of that name, it expressed excitement and exultation at the news of blacks' fighting back against their white persecutors in the recent Washington, D.C., and Chicago riots. These black defenders should be regarded as "courageous surgeons who performed the necessary though painful operation" of showing the country and the world that "the Negroes are determined to observe the primal law of self-preservation whenever civil laws break down." Justification for this was to be found in "the white man's own Bible that says 'Those who live by the sword shall perish by the sword.' " Two cartoons illustrated this spirit. One, caricaturing W. E. B. DuBois, James Weldon Johnson, and Robert Russa Moton, showed them advocating submissiveness in the face of rioting and lynching. The second cartoon depicted the New Crowd Negro firing on a white mob, "giving the 'Hun' a dose of his own medicine." Another contributor, exulting in the Washington riot, wrote that "for every Negro who lost his life in the race war, two white men have gone to that eternal sleep where the wicked cease from troubling and where they will think of lynching no more."[8]

The October issue of the magazine had similarly objectionable writing. A long article responded to South Carolina Congressman James F. Byrnes's warnings that the editors of the *Messenger* were Bolsheviks and advocates of political and social equality. Owen and Randolph gleefully admitted that "we would be glad to see a Bolshevik government substituted in the South in place of your Bourbon, reactionary, vote stolen, misrepresentative Democratic regime." On the issue of social equality the *Messenger* did not equivocate: "As for social equality, there are about five million mulattoes in the United States. This is the product of semi-social equality. It shows that social equality galore exists after dark, and we warn you that we expect to have social equality in the day as well as after dark." The editors promised that Byrnes would one day sup with blacks in a railroad dining car traveling through the Palmetto State. Echoing similar themes, former Lieutenant Colson wrote that the French accepted American blacks as social equals, with a resultant one to two thousand interracial marriages. In a different vein, a bitter poem by Archibald H. Grimké entitled "Her

Thirteen Black Soldiers," which DuBois had refused to print in the *Crisis,* commemorated the hanging of the soldiers implicated in the so-called Houston Riot in 1917.[9]

Other periodicals were singled out as purveyors of radicalism by worried Red-hunters, but none gained the detailed attention that the *Messenger* did. The *Crisis* received a hostile scrutiny not because its utterances were consistently seditious, but because it enjoyed a large and relatively prestigious circulation. DuBois was not a radical in the mold of Randolph and Owen, who were both good card-carrying members of the Socialist party. DuBois had socialist inclinations but no active party affiliation, was only halfheartedly in favor of the IWW, and was quite equivocal about the advance of Bolshevism. Neither did he wholeheartedly champion social equality. There is nothing to indicate that DuBois considered himself politically in the same league with Randolph and Owen; in fact, he avoided their company and repudiated their attacks on his leadership. And irrespective of what his personal principles and beliefs may have been, DuBois was held in rein by the board of directors of the NAACP, which was apprehensive lest he use the *Crisis* as a personal forum. Some board members were also genuinely fearful of the rise of radical influences among blacks.[10]

DuBois was probably the best-known black figure in America, and this Owen and Randolph had to bear in none-too-silent envy. They must have found consolation when the Attorney General branded the *Messenger* as far more dangerous than the NAACP's publication. Both Palmer and Lusk were hard put to label the *Crisis* subversive, although they recognized that the few "seditious" utterances they found in its pages reached a far wider audience than did the incessant rhetoric of the *Messenger*. The Red-baiters wanted to pin the subversive label on the *Crisis* but largely failed; with few exceptions they were not able to find what to them were genuinely radical articles.

The Lusk Committee and the Department of Justice similarly scrutinized other periodicals, chiefly the *Challenge,* the *Crusader,* the *Emancipator,* and the *Negro World,* and in the case of the Justice Department, the weekly newspaper press. Offensive articles were found in them all, although not as frequently as in the *Messenger*. But each of these journals was dangerous to one degree or another. They all displayed race pride; they all challenged the racial and social status quo, if not ex-

plicitly, then at least through the tenor of their vocabulary. It all boiled
down to a *racial* radicalism, distinct from other, equally dangerous
radicalisms. Whatever our age may think of them, there was something
about each article singled out for attention that profoundly disturbed
the individuals highly placed in the ruling Establishment in 1919 and
1920. To those who took the "Red menace" seriously these utterances
could not be ignored.

The *Messenger* and black radicalism were not all that Attorney General Palmer had to worry about. By late 1919 he and others of similar
political persuasion were acting on the assumption that the country
was on the brink of disaster and that in such revolutionary days national preservation took precedence over the niceties of constitutional
rights. The result was a wholesale perversion of traditional civil rights
that had its roots in the wartime period. During those years the Justice
Department had begun to decentralize its administration, which resulted,
then as later, in a wide variation in the zeal with which individual district attorneys carried out their office. Prosecutions were frequent and
enthusiastic in all areas where the IWW was active. An uneven pattern
of stern, sometimes summary punishment for "radicals" had been set
before the Red Scare. Palmer, once he perceived a renewed threat
from the Left—and this coincided with his growing ambitions to win
the presidency in 1920—became the single most important figure leading the country into a frenzied intolerance of dissenters. Although a
Quaker, he adopted decidedly un-Friendly methods and attitudes. He
personally rejected war on religious grounds but apparently had no
respect for those who opposed it for political reasons. He similarly
abhorred the practice of violence in any form, yet failed to perceive
the violence in his own actions as Attorney General.[11]

Palmer and the Justice Department performed a significant role in
creating the public stereotype of the radical agitator, a stereotype that
dovetailed with traditional nativism as well as with nervous fears engineered by the war and its disillusionments. Native Communist sympathizers, according to the Attorney General, "are composed chiefly
of criminals, mistaken idealists, social bigots, and many unfortunate
men and women suffering with various forms of hyperesthesia." Another Justice Department description of American-born radicals claimed

that "as a class they are less bloodthirsty and less given to violence than
the foreigners. Many of them border on insanity; many others are women with minds gone slightly awry, morbid, restless, and seeking the
sensational, craving for something, they know not what."[12] Such lurid
descriptions must have been comforting, for the aberrations the radicals allegedly displayed made it convenient to dismiss them as less
than fully American, as defective in mind and character. And one important defect, in the minds of many whites, was the radicals' interest
in black equality, particularly "social equality."

Reporting to Congress in 1919 on the activities of the Justice Department, Palmer warned that "from the date of the signing of the
armistice, a wave of radicalism appears to have swept over the country." Since that time more than fifty new radical publications had
been spawned. Of ominous significance was the fact that practically
all radical organizations looked on black America as a fertile ground
for conversion, and in many cases had already met with success. Palmer saw greatest evidence of this in the black press. In a section entitled
"Radicalism and Sedition Among the Negroes as Reflected in Their
Publications," he concluded that "the Negro is 'seeing red.' " The
power of this black press could not be ignored, especially in light of
its alleged wealthy backers. Many periodicals had taken deliberate advantage of the race riots during the summer of 1919 to utter "open
defiance and a counsel of retaliation." Pride in fighting back was a
frequent theme: "Defiance and insolently race-centered condemnation
of the white race is met in every issue of the more radical publications."
There could be little doubt as to the existence of a "well-concerted
movement among a certain class of Negro leaders of thought and
action to constitute themselves a determined and persistent source of
a radical opposition to the Government, and to the established rule of
law and order." Underlying all their attitudes Palmer saw an increased
emphasis on feelings of race consciousness, in some cases "always
antagonistic to the white race and openly, defiantly assertive of its
own equality and even superiority." Such assertions were to be read
most frequently in those journals edited by educated men, and therefore "the boast is not to be dismissed lightly as the ignorant vaporing
of untrained minds."[13]

Palmer's report distills the essense of the white Establishment's view of black radicalism: blacks were an easy target for conversion to subversive ideas or causes; black publications had white financial "angels" (that is, renegade whites were stirring up blacks); "defiance" of white authority and whites in general, retaliation in race riots, pride in fighting back, "insolent" speech toward the white race, all these could be defined as sedition because they attacked the racial status quo; finally, the black editors of the militant journals were "leaders" of their race. What all this adds up to is a challenge to white supremacy, expressed in ways strictly forbidden by the racial code: resisting whites; taking pride in one's blackness; denigrating the white (ideal) race. To the Establishment the black radicals were true subversives because they did not respect the fundamental assumptions of American life—theirs was as direct an attack on the white status quo as one could find.

The Attorney General was convinced that the *Messenger* was the most dangerous of the black publications. Printed on good paper, having few advertisements other than those from socialist sources, it nonetheless seemed to be thriving. By the publication of the May-June 1919 issue it was clearly an "exponent of open defiance and sedition," voicing "counsel to the Negro to align himself with Bolshevism." The September issue was even worse. "In some respects . . . [it] is more insolently offensive than any other of its issues. It is likewise more characteristically true to Negro type in its several instances of emotional abandon." The racial slur does not hide Palmer's fear of the language and meaning of Claude McKay's "If We Must Die" and of the exhilaration expressed by New Crowd Negroes in Washington, D.C., who killed riotous whites. And of course the rejoinder to Congressman Byrnes in the October *Messenger* was bound to excite Palmer, who in noting that this was the first time a black publication had openly approved of interracial sex, said that it was "marked throughout by a spirit of insolent bravado." As the Attorney General saw it, "no amount of mere quotation could serve as a full estimate of the evil scope attained by the *Messenger*. Only a reading of the magazine itself in all its several issues would suffice to do this."[14] Palmer had obviously done his homework.

The Department of Justice did not limit its efforts at exposing the sedition of radicals to its formal reports and bulletins. To supplement these it offered newspapers a free page of analysis and "news" stories, really thinly disguised propaganda, already written and engraved on plates ready for printing. A large circulation magazine was sent photostatic copies of documents purportedly showing the criminality of communism, with the personal suggestion from the Attorney General that it use this information, as well as any other it desired to receive from the Department of Justice, to expose the Red menace in print. In addition, the device of the informational press release was frequently used, with attribution to "federal sources" or "government officials." One such release, in late July 1919, warned of continuing propaganda efforts among blacks by the IWW, radical socialists, and Bolshevists and asserted that their campaigns were well financed. The logic here was less than perfect when it was claimed that the subversives were particularly attempting to reach uneducated Southern blacks through such dangerous weapons as pamphlets and newspapers! As evidence, several excerpts were quoted from the *Messenger,* although the press release did not identify that journal by name.[15]

The date on which the above was printed happened by coincidence to be the first day of the Chicago riot. Three days later Attorney General Palmer was quoted as saying that the violence was due to local conditions, not Bolshevik or radical propaganda, although the Bolsheviks were unsuccessfully spending considerable money and effort in the South. Yet four days later a front page story in the New York *Times,* again quoting unnamed government officials, took up the theme of radical agitation among blacks in the cities. The IWW was said to be engaged in heavy leafleting in New York and Philadelphia, using violent language and vicious cartoons; it was further claimed that nearly all IWW and left-wing socialist groups in the country were doing similar propagandizing. Again excerpts from *Messenger* articles were quoted, and again the source was not named. The flamboyance of its language was apparently too good not to use.[16]

In addition to formal reports, public statements by the Attorney General, and a steady stream of press releases, the Department of Justice had one other tactic in use against black radicals and suspected subversives: raids and similar threatening activities. More than once the offices of the *Messenger* were entered at night and ransacked, although whether for purposes of sheer intimidation, or to secure incriminating evidence, was never clear to the editors. Agents visited the NAACP offices and asked pointed questions about whether the association "received financial support from Bolshevick [sic] forces," whether there was any "Bolshevick talk" about the office, and if any of the staff had "Bolshevick" tendencies. Such intimidations, coupled with harassment by postal authorities, could hardly be taken lightly by those being threatened. As A. Philip Randolph later described his reactions, "I felt the force of the law and the force of public opinion . . . and I had no peace anywhere."[17]

Palmer sorted the attitudes expressed by radical black publications into five categories: (1) intemperate reactions to the race riots; (2) threats of retaliation for lynching; (3) a "more openly expressed demand for social equality, in which demand the sex problem is not infrequently included"; (4) identification with the IWW and other radical organizations, plus open advocacy of Bolshevik or Soviet doctrines; (5) "the [hostile] political stand assumed toward the present Federal administration, the South in general, and incidentally, toward the peace treaty and the league of nations."

Aside from the fact that Senator Henry Cabot Lodge fit most of the particulars of the fifth charge, this summary of attitudes is revealing of the misconceptions and assumptions that the Attorney General and, it is safe to assume, many other Americans entertained. First of all he labeled these the attitudes of "Negro leaders." Here Palmer generously gave notoriety to several individuals whose names were far from being household words in the black community. Probably many blacks knew of DuBois, but certainly few had ever heard of Owen and Randolph, much less the editors of the other black journals Palmer discussed. In calling these individuals leaders, Palmer both ignored and denigrated the status of well-known blacks like Robert Russa Moton, Emmett Scott, and Kelly Miller. Was this slight Palmer's way of criticizing them for not speaking firmly enough against the radicals? Perhaps he was so ignorant of the black community that he did not realize the roles they played. Or did he genuinely want the public to believe that blacks were in fact "seeing red" and that the whole race was being led by subversive "leaders" who edited seditious publications? Palmer may well have been prone to exaggerate and distort, for he was no uninvolved observer of the events of the day. Not only had his home been bombed, it is plain that he intended to ride the antiradical hysteria into the White House in 1920.[18]

The Attorney General, and probably the vast majority of whites in America, could not grasp the distinction between hatred of lynch law, Jim Crow, and disfranchisement, and actual race hatred. Palmer asserted that the black editors were motivated by hatred of the white race (which was particularly galling because it was so "defiantly" and "insolently" expressed). But the *Messenger* never expressed hatred of the white race. Southern racist politicians were singled out and vilified, but for the *Messenger* to attack the whole white race would have been to deny its socialist principles of the brotherhood of all exploited workers. Whites from Eugene Debs and Kate O'Hare to Roger Baldwin and Oswald Garrison Villard were praised in the pages of the *Messenger*. But an assault on fundamental American racial folkways could not be interpreted intellectually, only viscerally; outspoken attack on the worst examples of racists, lynchers, and demogogues like James K. Vardaman and Cole Blease was magnified in the mind of Palmer into hatred for the entire white race.

It is also obvious that anything that threatened to disrupt the racial status quo, which the Social Darwinists had taught was immutable, would be construed as a radical threat to the well-being of society. In this sense the import of the *Messenger* and occasionally even of the *Crisis* was certainly radical. Blacks arming themselves and fighting back against whites was not simply unheard of, it was unthinkable. Collective acts of violence, which the riots seemed to be, were even more threatening. And the demand for social, even sexual equality was so inconceivable to nearly all whites that it could not be dealt with on a rational level.[19] By 1920 this issue was in the open. But in being visible, it was all the more threatening to Anglo Saxon-American civilization. And Attorney General Palmer was not the only one who felt threatened.

In comparison with the Justice Department, the report of the Lusk Committee was somewhat less rabid, although this does not seem to be due to any particular liberalism on the part of its chairman. Clayton R. Lusk was an obscure upstate Republican senator who within nine months would be one of the best-known men in the state. He had no

previous experience in investigating radical activities. But he had undoubted conservative and nativist views, which were comforting to the
influential Union League Club, which had initially suggested to the
legislature that it investigate radicalism. It is likely that Lusk was chosen
not so much for his personal capabilities as to preserve the chairman-
ship of the committee for the upstate rural-Republican block which
controlled the Senate. And surely this group was as concerned as anyone
in the state about radicalism and pernicious alien influences in the
overgrown, immigrant-infested cities.

Beginning in May 1919, the Lusk Committee began to collect data,
monitor foreign-language groups, conduct raids and public hearings,
and dominate the front pages of at least the New York press with
allegation after allegation of this and that "Red plot."[20] Its revelations
about the loyalties of black Americans would be startling and frightening, for it discovered that dangerous attempts were being made to win
that impressionable group to communism. Its conclusions differed
little in substance from those of Attorney General Palmer, although
the Lusk Report avoided the obvious racial slurs of the latter and
made a deeper attempt to understand the social situation of blacks in
the United States and possible reasons for their discontent. This is
not to say that the committee's report achieved a balanced and insight-
ful social analysis—it did not—but its members seem to have taken the
trouble to probe a little deeper than did Palmer.

Having said about all that one can charitably say about the Joint
Legislative Committee Investigating Seditious Activities, it must be
noted that it ran roughshod over civil liberties and personal reputations,
either "unable or unwilling to distinguish between legislative and executive prerogatives." Through the abuse of search warrants, illegal de-
tainment of both persons and evidence, and especially the armed police
raid, it totally subverted constitutional practice in the search and seizure
process. None of this would have been possible without the knowing
cooperation of local magistrates and the legal system in general,
states and federal attorneys, the legislature and executive of the state,
and ultimately the tacit approval of the citizenry at large.[21]

One other tactic was of crucial importance to the Lusk Committee:
the use of spies and informers. Several of the former were employed
in Harlem, both male and female, usually white. The fact that white

radicals were tolerated and in some cases welcomed by the black population uptown made it relatively easy for white agents to observe meetings, if not to penetrate the inner circles of black activism. Local police
cooperation, not only in surveillance, but in actually preventing protest
meetings, was a corollary goal of the Lusk staff. The committee files
contain reports on several such gatherings, where speakers ranged
from Elizabeth Gurley Flynn and Norman Thomas to W. A. Domingo
and the two *Messenger* editors. Special agent Driscoll noted that at
one meeting over five hundred copies of the *Messenger* were sold as
various speakers urged blacks to join the IWW and alternately denounced the "Huns" of America and the signers of the Declaration of
Independence. Other functionaries monitored Owen and Randolph's
lectures at the Rand School. Agent Betty Thompson was assigned to
penetrate the *Messenger* circle and managed to interview the office
manager by posing as a journalism student.

Informers were of more dubious worth. One, a black person who
signed himself "A Staunch American," wrote to warn of the *Messenger*'s pernicious influence and offered the bizarre suggestion that the
office manager, Victor R. Daly, who was alleged to be an incipient
capitalist, be given downtown backing to start an enterprise of his
own. The reasoning here was that if the office manager was coopted,
the magazine would soon fold. Apparently the Lusk Committee did
not implement this suggestion. Another informer, this time a white
ex-agent of the American Protective League, reported an unusually
large number of blacks arriving at Grand Central Station and surmised
that they were riot veterans from Chicago coming to New York to
stir up similar disturbances. A committee agent was promptly dis-
patched to watch the metropolitan train stations, but found nothing
unusual. Judging from these examples, it would appear that the Lusk
Committee's more covert activities yielded relatively barren concrete
evidence, although a rich harvest of rumor and suspicion.[22]

The Lusk Report, as was typical in the Red Scare, jumped into the
subjects of radicalism, subversion, and sedition without bothering to
define terms. Perhaps the meanings, in the context of the day and the
hysteria, were assumed to be self-evident to anyone properly horrified
by the trend of events. Having thus dispensed with preliminaries, the

Lusk Report undertook, as one of its tasks, to expose groups "at work to stimulate race hatred in our colored population, and to engender so-called class consciousness in their ranks." This was not a reference to the Ku Klux Klan, which was nowhere mentioned in the 4,500-page report (probably with good reason, as the Klan was just then beginning a strong revival in Northern states like New York, particularly in rural, conservative areas that elected the likes of Clayton Lusk). What the committee had in mind was the radical organizations, particularly their publications. Hundreds of pages of the report were devoted to verbatim extracts from militant periodicals (the same technique used by Palmer) with annotations to point out particularly offensive or dangerous parts. It was acknowledged that some of the publications quoted in the report had not broken any specific law, yet even those that were not as dangerous as the most seditious ones should be criticized for giving aid and comfort to the revolutionary groups seeking to destroy the government and mislead the public.[23] This technique of "exposing" periodicals that had not actually done anything punishable proved a convenient method for Red-baiting the *Crisis,* which the Lusk Committee found difficult to place in the radical category.

"The most interesting as well as one of the most important features of radical and revolutionary propaganda is the appeal made to those elements of our population that have a just cause of complaint with the treatment they have received in this country." So began the section "Propaganda Among Negroes." This problem was said to be especially serious in New York, for in recent years a great number of blacks had migrated from both the West Indies and the American South. Generally speaking, they were well treated in the Empire State, claimed Lusk, but the fact that they often were ill treated where they had previously resided meant that they brought their resentments with them, and this resentment "has been capitalized [on] by agents and agitators of the Socialist Party of America, the IWW and other radical groups." The problem was exacerbated and encouraged by "well-to-do liberals" in "social uplift organizations"; the reference here was to the NAACP. Since many of the complaints of blacks were genuine, radical propaganda among them was all the more serious. Lusk advised that this "should encourage all loyal and thoughful negroes in this State to

organize to oppose the activities of such radicals. which cannot but
lead to serious trouble if they are permitted to continue the propaganda
which they now disseminate in such large volume."[24]

Like the Justice Department, the Lusk Committee felt that the *Messenger* was of special importance, devoted as it was "to the principles
of internationalism and the class struggle." The report's authors chose
their quotations well, for many of those they printed show the *Messenger* at its most militant, especially an editorial from the December
issue entitled "Thanksgiving." Printed nearly in its entirety by Lusk,
this piece gave nine reasons for thanks: (1) the Russian Revolution;
(2) the German, Austrian, Hungarian, and Bulgarian revolutions; (3)
world unrest, especially strikes in Britain, France, Italy, the United
States, and Japan; (4) the solidarity of labor, growth of industrial
unionism, and decline of trade unionism; (5) the rise of radicalism in
the United States and its part in encouraging the mine and steel strikes;
(6) the Seattle general strike; (7) the New Crowd Negro's fighting rioters and lynchers; (8) the declining influence of the Old Crowd Negro
and white leaders; (9) the speedy coming of the new social order. Lusk
warned that "it is this paper preaching these doctrines, advocating
these principles, that has commended itself to many of our intellectual liberals."[25]

A comparison of the offensive articles chosen for inclusion in the
Justice Department and the Lusk Committee reports shows that the
two agencies tended to stress different themes. The former was very
much concerned about the new radical consciousness displayed in
the *Messenger,* particularly that relating to demands for social and
sexual rights, as well as the encouragement of fighting back against
rioters and lynchers. The Lusk Committee, on the other hand, emphasized the possibility of blacks' becoming socialistic and part of a worldwide Bolshevik movement. Stated simply, Palmer's report displayed
more fear of blacks as blacks.

The Lusk Committee concluded that propaganda among blacks was
dangerous, partly because some of their grievances were valid, but primarily because the radicals were not really trying to remedy the conditions causing grievances but were only using them to appeal to class
consciousness and establish a social commonwealth. This was no indigenous social reform movement:

A study of the tactics and methods employed by revolutionary groups and organizations makes it clear that the present social unrest, with its revolutionary implications, is not the spontaneous development of economic causes. The growth of the radical and revolutionary movement is due largely to the effect of propaganda. False ideas respecting government and the present social order are being sold to the people of this country, as well as other countries, in much the same manner as a manufacturer or merchant sells his wares through the medium of advertising.

From the Establishment orientation of Lusk and his colleagues, anything that was subversive to the general status quo was radical because it posed fundamental changes and was also revolutionary because it demanded unacceptable alterations in the organization and fabric of society.[26]

This returns us to the differences in approach between the Lusk Committee and the Justice Department. Both agencies were equally alive to the dangers from subversion, but the latter, being the larger, had some agents focusing on alien radical seditionists, others on domestic troublemakers. The Department was thus more precise in defining the exact dangers of radicalism among blacks, and it spelled out these dangers in terms of challenges to the racial status quo. The Lusk Committee, attempting to cover all bases in one investigation, stressed the interdependency of the various radical groups and movements and saw the dangers of black militancy more in its association with the larger socialist-Bolshevik trend. Yet despite these emphases the two were in wholehearted agreement about the danger present and the inroads that had already been made. From this perspective, then, the two Red-hunting groups were cast in the same mold.

The most explicit linking of black radicalism to a threat to the racial status quo in 1919 was heard in the halls of Congress from, predictably, a Southern Congressman, Democrat James S. Byrnes of South Carolina. Scarcely a month after the July riots in Washington, Chicago, Harlem, Norfolk, Longview, Texas, and Bisbee, Arizona, Byrnes told his colleagues that the rise in antagonisms between the races was due solely to the malign efforts of black leaders through

their race's press. These persons were radicals who rejected the conservative advice of men like Moton (that is, rejected Bookerite accommodationism) and instead stirred up passions and incited to violence. Most
unfortunately, some of the heretofore conservative leaders had become
radical; here Byrnes had in mind none other than W. E. B. DuBois.

But even the *Crisis,* which Byrnes found irresponsible at best, was
not nearly as dangerous as the *Messenger.* The latter was condemned
for supporting the IWW, praising Eugene V. Debs, and praying for a
Bolshevik government in the United States. The fact that it was printed
on fine-quality paper and had few advertisements was proof that it must
be financed by the IWW, although where the IWW got the money to
subsidize such a venture Byrnes did not specify. Referring to a *Messenger* prediction that there would be more riots, he commented that such
statements "show that the negro leaders had deliberately planned a
campaign of violence." Referring to an article urging blacks to form
armed self-defense groups, Byrnes commented that if there was no legislation to keep such pernicious doctrines from the mails, it should be
enacted. "We can all believe in a free press, but we can recognize the
distinction between a free press and a revolutionary and anarchistic
press." The time was at hand for stopping the Bolsheviks of Russia
and the IWW from using the black press for their "nefarious purposes."
Other incendiary statements were found in the articles by Lieutenant
Colson, particularly the story of black troops bayoneting the image of
a Southern Congressman; apparently this struck too close to home for
comfort. Byrnes declared that this should lead one to consider carefully
whether black troops and officers should ever again be enlisted.

The Congressman went on to explain why he had given so much free
publicity to such heinous doctrines. First of all, whites should know
what blacks were doing. Second, responsible black leaders should be
warned not to act rashly for the purpose of furthering their own ambitions; rather, they should be encouraged to tell their race that political
and social equality were false hopes. Byrnes emphasized that the war
had not changed whites' attitudes toward the question of equality. A
long dissertation on the good treatment of blacks in the South followed,
including an assertion that lynching was almost universally condemned.
He then spoke to the North, allowing that that section could treat
blacks as it saw fit, but predicting that as soon as the proportion of

blacks reached the level where they might play a significant role in politics, then the North too would restrict the suffrage, for "this is a white man's country, and will always remain a white man's country. So much for political equality. . . . As to social equality, God Almighty never intended [it]."[27]

That other members of Congress were alert to the dangers of the new racial militancy, as well as possible connections between black and white radicals, can be seen from the legislation they introduced to try to cope with the problem. New laws seemed necessary because of the imminent expiration of wartime restrictions on offensive speech and action. During the war the question of radical or injudiciously independent publications or speech had been covered by espionage and sedition laws that empowered the Postmaster General either to ban a publication outright or to deny it a second-class mailing permit. Federal court interpretations of this legislation placed virtually no impediments to government censorship. These acts were to be used "in time of war," but the cessation of hostilities did not bring an immediate end to espionage and sedition prosecutions; not until the last day of his administration did President Wilson sign away the wartime powers. This explains why the second-class permit of the *Messenger,* which was lifted in mid-1918, was not returned until 1921, long after actual hostilities had ended. In this regard the magazine was by no means unique. Roger Baldwin has noted that these difficulties with the Post Office Department were "almost normal then for the Left."[28]

Soon after taking office, A. Mitchell Palmer announced that he would ask Congress to pass a peacetime sedition act, for he had come to believe that the date for actual revolution was close at hand. Clearly one of his motivations was the belief that practically every radical group was trying to appeal to black Americans, and he was afraid that the courts would not continue to sanction the use of the wartime legislation or various ancient (from the Civil War period) sedition laws. After appealing several times to Congress to initiate new legislation itself, Palmer finally sent his own draft to Capitol Hill in November. Legal scholar Zechariah Chafee, Jr., promptly termed the proposed bill a gross violation of First Amendment freedoms because it would "punish words merely for their assumed tendency to produce bad consequences in the remote future." Chafee voiced the same fears over a similar measure, the Graham-Sterling Sedition Bill, which proposed to exclude from the mails anything that would tend to justify or defend the use of force to accomplish some political, economic, or social purpose, or any material "whereby an appeal is made to racial prejudice, the intended or probable result of which appeal is to cause rioting or the result to force and violence." Such restrictions, Chafee reported, would prohibit the mailing of a history of the American Revolution, as well as "suppress all but the most carefully guarded presentations of the wrongs of the Negroes." Other similar bills were introduced in 1919 and 1920, including one authored by Representative Byrnes soon after his confrontation with the *Messenger.* So extreme was most of this legislation that even the New York *Times* had to oppose it; none of it ultimately found its way into law.[29]

Presumably to plug whatever cracks in the dike the proposed antiradical legislation overlooked, four bills authored by Representative Thaddeus H. Caraway of Arkansas were introduced a few days after the Washington, D.C., riot. The first would have prohibited enlistment of blacks in the armed services and required the discharge of those already so enrolled. The other three represented attempts to strengthen Jim Crow practices in the nation's capital. One prohibited intermarriage and prevented interracial couples from residing there. Another provided for the establishment of mandatory all-white and all-black residential districts, while the third called for the creation of a segregated street railway system. None of these achieved passage.[30]

From the perspective of the 1970s it seems inevitable that blacks would gain a new outlook from their wartime experiences, but probably the vast majority of white Americans in 1919 assumed that blacks would slip back into the same old position and role after the war. Thus the image of the returning black soldier, proudly wearing his uniform and believing that he had earned a new deal for himself and his race, had profoundly disturbing implications for whites. "The sight of a uniform on a brown man reminded the orthodox that the Negro soldiers in France had been taught . . . to rip Nordic bellies with their bayonets."[31] A major impediment to putting the black man in his prewar "place" was the persistent and supposedly well-organized and well-financed radical movement. The New York *Times,* by no means dispassionate on the subject, recognized that indeed there was a new mood in black America, and in essence this is what the whole white fear was about—the loyal, docile black population was no longer that, no longer predictable and unassuming and accommodating as it had seemed to be before the war. (For that matter, neither was the immigrant or the industrial worker. Militancy from these groups as well as from blacks prevented the Establishment in general from viewing their aspirations with equanimity.)

A news analysis in the *Times* in October 1919, coming after the summer of unprecedented racial violence, described the changed situation as follows:

> Out of the war has come a new negro problem—that, observers agree, is the first fact to be recognized in taking up the question. Before the war negro leaders, still under the influence of Booker Washington, were in the main for a policy of conciliation. For all the scattered injustice and oppression that the negro still suffered, the majority of the negro leaders still held in clear prospective [*sic*] the great benefits granted the negro race in this country, the fact that their freedom had been won by the sacrifice of an immense number of white men's lives, that in no other country in the world where a large colored population lived in contact with the white race did the principle of the laws confer equal recognition to the black man. In a word, there was still active among the negro leaders a sense of appreciation tracing back to the civil war period. Whenever friction threatened, leaders of this type, believing that by forebearance and thrift on the part of the black man a fair and harmonious adjustment of the two races would be attained, steadily argued conciliatory methods.

The *Times* went on to admit that domestic peace demanded that society work to eliminate the causes of the riots, and that a prudent course would be to encourage the old-style "responsible" Bookerite leaders who opposed the new generation of militants. But the trouble with this strategy, as the *Times* ruefully acknowledged, was that even the old-style leaders were now insisting on manhood rights, justice, and equal opportunity in uncomfortably frank terms.[32] There seemed no way out of this dilemma, for to conservative and even to moderate Americans, North and South, the goals of political and social equality for blacks were unthinkable. Even if they could have agreed to some alteration in the racial status quo, the turbulent months of the late teens were hardly the proper time to institute social innovations. Many saw, not the prospect of improving race relations, but worsening ones.

"Race War." Newspapers and magazines increasingly voiced this fear in article after article that followed the rioting of mid-1919. Whites read of the black veteran who remarked that "we fought for democracy [in Europe] and we're going to keep on fighting for democracy till we get our rights here at home. The black worm has turned."

"There is a high mortality among turning worms," replied his white interviewer. "We've got you people eight to one."

"Don't I know it?" answered the black man. "Thousands of us must die; but we'll die fighting. Mow us down—slaughter us! It's better than this."

Not all observers, to be sure, agreed that the ignition point was so close. But for many the worries could not be quieted. Too many people feared, too many believed. "Our Own Subject Race Rebels," "Why the Negro Appeals to Violence," "Are We Menaced by a New Race War?", "Our Own Race War," "The Negro at Bay," cried the magazines. New York newspapers, when they received the first word of the Elaine (Phillips County), Arkansas, pogrom against black sharecroppers, headlined their stories "All Whites Marked for Slaughter," "Planned Massacre of Whites To-day," and "Negro Plot to Massacre All Whites Found." The Southern press was just as explicit. During the prolonged steel strike in 1919 many newspapers spoke of impending race war in the mills. A newly frightful vocabulary was in vogue to describe the growing tensions. A "menacing" race problem. "Brute strength" in race relations. The "counsel of madness." A "revenge movement." Lothrop Stoddard's *Rising Tide of Color* and W. E. B. DuBois's new *Darkwater* agreed, if on nothing else, that there was a looming racial confrontation throughout the world. By the time of the Tulsa riot in 1921 the authorities, the press, and participants alike used military terminology to describe the events: skirmish lines, concentration camps, casualties, refugees, reconnaissance, prisoners.[33]

Whether Red-baiters like Palmer, Lusk, and Byrnes had created this spirit of fearful expectation, or whether widespread popular apprehension gave free reign to the professional anti-Communists and antiradicals, it is clear that a large part of the American public, black as well as white, agreed that the times were perilous and that stern measures should be taken. Whites, not unexpectedly, stressed that the status quo should somehow be reestablished. Yet how? The New York *Times* had no solution. *Vardaman's Weekly,* the vile outpouring of Southern racism, pinned the blame on the wartime experiences of black soldiers who had been "French-women-ruined": the old "social equality" nonsense again, aspirations to be "like white folks," to insinuate themselves into the bosoms of white families. This, perhaps more than anything else, worried white commentators. Why else, in yet another alarmed report on communist influence among blacks, was only one *Messenger* article quoted—the statement on five million mulattoes and the demand for social equality in the day as well as after dark? Why not print a *Messenger* editorial praising Soviet Russia? Which showed the more serious "Communist" influence? Obviously the former. The Houston *Chronicle* noted that the 1919 riots were in large measure due to the fact that "negroes . . . have been petted into an attitude of lazy conceit . . . the uniform has been permitted to give them an unprecedented degree of protection and consideration . . . high wages and allotments have tended to make them shiftless and irresponsible." One helpful Southerner took pains to discourage black pretensions by sending the following advice to the New York *Age*:

It would not be healthy for you to publish your paper in the South, if you did some fine morning a white man would walk up to you and lam you side the jaw with his fist and knock some of the ill manners and tomfoolery out of your head. The trouble with you Yankee niggers, especially the yellow brood, is that you are hankering after social equality with the white people. You would be tickled to death, John, if you could walk into some white man's parlor and snuggle up close beside his daughter. But don't do, John, if you

do we will hang you between the heavens and the earth. The best
medicine for a nigger that has the social equality bugs working in
his head is a good dose of hemp rope. We are good to our niggers
in the South as long as they stay in their place, but we are as mean
as all get out if they get out of their place.[34]

Less rabidly, but no less distinctly, analyst Glenn Frank wrote in the
Century that there was a new type of black man, the returned veteran.
In Europe he had been simply a white man in black skin, and his taste
of social equality there was "no doubt an exhilarating wine"; consequently he returned "still flushed with its intoxication." Such inebria-
tion was a direct cause of the race riots, for in cities like Chicago the
vice district had moved into the colored areas, resulting in the intimate
association of the races. "This mingling of black men and white women
fanned alive in many black minds the social equality idea and produced
a certain number of black braggadocios, whose swagger irritated the nearby whites. This black swagger and the white resentment were elements
[in causing the riots]."
    The old social equality bogey was a real burr under the white saddle,
an irritation that could not be salved. Attorney General Palmer focused
particularly on the social equality question, which he found trumpeted
in the *Messenger* with "insolent bravado." Lusk too, although to a lesser
degree, emphasized the same emotional issue. To many whites this preoccupation with the possibilities of interracial sexual relations reached
the proportions of mania. Black sociologist Charles S. Johnson found
that there existed three centrally held beliefs that controlled the thinking of nearly all whites: blacks were seen as mentally inferior, innately
immoral, and innately criminal, all by their biological nature. This
"information" about blacks, which we might term the cultural conventional wisdom, was passed from generation to new generation through
tradition, accumulated through "experience," and imbedded in the
mores of society both consciously and unconsciously. "These are the
background of recognition, of classification, and of behavior itself."[35]
Given such an "intellectual" substructure of white society, it is no surprise that the social equality demon reared its head in the Red Scare
days.

Many a black periodical pointed out, and not for the first time, that there was a difference between social equality and social intermingling. Most defended social equality (or "social justice") when it meant the right "to associate with one's fellowmen," in the words of DuBois. The Chicago *Whip* accurately summarized the situation by asking whether "it is the desire of the white American to keep the Negro inferior and subterfuge [*sic*] his every act on the ground of social equality?" The black Houston *Informer* answered the question by accusing whites of purposely confusing social equality and intermingling. "All this journalistic diarrhea about 'radical Negro editors' and 'race uplifters inciting Negroes to revolt against the white man,' etc., is unadulterated and unsophisticated bosh, buncombe, 'bull' and 'bull-sheviki.' "[36]

This leads to one further observation on why the *Messenger* and its editors were in the "most dangerous" category. The white Establishment was not greatly interested in or capable of exploring the complexities and differences among blacks and in black life. There is no wonder that the picture drawn by Lusk, Palmer, and Byrnes, as well as by journalists, was so often superficial and inaccurate. If one could pretend, as Palmer did, that Randolph and Owen were really race leaders, then one could fear them and attack them (and use them) all the more. In the final analysis the actual words printed by periodicals like the *Messenger* mattered less than the meanings read into them by alarmed white readers. Praise for the IWW or Soviet Russia, condemnation of lynchings and disfranchisement, advice to repel marauding white rioters and arm for self-defense, advocacy of the right to social and sexual equality with the white race—all these were simplified by the Establishment: blacks were restive; blacks were using white America's historic and current democratic rhetoric against America; blacks had friends and allies among subversives and radicals; above all, blacks were no longer what white Americans felt *they* had a right to define blacks to be. The sons and grandsons of slaves had been taught to shoot; blacks *had* ripped open Nordic bellies with their bayonets (and killed a few white Americans on city streets too). There *was* in fact a New Crowd Negro in the land.

The "Red Summer" of race riots ran concurrently with the Red

Scare, and out of the former was born, in the words of James Weldon
Johnson, "a spirit of defiance born of desperation. . . . a radicalism
motivated by a fierce race consciousness." Whites knew that unless
these gains were erased, these new lines of attack reversed, neither
the racial status quo nor American blacks would ever again be the
same. The *Messenger*'s task, on the contrary, was to consolidate the
gains and keep up the attacks on racist America. That it could not halt
the floodtide of reaction is no judgment of failure. The magazine functioned as symbol as well as combatant, and its courage and fearlessness
were not lost on a new generation of blacks, the first generation of the
new century of self-emancipation. Nor was its message lost on white
America either.[37]

The popular image has it that the Red Scare began to peter out by
mid-1920 when the Red-baiters' continued predictions of further violence
failed to materialize and the public repudiated their hysterical claims,
turning its attention instead to the business of Normalcy. There is some
truth to this image, for in fact the hysteria did subside after midsummer.
But the fears of Bolshevist and anarchist activities and black radicalism
did not quickly die, and in fact the Red Scare festered in pockets on
into the twenties. The complex of fears and apprehensions that surfaced
during the war and gave rise to 100 percent patriotism, which gained
new life in the postwar months as Bolshevism seemed to be marching
steadily westward across Europe and establishing beachheads on American shores, still seemed to have some logical basis in the early twenties.
As David Brion Davis comments, "clearly the idealistic visions and expectations of the past had been unfulfilled. America had not escaped
the class and industrial conflict of the Old World. . . . Wherever one
looked there was disunity, change, and uncertainty." Conservatives
could not risk letting the issue of radical threats vanish, for American
civilization was no safer than it had been when threatened by Imperial
Germany. The new 100 percent Americanism of the revived Klan and
the American Legion in the twenties was thus in good part the anti-
German feelings of the war years and the anti-Bolshevik fears of 1919
revived in a new uniform.[38]

The federal government did not dismantle its antisubversive machinery immediately after passions subsided in mid-1920. True, the virulence

of government persecution began to wind down in Harding's administration as Debs and other political prisoners were released and second-class mailing permits were restored, much to the relief of the *Messenger's* flagging finances. Antiradical raids were shelved for the time being, although the Bureau of Investigation continued to provide information on radical movements to state governments and private industry while it also maintained its links to private detective agencies. Undercover agents continued to infiltrate labor, radical, and leftist groups. It was not until President Coolidge appointed Harlan Fiske Stone as Attorney General in 1924 that these antiradical activities were curtailed.[39]

On the state level the Red Scare lasted into the twenties in certain areas, particularly in New York. This was the product of several factors. One was the concentration of radicals, black and white, in New York City as well as the strength of the Socialist party in electoral politics up to the early twenties. New York was also the chief entrepôt for the brief renewal of foreign immigration, so worried nativists would continue to be active up to mid-decade. Postwar economic conditions also helped to perpetuate the Red Scare. For months returned veterans stood in long lines at employment bureaus. A housing shortage was especially severe and led to ethnic conflicts. The business community worried about declining sales and profits while strikes, although declining from their peak in 1919, did not cease in the early twenties. Finally, a wide selection of nongovernmental patriotic organizations opposed radicalism, open immigration, pacifism, as well as the closed shop and labor militancy in general. The National Civic Federation, the American Defense Society, the American Legion, and the Ku Klux Klan all had ample finances and willing recruits in New York in the first half of the twenties. It was not until mid-decade that the passions of the Red Scare receded. But they did not disappear. For throughout the twenties Red-baiting was a convenient weapon to use against any unpopular group or dissenting idea, and it would be used on several occasions in efforts to halt or deny black militancy.[40]

Fears of conspiratorial and revolutionary movements among blacks never really had a chance to subside after the heady days of 1919 and 1920. The notion persisted in the Justice Department that the Garvey movement was tainted with Bolshevism; J. Edgar Hoover's Bureau of Investigation believed it to be "the communist party which is affiliated with the Russian Soviet Government." The Tulsa race riot in mid-1921 gave new life to old fears. The Fort Worth *Star-Telegram,* speaking for many other newspapers, declared that the Oklahoma blacks had been "inflamed by a violent propaganda against the whites which negro radicals in Chicago, New York, and other points in the East have been carrying on since the armistice." A Tulsan writing soon after the conflict explained that white radicals, agitators, Reds, and Bolsheviks had stirred up the colored population, while the city's police blamed both the IWW and the Communist-oriented African Blood Brotherhood for initiating the conflict.[41]

Concern over Communist attentions to the black population did not end here; the next year brought news that the Third International was as intent as ever on winning over "the oppressed colored peoples of the world" with promises of "race equality of the Negro with the white people, as well as . . . equal wages and political and social rights." A Communist party convention meeting at Bridgman, Michigan, was raided in 1922, and the evidence seized raised new alarms about Moscow's interest in the American racial situation. Unearthed was a directive from the International, purportedly signed by Bukharin, Redek, and Kluusinen, which ordered American Communists to stir up race strife. Although the *Messenger* was still considered a dangerous publication, more fear was manifested over the activities of the African Blood Brotherhood, whose program called for, among other things, absolute social equality. Here again was the feared equation: "Red" agitation plus blacks seeking social equality equals a threat to American society and security.[42]

A new radical, Communist-influenced organization came to the attention of white Americans in 1925: the American Negro Labor Conference. The ANLC program and impact will be discussed in a later chapter, but it should be noted here that again the Justice Department was in the forefront of spreading the alarm. It claimed there were more than one hundred paid Communist organizers in the country, financed by over a million dollars yearly, and that this effort was bearing fruit among blacks. Several members of the race had already been sent to Moscow for training, and now the party had started the ANLC. The New York *World* scooped the other white dailies by sending black correspondent Lester Walton to attend the ANLC convention in late

1925, and his dispatches were baldly anti-Communist, calling organizer Lovett Fort-Whiteman "the reddest Red of his race." Yet most of the newspapers surveyed by the *Literary Digest* professed to see little cause for panic: black Americans were not likely to rush to any Communist affiliation. Such a view indicates that the white public by mid-decade was no longer on edge at every rumor or whisper of radical agitation among blacks. Three years previously such a complacent attitude would hardly have been possible.[43]

A new "plot" was revealed in mid-1927 to white Americans by the headlines of their daily papers. The New York *Herald Tribune* ran the banner "Soviet Trains Negroes Here for Uprising" even though there was no evidence in the article about any planned uprising. The story revealed that a quiet campaign had been under way for several months to train selected American blacks in Bolshevik theory and practice at the "University of Far Eastern Peoples" in Moscow. Behind this scheme were Lovett Fort-Whiteman and Richard B. Moore of the ANLC. Upwards of a hundred students had already gone to Moscow, it was said, although most had not yet returned. Fort-Whiteman was supplied with plenty of money to pay for their passage to Russia, and it was alleged, had easy access to false birth certificates and other documents. Anticipating further expansion of its program, the ANLC was meanwhile setting up a school in Harlem with classes in imperialism, the Chinese Revolution, and the history of communism. Curiously, the day after this lengthy exposé the *Herald Tribune* editorialized that the Russians must have "an oversupply of ignorance and gullibility" if they thought they could radicalize the American black population. But why the scare headlines and story of the previous day? The New York *Age* had an explanation: every now and then the white press "has a spasm of seeing red" and taking alarm at alleged Soviet agitation among the colored population. Any attempt by blacks to better their social and economic conditions seemed to call for such sensational treatment. In fact, the *Age* suggested, the *Herald Tribune*'s "lurid speculations" might just be due to guilty white consciences. Much of the rest of the country's press was unconvinced that there was any danger in this latest flap, but some papers were taking it seriously enough, particularly those in New York.[44]

The persistence through the twenties of fears of Communism among the black population can be seen in the frequent Red-baiting of A. Philip Randolph when he began to organize the Brotherhood of Sleeping Car Porters in 1925. Randolph was vulnerable on this point: his early *Messenger* editorials praising the Soviet Union and his active participation in the Socialist party would not be forgotten. Practically the first effort of the Pullman Company to discredit the new organizer was to drag up his socialist past. Ministers were told that Randolph did not believe in God and were encouraged to denounce him for disbelief as well as for his political views. When Randolph and fellow-organizer Ashley Totten tried to speak to black congregations in Kansas City, they discovered that the Pullman propaganda machine had spread word they were "two men from Moscow who are coming to stir up race strife." At various times prominent figures in the black community were quoted as believing that the Pullman Company would recognize and deal fairly with the porters' new union if the radical, socialist Randolph resigned. This sort of Red-tagging was a continually serious problem, and the Pullman Company used it for all it was worth. That the black community was not unaffected by it only demonstrates that a decade of antiradical agitation from government, press, and the business community had a decided effect on the population as a whole. Yet Red-baiting could even be turned to Randolph's advantage on occasion. Shortly after the BSCP called off its strike threat in mid-1928, black and white Communist groups attacked Randolph for having sold out to conservative white labor (it was partly on the advice of AFL president William Green that Randolph "postponed" the strike). Communist attacks were just what was needed at that low point in the BSCP's precarious life—such attacks would help silence Pullman Company allegations that porter leaders were themselves Reds.[45]

The impact of the Red Scare of 1919-1920 on black America is clear. It served to draw public attention to the new militance growing within the race; yet it engendered not white sympathy, but fear and hostility. The racial status quo was under attack in 1919, and whites found themselves on the defensive. They could relax somewhat after 1920, but not completely, for the new black spirit, the New Crowd Negro, did not disappear with Normalcy. Consequently, whites continued to believe that Communists and other subversives were ever ready to exploit blacks' alleged passions for associating with whites and forcing themselves into the mainstream of white American society. To blacks, it was full participation in American life for which they were striving, not any narrow "social equality." But most whites were not perceptive enough to understand the real nature of black aspirations. So they turned for security to theories of conspiracy, to xenophobias and nativisms. These proved a convenient defense, a tactic that had been useful in the past in retarding the aspirations of other upwardly mobile groups. But previous groups had not had the "Red" label so tenaciously fastened to them. From 1919 on, this was to be one of the black man's burdens in white America. From that time to the present of Martin Luther King, Jr., any upsurge in black militancy has run the risk of being Red-baited. It is still a potent weapon.

NOTES

1. Rollin Lynde Hartt, "I'd Like to Show You Harlem," *Independent* 105 (April 2, 1921): 358; Claude McKay, *A Long Way From Home* (New York, 1937), p. 54; see also Theodore G. Vincent, *Black Power and the Garvey Movement* (Berkeley, Cal., n.d.), p. 44.

2. Robert T. Kerlin, *The Voice of the Negro: 1919* (New York, 1920), pp. 20, 23, 156; Washington *Bee*, August 2, 1919, p. 4; New York *Age*, August 2, 1919, p. 4; George E. Haynes, "What Negroes Think of Race Riots," *Public* 22 (August 9, 1919): 849; Henry Hugh Proctor, *Between Black and White: Autobiographical Sketches* (Boston, 1925), pp. 167-68.

3. The Chicago Commission on Race Relations, *The Negro in Chicago: A Study of Race Relations and a Race Riot* (Chicago, 1922), p. 476.

4. James Weldon Johnson, *Black Manhattan* (New York, 1969), p. 247; *Investigation Activities of the Department of Justice* (66th Cong., 1st Sess., Sen. Doc. XII, no. 153) (Washington, D.C., 1919), p. 172; Robert K. Murray, *Red Scare: A Study in National Hysteria, 1919-1920* (New York, 1964), pp. 100-102; New York *Times*, June 28, 1919, 1:2.

5. *Messenger,* May-June 1919, pp. 8-10.

6. Ibid., July 1919, pp. 4-5, 8-9, 14-15, 22, 24-25; August 1919, p. 7.

7. Ibid., August 1919, pp. 4, 10, 21-25, 27.

8. *Investigation Activities of the Department of Justice,* p. 179; *Messenger,* September 1919, pp. 4, 16-17, 28-29. The exhilaration of the summer's events even moved the moderate New York *Age* to suggest that an award be given to the plucky seventeen-year-old girl who had killed a white detective who broke into her bedroom during the night without a warrant. *Age,* August 2, 1919, pp. 1, 5.

9. *Messenger,* October 1919, pp. 11-14, 25-27.

10. Interview, A. Philip Randolph, July 13, 1972; Charles Flint Kellogg, *NAACP: A History of the National Association for the Advancement of Colored People, Vol. I, 1909-1920* (Baltimore, 1957), p. 256; Eugene Levy, *James Weldon Johnson: Black Leader, Black Voice* (Chicago, 1973), p. 274.

11. Stanley Coben, *A. Mitchell Palmer: Politician* (New York, 1963), p. 221; Harry N. Scheiber, *The Wilson Administration and Civil Liberties, 1917-1921* (Ithaca, N.Y., 1960), pp. 42-43, 48-49; Julian F. Jaffe, *Crusade Against Radicalism: New York During the Red Scare, 1914-1924* (Port Washington, N.Y., 1972), p. 176; Donald Johnson, "The Political Career of A. Mitchell Palmer," *Pennsylvania History* 25 (October 1958): 346-47.

12. "What is Attorney General Palmer Doing," *Nation* 110 (February 14, 1920): 190; Arthur Wallace Dunn, "The 'Reds' in America From the Standpoint of the Department of Justice," *American Review of Reviews* 61 (February 1920): 166.

13. *Investigation Activities of the Department of Justice,* 11-13, 162; *Annual Report of the Attorney General of the United States for the Year 1920* (Washington, 1920), pp. 177-78; *Attorney General A. Mitchell Palmer on Charges Made Against Department of Justice by Louis F. Post and Others* (Hearings before the Committee on Rules, House of Rep., 66th Cong., 2nd Sess., Pt. 1) (Washington, D.C., 1920), pp. 158, 189-90. Some of Palmer's allegations jibed with a secret report from the Chicago office of the U.S. Army Intelligence, which claimed that the riot in that city was caused by Bolsheviks and anarchists; see Allan H. Spear, *Black Chicago: The Making of a Negro Ghetto, 1890-1920* (Chicago, 1967), p. 217. As for the charge of black "superiority," a careful reading of these months fails to reveal any such sentiments. Palmer seems to have had personal anxieties about race consciousness and pride. In any case, the United States government was under pressure from the British government to curb racial radicalism, for Britain

feared, with some justification, that its Caribbean subjects would be influenced by the *Messenger* and other militant American black publications. See W. F. Elkins, " 'Unrest among the Negroes': A British Document of 1919," *Science and Society* 23 (Winter 1968): 66-79; Vincent, *Black Power and the Garvey Movement,* p. 35.

14. *Investigation Activities of the Department of Justice,* pp. 172-73, 179, 181-82, 184.

15. *Nation* 110 (February 14, 1920): 190-91; 110 (March 6, 1920): 285, 299; New York *Times,* July 28, 1919, 4:4.

16. New York *Times,* July 31, 1919, 2:3; August 4, 1919, 1:5, 6:1. To some extent Palmer was not well aware of what his eager subordinates, especially young J. Edgar Hoover, were doing. This may account in part for the inconsistency between these press reports. On Hoover's independence from his boss, see Coben, *A. Mitchell Palmer,* p. 222. The Justice Department's accuracy in gathering and evaluating information was not always the best. The Chicago office filed a report claiming that Big Bill Haywood had been invited to address the Urban League convention in Detroit in October 1919 and that the NAACP was planning to flood black neighborhoods with IWW literature. Chicago Commission, *Negro in Chicago,* pp. 574-75.

17. Interview, A. Philip Randolph; Carl S. Matthews, "After Booker T. Washington: The Search for a New Negro Leadership, 1915-1925" (Ph.D. dissertation, University of Virginia, 1971), pp. 183-84; Phyl Garland, "A. Philip Randolph: Labor's Grand Old Man," *Ebony* 24 (May 1969): 32.

18. *Investigation Activities of the Department of Justice,* p. 162; Coben, *A. Mitchell Palmer,* pp. 197, 203, 205-206.

19. For irrefutable evidence of the existence of white fear about social contact with blacks, see Chicago Commission, *Negro in Chicago,* Chapter IX.

20. Lawrence H. Chamberlain, *Loyalty and Legislative Action: A Survey of Activity by the New York State Legislature, 1919-1949* (Ithaca, N.Y., 1951) pp. 205, 211-12; Jaffe, *Crusade Against Radicalism,* pp. 120-22; Patricia W. Wingo, "Clayton R. Lusk: A Study of Patriotism in New York Politics, 1919-1923" (Ph.D. dissertation, University of Georgia, 1966), pp. iv, vii, 21, 26, Chapter 9.

21. Zechariah Chaffee, Jr., *Freedom of Speech* (New York, 1920), pp. 302-10; Jaffe, *Crusade Against Radicalism,* p. 123; Chamberlain, *Loyalty and Legislative Action,* pp. 13-20, 22-26, 28, 30, 36-39, 45-47, 51-52.

22. J.M. Pawa, "Black Radicals and White Spies: Harlem, 1919," *Negro History Bulletin* 35 (October 1972): 129-33.

23. New York (State) Legislature, Joint Legislative Committee Investigating Seditious Activities, *Revolutionary Radicalism: Its History, Purpose and Tactics, with an Exposition and Discussion of the Steps Being Taken and Required to Curb It* (Albany, 1920), 2: 1145, 1476; Kenneth T. Jackson, *The Ku Klux Klan in the City: 1915-1930* (New York, 1967), pp. 175 ff.

24. N.Y. Legislature, *Revolutionary Radicalism*, 2: 1476.

25. Ibid., 2: 1312, 1476-81.

26. Ibid., 2: 1143, 1519-20.

27. *Congressional Record* (66th Cong. 1st Sess., LVIII) (Washington, 1919), pp. 4303-4305.

28. Scheiber, *The Wilson Administration and Civil Liberties*, pp. 22-26, 28, 31-32, 34-35, 43-44, 53, 57; Jaffe, *Crusade Against Radicalism*, p. 62; Paul L. Murphy, *The Meaning of Freedom of Speech: First Amendment Freedoms from Wilson to FDR* (Westport, Conn., 1972), Chapters 5-6; Roger Baldwin to author, August 8, 1972.

29. Coben, *A. Mitchell Palmer*, pp. 241-44; *Investigation Activities of the Department of Justice*, pp. 6-9, 14; *To Punish Offenses Against the Existence of the Government of the United States* (66th Cong., 2nd Sess., House Report, I, no. 524) (Washington, D.C., 1920), p. 4; Chafee, *Freedom of Speech*, pp. 195, 203; Scheiber, *The Wilson Administration and Civil Liberties*, p. 54; Jaffe, *Crusade Against Radicalism*, pp. 217-18.

30. *Congressional Record* (66th Cong., 1st Sess., LVIII) (Washington, D.C., 1919), pp. 3463, 3547. Another indication of the narrow mood of Congress was the discovery by Senator Reed Smoot that "Red" literature was in the Howard University library. Smoot threatened never again to vote for any federal appropriations for the school. Howard's white president, J. Stanley Durkee, replied that the two books in question were authored by a pro-Russian and had been donated, not purchased. He agreed that such literature should be suppressed by the government and immediately ordered the volumes expurgated from the library. *Washington Bee*, January 17, 1920, p. 6.

31. Authur F. Raper and Ira De A. Reid, *Sharecroppers All* (Chapel Hill, N.C., 1941), p. 227.

32. New York Times (October 5, 1919):X, 10:1.

33. Rollin Lynde Hartt. "The New Negro: 'When He's Hit, He Hits Back!' ", *Independent* 105 (January 15, 1921): 59; " 'Our Own Subject Race' Rebels," *Literary Digest* 62 (August 2, 1919): 25; "Why the Negro Appeals to Violence," *Literary Digest* 62 (August 9, 1919): 11; "Are We Menaced by a New Race War?", *Current Opinion* 69 (July

1920): 82-85; "Our Own Race War," *North American Review* 210 (October 1919): 436-38; "The Negro at Bay," *Nation* 108 (June 14, 1919): 931; "Has the Negro Gone Bolshevik?", *World Outlook* 5 (October 1919): 12-13; Stephen Graham, "Militancy of Colour and Its Leader," *Nineteenth Century and After* 88 (November 1920): 909-13; "An English View of the 'Black Peril' in America," *Current Opinion* 70 (February 1921): 219-21; "Moving Toward Race War," *New Republic* 27 (June 22, 1921): 96-97; Herbert J. Seligmann, *The Negro Faces America,* 2nd ed., (New York, 1924), pp. 192-94, 205-206, 224; R. Halliburton, Jr., "The Tulsa Race War of 1921," *Journal of Black Studies* 2 (March 1972): 333, 337-38.

34. Hartt, " 'Our Own Subject Race' Rebels," p. 25; R. M. Whitney, *Reds in America* (New York, 1924), pp. 189-90; "What the South Thinks of Northern Race-Riots," *Literary Digest* 62 (August 19, 1919): 17-18; New York *Age,* January 11, 1919, p. 4.

35. Glenn Frank, "The Clash of Color: The Negro in American Democracy," *Century* 99 (November 1919): 89-91; Charles S. Johnson, "Public Opinion and the Negro," in *Proceedings of the National Conference of Social Work, 1923* (Chicago, 1923), pp. 498, 501.

36. Kerlin, *Voice of the Negro,* pp. 63-70; *Crisis,* November 1920, pp. 16, 18.

37. "A New Color Line," *Public* 22 (February 8, 1919): 129; Johnson, *Black Manhattan,* p. 246.

38. David Brion Davis, ed., *The Fear of Conspiracy: Images of Un-American Subversion from the Revolution to the Present* (Ithaca, N.Y., 1971), p. 208; Jaffe, *Crusade Against Radicalism,* p. 233.

39. Jaffe, *Crusade Against Radicalism,* pp. 224-26.

40. Ibid., pp. 77-78, 216-17, 227-28, 234-36; Davis, *Fear of Conspiracy,* p. 210.

41. "Mob Fury and Race Hatred as a National Danger," *Literary Digest* 69 (June 18, 1921): 9; Halliburton, "Tulsa Race War," p. 349; Edmund David Cronon, *Black Moses: The Story of Marcus Garvey and the Universal Negro Improvement Association* (Madison, Wis., 1955), pp. 98-99; Elton C. Fax, *Garvey: The Story of a Pioneer Black Nationalist* (New York, 1972), pp. 146-48.

42. Charles H. Wesley, *Negro Labor in the United States, 1850-1925: A Study in American Economic History* (New York, 1967), p. 278; Whitney, *Reds in America,* title page, pp. 189-94, 197. The same specter was raised two years later by Henry Cabot Lodge in a Senate speech in which he quoted from a letter, allegedly written by Leon Trotsky and

addressed to Claude McKay, that urged the training of black revolu-
tionaries. *Congressional Record* (68th Cong., 1st Sess., LXV, pt. 1)
(Washington, D.C., 1924), pp. 609-10.

43. "Bolshevizing the American Negro," *Independent* 115 (December 5, 1925): 631; New York *Times,* January 17, 1926, 2: 1-2; New
York *World,* October 26, 1925, pp. 1, 12; November 1, 1925, p. 11;
"The Plot to Make Our Blacks Red," *Literary Digest* 87 (November
21, 1925): 13-14.

44. New York *Herald Tribune,* June 29, 1927, pp. 1, 14; June 30,
1927, p. 20; New York *Age,* July 2, 1927, p. 1; July 9, 1927, p. 4; "To
Turn Negroes into 'Reds!'," *Literary Digest* 94 (July 30, 1927): 13.

45. Arna Bontemps, " 'The Most Dangerous Negro in America,' "
Negro Digest 10 (September 1961): 240; John Henrik Clarke, "A.
Philip Randolph: Portrait of an Afro-American Radical," *Negro Digest*
16 (March 1967): 19; Federated Press release, December 30, 1925, in
Administrative File, Subject File Labor, General, NAACP Papers, Li-
brary of Congress; A. Philip Randolph to Milton Webster, April 5,
1928, August 16, 1928, Brotherhood of Sleeping Car Porters Papers,
Chicago Historical Society.

4 | The *Messenger* and the Harlem Renaissance

Shortly before his death in 1973 poet Arna Bontemps looked back on the course of black cultural development and remarked on the significance of the Harlem Renaissance, noting that while black New York was spared the racial convulsions of 1919, it soon became the center of an even more telling assault on oppression than the bloody riots that occurred elsewhere. He was referring, of course, to the cultural volcano, previously alive but largely dormant, that erupted with such force in the twenties. Harlem, to many, became the greatest black city in the world, possessing not only magnificant churches, luxurious apartment houses, but also an intellectual community supporting Young's Book Exchange, popular forums at the Public Library, several newspapers, and three nationally circulated magazines that came to represent and typify Harlem to the black hinterlands. The Great Migration that had made the rapid darkening of Harlem possible had brought north not only the peasant masses but representatives of the Talented Tenth as well. Other Northern cities caught some of this tide, but what really distinguished Harlem from Chicago or Philadelphia or Boston was the magnetic image of New York: not only was it the nation's cultural and commercial capital, it was also black America's capital of protest and intellect. Langston Hughes acknowledged that it was difficult to sift out whether it was Harlem or New York itself that was the more powerful magnet. But in any case the black migrants *had* to live in Harlem unless they could pass for Mexican or Eurasian or live in the Village, so perforce Harlem became the primary, if not always the initial, focus. What better place for a Renaissance to flower?[1]

The growth in formal cultural and literary expression in the twenties needed organs of expression if it was to become a movement. Necessary were periodicals that would publish stories and poems by new authors as well as criticism that was neither overly harsh nor patronizing. White literary magazines, no matter what their intentions, no matter how much the "New Negro" was in vogue, could not begin to provide sufficient space and encouragement, much less an interested black audience. Fortunately a good part of these needs was satisfied by the three black monthlies founded for purposes other than cultural expression, but all of which, to varying degrees, recognized the burgeoning Harlem Renaissance for what it was. Many individuals saw in this movement "a star to which they could attach their wagons," in the words of Arna Bontemps,[2] and the same could be said for the magazines. The *Crisis* was the first seriously to launch into the publication of new black literature, under the impetus of W. E. B. DuBois and his literary editor, novelist Jessie Fauset. The magazine of the Urban League, *Opportunity,* which began publication in January 1923, also quickly turned to the same materials; the individual most responsible for this was Charles S. Johnson. The *Messenger* too became a periodical in which one could find poems, short stories, theater commentary, and literary criticism, although it enjoyed less prestige as a literary forum than the other two: a comparison of the authors and their writings in the three shows that *Crisis* and *Opportunity* published more of the works of authors who went on to establish firm reputations. But this is not to say that the *Messenger* was an insignificant literary magazine. It performed a valuable service in publishing new poets and authors and printed the best theater criticism to be found anywhere.

The *Messenger* was sympathetic to the Harlem Renaissance and the New Negro spirit but never committed itself to them wholeheartedly.

It would be more accurate to say that while the *Messenger* opened its
pages to new talent as well as old and provided space for a certain
amount of cultural criticism and comment, its editorial columns never
embraced the cultural movement or attempted to spell out a coherent
philosophy for it. What philosophy did appear was incidental, the product of columnists and reviewers, chiefly drama critic Theophilus Lewis.
In other words, the new movement was neglected in the editorial section, yet recognized by individual contributors. The magazine's political-
economic orientation always overshadowed official recognition of the
Renaissance because it viewed cultural nationalism as secondary to more
pragmatic approaches and only one manifestation of a larger "New
Negro" spirit. From the *Messenger's* perspective the New Negro was
not a concept newly coined in the twenties; it was instead the attitude
of militance that had been born in the war and nurtured on the "Red
Summer" of 1919. The magazine had used the term "New Crowd
Negro" in that year to describe a militancy that demanded full political rights, economic opportunity, and complete social equality. This
concept of the New Negro as a politicized being continued to find cur-
rency in the magazine throughout the twenties. It is understandable,
then, that its editorial analysis of *Survey Graphic's* now famous Harlem
issue focused on increasing white interest in the "Negro problem"; it
missed entirely the point that the articles constituted a series of procla-
mations on black culture and nationalism. Likewise, when a reviewer
discussed the same materials expanded in book form by Alain Locke as
The New Negro (1926), he lamented that the "virile, insurgent, revolutionary spirit peculiar to the [New] Negro is missing."[3] In the hands
of one of the magazine's more perceptive writers the volume's import
would have been recognized.

    The most thought-out and consistent commentary on black theater
to be produced during the Harlem Renaissance was the drama criticism
of Theophilus Lewis. From September 1923 to July 1927 he wrote
monthly columns that dissected in honest yet sympathetic ways the
foibles and shortcomings of the black theater as well as the white stage
that produced works on black themes. Mere criticism was not his end;
rather, he intended to provide an ideology for the development of a
national black theater that would be both a source of a racial ethos and
a repository of the race's genius. In so doing Lewis was articulating a

primary goal of the New Negro spirit: racial self-assertion in the arts would provide blacks a cultural foundation derived from their own historical and cultural roots. Lewis's tools were alternately satire (of white stereotypes and of the lingering "slave psychology" among blacks), compassion and sympathy (for the often amateurish efforts of little-theater groups), and exhortation (of playwrights to write serious drama, and of actors to demand serious and racially meaningful roles). His columns—urbane and witty, biting, but never malicious—showed the impact of Mencken's *Smart Set.* His fundamental theme, that the primary need of blacks in establishing their cultural independence was for a national black theater grounded in the works of black playwrights, was a justifiable criticism.

Theophilus Lewis's knowledge of the theater was more intuitive than scholastic. A native of Baltimore, born March 4, 1891, Lewis had little formal schooling but from the beginning had a great interest in the theater. He liked to go to shows, and as a teenager attended whatever and whenever he could: vaudeville, burlesque, anything that was available and that he could afford. Lewis came to New York before World War I and there met A. Philip Randolph and Chandler Owen, who were soon to begin publishing the *Messenger.* When the United States became involved in the war, Lewis went into the service and was sent overseas. Returning to New York in 1922, he secured a job in the post office.

Lewis started writing for the *Messenger* almost by chance. Given his longstanding interest in the theater, he naturally was drawn to the Lafayette Theater in Harlem and soon was a frequent visitor there. One day, after seeing a performance, he wrote a review of the play on a whim and showed it to his friend Randolph, although he had never before written any theater criticism. The editor of the *Messenger* liked the review and asked whether Lewis would write such pieces on a regular basis. There could be no remuneration, given the precarious finances of the magazine; all the magazine would do was pay for the tickets. And naturally Lewis would have to do his play-viewing and writing after his regular work at the post office. But Lewis was nonetheless interested, and thus began a fruitful association.[4]

The *Messenger* was lucky to have the services of Lewis. Like the other black monthlies, it was not founded as a literary periodical, but nonetheless noticed cultural developments as new writers began to emerge and demand publication of their works. All three monthlies began to print a considerable volume of the new poetry and fiction as well as book reviews and criticism, but the *Messenger* was the only one to have a regular drama critic. In addition to theater criticism Lewis also reviewed important books such as Langston Hughes's first two volumes of poetry, and he brought to literary criticism the same New Negro perspective to be found in his theater reviews. Lewis also had modest aspirations as a creative writer and published four of his own short stories in the magazine in addition to collaborating with George S. Schuyler on the latter's satiric column, "Shafts and Darts."

However much Lewis may have lacked a formal education, he possessed considerable gifts that did not go unnoticed in the literary world. Arna Bontemps remembered him as an intellectual whose mind was widely respected among the black intelligentsia of Harlem. In particular, Wallace Thurman, who later joined the *Messenger* staff through Lewis's influence, considered him to be a real scholar of the theater; so, too, did Langston Hughes and George Schuyler. And despite the fact that the *Messenger* was not as well known as the *Crisis* or *Opportunity*, the word circulated among young artists and writers that Lewis was the only drama critic they could take seriously. The other "critics" rarely displayed any discrimination and did little more than promote any show that promised to be successful.[5]

Harlem was the capital of formal black culture in the country, just as was New York for the nation as a whole. What passed for a national black stage (which played a circuit of New York, Philadelphia, Washington, and sometimes Chicago) had its inspiration and headquarters in Harlem. The most common and most popular type of theatrical entertainment was the musical revue, and most of them played either at the Lafayette or Lincoln theaters, both white-owned and -operated. They usually consisted of a series of dance and musical numbers with an inevitable chorus line of beautiful girls. The degree of excellence of acting, dance, and music, as well as taste, ran an expected full gamut. High theater it was not, but Lewis and others recognized that its best examples provided something invaluable to black audiences, if only productions composed, written, and acted by blacks.

Lewis was of two minds about the revues and low-humor comedies. Some were often cheap and tawdry, yet others could be elevating in their joy, mirth, and infectious music and dancing. They might provide

absolutely no challenge to acting skills, yet still be perfect vehicles for
such genuine stars as Florence Mills and Irvin Miller. The major drawback to the revues was that the supply of fresh ideas and new dance
combinations was easily exhausted. Programs at the Lafayette and the
Lincoln changed frequently, because of the almost insatiable demand
for new revues, and the productions were not presented in repertory
fashion; as a consequence, Lewis noted, even the best-known and most-
talented writers and producers borrowed shamelessly from previous
successes. One of the better revues was *The Sheik of Harlem,* starring
Hattie King Reavis and Irvin Miller, which allowed mid-1923 audiences
to see "the frothy side of Harlem life" with all its foibles and vices
prominently displayed, as well as a chorus of "sweet baby vamps."
(Lewis's commentary, while not always employing flapper terminology,
was usually spicy and interlarded with his admiration for the charms
and beauties of the female form.) Unfortunately the shoddy or imita-
tive revues outnumbered the finer ones, although the audiences seemed
to enjoy them all; this only proved to Lewis how fastidious were the
tastes of the Harlem show-going public.[6]

The best examples of the revue, however, served good purposes and
could be justified as art. Lewis was honest enough to admit that he
more often than not enjoyed the dancing, bawdy jokes, and shedding
of clothes, as well as the fine comedy and music of artists like Noble
Sissle and Eubie Blake. He recognized the special liberties allowed by
the Roaring Twenties and that its freedoms and joys might well not
last:

> I look upon these musical shows and call them good. It is the busi-
> ness of the theater to satisfy spiritual craving. Whether the craving
> is refined or ethical is beside the point, so long as it's human. Since
> these shows satisfy a very definite and intense desire they are sound
> theater. So let us enjoy their verve, beauty and sin while we may,
> for the drear and inevitable day is coming when they will be against
> the law.

One revue that reached this higher plane was *Gay Harlem* (1927), not
simply entertaining but intelligent in its humor and poking satire. It
displayed neither racial buffooneries nor stereotypes, but portrayed in

honest fashion the foibles and rakishness of black life. As such, Lewis unreservedly defended its seminudity against the charge of encouraging a decline in modesty. Rather, a general societal decline in modesty had resulted in nudity on the stage. And that was precisely why the scantily clad performers were a valuable contribution to contemporary life and theater, for this was nothing less than art holding up a mirror to life. This was the musical revue at its best.[7]

One of Theophilus Lewis's pet crusades was against the belief that only light-skinned women were "beautiful." Nowhere was this color line more in evidence than in the revues. The chorus was often the highlight of an otherwise pedestrian production, and for many its scarcely clad, long-legged members were the main attraction of the evening's entertainment. But to see even a medium-brown girl was a rarity. The otherwise mediocre *Come Along, Mandy* had the "theatrical sensation of the decade—colored girls in the chorus!" The girls in *Club Alabam*, however, were the usual "high yaller." And of the whole cast of *Blackbirds of 1926*, ironically, all the females but the two stars were "biological whites." Lewis attributed this discrimination to a psychology rooted in slavery, and it was certainly not confined to the musical stage. Suffice it to say the New Negro perceived that along with a new definition of black culture would have to come new standards of aesthetics, of which color was a major component.[8]

The musical stage was not without importance, but Lewis, and probably any other serious student of the drama, would have insisted that it hardly served the functions of a race theater. It did provide employment for many actors and actresses and dancers, but only in the realm of comedy. The same held true for playwrights: the musical stage was not the place for serious drama. And despite the protestations of James Weldon Johnson that the best musical revues broke completely with the minstrel tradition, there was certainly enough that was similar for younger critics to view it as a limited and stereotyped medium. It was clear to Lewis that a truly racial theater based on black values and rooted in the black consciousness would come about primarily through the medium of serious drama, for serious drama was the repository of a society's (or race's) collective spiritual life, culture, and character.[9]

Several significant advances in the serious portrayal of blacks in drama were recorded by Lewis in the mid-1920s. There was promising activity

coming from (often short-lived) little-theater groups, as well as the occasional play written by a white, that presented blacks as believable and
sympathetic characters and provided roles that were at the same time
challenging to the competent actor, also sometimes white. Such a play
was *Roseanne,* white-authored and starring in its original production
in 1924 a white actress portraying a black character. Despite the lack
of black personnel, Lewis praised it because it portrayed a believable
Negro character "without sentimentality or exaggeration." In the same
year Eugene O'Neill's *All God's Chillun Got Wings,* although suffering
by comparison with *The Emperor Jones,* was hailed not only as a vehicle for Paul Robeson's considerable talents, but also for showing that
black people led lives, not in a vacuum, but in juxtaposition to others
and to society. In addition the play gave black actors four major roles
and in so doing greatly enriched black acting experience.[10]

That Lewis could praise white-authored plays for contributing significantly to black drama does not mean that he disregarded the New
Negro goal of developing black playwrights in order to ensure that the
race's life would be accurately portrayed. The critic spent no little
energy decrying the paucity of serious black dramatists and showed
clearly how vital this was. To Lewis the playwright was more important
than the actor in the long run, and thus acting should not be developed
at the expense of composition. Actors contributed little to civilization
except the moment of their performance, although exceptional examples occasionally become tradition. But great drama, great plays were
enduring in tangible form. A playwright could create "the idealization
of race character which in the last analysis is the real meaning of Negro
drama." So the first item of importance in the theater was the drama;
then came acting, audience, and production. There were many causes
for the lack of black dramatists—little public support, competing white
drama, public tastes—all of which were valid complaints. But on occasion Lewis could not contain his frustration and disgust at the sorry
state of black playwriting. In reviewing a play so bad he did not even
name it, yet noticing that Charles S. Gilpin, probably the finest black
actor then playing, had transformed his part into a thing of beauty,
Lewis despaired that Gilpin was condemned to perform in such trash.
Blacks simply would not write enough good theater to keep a fine
artist like Gilpin well employed.[11]

Another obstacle to the development of black theater was the matter of audience. At whom should the theater be aimed? The answer to this question depended on several variables, such as the affluence of patrons, the types of themes available, and the type of drama to be presented. In general, Lewis was distrustful of the willingness of the black middle and upper classes to support meaningful theater. Those groups had strenuously objected to the miscegenation theme of *All God's Chillun Got Wings*, focusing on propriety instead of the craftsmanship of the entire production. On the other hand, since so much of the black audience was uncultured, a large number of black entertainments naturally catered to this level. The result was that the more sensitive and intelligent actors were driven out of the theaters. Things would be better if the higher classes attended more often and in so doing demanded a higher degree of fare. This might have the effect of raising the mean of race culture, although it might merely result in the type of Victorian censorship suggested above. The fundamental problem with the upper-class or "higher-intellect" black theater patron, Lewis noted, was that he went to the theater and often ignored his own tastes as well as the desires of the lower classes in the audience and demanded instead that the performance be geared to a set of standards alien to both—to white standards. This patron often insisted that the black theater copy the suave manners and conventions of the white theater, which at base reflected the racial experience and heritage of a different tradition. The result was sterility and artificiality.

Lewis recognized that in the long run it would be best to reach out to those with lower but nonetheless genuine standards. After all, the less-educated group was the greater in number—and numbers pay. Such drama would be much more healthy than a snobbish, artificial "high" theater, and it would also keep more theaters in existence and provide a corps of competent performers. All this was not to say that the problems of a paucity of playwrights and of well-constructed plays and good roles would immediately cease to exist.[12]

Lewis drew attention to two additional weaknesses of the black theater. One was the absence of actors with an understanding of the dignity of their calling. There were in fact plenty of black actors, but all too many were willing to play for low humor or obscenity. And it was plain that the black stage had more than enough low comedy already, even though the best of it far surpassed that found in the white theater, and in this respect the black stage enriched and helped to liberate the sexually repressed white world. A second, related weakness concerned the ownership and control of the theaters in Harlem. Lewis cited figures showing that white owners controlled 50 percent of the theaters and 75 percent of the patronage of blacks in New York. These whites were not cultured persons linked to the white stage—they were cheap vaudeville entrepreneurs and sideshow vendors. Most of the black owners were alleged to be of the same generally low character. Neither was qualified to make cultural contributions to the community. If they managed to uplift the theater, it would only be because that would pay immediate profits, which was very doubtful; experimental and high-level theater was bound to lose money and would have to be underwritten by money-making popular theater. The influence of the white theater promoters was doubly pernicious. Not only did they produce jaded theater, but they produced it in part for the tastes of voyeuristic whites who were titillated by risqué black-and-tan entertainment. The lesson was clear to Lewis: "Without economic autonomy the Negro stage can never become the flexible medium for the expression of the spirit of Negro people it ought to be."[13]

If Harlem's established theaters could not be depended to sponsor serious and probably unprofitable drama, the task then lay with little-theater groups. Lewis paid attention to such groups and was often solicitous of their efforts even in the face of pedestrian and amateurish performances. He always managed to say something good about a particular evening's offering, for he regarded the little-theater movement as perhaps the only foundation on which a truly national black theater could be built. So even the most pathetic attempts offered some encouragement and hope.

Lewis's prescription for the health and vitality of the little-theater movement was a simple one: perform, perform, and perform some more. During its first year(s) of existence the most important thing was to keep putting on plays, mediocre though they be. This would develop actors, who as they became more accomplished would inspire dramatists to write good plays for them. And the frequent performances would create and begin to hold a public. All of this could be done without resident geniuses in either the acting or the playwriting departments.

Several famous white little-theater groups, Lewis noted, had succeeded without such exceptional talent. The crucial task was to develop competent acting quickly. But to do this any company would have to become at least semiprofessional. Good acting could be acquired in only two ways: hire already trained and competent professional actors; or pay resident amateurs who showed promise, so that they could afford dramatic training. In either case money was necessary. Who would provide funds? Lewis was confident that there was a segment of the population that could be induced to support such endeavors, but in order to secure its cooperation the productions of the group should be geared in their direction. Lewis defined that group as those who desired theater entertainment but were so dissatisfied with what was currently available that they would contribute toward subsidizing new theater more in accord with their tastes. But that returned the matter to the dilemma of the sophistication of the audience and its various ideas of artistic taste. There was no easy answer, and Lewis was perhaps more optimistic than was warranted; it was not easy to keep a little theater alive without some outside patronage or support that might or might not have strings attached.[14]

Lewis saw the little-theater movement as a precursor and component of what he hoped would become a national black theater. To develop a race theater meant that a national theater must be constructed. It would have to be grounded on indigenous drama by its own playwrights, or else it would become only the "sepia province of American Theater." Yet it must not isolate itself and address its appeal exclusively to black audiences. The problem could be seen in the nature of Harlem, where conditions were admittedly most propitious for the development of a black theater. Even there only a fraction of the population, perhaps no more than five thousand, would initially support serious theater. Thus it must be on a low budget and repertory basis. It would have to educate and win its audience, and since much of that audience was conditioned by movies, the initial plays should be mostly melodrama, mysteries, and farce. But when the audience had been won over, more serious productions could be attempted. Finally, a nationwide network of repertory companies should be organized so that productions could be exchanged. This was the stage at which a national race theater would come into being.[15]

What was to be done about the matter of popular taste? First, the race theater would have to develop outside the houses controlled by whites. The more serious problem lay in the concept of legitimacy. Lewis went to the heart of the matter when he noted that one of the fundamental causes of weakness in the black theater was its unwritten philosophy that the only "legitimate" theater was the white stage, particularly Broadway. The black theater had wrongly tried to excel at the things Broadway did, even though the white stage usually portrayed blacks only in caricature. The Lafayette Players, the only permanent company of adult performers in Harlem, took their cues from Broadway and performed ten-year-old, castoff plays. Not only did the Lafayette group fail to encourage black playwrights, it did not even keep pace with the white theaters it set out to emulate. Instead of crying for a "chance" on the white stage, Lewis asked, why not produce black drama on the black stage for black audiences? With a contribution of a hundred dollars monthly from the five richest black churches in New York City, a resident company would employ Charles Gilpin and Paul Robeson on a regular basis and offer the finest of drama to black audiences. But did the public really want this? Aside from his own fulminations on the subject and an occasional column in *Opportunity,* Lewis claimed to have heard no complaint from either public or cultural figures. He described the result in September 1924: "What we call the Negro Theater is an anemic sort of thing that does not reflect Negro life, Negro fancies or Negro ideas. It reflects the 100 percent American Theater at its middling and cheapest."[16]

The cultural ethos of the New Negro balanced two views on the subject of the race's contributions. On the one hand, blacks should strive to develop their own cultural institutions and ideals so that for the first time an accurate representation of black life would be available. Thereby the spiritual part of the racial heritage would be preserved and fostered. On the other hand, the contributions blacks made to culture would be to the whole of culture. The New Negro saw himself as contributing not only to his race but also to American (and world) culture. It was not to be a separatist movement. Theophilus Lewis described the process of enriching the racial heritage, advising that "the Negro stage should be a vital force in the spiritual life of the race; it should constantly delight . . . and . . . exalt . . . and it should crystallize that delight and exaltation in a form worthy of being preserved as a part of our racial contribution to the general culture of mankind."[17]

But he also saw the issue from a more radical position, in which blacks would hold themselves somewhat aloof from American civilization, contributing to it, yet reserving judgment on whether to join it wholeheartedly:

> Now the Negro Problem is this: It is the question whether a youthful people living in the midst of an old and moribund civilization shall die with it or find themselves able to shake loose from its complexities and build their own culture on its ruins. . . . This condition of doubt will find its esthetic expression in dissonances of sound and color, and such explosive comedy and tragedy as results from the struggles of a passionate people to escape the restraints of the Calvinist version of the Ten Commandments.
>
> The task for the Negro artist, then, is to observe the confusion of rusting flivvers, vanishing forests, migratory populations and expiring faiths which confronts him and reveal its meaning in a felicitous manner. He will show us, perhaps, the convulsions of a world breaking down in chaos. Perhaps the nuclei of a new world forming in incandescence.[18]

Lewis did not confine his commentary to the theater; both poetry and fiction also fell within his self-taught expertise. Here, as with the theater criticism, his views were as consistently New Negro as could be found in the *Messenger*. Again his asset was not formal training but instead a well-developed intellectual sense both of the aesthetic and of the prospects for an autonomous black culture. His larger view of the Harlem Renaissance was critical yet charitable; from today's perspective his criticism seems well founded.

Writing in late 1926, and the date is significant, Lewis declined to get on the bandwagon and celebrate a renaissance in the black arts. He pointed out that the spirituals were not at all triumphs of art, that he knew of no first-rank black musicians, that blacks had no special talent for dramatic art, and that only two writers under forty were producing genuine literature: George S. Schuyler in humor and Jean Toomer in short fiction. Judging from these criteria, the talk of a renaissance was built on very thin evidence. Only poetry justified such optimism. Langston Hughes, Countee Cullen, Georgia Douglass Johnson, Claude McKay, Arna Bontemps, Wallace Thurman, Gwendolyn Bennett, Helene Johnson, and half a dozen more were producing poetry every bit as good as that written by Edgar Lee Masters and his generation. The reasons why there was good poetry yet meager contributions in other art forms could be seen in the historical background of black Americans. Poetry, Lewis explained, evolves from a folk sooner than does prose; poetry, on the whole, expresses emotion whereas prose expresses ideas. Thus the poet finds the language and thought patterns prepared for him earlier than does the novelist or essayist. And as for cultural ideas which grow out of a refined way of living, blacks had produced none at all. To Lewis the black background was one rich in feeling but so far barren in ideas, which made it no surprise to see many respectable poets but few notable writers of fiction.

Lewis's criticism, taken in the context of 1926, seems neither incorrect nor uncharitable. Up to that time poetry was indeed the finest product of the young writers. Prior to that year not much prose besides Toomer's stories had emerged from the Renaissance. One may quarrel with a few of the names included in Lewis's list of notables—posterity has not given Schuyler a rank with Toomer, and Wallace Thurman never became a poet of distinction—but his vision was essentially correct.[19] His appreciation of some of the best poetry of the period, as well as the perceptiveness of his New Negro vision, can be seen in his reviews of Langston Hughes's first two collections.

In reviewing *The Weary Blues,* Lewis placed Hughes in the category of those poets who bear unmistakably the marks of race, as opposed to those who voice universal human feelings. The former, Lewis thought, would ultimately prevail over the latter, and Hughes showed why. He had gone directly to life for his themes and harmonies, not life past, but life "in its current incandescence as it roars and blazes in the bosoms of the new race of American blacks." In giving expression to the incoherent feelings and impulses of his people, Hughes was a unifying spiritual agent. Some of his verse came "straight from the guts of 133rd Street." In using a Charleston rhythm in one poem, he literally made it dance. When Lewis read *Fine Clothes to the Jew* a year later, he was prepared to be disappointed by another volume of blues poetry, fearing that Hughes had become ensnared in a cabaret-nightlife trap. But Hughes had discovered another side of blues life, a more subdued one, one characterized by wistfulness. These poems, Lewis thought, were in fact more original than those in the first volume, for Hughes seemed to have probed even deeper into life and found things others could not perceive. For that reason people might regard his poems as freakish or strange or startling compared to the conventional forms, but this very quality was what Lewis predicted would make Hughes's work enduring. Lewis's prediction about the reactions of others was accurate. Most black "critics" thought *Fine Clothes to the Jew* vulgar: the Pittsburgh *Courier* headlined its review "Langston Hughes' Book of Poems Trash," and the New York *Amsterdam News* wrote of "Langston Hughes—The Slum Dweller."[20]

Plainly Theophilus Lewis had a clear and consistent vision of the direction and destination of black culture. But what was his relationship to the *Messenger?* Was he articulating the collective voice of the journal, or was the part-time critic and full-time postal clerk merely being allowed to air his personal views and lend a veneer of culture to the publication? The latter is closer to the truth. There was for a long time no regular book reviewer or poetry or fiction critic. Wallace Thurman was the only other person writing from a consciously New Negro perspective, and his tenure was all too short. George Schuyler had the wit and wisdom to be a fine critic but was too cynical about the "Negro Art Hokum" to be a sympathetic champion of the Renaissance. When "The World's Greatest Negro Monthly" published incisive and forward-looking criticism and commentary, it was more by fortuitous circumstance than by conscious design. Without the presence of Lewis the *Messenger* would have had precious little cultural analysis of enduring interest. He was, in Arna Bontemps words, the "literary brain" of the magazine. Known and valued by those who could appreciate him in the twenties, his subsequent neglect by critics like Harold Cruse is entirely undeserved.[21]

It would be incorrect to assume that not until the emergence of a visible cultural movement did fiction and poetry appear in the *Messen-*

ger. In fact the first issue, in November 1917, featured a short story, poems, and theater news in addition to the dominant political concerns. A pattern of occasional literary contributions persisted up to the time when the *Messenger* recognized the Renaissance and encouraged culture in a more systematic manner. The early pieces, especially the poems of Claude McKay and Walter Everett Hawkins, contained anti-Establishment or radical themes. While these poems were printed more for politics' than for art's sake, their impact was nonetheless an important one. McKay's militant poems moved young blacks to introspection and anger. Arna Bontemps recalled that everyone's blood came to a boil when reading "If We Must Die." This and other poems opened the eyes of Bontemps and his contemporaries to aspects of themselves and their race they had not previously seen. It was a result the *Messenger* would have appreciated.[22]

A consistent interest in fiction and poetry for its own sake cannot be seen in the *Messenger* until about late 1923, a date that roughly corresponds with the opening works of the Harlem Renaissance. Theophilus Lewis joined the staff around September 1923, when his first drama criticism appeared. By March 1924 the magazine was definitely aware of the cultural awakening, as two poems by Langston Hughes and one by Countee Cullen appeared in that month's issue. From then until the demise of the magazine in mid-1928 every issue had some poetry or cultural commentary and usually both.

At least four persons were responsible for the literary emphasis of the *Messenger* in the mid-1920s. The most ambiguous role was played by A. Philip Randolph. Arna Bontemps credits him with the original literary impulse of the magazine. It is probable that, given his partiality to literature, it did not take much to convince him that the *Messenger* should print the efforts of new writers and poets.[23] But having said this, it must be noted that neither Randolph nor Chandler Owen ever considered cultural nationalism to be a primary solution to the race's difficulties in America. The early inclusion of literature in the *Messenger* either buttressed political themes or was simply a favor to would-be litterateurs. Art for art's sake played no part in it. Randolph could recognize Theophilus Lewis's critical talents, even his conscious New Negro perspective, see that they added breadth to what was becoming something of a family magazine, without himself being a cultural New

Negro. His whole existence was issue oriented, change oriented, and quite naturally politics and economics were his foci. If cultural developments might aid in achieving concrete goals, then they could be welcomed. But if they were perceived to be harmful, as Randolph seemed to view black popular music, then they should be forthrightly criticized. A political consistency thus stands beside a cultural inconsistency.

Theophilus Lewis's usefulness to the magazine went beyond his own columns. The reputation his criticism enjoyed helped develop contacts that brought in more poetry and fiction. A third influence was George S. Schuyler, who served as managing editor, in fact if not in name, for much of the period from mid-1923 to 1928, often doing what a literary editor might on another magazine. It was he who decided what poems and short stories were printed and who should review new books. Despite the fact that only on rare occasions was there any money to pay authors, artistic criteria were applied as far as was possible. Not every unsolicited contribution was printed, and there was a definite effort to achieve literary excellence. Finally, Wallace Thurman had some influence on the literary course of the magazine, becoming associated with it through the recommendation of his friend Theophilus Lewis. Although on the staff for only a few months in mid-1926, he had important contacts with leading literati and was responsible for soliciting contributions from, among others, Hughes and Bontemps.[24]

Over its span of eleven years and 101 issues the *Messenger* published more than 250 poems written by about 90 different individuals. The majority of these poets is unknown today, and it is safe to assume that they neither lived in Harlem, Washington, D.C., or Boston (the three cities with well-known active literary circles) nor had other connections to an organized literary "movement"; nonetheless they were aware of the emerging Renaissance, felt a part of it, and wanted to add their contributions to it.[25] Yet despite the volume of unsolicited poetry, not all of which was accepted, the magazine also printed a sizable amount of verse by writers who had or were in the process of establishing literary reputations. Most of the poetic lights of the Renaissance showed up in the *Messenger*'s pages at one point or another.

Young Langston Hughes, while not yet out of Lincoln University, was recognized as literary "hot property" by the *Messenger,* which, especially during Wallace Thurman's tenure as managing editor, was eager

for anything from his pen. Sixteen of his poems found publication in
the magazine, as did eight by fellow Lincoln poet Edward L. Silvera.
The Washington, D.C., literary circle surrounding Georgia Douglass Johnson was also well represented in the *Messenger*; sixteen of her poems
appeared, as did several by Angelina Grimké, Lewis Alexander, and
Walter Everett Hawkins. Of the Harlem group, besides Hughes and
McKay, the *Messenger* published a handful of poems by Countee Cullen,
Arna Bontemps, Wesley Curtwright, Johnathan Henderson Brooks,
artist Bruce Nugent, and Wallace Thurman.

Boston's Saturday Evening Quill Club was represented in the poetry
category by Helene Johnson, while other members of that circle made
different contributions: Eugene Gordon edited a monthly feature on
the best editorials in the black newspaper press, and Dorothy West,
cousin to Miss Johnson, sent one of her many short stories. In all,
twenty-three authors published a total of thirty-five short works of
fiction in the *Messenger,* and several came from the pens of talented
writers like Miss West, Zora Neal Hurston, Hughes, Thurman, and
Eric Walrond. Hughes's three short stories, the first ones he published,
are of particular interest because of their autobiographical nature, describing the adventures of a young man away from home alone for the
first time, bound for the African coast on a tramp steamer. Many of
the details in these stories would be familiar to readers of *The Big Sea.*

An author in a category all his own was George S. Schuyler. His
monthly column "Shafts and Darts" was always satiric in tone and
usually quite witty, displaying his debt to H. L. Mencken. In the same
vein was a one-act play, *The Yellow Peril,* concerning a "high yaller"
courtesan and her eventual (and humorous) downfall from having too
many irons in the fire. To Langston Hughes, Schuyler's satire and bite,
"verbal, vigorous brickbats," were the most interesting thing in the
Messenger, and no doubt many readers, excluding frequent targets
like Marcus Garvey, looked forward to seeing whose hide would be
pierced by the next month's "Shafts."[26]

The *Messenger* viewed with benevolence the increasing production
of poetry and fiction, and in general the avant-garde works received a
more sympathetic review than those cast in a traditional mold. This was
due in good measure to the efforts of Wallace Thurman and Theophilus

Lewis. But the opposite was the case with music. Here the magazine concluded that the newer musical forms—jazz and the blues—were little credit to the race. This orientation illustrates well one of the central dilemmas of the Harlem intellectuals: Was their product to be "high culture," a folk oriented culture, or some new synthesis of the two? On the whole, the *Messenger* took a conservative stance.

Nathan Huggins has recently noted that Western societies in the early decades of the century all presumed that culture (literature, music, art) was the way in which civilizations were to be measured. The Harlem artists with few exceptions used this yardstick as their guide, as did many white artists. Consequently, most of them focused overwhelmingly on "high culture," not on the culture of the common people. Given this orientation, it was hard to escape the white cultural definitions, for most of the black intellectuals saw themselves not only as blacks in search of a new identity, but also as Americans and builders of an American civilization. Only Langston Hughes among the major figures took jazz seriously. Everyone, of course, recognized jazz as "background," as a source, but an unrefined source from which a higher, truer art would come. Jazz and the blues, then, were to most artists and commentators the raw materials from which a higher culture could be built.[27]

The *Messenger* at times shared this building-block view, and at other times it took an even more reactionary stance. Early in 1923 Josephine Cogdell (later Mrs. George Schuyler), a young white would-be critic, wrote on "Truth in Art in America" and had the following to say for jazz:

> Our prohibited instincts riot disgustingly here like thirsty men in a desert oasis; we revel in "Jazz." This "lets off steam" but it deplorably cheapens our instincts and corrupts the true spirit of music. Jazz is essentially a capitalistic production, it steals its melodies from all sources, the Masters, the Negroes, the Orient, with naïve greed and unconcern, then proceeds to ruin them. It is as noisy and rapacious as the system that creates it.

The fact that "The World's Greatest Negro Monthly" allowed an uninformed white to pass unfavorable judgment on jazz shows how far the magazine was from a sympathetic understanding of what music meant to the New Negro, much less to the masses of the black population. The commentary of a black critic the following year managed a slightly more positive view. Composer W. Astor Morgan wrote that the blues were often crude, illiterate, and vulgar, but he was confident that some day classically trained composers would build on the musical genius that resided in the blues to create a really fine modern music. If unlettered persons could improvise pleasingly on the blues, what could a classically trained composer do by adding counterpoint, harmony, and structure? The blues might be an embarrassment today, but tomorrow could find them the raw material for a new Verdi or Handel![28]

Two editorials, voicing Randolph's opinions, contained similar views. One deplored the fact that black audiences did not seem to want anything "High Class"; rather than view serious drama or music, audiences preferred "Mamie Smith and various blues singers whose offerings range between the racially derogatory or the vulgar." Another editorial shows how conventional and bourgeois the tastes of the *Messenger* had become by 1924 and how out of touch the magazine was with the new spirit of black people and black music. The blues were simply "musical pablum." By comparison, the cultural food of immigrants and native whites was alleged to be a steady diet of opera. Opera represented culture, poetry, and art; the blues represented only what was "loud, boisterous, cheap, tawdry, [and] unmusical." Taking a broad swipe at the black folk heritage, the writer observed that it took a good deal more education to write operas than to create the blues. The lesson of all this was ominous: "A race that hums operas will stay ahead of a race that simply hums the 'blues.' "[29]

Encouragement was not lacking for blacks to take an interest in classical music. An inspiring biography of the composer Samuel Coleridge-Taylor portrayed his perseverance from humble beginnings to international fame. An article on pianist Helen E. Hagen honored her as a model of what representative black art should be, rather than the "clownism and buffoonery of Negro buck and wing dancers, rag-time piano plunkers, black-faced comedians and questionable jubilee singers." Roland Hayes was lauded as the first black artist to sing with the Boston Symphony Orchestra. This was proof, Randolph wrote, that blacks could be trained and sing as well as whites; to whom this needed proving is unclear. And Robert Nathaniel Dett, "the greatest composer the Negro race has produced since S. Coleridge-Taylor," was honored in the *Messenger*'s Afro-American Academy, a black hall of fame.[30]

Clearly Randolph was the major influence steering the magazine in this direction. As a youth he had been exposed to "classical" literature and began to acquire an Oxford accent; as a young man in Harlem he performed the classics of English-speaking culture. So his personal predilections lay in a definite direction. Beyond that he apparently believed, with many members of the Talented Tenth, that the race would progress fastest as it put its best foot forward. Thus the note of pride (and perhaps of relief?) that Roland Hayes could indeed sing as well as a white tenor. There is nothing inherently reactionary, of course, in preferring classical music; but in dismissing jazz and the blues, the magazine was clearly rejecting both the New Negro interest in "pop" and folk forms as well as the musical idioms most meaningful to the masses. It does not appear that Randolph, the self-appointed spokesman for black working-class interests, ever appreciated either the inconsistency or the insult inherent in his judgment on contemporary black music.

Granted that the contemporary spirit was denied in the *Messenger*'s analysis of black music; this example notwithstanding, the magazine's contribution to the growth and nurturing of the Harlem Renaissance was important. Theophilus Lewis's criticism stands in the front rank of its day. But above all, the simple fact that the *Messenger* was willing to take culture seriously and open its pages to both established and aspiring writers signifies that it was a real asset to the black community in the twenties. The weekly black press could not be depended on for serious literary or theater criticism or book reviews, nor did it have space for publication of poetry, short fiction, and drama. So it fell to the three national magazines, and to a handful of other, short-lived periodicals, to fill this gap. Only three of the major white periodicals— *New Masses, Modern Quarterly,* and the *American Mercury*—were truly open to black writers in the twenties, and their (less than full) embrace of black letters could not begin to satisfy the need for publication. In a sense, neither could the *Messenger,* the *Crisis,* and *Opportunity,* for while they all welcomed black literary efforts, none was a strictly literary periodical.[31]

In volume of poetry, fiction, and plays the three monthlies published approximately the same amount of works. The number of poems the *Crisis, Opportunity,* and the *Messenger* printed for the time period January 1923 through June 1928 was 194, 202, and 226, respectively. For the same span the number of works of short fiction published was 30, 30, and 32. The pattern differs in the number of plays published; here the figures are 5, 4, and 1.

The volume of criticism—of art, theater, literature, poetry—published by the monthlies offers a further basis for comparison. The *Crisis* had fewer articles than the other two; most of its criticism appeared in the monthly column "Horizon," and much of its content centered on DuBois's pet project, the Krigwa little-theater group. *Opportunity* carried more articles on the visual arts than the other two magazines combined, with a considerable emphasis on African art. It also commented on such important topics as folk and dialect questions, white theater on black themes, and the new writers. The *Messenger* featured somewhat more writing on general cultural topics as well as the extensive drama criticism of Theophilus Lewis, but lagged behind *Opportunity* in in-depth analyses on other topics. The generalization can be made, then, that the most extensive cultural critique in the mid-1920s among the black magazines was to be found in *Opportunity,* with the exception of theater commentary, which was strongest in the *Messenger.*

The two brightest lights among the young poets, Langston Hughes and Countee Cullen, published much more in the *Crisis* and *Opportunity* than in the *Messenger.* The same was true of Claude McKay, Arna Bontemps, and Lewis Alexander. But for other poets this was not the pattern. Georgia Douglass Johnson published as many poems in the *Messenger* as she did in *Crisis,* and less than half as many in the third magazine. Some writers published in the *Messenger* and *Opportunity* but not at all in *Crisis* during the period 1923 to mid-1928; included in this category are Helene Johnson, Wesley Curtwright, Wallace Thurman, Zora Neal Hurston, Dorothy West, and Eric Walrond. A rough generalization can be drawn from this: for the fullest selection of poetry by new authors, one would turn first to *Opportunity,* then to the *Crisis,* and third to the *Messenger;* none of the three, however, should be ignored, for all printed important works.

Different writers had varying criteria for deciding which poems or stories to send to which magazines. Arna Bontemps recalled that on one occasion he sent the *Messenger* two poems that had already been rejected by periodicals like the *Crisis* and *Opportunity,* and noted that other writers had done the same. The two poems in question were published, but never subsequently included in any of Bontemps's collections. Langston Hughes exercised a somewhat different option when he sent his first tentative efforts in short fiction to Wallace Thurman, the managing editor of the *Messenger*. Thurman accepted Hughes's first short stories, paying ten dollars apiece for them, with the comment that they were very bad but that the magazine could find nothing better.[32]

Hughes published 16 poems in the *Messenger,* 62 in the *Crisis,* and 24 in *Opportunity* during the period being surveyed. What is more significant is the number that he chose to include in his first two collections. The first volume was *The Weary Blues* (1926), and whereas it contained no *Messenger* poems, 20 poems published in the *Crisis* and 7 from *Opportunity* appeared. *Fine Clothes to the Jew* (1927) featured one poem first published in the *Messenger,* three from the *Crisis,* and two from *Opportunity*. It seems reasonable to hypothesize that Hughes regarded the poems published in the *Crisis,* and to a lesser extent in *Opportunity,* as being more worthy of preservation in collected form than those he sent to the *Messenger*. This does not unequivocally demostrate that Hughes sent only his rejects to the *Messenger,* but it does indicate that he had a higher regard for the other two magazines from the standpoint of a literary platform.

The case of Georgia Douglass Johnson is different, however. While not generally ranked with Hughes, she is nonetheless an important poet of the times. Her only collection in this period was *An Autumn Love Cycle* (1928), in which she included two poems first published in the *Messenger,* three from the *Crisis,* and none from *Opportunity*. What conclusions are to be drawn from this? Considering the fact that she had printed sixteen poems in both the *Crisis* and the *Messenger* and only five in *Opportunity,* is one to assume that *Opportunity* rejected most of her poems, which she then sent elsewhere? Probably not, or else why would she not preserve any of the *Opportunity*-published poems in her collection if that magazine had such superior standards? Or did she have a special relationship with the *Crisis* and the *Messenger* and favor them with her poems for reasons other than the literary reputation of the periodicals? These possibilities lead one to question the generalization advanced by Bontemps that authors tended to send only their second-rate productions to the *Messenger*.

This selective process would only have operated for those writers who already enjoyed ready access to the *Crisis* and *Opportunity* and whose talents were sufficiently recognized by others. Yet the literary editors of these two magazines were not infallible; the mere fact that a poem was rejected by either is not proof that the poem had no literary merit. What is true is that the *Crisis* and *Opportunity* tended to print more of the works of the well-known authors, and proportionally more of these poems were collected in the authors' volumes of poetry. Despite this, the *Crisis* and *Opportunity* printed many stories and poems by persons who today are unknowns, many of the same "unknowns" who also published in the *Messenger*. And in a few cases the *Messenger* published the work of important authors who did not publish in *Opportunity* or the *Crisis* at all in this period. So it would be wrong to categorically state that the *Messenger* commonly got the dregs of an author's writings.

The question of the reputation of the magazines is nonetheless important, and there are clear reasons for the differences between the three. A major factor was that the *Messenger* was so meagerly financed that it never employed a person who functioned exclusively as literary editor. This was definitely an advantage for the other two, which had Jessie Fauset (*Crisis*) and Charles S. Johnson (*Opportunity*). Schuyler was no unlettered man, but he did not have unlimited time to devote to encouraging and seeking out new writers; neither did Theophilus Lewis, who had more than enough to do working in the Post Office by day and going to shows at night. Wallace Thurman did not stay with the magazine long enough to have a permanent impact.

A second factor has to do with the audiences of the magazines. Both the *Crisis* and *Opportunity* had a greater circulation than did the *Messenger;* they enjoyed as well a more national readership because they were the organs of integrated racial-uplift groups. While the *Messenger* did have some white readers, its audience in the mid-twenties was primarily black. The *Crisis* and *Opportunity,* on the other hand, reached a much greater white public. It is natural to suppose that young writers beginning to establish reputations would hope to have themselves well known not only among their race but also in the white literary world, which held a far greater potential audience. One might thus naturally prefer to publish in the *Crisis* or *Opportunity,* without having to draw the conclusion that the *Messenger* was a second-rate periodical. And in fact it was not. Its canons of taste and discrimination in literary merit were not below those of the other two. In drama criticism it was surpassed by none. The *Messenger* needs no apology simply because it did not enjoy as high a reputation in literary circles as did the other two; on the contrary, the most significant point is that all three magazines were of crucial importance to spreading the works of the Harlem Renaissance and giving encouragement to aspiring artists. Had any one of the three not so opened its pages, the New Negro cultural movement would have been that much poorer.

NOTES

1. Arna Bontemps, "The Awakening: A Memoir," in Bontemps, *The Harlem Renaissance Remembered* (New York, 1972), p. 5; Rollin Lynde Hartt, "I'd Like to Show You Harlem," *Independent* 105 (April 2, 1921): 334-35; Nathan Irvin Huggins, *Harlem Renaissance* (New York, 1971), pp. 18, 21, 22; Langston Hughes, "Harlem Literati in the Twenties," *Saturday Review* 22 (June 22, 1940): 14.

2. Interview, Arna Bontemps, April 22, 1970.

3. *Messenger,* April 1925, p. 156; April 1926, pp. 118-19.

4. Interview, Theophilus Lewis, September 28, 1970; *Catholic World* 153 (May 1941): 239.

5. George S. Schuyler, *Black and Conservative: The Autobiography of George S. Schuyler* (New Rochelle, N.Y., 1966), pp. 142-43; "The Reminiscences of George S. Schuyler," Oral History Research Office, Columbia University, 1962, pp. 81-82, 129; interview, Arna Bontemps, April 22, 1970; interview, Theophilus Lewis; *Messenger,* May 1927, p. 171.

6. *Messenger,* September 1923, pp. 818, 821; December 1923, p. 923; March 1924, p. 74.

7. Ibid., March 1927, p. 85; June 1927, pp. 193, 200.

8. Ibid., February 1924, p. 43; June 1924, p. 182; May 1926, p. 150; February 1925, p. 92.

9. James Weldon Johnson, *Black Manhattan* (New York, 1968), p. 196, referring to *From Dixie to Broadway; Messenger,* October 1926, p. 302.

10. *Messenger,* March 1924, pp. 73-74; July 1924, p. 223.

11. Ibid., December 1923, pp. 923-24; July 1927, pp. 229, 243; December 1924, p. 380.

12. Ibid., April 1924, p. 110; July 1926, pp. 214-15.

13. Ibid., October 1926, p. 301; September 1926, p. 278.

14. Ibid., December 1926, p. 362; November 1926, pp. 334-35.

15. Ibid., December 1923, p. 924; July 1927, pp. 229, 243.

16. Ibid., September 1924, p. 291; January 1925, pp. 14-15.

17. Huggins, *Harlem Renaissance,* p. 11; *Messenger,* July 1926, p. 214.

18. *Messenger,* June 1925, p. 230.

19. Ibid., October 1926, p. 312. Lewis soon came to a different appraisal of his friend Thurman. Shortly after the latter's death in 1934, Lewis wrote that "as editor, novelist and playwright, he was the most versatile of contemporary Afro-American literary men" although "he wrote lousy poetry." Lewis, "Harlem Sketchbook," New York *Amsterdam News,* January 5, 1935.

20. *Messenger,* March 1926, p. 92; March 1927, p. 95; Langston Hughes, *The Big Sea* (New York, 1940), pp. 264-68.

21. Interview, Arna Bontemps, April 22, 1970. Lewis's career after leaving the *Messenger* was a varied one. He continued to work for the post office until retirement, for a black theater critic could hardly make a living in that profession. But he continued to write occasional drama criticism for the *Catholic World, Commonweal, America,* and the Pittsburgh *Courier.* In addition, he was one of the original members (in the 1950s) of New York City's Commission on Human Rights. Interview, Theophilus Lewis. For a more detailed analysis of Lewis's theater criticism, see Theodore Kornweibel, Jr., "Theophilus Lewis and the Theater of the Harlem Renaissance," in Arna Bontemps, ed., *The Harlem Renaissance Remembered* (New York, 1972). Regarding Harold Cruse, he has been harshly critical of the Renaissance for being too little concerned with developing the sort of cultural nationalism that Lewis was speaking of. Cruse seems not to have known of either Lewis or his writings. Harold Cruse, *The Crisis of the Negro Intellectual* (New York, 1967), pp. 36-37.

22. Bontemps, "The Awakening," p. 7.

23. Interview, Arna Bontemps, April 22, 1970; interview, Theophilus Lewis; "Biographical Sketch: A. Philip Randolph" (New York: A. Philip Randolph Institute, n.d.); John Henrik Clarke, "A. Philip Randolph: Portrait of an Afro-American Radical," *Negro Digest* 16 (March 1967): 17.

24. Interview, George S. Schuyler, October 16, 1970; Lewis, "Harlem Sketchbook"; Mae G. Henderson, "Portrait of Wallace Thurman," in Bontemps, ed., *The Harlem Renaissance Remembered*, p. 150.

25. Interview, Arna Bontemps, April 28, 1970.

26. Hughes, "Harlem Literati in the Twenties," p. 13.

27. Huggins, *Harlem Renaissance*, pp. 5, 9-11.

28. *Messenger*, March 1923, p. 636; February 1924, pp. 57-59.

29. Ibid., January 1925, p. 20; March 1924, p. 71.

30. Ibid., July 1926, p. 200; September 1926, pp. 266-67; October 1926, pp. 298, 319; January 1927, pp. 8-9; October 1921, p. 260; January 1924, p. 21; February 1928, p. 34.

31. Hughes, *The Big Sea*, pp. 235-37; Hughes, "Harlem Literati in the Twenties," pp. 13-14; Dorothy Deloris Boone, "A Historical Review and a Bibliography of Selected Negro Magazines, 1910-1969" (Ed.D. dissertation, University of Michigan, 1970), pp. 29-30, 41, 43-45, 100; Haim Genizi, "V. F. Calverton, A Radical Magazinist for Black Intellectuals, 1920-1940," *Journal of Negro History* 57 (July 1972): 241-53.

32. Interview, Arna Bontemps, April 22, 1970; Hughes, *The Big Sea*, pp. 233-34; Hughes, "Harlem Literati in the Twenties," p. 13; Wallace Thurman to Langston Hughes, undated, Hughes Papers, James Weldon Johnson Collection, Yale University.

5 | The "Garvey Must Go" Campaign

Harlem residents in July of 1922 were greeted with a handbill guaranteeing an extraordinary event, Marcus Garvey's climactic and, unintentionally, most uproarious annual convention. It promised to be

A ROYAL NIGHT
for the
Four Hundred Million Negroes of the World
GRAND OPENING OF THE
THIRD ANNUAL INTERNATIONAL CONVENTION OF THE
NEGRO PEOPLES OF THE WORLD
150 THOUSAND DEPUTIES, DELEGATES AND MEMBERS OF THE UNIVER-
SAL NEGRO IMPROVEMENT ASSOCIATION WILL BE IN ATTENDANCE
AT THE OPENING OF THIS GREAT CONVENTION
DEPUTIES AND DELEGATES ARE COMING FROM AUSTRALIA,
ASIA, EUROPE, AFRICA, CANADA, UNITED STATES OF AMERICA
SOUTH AND CENTRAL AMERICA AND THE WEST INDIES
THIS WILL BE THE BIGGEST ASSEMBLAGE OF NEGROES EVER SEEN

NO REAL, LIVING NEGRO CAN AFFORD TO MISS SEEING
THE GREAT INTERNATIONAL DEMONSTRATION
FAMOUS ORATORS AND RACE LEADERS FROM AFRICA, AMERICA AND
THE WEST INDIES WILL SPEAK ON THIS NIGHT
COME & HEAR THE GREATEST CHAMPION
of Race Rights Speak for the Liberty of the NEGRO
THE NEWS OF WHAT HAPPENS ON THIS NIGHT WILL BE FLASHED
AROUND THE WORLD
BE AN EYE-WITNESS TO THE GREAT DEMONSTRATION
THOUSANDS OF OFFICERS AND MEN OF THE UNIVERSAL AFRICAN
LEGION WILL BE ON REVIEW
as also
THOUSANDS OF LADIES OF THE UNIVERSAL AFRICAN MOTOR CORPS
AND AFRICAN BLACK CROSS NURSES
THIS WILL BE THE GREATEST CIVIL AND MILITARY DISPLAY OF
AWAKENED ETHIOPIA
PEOPLE ARE TRAVELLING AS FAR AS SIX THOUSAND MILES
TO WITNESS THIS GREAT DEMONSTRATION AT
THE 71st REGIMENT ARMORY
BIG MUSICAL PROGRAM
IF YOU FAIL TO BE AT THE ARMORY ON THIS NIGHT
OF NIGHTS THEN YOU MIGHT AS WELL BE DEAD
GOD SAVE AFRICA!   LONG LIVE THE NEGRO RACE!

The "Greatest Champion" of the race, of course, was "His Excellency
Hon. Marcus Garvey (Provisional President of Africa and President-General
of the Universal Negro Improvement Association—the World's Greatest
Orator),"[1] whose immodest invitation engendered a combination of embarrassment and chagrin in the minds of New York's established black
leadership and press. To many, Garvey came all too close to the unflattering white stereotypes about blacks; at the same time he seemed to drain
precious energy from the ongoing struggle for improvements in the race's
political, economic, and social position in America. It is no wonder, then,
that organized opposition to this West Indian and his followers reached
its peak at the same time as did the Universal Negro Improvement Association (UNIA), a peak of inflamed rhetoric, bitter charge and counter-denunciation, mob and bully tactics, even of enlisting the support of
"the Man" in the effort to "get Garvey."

The Garvey movement has usually been seen in the context of its leader's mistakes and blunders. The standard interpretation is that he enjoyed great success as an organizer but through errors in judgment and unwise business dealings brought about his own downfall. There is much truth to this perspective, but it leaves out an important consideration: Garvey was an enormously popular leader who aroused a great deal of jealousy and petty hatred as well as ideological opposition among other leaders and black intellectuals. It may be true that Garvey's activities in the United States would have come to ruin unaided, but that question is a moot one since it is clear that his downfall was encouraged by the active opposition of certain public figures. The *Messenger* was a leading voice in the anti-Garvey campaign, and while not the sole publication that took it upon itself to expose the West Indian organizer, it kept up what was probably the most continuous attack. Once the *Messenger* seized on the Garvey issue, it did not relent until the public was plainly tired of the question, and by then Garvey was only a few steps away from the federal penitentiary in Atlanta. The magazine used many weapons, some fair, a few foul. It is a chapter in the periodical's history that is vivid with controversy and invective; it is also a chapter that has its sordid features, one that sullies the reputations of both the magazine and its chief editors.

The story of this conflict has three facets: the development and climax of the struggle; the ideological undercurrents beneath the contest; and the abrupt termination of active warfare. Familiarity with the rhetoric is important for an understanding of all three, for the language used cannot be separated from the larger issues. The words of fifty years ago, imparting the flavor of the times and the smell of battle, can scarcely be improved upon.

The precise nature of the early contacts between Marcus Garvey and the editors of the *Messenger* is obscure, but it is known that their paths crossed more than a year before the magazine moved into active opposition to the West Indian. A. Philip Randolph addressed a UNIA meeting in 1919 called to generate interest in securing a black representative to the Paris Peace Conference. He later justified his appearance by insisting that he spoke merely to educate the UNIA membership "in the class struggle nature of the Negro problem" and to encourage a socialist perspective. In any case, the UNIA deemed Randolph either sufficiently sympathetic or sufficiently well-known to name him one of its delegates to the peace conference, although he never attended it.[2]

Another early contact between the later antagonists occurred when Garvey attended a conference organized by Randolph in the immediate postwar months that led to the formation of the short-lived International League of Darker Peoples. The league's goal was to ensure " 'Africa for the Africans' through the instrumentality of a league of darker peoples, reinforced by an alliance with the white radical, liberal and labor movements of the world." Both Garvey and the *Messenger*'s editors were publicly encouraging rebellion of the oppressed peoples of the world in 1919, although Randolph included insurrection in Europe and America as well as in Africa and Asia. The later opponents also shared New Negro rhetoric, which was spread over the pages of the *Negro World.* Garvey approved of retaliation against white rioters in the summer of 1919 and told a crowd of twenty thousand at Madison Square Garden a year later that "We New Negroes, we men who have returned from World War I, we will dispute every inch of the way until we win."[3]

By the time the *Messenger* first took notice, in September 1920, the UNIA was already the largest, most powerful black mass organization ever formed in America, as well as one of the largest all-black businesses then in existence. The magazine's initial article set out the theoretical basis for much of the less emotional criticism of Garvey that was to follow in the next three years. Garvey's African panacea, it was claimed, was based on simplistic reasoning. Oppression throughout the world was not primarily racial. As far as exploitation and oppression went, no race had clean hands, not even the black race. Nations oppressed others out of profit, and black nations were as prone to this as any others. Capitalistic gain was what motivated imperialism in Africa, and since England was the chief exploiter of that continent even though only very few Britons benefited from the exploitation, a more sensible program of African redemption would be to work against English and other imperialists by boycotting their goods. Only practical methods should be used. To really do what was best for Africa, one would have to consult, in secret, with native leaders. Emotion, personal ambition, and ignorance of the true conditions in Africa were poor weapons against British capital and munitions. The magic word "unity" would prove of little use without more practical considerations.[4]

A socialist critique of the domestic implications of Garvey's budding black nationalism appeared in the *Messenger* later in the year. The attack centered on Garvey's proposal for an all-black Liberty party. Since such a party could never become the majority party in the United States, it would never be effective in either winning national elections or outlawing Jim Crow and lynching. Such a faction would also produce its own counter-irritant, an all-white party, which would play into the hands of racists. An all-black party might make sense in the West Indies, where blacks were in the majority, but still would be no guarantee of improvement; a black king or czar was hardly better than a white one. The answer did not lie in racial parties, for parties were based on economic interests, not race lines. Blacks should organize along socialistic lines.[5]

For the next year and a half the *Messenger* discussed Garvey and the UNIA only infrequently. The magazine's editors were not unwilling to admit that some good had come from the movement, particularly the example of successful racial organizing. Garvey's stimulation of black pride also did not go unnoticed. But granted these positive points, the movement was said to be based on fallacies and guided by poor judgment. The plans for the redemption of Africa were deemed totally unrealistic, and the "Negro first" doctrine, to replace an emphasis on "white man first," was viewed as politically counterproductive and likely to retard the march of radicalism. At heart, so the *Messenger* believed, Garveyism broadened the chasm between black and white workers and increased the likelihood of more race hatred and violence. These questions were discussed in tones of relative moderation, if not respect.[6] But all this changed abruptly in mid-1922 as Garvey took off on a new and strange tangent that was guaranteed to earn the unmitigated hatred of many blacks, radicals and otherwise.

"Marcus Garvey! The Black Imperial Wizard Becomes Messenger Boy of the White Ku Klux Kleagle." Thus headlined, the lead editorial in July stated the magazine's new position on Garvey: "Here's notice that the *Messenger* is firing the opening gun in a campaign to drive Garvey and Garveyism in all its [*sic*] sinister viciousness from the American soil." At issue were Garvey's relations with the Ku Klux Klan. He admitted that he conferred with Kleagle Edward Young Clarke in Atlanta early in 1922, and although he promised to make public the substance of the conversation, the exact details were never revealed. Here was Garvey, a figure of undeniable influence, meeting with the head of the race's most outspoken foe. The July editorial referred specifically to a speech that Garvey made on his trip South in which he asserted that since blacks had not built the railroads, they had no cause to complain as to how they were accommodated on them; in other words, they should observe the white man's rules on the white man's trains.

To the *Messenger* such a statement was unconscionable. Too long had public figures been lenient with the Garvey nonsense, fearing a loss of trade with his following or being attacked in the pages of his *Negro World.* Furthermore, the fact that most of his followers were West Indians was no justification for failing to take the Garvey menace seriously. The *Messenger* promised an unremitting campaign to expose in detail all of Garvey's spurious schemes, "from his row-boatless steamship line to his voteless election to the Presidency of a non-existent nation." Every American, West Indian, African, South American, and Canal Zone black person should become appraised "of the emptiness of all this Garvey flapdoodle, bombast and lying about impossible and conscienceless schemes calculated not to redeem but to enslave Africa and the Negro everywhere." Thus a new tone in the debate was set: rhetoric and emotion were escalated and the "Garvey Must Go" campaign was about to be launched. This was the first low attack on Garvey by the *Messenger* and the first mention that the ultimate goal was deportation. "Politics of the gutter" became the order of the day on both sides.[7]

Besides the pages of the *Messenger,* another avenue of attack against the West Indian was the Friends of Negro Freedom, a black-led civil rights and propaganda organization founded in 1920 by Randolph and Owen. The FNF issued a direct challenge to the UNIA by promoting anti-Garvey meetings and speakers to coincide with the annual UNIA convention, and even went so far as to invite convention delegates so that they might learn the "truth" about their leader. Not solely a Harlem organization, FNF branches across the country were expected to also join in the campaign against Garvey. There were other important elements of opposition as well. Article after article criticizing Garvey could be found in the major newspapers by mid-1922. The Chicago *Defender* and the New York *Age* in particular gave Garvey no quarter, while others printed anti-Garvey press releases furnished by Cyril Briggs's Crusader News Service. Brigg's organization, the African Blood Brotherhood, which had briefly been

allied with the UNIA before being expelled, sponsored hostile street meetings and demonstrations in New York City. Opposition to Garvey was
mighty indeed.[8]

As soon as the UNIA convention began in August, street meetings,
social gatherings, and FNF "forums" took up the cry of "Garvey Must
Go." Garvey responded to this blatant threat to his organization and convention by publishing "A Warning to the Enemy" in the *Negro World* on
August 5:

> We say, therefore, to the Negro enemies of the past, we are ready for
> you, and before the 31st of August comes we are going to give you
> your Waterloo. They threaten to smash the Universal Negro Improve-
> ment Association. Let me tell you somebody is going to be smashed
> in New York between the 1st and 31st of August. We have never yet
> gone out of the way to interfere with any organization or any Negro
> individual, but any Negro individual or Negro organization within the
> bounds of the United States of America that thinks it can fight and
> intimidate the Universal Negro Improvement Association—let you be
> the Negro Association for the Advancement of Colored People—let
> you be Negro Socialists—let me tell you, you are preparing for your
> Waterloo. We do not want a fight among Negro organizations; we do
> not want a fight among Negroes, because it does not help the Race;
> but it will appear that some people desire a fight. If you want a fight
> you are going to have it. So you will understand whether it be [Wil-
> liam] Pickens or whether it be Chandler Owens [*sic*], the Universal
> Negro Improvement Association has no fear of anybody, and when
> you interfere with the Universal Negro Improvement Association you
> will take the consequences.[9]

Whether, as one Garvey biographer states, his followers took the
"Waterloo" utterance as a caveat to disrupt the anti-Garvey meetings
or whether the FNF-*Messenger* attacks were provocative enough in themselves, there was considerable disorder at the four large meetings sponsored
by the FNF in August. The opening forum, which featured an address by
Pickens on "What to Do When Negro Leaders League with Negro Lynchers," drew more than two thousand listeners and was punctuated by frequent attempts at interruption by Garvey supporters. Several policemen

had to be stationed in the audience to keep order. Pickens alleged that
he had received many threats on his life since repudiating Garvey's offer
of a titled position in the UNIA, and at each mention of these threats the
police had to warn the noisiest objectors that they faced ejection. "Throughout the meeting there were many cries of 'Garvey must go,' and in each
instance it was several minutes before order was restored and the speaker
could continue."[10]

On succeeding Sunday afternoons Randolph spoke on "The Only Way
to Redeem Africa"; Robert W. Bagnall, another FNF member and like
Pickens an NAACP official, diagnosed "The Madness of Marcus Garvey";
and the series ended with Chandler Owen explicating "A Practical Program for Negroes Everywhere." It was no wonder that violence characterized these meetings, that fights between Garvey opponents and proponents
had to be broken up by the police. At one forum Randolph called the
West Indian "either a crook or a liar," and UNIA members in attendance
did not take this sitting down. In his speech on August 27 Owen announced that the Friends of Negro Freedom would soon petition the
Department of Justice to bring Garvey to an early trial on his mail fraud
charge. "Marcus Garvey has become the worst type of *me-too-boss* and
hat-in-hand good 'nigger' the race has ever been bedeviled by. A menace
to sound, democratic racial relations, a race baiter and a race traitor,
Garvey must go. The sooner the better."[11]

The logic of the "Garvey Must Go" campaign dictated that the *Messenger*-FNF group support the principle of deportation of undesirable
aliens. The stand taken on this issue shows how far the magazine had
traveled from its position during the Red Scare. (This gradual erosion of
the radicalism of 1919 is the subject of Chapter 7.) Chandler Owen explained that historically radicals had opposed deportation only in cases
of expression of political or class war opinions. There was nothing wrong
in deporting Napoleon to St. Helena. Even the Soviet Union favored
"deportation": it had recently allowed over a thousand recalcitrant intellectuals and counterrevolutionaries to leave the country. Despite these
justifications, the *Messenger* was clearly violating its earlier principles; it
seems clear that Garvey *was* being persecuted for his ideology.

Owen also justified deportation for Garvey on the basis that he was
an anarchist. The *Messenger* editor saw "anarchism" in Garvey's prediction of a "Waterloo" for his tormentors, interpreting this as an invitation

to UNIA fanatics to assassinate the opposition. Further proof of such "anarchistic" beliefs was a speech by UNIA official William Sherrill in which he warned that "black folk as well as white who tamper with the Universal Negro Improvement Association are going to die." Obviously Garvey was no anarchist by any common definition; Owen seems to have used the term merely to Red-bait his enemy.

If these were not grounds enough for deportation, Owen was certain there were other ways to snare Garvey. He quoted from a law authorizing deportation for disbelief in organized government, being a public charge, or being insane. Garvey qualified under all three. His support of the KKK was seen as a rejection of established government; preying on innocent and gullible persons definitely made him a public charge; and a New York judge had already suggested he was a paranoiac. Further evidence of Garvey's criminal activities was the alleged encouragement to his followers to break up opposition meetings and thereby commit trespass, assault and battery, and disorderly conduct. In the name of free speech, according to Owen's logic, Garvey must be deported.[12]

The *Messenger*'s position in demanding deportation for Garvey was undoubtedly extreme. Not even everyone connected with the FNF approved of that goal. Clearly the magazine had taken a position far in advance of most Garvey critics at that point.[13]

A grizzly note was introduced into the drama in early September when Randolph received a package in the mail postmarked New Orleans and sent "from a friend." Fearing that it was a bomb, Randolph called the police, and upon examination the package was found to contain the severed left hand of a white man. An accompanying note warned that if Randolph did not become a paid-up member of the UNIA, his own hand would be sent to someone else. Although the note was signed by the KKK, it was generally assumed that the sender was a black Garveyite. To this suspicion Garvey only replied that the *Messenger* group had come up with a good publicity stunt. A week after receiving the hand, Randolph got a letter, written in red ink and signed by the Klan, saying that he would not live to see the new year, for "we don't want niggers like you here." Again the postmark was from New Orleans. This throws doubt on any Garveyite implication in the macabre affair, but the incident nonetheless provided new ammunition that was used to full effect in anti-Garvey meetings.[14]

The attacks on Garvey continued in the *Messenger* with "The Only Way to Redeem Africa", which was serialized from November 1922 through

February 1923. Four new themes emerged in the series. Not only was Garvey accused of stirring up prejudice of whites against blacks; he was charged with fostering intraracial prejudice between West Indians and natives where, it was implied, none had existed before. In addition, Garvey denigrated American citizenship and advised West Indians not to take out American papers; this, Randolph charged, would surely demoralize the struggle for black rights in America. Third, if Garvey were really serious about liberating blacks from the oppressive yoke of the white race, he should more logically start with a place like Jamaica, where the blacks and coloreds outnumbered the white population by forty-two to one. Finally, Randolph showed a fundamental antipathy to the whole style of the Garvey movement, its ceremony and paraphernalia, titles and royalty. The pretentiousness of it was highly repugnant to the black socialist.[15]

On January 15, 1923, eight individuals sent and made public a letter to U.S. Attorney General Harry M. Daugherty urging the government to get on with its prosecution of the year-old case against Garvey for mail fraud. It was an amazing document by any account. The letter accused Garvey and the UNIA of stirring up prejudice within the black race as well as between black and white. The UNIA, it was said, approved of violence to achieve its ends. The "most primitive and ignorant" West Indian immigrants and native blacks made up its membership. The letter averred that thirteen specific acts of violence or intimidation had been perpetrated by the UNIA on its opponents, including an attack on Chandler Owen in Pittsburgh while on a speaking trip, the murder of an ex-Garveyite-turned-opponent in New Orleans, and an attempt at intimidation of William Pickens while he was speaking in Toronto. Garvey himself was accused of victimizing the ignorant with his wild schemes and promotions. It was noted that he had affiliations with the KKK, and that, if possible, the UNIA was a more despicable organization. Paragraph 25 of this long letter read as follows:

For the above reasons we advocate that the Attorney-General use his full influence completely to disband and extirpate this vicious movement, and that he vigorously and speedily push the government's case against Marcus Garvey for using the mails to defraud. This should be done in the interest of justice; even as a matter of practical expediency.

The letter came from a committee of whom Chandler Owen was the secretary. The signers included Harry H. Pace, president of the Black Swan Phonograph Corporation; John E. Nail, a well-known New York realtor; and Julia P. Coleman, president of a black cosmetics firm. These three were frequent advertisers in the *Messenger*. The others were Robert S. Abbott, publisher of the Chicago *Defender* and a longtime opponent of Garvey; William Pickens and the Reverend Robert W. Bagnall of the NAACP; and George W. Harris, New York Alderman and editor of the New York *News*.[16]

The participation of Pickens and Bagnall in the anti-Garvey activities was not meant to commit the NAACP, but behind the scenes James Weldon Johnson and Walter White, as well as the association's top legal talent, Arthur B. Spingarn, were deeply implicated in the letter to the Attorney General. Spingarn was asked to make sure the letter was not libelous, and he provided some helpful suggestions. When Garvey sued Owen, Randolph, and Bagnall in late August, Spingarn privately offered them his services so as not publicly to commit the Association. Perhaps because of rumors of NAACP implication, perhaps also because Garvey later charged he was denied a fair trial because the judge was an NAACP member, James Weldon Johnson found it necessary to assure the court that the association had never taken an official stance in opposition to Garvey. While this is true on the surface, its hands were in fact not entirely clean.[17]

How could "radical" Chandler Owen make such an appeal to the Attorney General? True, the incumbent was no longer A. Mitchell Palmer, but could Owen have forgotten how hostile the Justice Department had been to black aspirations in 1919 and 1920? It was an intemperate letter, more intent, as the New York *Age* clearly perceived, on persecution than on prosecution. The West Indian deserved a fair trial without such documents to prejudice the case against him. "Marcus Garvey should be tried in the courts, not lynched by petition or otherwise." It is doubtful whether the letter in fact made any difference in the outcome of Garvey's trial. But it shows how worried were the signers: Garvey threatened racial progress, and on that account had to be stopped.[18] But to invite the Department of Justice to prosecute one's black opponent was nearly as despicable as inviting the Klan to do so.

Garvey's rebuttal to the letter scored many well-earned points against the Eight. "Like the good old darkey, they believe they have some news to tell and they are telling it for all it is worth." He noted that the Eight seemed naïvely unaware of how bad a precedent it was to encourage the government to destroy a black organization. As for the charges that only the ignorant were members of the UNIA, Garvey astutely saw that in harping on this theme, his opponents showed ambivalence about their own blackness and seemed eager to put as much distance between themselves and the dark masses as possible. Addressing himself to the signers of the letter, Garvey charged each with various offenses against race solidarity and race pride, or simply with being dishonest or immoral. Not all the allegations were accurate, but there was at least a kernel of truth in the charges against Abbott, Nail, Coleman, and Bagnall. Garvey could not resist the parting shot of noting that the Eight were nearly all octoroons and quadroons, or married to such. It should also be added that Garvey had long before tangled with Harris, Owen, Abbott, Pickens, and Bagnall, having filed several libel suits against these "miscegenationists" (Garvey's word).[19]

Curiously, the *Messenger* never mentioned the letter to the Attorney General or printed its text. Perhaps Owen became embarrassed by its implications; perhaps he recognized how deeply it contradicted the magazine's original radical spirit. In any case, as Amy Jacques-Garvey pointed out years later, it was more than ironic for Owen to appeal to Attorney General Daugherty in 1923 and a year later condemn him in the *Messenger* as a political crook.[20] One wonders if Owen ever saw the irony.

Meanwhile, the West Indian-American Negro issue provoked a breach between W. A. Domingo and Chandler Owen, resulting in Domingo's departure from the *Messenger*. Domingo was a Jamaican who had ties to the largely West Indian and communist-oriented African Blood Brotherhood, yet despite having gravitated toward Moscow after 1919 he continued to have associations with the Socialist party-oriented *Messenger* group and remained on the masthead as a contributing editor. He disliked Garvey, and as editor of the *Crusader* had been one of Garvey's earliest and most persistent critics. Domingo was disturbed, however, by the increasing pejorative use of the term "West Indian" to describe the UNIA membership and the related inclination of the *Messenger* to impugn the intellectual abilities of Garvey's followers.

Stereotyping of West Indians was widespread in the magazine, Domingo charged. Furthermore, the socialist faith of the periodical had been betrayed by advocating deportation and emphasizing the nationality of one's

opponent. Whether or not the *Messenger* intended to generate hostility
toward West Indians, such hostility had in fact increased. Had not American blacks long protested against cruel and distorted newspaper carica-
tures of blacks, and was not the *Messenger* now employing such stereotypes? The old *Messenger,* which Domingo wrote for and respected, had
prided itself on its internationalism; this too had been betrayed. Was not
the magazine ignoring all the financial, intellectual, and moral support
given to it by black aliens since 1917? Who had been among the most
persistent and earliest critics of Garvey? West Indians like Domingo and
Cyril Briggs. He also pointed out that most of the higher officials in the
UNIA were native Americans, and so were most of those who received
titles. In all these charges Domingo was substantially correct.

Chandler Owen's rebuttal evaded the questions raised by Domingo
and served only as a personal attack on his staff associate. Randolph suggested that the two debate the issues at a Friends of Negro Freedom
forum, but the public confrontation never materialized. Needless to say,
that same month Domingo's name was dropped from the masthead. All
in all, the affair reflected little credit on Owen.[21]

March 1923 marked the date of the *Messenger*'s most scurrilous attack
on Garvey. The author, the Reverend Robert W. Bagnall, penned one of
the most famous and vicious sketches of its subject:

> A Jamaican Negro of unmixed stock, squat, fat and sleek, with pro-
> truding jaws, and heavy jowls, small bright pig-like eyes and rather
> bull-dog-like face. Boastful, egotistic, tyrannical, intolerant, cunning,
> shifty, smooth and suave, avaricious; as adroit as a fencer in changing
> front, as adept as a cuttle-fish in beclouding an issue he cannot meet,
> prolix to the 'nth degree in devising new schemes to gain the money
> of poor ignorant Negroes; gifted at self-advertisement, without shame
> in self-laudation, promising ever, but never fulfilling, without regard
> for veracity, a lover of pomp and tawdry finery and garish display, a
> bully with his own folk but servile in the presence of the Klan, a sheer
> opportunist and demagogic charlatan.

Bagnall went on to list classical cases of insanity, figures like Nero, Alexander, and Don Quixote, who appeared normal some of the time but who
were nonetheless insane. Was Garvey also? Bagnall saw all the symptoms;

egomania, delusions of grandeur, delusions of fact, and a persecution complex. "If he is not insane, he is a demagogic charlatan, but the probability is that the man is insane. Certainly the movement is insane, whether Garvey is or not."[22]

Garvey's long-delayed trial finally began in May 1923. By then the *Messenger* had long since run out of things to say, whether constructive or not. Surprisingly, the trial was not reported, although there was much that the flamboyant West Indian said and did during the lengthy proceedings that would have made exciting copy. A guilty verdict was returned in late June, and the *Messenger* marked the conviction with a short, derisive editorial. Plainly interest was waning, however, for there was no extended comment, no rehash of old arguments, no analysis of the steps Garvey had taken to his downfall. Ironically, the same page carried an editorial entitled "Political Amnesty": "The United States still holds men in bondage for the expression of their economic and political beliefs during the war. What a shameless disparity between our practice and professions!"[23] What a disparity indeed! Did the *Messenger* editors really believe that they had hounded Garvey because he was illegally promoting stock through the mails? Or had they not persecuted the man for his "economic and political beliefs"?

Garvey's imprisonment, once his appeals were denied, brought him sympathy from many who had earlier been his opponents. Several of the once-hostile periodicals began to agitate for his release from Atlanta Penitentiary, coming to the view that Garvey had been unjustly convicted in a white man's court and that his incarceration only proved what he had said all along about the futility of seeking justice in America. William Pickens was the only one of the *Messenger* circle who joined in the campaign for clemency or pardon. Writing to the *New Republic* in mid-1927, presumably to gain the support of white liberals, Pickens stated that no useful purpose was being served by keeping Garvey imprisoned; even his enemies should now admit that he never had had deliberate intentions of defrauding the public. His was the case of a bold, yet foolish visionary. Being West Indian, he probably had not understood the technicalities of American law on the subject of improper use of the mails. The real criminals had been those in the UNIA who had known what the law said.

Such forgiveness was not universal, however. The *Messenger* opposed mercy, as did the moderate New York *Age*, which noted that the effects of Garvey's offense were long-lasting. Many who had been duped by his schemes and had invested their savings were undoubtedly still suffering. Pity for the victims, yes, but not for their victimizer. Garvey's crime was against the whole race, "a mortal blow at all similar efforts for race building." Betrayal of the faith, abuse of the trust of the race, were indeed Garvey's offenses, for which his critics never forgave him.[24]

The debate between Garvey and the *Messenger* circle could never have been so sustained or antagonistic had there not been fundamental differences of philosophy between the two. Nearly all of the magazine's comment on Garvey was making some ideological point, even if it was too often beclouded by needless venom. Bitter rhetoric was inevitable, given the many conflicting factors of personality and program. The pity of it is not so much that it became a sordid exchange, but that it all ended so unproductively.

One important source of conflict centered on the questions of socialism and capitalism. The position of the *Messenger* is clear: nonsocialist panaceas to the problems of blacks in America and elsewhere would have little hope of success. Some form of collectivism was essential. An all-black party, as Garvey conceived it, was unrealistically based on race lines, not economic class interests. The socialism issue was clearly drawn in relation to Africa. The real danger to Africa of the Garvey movement, in the very unlikely event that it should succeed in gaining some part of that continent, was that a black emperor would be substituted for a colonial administration and be just as despotic. The only hope for blacks everywhere was in a worldwide liberation movement of the enslaved and downtrodden of all races, creeds, and colors. Only the abolition of imperialism would free Africa. White and yellow imperialism should not be abolished only to substitute black imperialism. Radical socialism and international labor movements would be the only feasible means.[25]

Garvey's orientation leaned more toward capitalism than socialism, but he stopped short of wholehearted approval of the former. A Bookerite at heart, he never abandoned the emphasis on self-help and economic improvement, which, of course, was a traditional American virtue. As a young man he was deeply impressed with Booker Washington's economic nationalism, and Claude McKay credits this orientation with primary responsibility for making Garvey unpalatable to Northern black intel-

lectuals. Yet he was no advocate of extreme wealth; capitalism should
be limited so that no individual could invest or control more than a
million dollars, and no corporation have assets of more than five million.
He realized that both capitalists and socialists were capable of imperialist exploitation, and perceived that an industrialized socialist nation
would likely exploit the underdeveloped countries from which it got raw
materials and to which it sold finished goods. At the same time he came
down hard on traditional black petit-bourgeois capitalists: "The Negro
people are suffering under exploitation by a privileged class of Negroes,
businessmen and professional men who have no more consideration for
their own unfortunate people than the white exploiter. . . . The Negro
real-estate man in New York is the greatest devil we have to combat."
Garvey explicitly disavowed support from black businessmen and prohibited large investments in UNIA enterprises like the Black Star Line. He
intended his business ventures to be cooperatives, not corporations. The
Messenger, too, favored cooperative businesses, but only as a step in the
march toward full socialism. Garvey's disavowal of a socialist future
placed him at irreconcilable loggerheads with the magazine and its editors;
no qualifications on the subject of capitalism could diminish their conflict. Garvey was not alone in his views; Harold Cruse has observed that
most West Indians were basically economic conservatives.[26]
    In addition to preferring a benevolent form of capitalism, Garvey re-
jected trade unionism as it existed in the United States because of its
white domination. The only white friends black workers might have
would be employers. The latter, being selfish, were willing to give jobs
to blacks at a lower wage scale. With this blacks must be satisfied, for
if they were to unionize with whites and attain the same wage scale,
white employers would inevitably exercise race loyalty and hire only
white workers and discharge the blacks. Such sentiments, of course, were
anathema to the *Messenger.* Garvey similarly rejected communism as a
solution to the race's plight, concluding that white Communists were as
likely to draw the color line once they had gained power as any white
Republican or Democrat. As for black Communists, the African Blood
Brotherhood made several overtures to the UNIA, all of which Garvey
eventually rejected.[27]
    Marcus Garvey was by far the most successful organizer of the masses
of the black race of his generation, and he accomplished this on a non-

socialist basis and largely without resort to conventional class-conflict rhetoric. Jealousy of this accomplishment will be discussed in detail below, but it may be noted here that the opposition of persons like Owen and Randolph drew in part on their frustration at observing such a grand mobilization of the black population being turned to reactionary purposes.

From an early date the West Indian influence in the UNIA became a source of ugly nativism. The *Messenger* was not immune to such a response, although its early inclination was to warn against anti-West Indianism. The initial posture of the magazine took no particular significance in Garvey's background or the nativity of many of his supporters, and as late as April 1922, only a few months before the initiation of the "Garvey Must Go" campaign, the *Messenger* was warning against maligning West Indians as a group. But despite its plea for tolerance it slipped, perhaps unconsciously, into negative stereotyping.

The July 1922 editorial calling Garvey the "Messenger Boy" of the Klan was the vehicle for announcing the drive to have him deported. Here the nativity of Garvey and his followers was first mentioned in a pejorative fashion: he was called "a blustering West Indian demagogue who preys upon the ignorant, unsuspecting poor West Indian working men and women who believe Garvey is some sort of Moses." To this was added the disclaimer that there were indeed many intelligent and courageous West Indians who would never stoop as low as had Garvey. But the concept of deportation for a political-ideological opponent was in fact a form of antiforeignism, especially when coupled with the tasteless rhetoric of an article two months later entitled "Should Marcus Garvey be Deported?" written by Chandler Owen:

> Now Garvey and his *Uninformed Negroes Infamous Association* meet in Slavery Hole (sometimes incorrectly termed Liberty Hall— liberty to make a fool of one's self) every night. We intelligent and honest American and West Indian Negroes are opposed to almost everything they do and say. Still we never interrupt that motley crew of Negro ignoramuses. No one ever attempts to interfere while the nefarious Negro lizard is making a report to his universally ignorant Negro savages from his imperial boss, the infamous white wizard. We grant them free speech—hardly a citizen among them.

Even Garvey's most outspoken West Indian opponents only wanted him imprisoned for fraud. To them the concept of deportation could only mean an attack on their right to remain in the country and discrimination against them solely because of their nativity.[28]

Perhaps the *Messenger* had some brief thoughts about such scurrilous rhetoric; in any case, a month later, it claimed that the Friends of Negro Freedom, whose chief task by that time was to hound Garvey, held no prejudice against him on account of his origins, and that it was merely coincidental that the FNF was fighting mainly against foreigners.[29] Despite this, prejudice against Garvey's nationality became if anything more clear in the title of the lead editorial in the January 1923 issue: "A Supreme Negro Jamaican Jackass." In fairness to the *Messenger*'s editors, however, it must be admitted that Garvey's latest antic was unforgivable.

Garvey had been the featured speaker at the North Carolina Negro State Fair the previous October, and what he told his black audience was taken up with undisguised joy by the regional white press. Garvey thanked the white South for having "lynched race pride into the Negro." The Jews and Irish, he noted, were also oppressed groups that possessed race consciousness, but only blacks required a beating to accomplish this. Other advantages accrued to blacks in the South; their only business opportunity lay there, thanks to segregation, which forced the race to build up its own manufacturing and commerce. Urging his listeners to greater efforts, Garvey said that "the southern white man despises [you] and is frank enough to tell you so. He has everything and you have nothing. Don't blame him for despising you. He has contempt for you because you won't do anything for yourselves." If he had had to rely on blacks, Garvey said, it would have taken him six months to get to North Carolina. Turning to his own program, Garvey warned, "Don't think I want all of you to go to Africa. . . . no, no, there are lots of lazy niggers whom we don't want over there. You just stay here where it suits you." To the *Messenger,* this pandering to white racism, use of the word "nigger," and faulty logic could only come from the "diseased brain of this Supreme Negro Jackass from Jamaica."[30]

Another strain of anti-West Indianism emerged in the following month when Garvey was charged with stirring up intraracial prejudices within the United States. The *Messenger*'s logic was that since native blacks were aware of Garvey's alliance with the Klan—their enemy—they could

easily conclude that therefore all West Indians were their enemies too.
Of course, the magazine said innocently, this was not true. Others made
related accusations. William Pickens noted that Garvey had arrived on
American shores with a chip on his shoulder against persons lighter-skinned
than he, and the New York *Age* saw this creation of divisions between
lighter and darker blacks as the very backbone of Garvey's propaganda.
Garvey did encourage divisions; yet the *Messenger*'s use of them to brand
him and his West Indian followers was hardly more scrupulous.[31]

W. A. Domingo's exchange with Chandler Owen over the anti-West
Indianism displayed in the *Messenger* raises some interesting questions
about the periodical's attitude toward blackness in general. The language
of "Should Marcus Garvey Be Deported?" spoke of a "motley crew of
Negro ignoramuses," of "the nefarious Negro lizard," and of "universally ignorant Negro savages." In each case the word "Negro" is used as a
pejorative adjective and is especially cruel in the context of the last-quoted
phrase, coupled with the traditional pejorative "savages." Again, "A Supreme Negro Jamaican Jackass" uses the racial term and country of origin
as pejoratives modifying the characterization of Garvey as a stupid beast.

Garvey always claimed that his opposition came from mulatto elements,
that "unfortunately there is a disposition on the part of a certain element
of our people in America, the West Indies and Africa, to hold themselves
up as the 'better class' or 'privileged' group on the caste of color." Such
slaps at mulattoes was never acknowledged by the *Messenger*. But did they
touch a tender spot nonetheless? Is the reaction to Garvey's criticism of
"so-called leaders" to be found in the *Messenger*'s derogatory usages of
"Negro"? How comfortable was Chandler Owen, himself comparatively
light-skinned, with the criticism of mulatto leaders? He was the author of
the article advocating deportation; it was he who defended the *Messenger*'s record against Domingo's criticism. It would be unwarranted to ac-
cuse the magazine of initiating anti-West Indianism, but it must be ad-
judged guilty of having employed it in the campaign to silence and banish
Garvey. In this respect Chandler Owen bears the major responsibility.[32]

A demographic perspective helps in understanding both the prominence
of the foreign-born element in the UNIA and the ugly stereotyping of the
anti-Garvey campaign. The 1930 census, reflecting the previous decade,
indicates that 16.7 percent of the black population in New York City
was foreign-born, so it was indeed a "visible" element within the race. The
census showed that 65 percent of the nation's black immigrant population

lived in New York State and nearly all of that number in metropolitan New York. In 1923 roughly two-thirds of the immigrants entering the country declared their intention to settle in New York.[33]

It was, therefore, entirely natural for Garvey to begin his organizational work by appealing in terms that were understandable to West Indians. But his message was by no means restricted to the immigrant population, for it was based on psychological and circumstantial denominators that were to be found in both the native and foreign-born black populations. First of all, Garvey appealed to those who were suffering prejudice (although obviously not all persons so burdened were receptive to him). Migrants from the Southern states knew whereof he spoke when he talked of discrimination. As for the immigrant population, it experienced tangible prejudice emanating not only from the white world but also from the American black group. If the American-born white populace was disposed to view white immigrants in nativistic terms, why should not the native black population react similarly to black foreigners? And it was quite possible for American blacks to see immigrant blacks in the same threatening way that many white Americans viewed recent arrivals. For example, native blacks often complained that West Indians were clannish and exhibited too much insular solidarity: when one of them secured a job, he managed to bring all his West Indian friends and relatives into it. Other stereotypes followed easily. In truth, however, intrainsular rivalries among the various West Indian groups prevented the degree of solidarity that native blacks feared. But the existence of stereotypes clearly shows that the immigrants were threatening in a number of ways.[34]

The West Indian immigrant was also subjected to prejudice because of his blackness, and it is here that the *Messenger*'s position comes into focus. Garvey used the Jamaican social analysis of black-mulatto caste subdivisions. DuBois, for one, claimed that it had no relevance in the United States, but in fact this conflict had long been present as an undercurrent of intraracial relations;[35] for very dark blacks Garvey's race chauvinism might well have a powerful, soothing psychological effect. Certainly the pejorative usage of "Negro" in the *Messenger* could be threatening to light-skinned West Indians in whose background "Negro" implied a much lower status than that of "colored" (mulatto).

Garvey's appeal was also to those oppressed by social class discriminations, and it is hard not to conclude that the *Messenger* encouraged such reactions with its incessant harpings on "ignorant" West Indians, or more generally, Garvey's "ignorant" followers. Black intellectuals opposed Garvey for leading what was in effect a racial-class movement, composed almost exclusively of lower-strata persons. The possibility of a successful exclusively lower-class movement was not without threat to many black leaders. Garvey did lay bare some of the socioeconomic differences in the black community, directing his fire at the more prosperous and advantaged of the race, saying that they had betrayed their less prosperous brothers in return for crumbs from the white man's table. Part of the reaction of the intellectuals was also directed against Garvey's inversion of color prejudices, putting down the (light-colored) upper strata and elevating the (black) lower strata while implying that mixed-bloods were mongrels displaying all the unfortunate characteristics of race mixture.[36]

The least assimilated elements of the Northern black population were often attracted to Garvey, and the import of his message was to discourage further assimilation into the American mainstream. According to Ira Reid, the Garvey movement "both undermined the national patriotisms of the native and foreign born groups, and arrested the conscious assimilation process of the immigrants." The same point could be made for recent migrants from the South. Here the Garvey movement resembles a revitalization movement, where messianic leadership and emphasis on a future national homeland displace concentration on the trials of the present life and country. The preoccupation with Africa in the Garvey ideology meant that comparatively little attention was paid to problems in America. And since Garvey did not himself file citizenship papers, nor for several years did he advise his alien adherents to do so, he was obviously not advocating assimilation.

This was yet another reason why a broad range of middle-class and liberal blacks opposed Garvey, given the increasing concern for civil rights in the twenties. For Randolph and Owen it was vital that all blacks be "assimilated" so that they might become more militant fighters for civil rights and ultimate (social) equality. Garvey began to give ground on this question after his conviction and while his appeal was pending: "If DuBois and James Weldon Johnson, with only two hundred thousand followers, can send one Negro to jail, the UNIA, with two million voters, will be able to send that many more. When we are all voting we can demand that the Government send us back to Africa." Garvey erred in attributing his conviction to the NAACP's black leadership, but he may have been accurately gauging the sentiments of at least native-born blacks on the issue of political participation. The UNIA convention in the summer of 1924 created a Negro Political Union that was to endorse and campaign for specific candidates and issues on the local, national, and international level. Filing for citizenship was now a duty of UNIA members.[37]

It must have been frustrating for militants like Randolph and Owen to compare the meager support for their magazine and the FNF to the popularity of Garvey's movement. The UNIA was literally weaning away the folk on which a mass movement would have to be based. Instead of becoming radicalized, the masses were turning in droves to a reactionary demagogue. Does this mean that the typical West Indian immigrant was a conservative (acknowledging that those associated with the African Blood Brotherhood were atypical)? Harold Cruse's recent view to the contrary, it seems more likely that the Islanders were "a spirited aggressive culture-type, whose program and principle of accommodation has been singularly different from that of the American Negro." This was the view of Ira Reid, who had the benefit of considerable first-hand contact with black immigrants in this period. There is little reason to doubt his feeling that, with this background, West Indians (by definition "unassimilated" to the new culture) were so prone to protest against injustice that they were often more radical than natives. A good proportion of immigrants might well become active in social and political protest since so many were educated, had white-collar skills, and were upwardly mobile. They resented the new segregation patterns in America, which were often more galling than the caste-status restrictions of the Islands, since the new segregation often meant a decrease in relative status. From this evidence Garveyism was not a mudsill movement, for few immigrants came from the lowest social stratum.

From a totally different perspective, if such militant persons joined with Garvey (and to what precise extent they did cannot be measured), then one must view the UNIA as in some respects an extreme protest against American conditions. It is possible to be so militant about conditions that one sees absolutely no hope for their change and is compelled to seek a totally different alternative. One would do well to treat with caution the impression left by the *Messenger* that most West Indians were docile and unmilitant.[38]

In one respect nearly all West Indians had to be militant. Although they might be very much divided on Garvey, they were forced to stick together in defense of their citizenship status. It is doubtful whether any

West Indians could comfortably support the idea of deporting Garvey.
Deportation was the weapon over which one had no influence, one that
in those years was deliberately devoid of due process. For the immigrant,
especially the African Blood Brotherhood militant, deportation could
well mean Garvey today, himself tomorrow.[39]

Another major source of conflict between the *Messenger* and Garveyism concerned what racial program was best for American blacks. It involved a question of emphasis—on domestic issues or on Africa, on integrationist goals or goals fostering group separatism. Were Garvey's programs visionary yet within the realm of attainment, or merely escapist?
On all of these questions, sharp differences early emerged.

The problem for historians is to discover whether Garvey in fact had
a positive and far-reaching program for blacks in the United States. Recent
historians have pointed out that the UNIA was on record as opposing various discriminations, forced segregation, lynchings, and other forms of
mistreatment, and that these issues were not infrequently discussed in
the pages of the *Negro World.* The Declaration of Rights of the Negro
Peoples of the World, drafted at the annual convention in 1920, included
demands for the same civil rights the NAACP was working for. The difference between the UNIA and the NAACP on this score, however, is the
significant point: whereas the NAACP was working for an integrated
future, the UNIA was seeking legal protections for the struggle for separatism. On one level, then, it could be said that the UNIA did have what
amounted to a domestic program. But the evidence points to the view
held by contemporary critics, including Randolph and Owen, that the
Garvey movement at the top level was not primarily concerned with the
day-to-day problems of black people in the United States.

The rhetoric of the Declaration of Rights was noble enough, but it
was not backed up by the enthusiasm of the top leadership in actively
developing strategies to deal with lynching, forced segregation, and similar indignities. To the New York *Age,* the UNIA did not really address
itself to the major concern of American blacks—their future in America.
This lack of domestic program was responsible, over the years, for a not
insignificant steady defection from the UNIA. It was not until the last
year of Garvey's imprisonment that the UNIA approved the principle of
branches' working with other black organizations on issues of political
rights, employment, and housing.[40]

Marcus Garvey plainly put the attainment of civil rights in the United States at a relatively low priority. His address to the North Carolina Negro State Fair demonstrates this, as does the almost total preoccupation with an African destiny in his published writings. As he saw it, "the masses of Negroes think differently from the self-appointed leaders of the race. . . . The people desire freedom in a land of their own, while the colored politician desires office and social equality for himself in America." Given this orientation, Garvey put no high premium on the attainment of citizenship. This coincided with a tendency among West Indian immigrants to disfavor naturalization. (The percentage of black immigrants naturalized was lower than the rates of nearly every white immigrant nationality.) As for the proper sort of organization for blacks within the United States, Garvey felt that the UNIA filled a near void, for with the exception of those led by strict Bookerites, all other organizations were tainted with the desire for social equality to be achieved through aggressive political agitation. Of course it was just such agitation that the *Messenger* fancied it excelled in, and for that reason alone it would have opposed this conservative aspect of Garveyism.[41]

Almost from the beginning, Owen and Randolph saw that Garvey deemphasized agitation of political or social questions. They feared that his movement would take the steam out of the groundswell of activism and militancy by shifting the vision of blacks away from America-now to Africa-in-the-future. In this respect the magazine correctly gauged that the UNIA had no active domestic political program (and for that matter did not even have a viable program for blacks in the West Indies). The noncitizenship policy demoralized the drive for full black citizenship, and even after Garvey was convicted the magazine continued to urge the suppression of the UNIA for this reason.[42]

Was the Garvey movement merely escapist, and if so was there any justification for such an orientation? The *Messenger* believed that every aspect of Garvey's program was illusory. It pointed out, accurately, how unrealistic it was to expect that the Klan or any other group in the South would aid a repatriation scheme. The South had hardly welcomed Northern labor agents attempting to recruit black workers in the teens! The magazine also pointed out, again correctly, that if Garvey wanted the best opportunity to attain self-government and an autonomous black society, he would have a more fertile field, and better initial chances, in Jamaica. As Ira Reid saw it, Garvey's movement flourished precisely be-

cause it *was* escapist, providing newly urbanized peasants with a mystical
status in a white world that relegated it to the fringes.[43]

There is something to be said for Garvey's analysis of the future of
blacks in America. He had come to conclusions that were in fact quite
applicable in much of the country in the twenties: "There is no guarantee
of the safety of any such Negro, because by mob violence and lynch law,
the outcome of race prejudice, one's success can be overthrown overnight,
and one transformed from a prosperous subject or citizen, to a refugee."
Was not the search for genuine first-class citizenship, particularly in the
South, still largely futile? Was Garvey's mistake not so much that he mis-
read the character of the nation, but that he assumed that a basically accommodationist program viable for one section was viable for the whole?
This was the same miscalculation that had made Booker Washington unpalatable to many intellectuals in the North. Certainly things were not
quite as desperate as Garvey depicted in a place like New York City, even
though institutional prejudice and overt racial antagonisms were on the
rise in the early twentieth century. The flaw in the Garvey program, then,
was not that it was escapist, but that in the process of planning a strategic
retreat to Africa it neglected its flanks and rear in America.[44]

Garvey's stand on social equality was based in part on a belief in racial
purity and in part on a not unrealistic view of race relations in the United
States. Again using DuBois as his chief focus, but not excluding the *Messenger* group, he charged that so-called leaders were demanding social
equality up to and including intermarriage and black members of government.

> All these, as everybody knows, are the Negroes' constitutional rights,
> but reason dictates that the masses of the white race will never stand
> by the ascendency of an opposite minority group to the favored posi-
> tions in a government, society, and industry that exist by the will of
> the majority; hence the demand of the DuBois group of colored leaders
> will only lead, ultimately, to further disturbances in riots, lynching
> and mob rule. The only logical solution therefore, is to supply the
> Negro with opportunities and environments of his own, and there
> point him to the fullness of his ambition.

It is likely that this rejection of social equality, coupled with the Klan
issue, was responsible more than anything else for driving the *Messenger*

into unremitting opposition to Garvey. To the magazine social equality was the *sine qua non* of American citizenship, no goal to be hushed up and relegated to the far misty future.[45]

A repudiation of social equality was necessary for the achievement of racial purity. Here Garvey imbibed the popularized racial theories of the early twentieth-century eugenists. The destiny of all races depended on a pure stock; this was the way evolution took place. The great day of the black race was just beginning to dawn, and in its hands lay its own evolutionary development. The *Messenger* did not share such grandiose hypotheses. Working for social equality was an integral part of fighting all descriminations. Emphasizing racial purity would easily become an excuse for all manner of indignity. "Without social equality the Negro will ever remain a political and economic serf."[46]

The social equality question gradually became displaced by the Klan issue as the details of Garvey's links to that organization became broadcast. To the *Messenger* they spelled race betrayal; to the present reader Garvey's actions seem misguided idealism at best and an incredibly stupid maneuver at worst. The Klan-Garvey chapter reflects precious little credit, and about all that can be said in his favor is that Garvey seemed to have been sincere in doing what he thought best for the black race.[47]

Garvey felt that he could deal honestly with the Klan and be dealt with similarly, and he naïvely believed that the Klan would be glad to aid in the expatriation of blacks to Africa. But he also believed, on more realistic grounds, that the Klan was as interested in the purity of the races as he was, and that the effort of both races was required to achieve this purity. Garvey had no exaggerated respect for them, but he believed the hooded knights were basically more truthful Caucasians than most and could be depended on to say what they honestly believed. What, then, was wrong in seeking cooperation toward the mutual objective of permanently separating the races to prevent amalgamation? Garvey's most naïve mistake was in not realizing the effects that his dealings would have on black morale.[48]

The *Messenger* reserved some of its choicest rhetoric to describe Garvey's connections with the Klan. A typical piece labeled Garvey "the chief hat-in-hand, me-too-boss 'good nigger' puppet of Kleagle Clarke of Georgia." This hateful epithet, about the worst the magazine could come up with, was reserved for only the most notorious race traitors.[49]

Irrespective of Garvey's motives, his dealings with the Klan were by

far his worst mistake. William Pickens noted that until Garvey's connection with the Hooded Empire became known, most American blacks not
UNIA members were perhaps amused, but not greatly threatened or
worried, by Garveyism. But all this quickly changed as it appeared that
Southern blacks in particular, but all blacks ultimately, could be robbed
of their slowly improving position by this tack that, at the least, lent
legitimacy to the Klan. Garvey's stress on racial purity, and the language
he used, threatened to provoke renewed racial aggression. When he charged
that his black opponents desired the "amalgamation" of the two races,
and called this "a crime against nature," he was using the lynch-provoking
language of racists. In echoing the worst race-haters, even to using the
same charged language, Garvey made himself a menace to racial progress,
no matter whether one ultimately desired an integrated or a separated
society. Such rhetoric could not possibly bring productive results.[50]

Perhaps the most widely known feature of Garvey's program was his
dream of a black steamship line, and on no part of his movement was
more ridicule heaped. The Black Star Line and its successors were to
be the vehicles for welding together the black peoples of the globe, spirit-
ually as well as commercially. The primary idea behind the line was not
to transport massive boatloads of expatriates to Africa, although a fleet
would be invaluable in the eventual African redemption. Rather, it was
to be the model of a black-owned, black-operated, and black-financed
business cooperative, one of the cornerstones of Garvey's future black
economy.

Garvey's critics found much in the operations of the line that was
comical, as well as much that was tragic. The *Messenger* noted with accuracy that the postwar period was not an auspicious one for beginning
a new ship line, given the glut in the shipping market and the domination of that market by a few major lines. Another criticism charged
Garvey with playing on the ignorant masses and picking their pockets
of hard-earned savings, and the Friends of Negro Freedom vowed to aid
duped investors bring suit to recover their money. What made it easy for
Garvey to raise money was the fact that he exploited race pride. But
successful black business, in the magazine's analysis, could not be long
based on the race chauvinism of its patrons, only on the efficiency of
the particular enterprise. This was demonstrated when the UNIA's laun-

dries failed to compete with the white chains. Apparently few blacks were willing to pay a few pennies more to have their wash done at a race establishment.[51]

Ridicule was not stinted in attacking the Black Star Line. The irregularity of the sailings and disrepair of the ships, as well as the court battles to keep the vessels in BSL hands, provided ample opportunity for wit, and its vessels were torpedoed in no less than twenty of George Schuyler's "Shafts and Darts" columns.

There were at least two redeeming virtues in the Black Star Line to which the *Messenger* was insensitive. Garvey pointed out that black travelers had to undergo considerable indignities in getting and enjoying ocean passage. Randolph cavalierly dismissed this point by asking how many blacks did or could make use of ocean travel. More importantly, the magazine could never see any psychological justification for, or understand the economic principle behind, a black steamship line. Notwithstanding the justified criticism of starting a steamship company in the face of almost insuperable odds, for many West Indians such a venture still made sense. Steamers were the usual means of communication and commerce between the Islands; black crews were common, and black masters not unknown. A black-owned fleet of vessels might well have played a viable economic, not to mention spiritual, role in more prosperous times. But the *Messenger* was unwilling to entertain these possibilities.[52]

Randolph, Owen, and other critics like William Pickens implied that Garvey was crooked and dishonest in promoting the Black Star Line. There was plenty of dirt that Garvey's critics could mine for suspicions of scandal. He did at times mislead the public, and his advertising and promotional claims were often exaggerated. It was also easy to speculate that Garvey was feathering his own nest financially. But biographers have found no substantial evidence that he personally profited in any significant degree from the UNIA businesses or that he was personally dishonest. His chief fault was the propensity to believe his own rhetoric.

Another basic difference between Garvey and his critics centered on the UNIA's black nationalism and the cultural pluralism and integrationist goals of its opponents. Garvey put it succinctly: "We differ from the other organizations in America because they seek to subordinate the

Negro as a secondary consideration in a great civilization." Such a subordinate role would mean eventual extinction for blacks in America.
Speaking of the white majority, he said that "no race in the world is so
just as to give others, for the asking, a square deal in things economic,
political, and social." Clearly the hope of the black race lay in the new
(pure) blood and the new future—in Africa. In Garvey's criticism of those
who rejected a consistent black nationalism with Africa as the goal, he
hit particularly at leaders who, he believed, advocated social equality.
Such persons

> feel that it is too much work for them to settle down and build up a
> civilization of their own. They feel it is easier to seize on to the civili-
> zation of the white man and under the guise of constitutional rights
> fight for those things that the white man has created. . . . As for in-
> stance, Dr. W. E. B. DuBois, who has been educated by white charity,
> is a brilliant scholar, but he is not a hard worker. He prefers to use
> his higher intellectual abilities to fight for a place among white men
> in society, industry and in politics, rather than use that ability to
> work and create for his own race that which the race could be able
> to take credit for. He would not think of repeating for his race the
> work of the Pilgrim Fathers or the Colonists who laid the foundation
> of America, but he prefers to fight and agitate for the privilege of
> dancing with a white lady at a ball at the Biltmore.

Nor was Garvey solely concerned with an economic and political black
nationalism; the cultural emphasis also was important. "History is written
with prejudices, likes and dislikes; and there has never been a white historian who ever wrote with any true love or feeling for the Negro."[53]
   The majority of black intellectuals opposed Garvey not only on organizational and personal grounds, but on the ideological ground of black
nationalism. The *Messenger* group, the Bookerite and Talented Tenth
schools as well, believed in the possibilities of an American future devoid
of lynching and Jim Crow, discrimination and prejudice, a dream in which
black Americans would become (sometimes autonomous) contributors
to the general culture. Garvey's vision was fixed on an opposite pole,

and his nationalism was far broader than theirs. He combined in one
ideology a cultural nationalism stressing the intellectual, political, and
military achievements of the race; economic nationalism, emphasizing
a separate-economy ideal in the United States as well as a worldwide
colored economy; and political nationalism demanding a separate state
in Africa where the cultural, social, and spiritual life of the race could
be rebuilt.[54]

In opposing Garvey, the bulk of the intellectuals were fighting not
only for the cause of blacks in America, but personally, for themselves
as well. Garvey's "extreme" position forced them into having to assert,
more positively than they would have otherwise, that America held
promise for the black race. And there was an additional trap. For just
as Garvey's opponents had to assert all the more strongly their American
identity and future, his central theme was to call them back to Africa,
and more basically, back to their own blackness. He was calling them
back to themselves, asking them to stop seeking their reflection in the
white man's mirror. But how could one feel comfortable in seeking a
radical black identity at precisely the time when one had to defend the
black man's future in white America? The *Messenger* group had to reject
Garvey on this ground; the dilemma he exposed was too difficult to
reconcile.[55]

Garvey's call was a messianic message to all black brothers; Africa
beckons, and the future is there: "I come to the people in the role of
the reformer and say to them, 'Awake! the day is upon you, go forth in
the name of the race and build yourselves a nation, redeem your country
Africa, the land from whence you came and prove yourselves men worthy
of the recognition of others.' " But Africa did not beckon strongly enough
to Randolph and Owen. They, like DuBois, were unwilling to be the new
Pilgrims to a distant continent. To them Garvey's repatriation scheme
was totally unrealistic. This does not mean that there was no thought of
Africa among intellectuals before or after Garvey; DuBois's interest is
well known, and Richard Moore recalls that Harlem, before Garvey,
gained a sophisticated awareness of Africa through the press of that city,
including the *Messenger.*[56]

A. Philip Randolph knew enough about the realities of colonialism
to see the futility of trying to liberate Africa by mere promises.

It ought to be apparent to even the most ardent and superficial Garvey-ite that the interest of one [colonial] Power in preventing the establishment of an African State is the interest of all of the Powers; and if all of the Powers are interested in maintaining the status quo in Africa, that the redemption of Africa by Negroes who are unarmed, unorganized, uneducated, a minority in numbers to their oppressors, divided, both in and out of Africa by languages, custom, history, and habits, is a will-o'-wisp, an iridescent dream which could only be born in the head of an irresponsible enthusiast.

Even the Senegalese French Deputy, Blaise Diagne, agreed that Africa was too diverse and fragmented for Garvey's black Zionism to be realized. From the perspective of Randolph's internationalism, Garvey's schemes for Africa were simply wrong-headed. Whether he interpreted the UNIA program correctly or not, Randolph saw a hope of isolation from the white world that was neither desirable nor possible. Quarantine would inevitably mean decay, as China's history had shown. Separation was precisely the opposite of what was needed; a really free Africa would come only with the worldwide overthrow of capitalism. In the interim, those interested in that continent's welfare should concern themselves with international efforts to abolish forced labor and preserve lands for native Africans.[57]

Garvey's argument was indeed as vulnerable as Randolph charged. His ideas were noticeably vague when it came to the specifics of how African redemption would be achieved. He referred to some hazy future confrontation with the colonial powers, stating that the race had "reared many Fochs between 1914 and 1918 on the battlefields of France and Flanders. It will be a question later on of Foch meeting Foch." But this was no program, no strategy, merely a prophecy. It is true that Garvey did not intend to expatriate the whole black American population to its ancestral homeland within the foreseeable future; at the most the UNIA expected to send a few hundred thousand to Africa, persons who could provide technical aid and assistance. But even the hazy plans for this exodus were noticeably lacking in realities.

It is not at all clear that a significant portion of the UNIA membership even desired to return to Africa. With the exception of the ill-fated

technical mission to Liberia, no Garveyite pioneers were ever sent to
Africa, and there was apparently no pressure from the membership at
large for such passage, even when the cash to charter a ship or two was
available. The American-born membership was plainly apathetic, as were,
probably, a significant majority of all black Americans. Kelly Miller, speaking for the moderate leadership, noted that the educated black "resents
as a reflection upon his American birthright any suggestion that he has
a special and peculiar interest in the dark continent" and quoted Frederick Douglass as saying, " 'I have none of the banana in me.' " James
Weldon Johnson wrote that while American blacks were angered and
stirred by the European rape of Africa, they nonetheless saw the United
States as their home. And while the notion of returning was a traditional Afro-American theme, a secularization of the "other-world" view
purveyed by the churches, it was plain that most racial militants had no
urge to pick up and leave. Eric Walrond noted the same. From what population, then, would Garvey get his twentieth-century Pilgrims?[58]

The complexities of Africa's ethnography and political development
were slighted in Garvey's superficial view of that continent. Tribal, religious, linguistic, and ethnic divisions among the black groups, much
less those that did not identify themselves as Negroid, were glossed over.
How could the different national traditions be unified? William Pickens,
observing that "there is no more in common between South Africa and
North Africa than between Texas and Turkey," concluded that Garvey
"had not a grammer grade understanding of Africa." An uncharitable
statement, yes, but Garvey's tutelage under Duse Mohammed Ali was
not well reflected in his public statements on African redemption.

Garvey also seemed unaware that he was frightening middle-class,
educated Africans, the group that would eventually have to begin the
process of decolonization. He was not too radical for them, only utterly
visionary. These Africans preferred DuBois's version of Pan-Africanism,
which encouraged a more gradual movement toward independence and
self-determination through piecemeal reforms and cooperation with
liberals in Europe and elsewhere. Plainly any hope for cooperation from
Liberia would have to come through such gradualism. There was simply
no way, whether politic or not, that Garvey could appeal to the African
masses; they were in no position yet to take the forefront in the libera-

tion of their continent. Extremism at that early point seemed suicidal.
In the words of Senegalese Deputy Blaise Diagne and his colleague from
Guadeloupe, Gratien Candance, "We do not hate the white race. What
we seek is conciliation and collaboration. Our evolution and development
depends upon relations with the white race. We would lose everything
if we were isolated in Africa."

On a final point Garvey managed to alienate himself from important
parts of native African leadership: "We are not favorably impressed with
the unmitigated presumption of this man, Garvey, in electing himself
provisional President of Africa." These words, spoken at anti-Garvey
rallies in 1921 by Mokete Manoedi, a native of Basutoland, mirrored a
very real apprehension. What could the self-annointed saviour of Africa
really offer that continent, other than grief in the form of retaliation from
the imperialist powers or a substitution of black oppression for white?
Randolph, Owen, and other critics had ample justification for distrusting
Garvey. In the absense of cooperation or even discussion with native
African leadership, in the absence of any realistic scenario for African
self-development, and in the absence of a recognition of world power
politics, one cannot credit Garvey with having the answer for Africa.[59]

A final source of conflict that pitted the *Messenger* against Garvey
involved the type of leadership appropriate for blacks in America. Garvey
had two images of himself, at times the popular figure elected by the
people to spearhead their movement, and at others the messianic, self-
appointed leader. Garvey took his own "election" as President General
of the UNIA seriously and contrasted himself to "self-appointed" leaders.
But of course there had never been any doubt that he would be "elected,"
and he probably did not fool himself much, for the other strain comes
through much clearer. Throughout the two volumes of *Philosophy and
Opinions* Garvey compared himself to Christ; both were persecuted by
the authorities after being betrayed by their fellow men; both were only
trying to work humbly for the benefit of their people; both were men
of singular vision.[60]

Garvey might see himself as a Christ, but others compared him to less
flattering images, and he bewildered followers as well as foes "by acting
as a democrat one moment and a revolutionary dictator the next." Robert

Bagnall likened him to such notorious madmen as Nero and Alexander. Joel A. Rogers, a lifelong friend, admitted that Garvey was a potential Hitler or Mussolini whose cause was just but whose methods, which amounted to racial fascism, were "perverse." A third contemporary spoke of his "Napoleonic urge for personal power," and it is no accident that Garvey proclaimed the French dictator his "ideal hero." More than one critic used megalomania to describe his personality. Above all Garvey understood and used mass psychology with adroitness; his oddly lyrical style had the power to move and sway and transport audiences. This hypnotic influence stemmed from the fact that he was simultaneously the object of adoration and of fear. Certainly all this was far different from the leadership of DuBois or Randolph or Owen, for several reasons, not the least of which was that none of them could muster a mass following behind his program.[61]

The fascistic underside of Garveyism worried not a few observers. The "Waterloo" threat against Chandler Owen and William Pickens could not be dismissed as Garvey's usual verbosity. Such statements give license to UNIA thugs who perpetrated at least one murder and innumerable lesser intimidations. In mid-1920, black preachers who opposed Garvey found their church services disrupted by verbal abuse and threats. The 1924 annual convention discussed the movement's opponents and ways of "putting them away," and some of the intended victims were even identified by name. That same year a prominent Garveyite was quoted as saying that soon it would be unsafe for any black person to walk Harlem's streets without wearing a UNIA button. Even as late as 1928, with Garvey deported from the country, his followers still resorted to terror tactics. Militant members, attending a forum on Garvey being conducted by a Harlem minister, broke chairs, smashed windows, destroyed hymnbooks, and blackjacked the hapless preacher when they objected to what was being said. It may be unfair to charge Garvey with direct responsibility for all these occurrences, but his heavy-handed rhetoric must bear some burden for having incited such a spirit of ruffianism.[62]

Garvey's critique of other organizations and leaders was predictably harsh, but not without some grains of truth. Beyond basic differences over integrationist versus black nationalist goals, other points could be made:

Nearly everyone who essays to lead the race at this time does so by
first establishing himself as the pet of some philanthropist of another
race, to whom he will go and debase his race in the worst form, humil-
iate his own manhood, and thereby win the sympathy of the "great
benefactor," who will dictate to him what he could do in the leadership of the Negro race.

It is not clear whether Garvey realized that the figure he most respected
outside himself, Booker Washington, also fit these unflattering stereotypes. But aside from that, Garvey was the first leader to succeed in making blacks pay for black agitation. Despite all the furor over his supposed
connections with the Klan, it can be safely assumed that the UNIA's
funds came entirely from the pockets of black folk of poor or modest
means, not from any Rosenwalds, Spingarns, or white socialists. If, as
Nathan Huggins suggests, the association of the established black leadership with white philanthropists and reformers "compromised" them in
the eyes of the black masses, then Garvey's independence from white
support may have been one of his greatest attractions. But of course he
was not criticizing merely the patronage of black leaders by white philanthropists. His enmity went far deeper: "It amuses me sometimes to
hear the biggest crooks in the Negro Race referring to me as a criminal.
As I have said before, Negro race leaders are the biggest crooks in the
world." And there the argument ended.[63]

A frequent charge made by Garvey's opponents was that the UNIA
was composed of the most ignorant of the race, and more specifically,
ignorant West Indians. Part of this has to do with anti-West Indianism,
but part was due also to a genuine revulsion at the lack of intellectual
content that many perceived in the movement. The *Messenger* frequently
voiced this notion of ignorant followers, while sometimes also mention-
ing that most intelligent West Indians opposed him. Yet a more dispassionate analysis of some of Garvey's thought, scattered in the two volumes of *Philosophy and Opinions*, uncovers ideas both original and
prescient. Garvey's antagonism toward his well-educated black critics
was not out of an innate dislike of intellectuals—after all, he probably
fancied himself one—but out of a deep and well-grounded distrust of

them. It certainly was not true that he appealed only to the illiterate;
on the contrary, at an early date he offered a noble role to the educated:
"I appeal to the higher intelligence as well as to the illiterate groups of
our race. We must work together. Those of us who are better positioned
intellectually must exercise forebearance with the illiterate and help
them to see the right." Yet years of frustration and opposition led ultimately to the point of anathema:

> The present day Negro or "colored" intellectual is no less a liar and
> a cunning thief than his illustrious teacher [whites]. His occidental
> collegiate training only fits him to be a rogue and vagabond, and a
> seeker after the easiest and best by following the line of least resist-
> ance. He is lazy, dull and un-creative. His purpose is to deceive the
> less fortunate of his race, and, by his wiles ride easily into position
> and wealth at their expense, and thereafter agitate for and seek
> social equality with the creative and industrious whites.[64]

Were Garvey's followers an uneducated lot? Ira Reid found that 98.6
percent of adult black immigrants in 1923 passed the Bureau of Immigration's none-too-easy literacy test; so if, as was frequently claimed, a majority of the UNIA membership was West Indian, then that membership
was comparatively well educated. Joel A. Rogers adduces evidence of the
intellectual abilities of at least a portion of the movement's converts; the
Negro World, he noted, was edited by some of the "brightest Negro minds"
and over the years featured the writings of William H. Ferris, Hubert H.
Harrison, Eric Walrond, W. A. Domingo, Cyril Briggs, and William Pickens.
If Garvey's followers were so ignorant, who read the *Negro World*? This
emphasis on allegedly "uneducated" Garveyites betrays a real ambivalence
about the great unwashed masses who flocked to Garvey's standards. In
Nathan Huggins's words, "the Harlem intellectuals had been anxious to
make those class distinctions which would mark them as different from
their black brothers further down. So while proclaiming a new race consciousness [and, one might add, at times justifiably criticizing the Garveyite program], they had been wearing the clothes and using the manners
of sophisticated whites, thereby earning the epithet 'dicty niggers' from

the very people they were supposed to be championing." This flaw in
the Talented Tenth leadership spilled over to more radical figures like
Randolph and Owen when the subject was Garvey.[65]

Overshadowing all other conflicts between Garvey and his critics was
his challenge to the Talented Tenth's pretensions to race leadership. Nearly all black intellectuals, including those in the *Messenger* circle, were by
definition part of that segment of the population, and Garvey explicitly
denied their right to lead by denying the presumptions on which their
leadership was based. Many of them had identified race progress as the
sum of their personal progress; individual betterment did not connote
simply a life of ease and bourgeois indulgence, but in fact the building
blocks of advancement for the whole race. Achieving would level barriers
for those to come, and when enough had reached that achieving position,
the floodgates of racial goodwill would swing open. The final end of
successful blacks was to influence white people for the good of the race,
and their examples of success and propriety would be the chief instru-
ments of persuasion. Garvey rejected these presumptions. Perceiving
danger, the Talented Tenth reacted like a threatened Establishment, using
all the weapons an Establishment possesses. A handful hoped for cooperation with Garvey, but most could only conceive of implacable opposition.[66]

Garvey was not interested in cooperating with the other organizations;
on the contrary, he was proud of the fact that the UNIA cut into the
Talented Tenth movements' grass roots support. His movement rejected
the black Establishment's future, and the intellectuals personally, by
reserving no leadership place for them in it. The UNIA was essentially a
one-man show. With few exceptions, such as Dr. Leroy Bundy, UNIA
leadership developed indigenously and not from already-well-known
figures in the black Establishment.[67]

Nearly all middle-class and aspiring-to-middle-class blacks rejected
Garvey, at least in part on the basis of class differences. In unguarded
moments his critics displayed, if not genuine repugnance, then at least
disdain for the masses.[68] That these attitudes existed demonstrates the
effect of caste restrictions in America, which serve to overemphasize
class distinctions within the black world. To varying degrees members
of the *Messenger* circle shared this middle-class perspective. If a magazine
of socialist birth could, by November 1923, dedicate its whole issue as

a panegyric to black capitalism, if it opposed Garvey in part because of
the alleged uncouthness of his followers, was it not flirting dangerously
with the bourgeois world? This evolution would be arrested in 1925 when
the magazine turned its attention to the Pullman porters, but it would
never again be as proletarian as it had been in 1919. Whatever purely
working-class character remained to the magazine after 1920 was soon
lost in the effort to "get Garvey."

   One cannot generalize about the well-intentioned goals of the anti-
Garvey campaign and neatly ignore the sordid methods. Means and ends
became inextricably entwined in the whole affair, on both sides, and
scrupulous honesty and charity in debate were the casualties. To call
Garvey a "half wit, low grade moron, whose insufferable presumption
is only exceeded by his abysmal ignorance" reflects no credit on A. Philip
Randolph. Had the *Messenger* felt less threatened by Garvey, it need not
have resorted to such scurrilous epithets. Cronon makes the point that
very few of Garvey's critics charged him with dishonesty; yet Randolph
on occasions impugned his character as well as his honesty. Garvey would
never understand how his enemies could, as he saw it, sacrifice the prestige
of the race in order to destroy his leadership. While we need not take
Garvey's innocence at face value, the point is valid: The *Messenger*'s anti-
West Indianism *did* degrade the race, as did the language used to describe
Garvey.[69]
   Consistency was also lacking in several of the major arguments used by
the *Messenger*. Garvey was chided for not keeping the controversy on an
elevated plane and sticking to relevant issues, but the periodical was itself
guilty of precisely that. More seriously, the *Messenger* advocated denying
free speech to Garvey because he endangered free speech. The Eight "defended" the race by bringing its supposedly "worst" characteristics before
the white authorities. The *Messenger* agitated for amnesty for political
prisoners while demanding Garvey's deportation.
   A final question can now be posed: Was the opposition to Garvey
based not only on ideological and organizational grounds, but also on
pure jealousy of an enormously successful man? He, an alien of obscure
background, had collected millions of dollars, while other "leaders,"
many of whom were college-educated, had to rely on white philanthropy.

At the same time he cut into the grass roots base of the Friends of Negro Freedom, black labor unions, and the NAACP. Both the UNIA and the FNF aspired to be militant, mass-based, and against the status quo, but only the former enjoyed substantial success. As Kelly Miller acknowledged in 1927, no movement launched by intellectuals or the Talented Tenth managed to penetrate the masses in the twenties, Randolph's work with the Pullman porters to the contrary notwithstanding. Garvey became the most exciting personage in Harlem, drawing thousands to his rallies and parades. Poor DuBois's Pan-African Congresses were often confused with UNIA programs, and while the UNIA drew hundreds of thousands, Du-Bois's movement barely survived. Garvey realized, despite the bombast, where things stood: "My success as an organizer was much more than rival Negro leaders could tolerate." Here was a mass movement the size of which Randolph and Owen and DuBois had long dreamed about—and they had no part in it or of it. Here was an organization based on the working class, and it was not socialistic. What better reason could they have for being envious, what better reasons for trying to get rid of him?[70]

A. Philip Randolph charged that Garvey would never have gotten a start had he not ridden on the coattails of the *Messenger,* that it was Randolph himself who gave Garvey his first knowledge of African problems. But Garvey knew this wasn't true, and whether Randolph really believed it or not, he had to suffer Garvey's subsequent successes in none too graceful silence. In the second volume of *Philosophy and Opinions* a photograph shows the top officials of the UNIA, including Garvey, watching a parade during the 1922 Convention of the Negro Peoples of the World. The reviewing stand was situated on the steps of the association's publishing house. Unhappily for Owen and Randolph, the second floor of that same building housed the offices of the *Messenger.* Owen and Randolph are seen in the photograph standing to the rear of the UNIA dignitaries.[71] What bitter gall it must have been for the two young editors to witness one of Garvey's greatest successes, to share the same building with their (in a literal *and* a figurative sense) *bête noire.* They could not escape his parade on that day; they could not, apparently, escape his presence. It is this latter point that needs stressing: Randolph and Owen, for ideological, political, and organizational reasons, but also for deeply personal reasons, for reasons of envy as well as reasons of program, had to attack and destroy Garvey. They succeeded, but at a cost in integrity.

NOTES

1. The handbill is in the Administrative File, Subject File Garvey, NAACP Papers, Library of Congress.

2. *Messenger,* December 1920, p. 170.

3. Ibid., August 1922, p. 470; Theodore Vincent, *Black Power and the Garvey Movement* (Berkeley, Cal., n.d.), pp. 41, 43, 45, 114; Eric D. Walrond, "Imperator Africanus: Marcus Garvey, Menace or Promise?", *Independent* 114 (January 3, 1925): 8; New York *Times,* August 3, 1920, 7:2; Rollin Lynde Hartt, "The Negro Moses and His Campaign to Lead the Black Millions into Their Promised Land," *Independent* 105 (February 26, 1921): 206. New Negro utterances of Garvey were reprinted in New York (State) Legislature, Joint Legislative Committee Investigating Seditious Activities, *Revolutionary Radicalism: Its History, Purpose and Tactics, with an Exposition and Discussion of the Steps Being Taken and Required to Curb It* (Albany, 1920), 2: 1512-14.

4. *Messenger,* September 1920, pp. 83-84.

5. Ibid., October 1920, pp. 114-15; December 1920, pp. 170-72. Theodore Vincent has pointed out that this article may have undertones of actual political rivalry, for Randolph was on the Socialist party ticket in 1920 at the same time that the left-wing Garveyites running the Liberty party also put up a ticket. Letter to author, June 16, 1972.

6. *Messenger,* September 1921, pp. 248-52.

7. Ibid., July 1922, p. 437; Vincent, *Black Power and the Garvey Movement,* p. 194.

8. Vincent, *Black Power and the Garvey Movement,* pp. 191-93.

9. Quoted in Chicago *Defender,* August 12, 1922, p. 2.

10. Edmund David Cronon, *Black Moses: The Story of Marcus Garvey and the Universal Negro Improvement Association* (Madison, Wis., 1955), p. 180; New York *Times,* August 7, 1922, 7:1.

11. Chicago *Defender,* August 12, 1922, p. 2; August 26, 1922, p. 8; New York *Times,* August 28, 1922, 13:5; *Messenger,* August 1922, pp. 457-58, back cover; Cronon, *Black Moses,* pp. 100-101.

12. *Messenger,* September 1922, pp. 479-80.

13. See Ibid., December 1922, pp. 550-52, for the results of a poll on how to deal with Garvey.

14. J. A. Rogers, *World's Great Men of Color* (New York, 1947), 2: 603; New York *Times,* September 6, 1922, 19:4; September 11, 1922, 19:7; Cronon, *Black Moses,* pp. 108-109; *Messenger,* October 1922, pp.

499-500; New York *Age,* September 9, 1922, p. 1; September 16, 1922, p. 1.

15. *Messenger,* December 1922, p. 542; January 1923, p. 569; February 1923, p. 612.

16. See Amy Jacques Garvey, ed., *Philosophy and Opinions of Marcus Garvey* (New York, 1969), 2: 293-300, for the full text of the letter.

17. The following documents in the NAACP Papers, Library of Congress, reflect this activity: White to Randolph, August 7, 1922; White to Spingarn, August 16, 1922; Randolph to White, August 25, 1922; Bagnall to Spingarn, September 1, 1922; copy of the letter to the Attorney General with marginal comments by Spingarn, dated January 15, 1923; White to Johnson, May 17, 1923; Johnson to Judge Julian W. Mack, May 17, 1923, all in the Administrative File, Subject File Garvey; White to Randolph, August 23, 1922, in Administrative File, General Correspondence; Spingarn to White, August 17, 1922, August 23, 1922, in Administrative File, Special Correspondence, Spingarn, Arthur B.

18. New York *Age,* February 24, 1923, p. 4; Elton C. Fax, *Garvey: The Story of a Pioneer Black Nationalist* (New York, 1972), p. 172.

19. Garvey, *Philosophy and Opinions,* 2: 240, 300-308. Garvey was not above Red-baiting and social-equality-baiting his opponents. See especially ibid., 2: 240, 308.

20. *Messenger,* June 1924, p. 178; Amy Jacques Garvey, *Garvey and Garveyism* (Kingston, 1963), pp. 102-103.

21. *Messenger,* March 1923, pp. 639-45; interview, Bernice Wilds, October 16, 1972.

22. *Messenger,* March 1923, pp. 638, 648. For a short biography of Bagnall, see Theodore Kornweibel, Jr., "Robert Wellington Bagnall," in Rayford W. Logan, ed., *Dictionary of American Negro Biography* (New York, 1977).

23. *Messenger,* July 1923, p. 759.

24. *New Republic* 52 (August 31, 1927): 46-47; New York *Age,* November 5, 1927, p. 4. Kelly Miller's arguments for pardoning Garvey are typical; see New York *Amsterdam News,* August 24, 1927, p. 15.

25. *Messenger,* December 1920, p. 172; January 1922, pp. 334-35.

26. Claude McKay, *Harlem: Negro Metropolis* (New York, 1940), p. 158; Garvey, *Philosophy and Opinions,* 2: 72-73; Harold Cruse, *The Crisis of the Negro Intellectual* (New York, 1967), pp. 132-33; Nathan Irvin Huggins, *Harlem Renaissance* (New York, 1971), p. 41; Vincent, *Black Power and the Garvey Movement,* pp. 18, 24-27.

27. Garvey, *Philosophy and Opinions,* 2: 69-71, 334-35, 357; Garvey,

Garvey and Garveyism, pp. 129-31. Vincent, *Black Power and the Garvey Movement,* pp. 172-73, notes that Garvey did favor interracial unionism in Jamaica and Trinidad where blacks were in the majority. See the same author, pp. 78-84, for details of the tortured relationship between the UNIA and the African Blood Brotherhood.

28. *Messenger,* April 1922, p. 387; July 1922, p. 437; September 1922, p. 480; Cruse, *Crisis of the Negro Intellectual,* p. 124.

29. *Messenger,* October 1922, pp. 501-502.

30. New York *Age,* November 11, 1922, p. 1; *Messenger,* January 1923, p. 561.

31. *Messenger,* February 1923, p. 612; New York *Age,* July 7, 1923; William Pickens, "The Emperor of Africa: The Psychology of Garveyism," *Forum* 70 (August 1923): 1794.

32. Interview, Bernice Wilds; Garvey, *Philosophy and Opinions,* 2: 42, 55-61, 85.

33. Ira De A. Reid, *The Negro Immigrant: His Background, Characteristics and Social Adjustment, 1899-1937* (New York, 1939), pp. 85, 245, 248.

34. Cruse, *Crisis of the Negro Intellectual,* p. 131; Reid, *Negro Immigrant,* pp. 107-109.

35. Elliott M. Rudwick, *W. E. B. DuBois: Propagandist of the Negro Protest* (New York, 1968), pp. 217, 230.

36. Wilson Record, "The Negro Intellectual and Negro Nationalism," *Social Forces* 33 (October 1954): 16; Garvey, *Garvey and Garveyism,* pp. 129-31.

37. Reid, *Negro Immigrant,* p. 151; New York *Age,* October 6, 1923, p. 4; Roi Ottley, *"New World A-Coming": Inside Black America* (New York, 1968), p. 80; Vincent, *Black Power and the Garvey Movement,* pp. 204-205.

38. Cruse, *Crisis of the Negro Intellectual,* p. 119; Reid, *Negro Immigrant,* pp. 49, 84, 111-12, 221.

39. Cruse, *Crisis of the Negro Intellectual,* p. 122.

40. New York *Age,* August 14, 1920, p. 4; Vincent, *Black Power and the Garvey Movement,* pp. 17, 19, 116 ff., 124, 212-13, 217-19.

41. Garvey, *Philosophy and Opinions,* 2: 38, 41; Reid, *Negro Immigrant,* pp. 164, 249.

42. *Messenger,* September 1921, p. 251; December 1922, pp. 241-42; February 1923, p. 613; August 1923, p. 782.

43. Ibid., September 1922, pp. 477-78; Reid, *Negro Immigrant,* p. 154.

44. Gilbert Osofsky, *Harlem: The Making of a Ghetto: Negro New York,*

1890-1930 (New York, 1966), pp. 40-41; Garvey is quoted in Charles W. Simmons, "The Negro Intellectual's Criticism of Garveyism," *Negro History Bulletin* 25 (November 1961): 33-34.

45. Garvey, *Philosophy and Opinions,* 2: 4, 39.

46. Ibid., 2: 286; *Messenger,* October 1921, p. 259; September 1921, p. 252.

47. Joel A. Rogers, who knew Garvey personally, asserts that Garvey allied himself with the Klan to gain revenge on his black opposition. Given his sincerity in other contexts, such base cynicism as Rogers suggests is to be doubted. *World's Great Men of Color,* 2: 605.

48. Garvey, *Philosophy and Opinions,* 2: 41, 71, 338-49; Cronon, *Black Moses,* pp. 188-89.

49. *Messenger,* September 1922, p. 478.

50. Pickens, "The Emperor of Africa," p. 1798; New York *Age,* September 24, 1921, p. 4; November 10, 1923, p. 4.

51. *Messenger,* July 1922, pp. 439-40; August 1922, p. 466; September 1922, p. 480.

52. Ibid., September 1921, p. 250; Reid, *Negro Immigrant,* p. 151.

53. Garvey, *Philosophy and Opinions,* 1: 2, 10; 2: 43, 82, 97.

54. Record, "Negro Intellectual and Negro Nationalism," pp. 15-16.

55. Harold R. Isaacs, *The New World of Negro Americans* (New York, 1964), pp. 137, 143-45; Huggins, *Harlem Renaissance,* pp. 305-306.

56. Garvey, *Philosophy and Opinions,* 2: 99; Richard B. Moore, "Africa-Conscious Harlem," *Freedomways* 3 (Summer 1963): 320.

57. *Messenger,* January 1922, pp. 334-35; December 1922, pp. 538-39; September 1921, p. 250; November 1922, p. 522; February 1923, p. 614.

58. Garvey, *Philosophy and Opinions,* 2: 114; Vincent, *Black Power and the Garvey Movement,* p. 16n; Fax, *Garvey: The Story of a Pioneer Black Nationalist,* p. 215; Kelly Miller, "After Marcus Garvey—What of the Negro," *Contemporary Review* 131 (April 1927): 497; New York *Age,* August 21, 1920, p. 4; Eric D. Walrond, "The New Negro Faces America," *Current History* 17 (February 1923): 788; Huggins, *Harlem Renaissance,* p. 42.

59. Huggins, *Harlem Renaissance,* pp. 44, 46; Pickens, "The Emperor of Africa," p. 1794; New York *Times,* August 4, 1920, 10:5; New York *Age,* September 10, 1921, p. 2; July 26, 1924, p. 4; Fax, *Garvey: The Story of a Pioneer Black Nationalist,* pp. 143, 145-46, 213.

60. Garvey, *Philosophy and Opinions,* 1: 61; 2: 41, 99.

61. *Messenger,* March 1923, p. 638; Rogers, *World's Great Men of Color,* 2: 602, 608; Moore, "Africa-Conscious Harlem," p. 322; Reid,

Negro Immigrant, p. 148; Vincent, *Black Power and the Garvey Movement,* p. 212; Walrond, "The New Negro Faces America," p. 787; Pickens, "The Emperor of Africa," pp. 1791, 1795-96; Arna Bontemps, "The Awakening," in Bontemps, ed., *The Harlem Renaissance Remembered* (New York, 1972), p. 8.

62. New York *Age,* August 28, 1920, p. 1; August 16, 1924, p. 4; September 6, 1924, p. 4; January 31, 1928, p. 3; February 4, 1928, p. 4.

63. Garvey, *Philosophy and Opinions,* 1: 29; 2: 24-25, 104; Rogers *World's Great Men of Color,* 2: 604; Huggins, *Harlem Renaissance,* p. 50.

64. Garvey, *Philosophy and Opinions,* 1: 67; 2: 123.

65. Reid, *Negro Immigrant,* p. 84; Rogers, *World's Great Men of Color,* 2: 610; Huggins, *Harlem Renaissance,* pp. 305-306.

66. Record, "Negro Intellectual and Negro Nationalism," p. 16; Carl S. Matthews, "After Booker T. Washington: The Search for a New Negro Leadership, 1915-1925" (Ph.D. dissertation, University of Virginia, 1971), pp. 2, 215; Huggins, *Harlem Renaissance,* pp. 6, 49-50.

67. Record, "Negro Intellectual and Negro Nationalism," p. 17; Vincent, *Black Power and the Garvey Movement,* pp. 91, 155.

68. See the article by Robert Minor in the *Daily Worker,* quoted in Garvey, *Garvey and Garveyism,* pp. 129-31.

69. *Messenger,* August 1922, pp. 267-68; Cronon, *Black Moses,* p. 208; Garvey, *Garvey and Garveyism,* p. 102.

70. Rogers, *World's Great Men of Color,* 2: 604; Garvey, *Philosophy and Opinions,* 2: 132, 313, Rudwick, *W. E. B. DuBois: Propagandist,* pp. 224, 226, 230; Miller, "After Marcus Garvey—What of the Negro?", p. 499; Jervis Anderson, "Early Voice," *New Yorker* 47 (December 16, 1972): 40.

71. *Messenger,* August 1922, p. 470; Garvey, *Philosophy and Opinions,* Vol. 2, facing page 281.

6 | Black Labor, White Labor and Black Business

Popular history teaches us that the 1920s were a "Prosperity Decade," and we call to mind the image of good times, frivolity, flappers, and Fords. But this is the view from "white history"; as far as black Americans were concerned, those ten years contained about as much adversity as previous decades, which was considerable. The ticker tape at Times Square may have convinced whites that the better life had arrived, but many blacks, including the editors of the *Messenger,* labored under no exaggerated delusions of a bright tomorrow. On the contrary, they saw in stark relief the forces of reaction and indifference that weighed heavily on the working population of the country and particularly on blacks. The major preoccupation of the *Messenger* in the twenties concerned the race's continuing economic problems. For black laborers and entrepreneurs the decade contained new pitfalls and new competitors, as well as the ever-present burden of American racism. The *Messenger*'s self-appointed task was to find a way out.

Black America suffered a series of economic fluctuations in the twenties that contradicted the image of good times and made the assimilation of the 1.5 million migrants who flocked north between 1915 and 1929 all the more problematical. Between 1919 and 1924 two complete cycles of prosperity and depression raked the population, and similar uncertainties continued throughout the rest of the decade. Blacks suffered more than any other major population group from a lack of skills and seniority in industry, while those remaining on the farms fared little better. The economy in general was moving away from manual to nonmanual employment, from blue-collar to white-collar work, but the proportion of blacks in white-collar occupations was decreasing. The growth of technological unemployment in the twenties hit blacks harder than it did whites. Overall, the percentage of black workers in industry, trade, and transportation in the North declined from 1920 to 1930. Whites, not blacks, were taking up the slack created by the cutoff of foreign immigration. On the whole, white labor was unsympathetic to the plight of black workers. In an era when company unionism and the open shop put organized labor on the defensive, hostility of white to black workers was not likely to abate. As for the black business community, it started the twenties occupying an insignificant part of the total commercial picture and ended the decade in the same vestigial position.[1]

Where were black workers and entrepreneurs to turn? With labor hostile, with Horatio Alger only a myth, with government indifferent to economic distress, the options were few and never promising. Despite this the *Messenger* determined to find a way out, to build some basis either for intragroup strength or aid and sympathy from the white world. Drawing particularly on the idealism of A. Philip Randolph, it tried several avenues: radical interracial unionism; all-black independent unionism; cooperation with the white trade union movement; cooperative business; even the encouragement of black capitalism. That partial success came from only one of these approaches—organization of the Pullman porters with undependable AFL "support"—is no comment on the "failure" of the magazine to find a way out; rather it is proof that there *was* no way out in the twenties. No segment of white society was willing to challenge folkways and begin to offer black America even the opportunities formerly offered to European immigrants. The economic and social problems of the black community, the *Messenger*'s efforts notwithstanding, would not begin to be solved until the next two decades.

World War I dictated the *Messenger*'s first broad policies and goals. Randolph and Owen set out a dual role for themselves: help bring the

war to as quick a halt as possible; and ensure that the postwar reconstruction would solidify recent economic and social gains and pave the
way for further advances for all workers and for blacks in particular.
Soon after the Armistice the editors wrote a lengthy pamphlet entitled
"The Negro and the New Social Order: Reconstruction Program of the
American Negro."[2] Demobilization must be carefully planned, they said.
Public works projects, a thirty-four-hour week, and social insurance
would be necessary to prevent unemployment. Permanently improved
conditions would not prevail until peonage, the company store, tenant
farming, and private ownership of grain elevators, stockyards, and packing-
houses were eradicated. Other reforms needed were the single tax, agricultural unions, agricultural labor laws, blacks and whites in labor unions
on an equitable basis, an end to child labor, protection of female labor,
equal pay for equal work (referring to sex and race), equal employment
opportunity in government, a minimum wage, and social security.

The *Messenger* editors were by no means the only blacks recognizing
the need for comprehensive postwar planning, but their proposals were
much more far-reaching and socialistic than the majority black viewpoint.
The Division of Negro Economics, under the directorship of George E.
Haynes, was alive to the problems of a labor surplus, cutbacks in arma-
ments production, and imminent layoffs for women workers, but its
emphasis was more on how the individual through his own efforts could
maintain a competitive position. This mirrored Haynes's Urban League
background, and that organization's approach to postwar difficulties
similarly stressed individual improvement: cultivate thrift, industriousness, and efficiency. In the end the nation's decision makers listened to
neither the radical nor the moderate views. There was no black voice on
the special council considering postwar demobilization of industry, and
the black worker found himself at an increasing competitive disadvantage
in the changing order.[3]

The union that showed the most promise was the Industrial Workers
of the World. In numerous articles throughout 1919 and continuing to
mid-1921, the *Messenger* praised the IWW and urged blacks to join it. To
the magazine, and to many who were aware of the AFL's hostile or indifferent attitude toward the unionization of blacks, there were good
reasons for blacks to join the Wobblies. The IWW was the only labor
organization that drew no race or color line. Its constitution and by-laws

encouraged all races and both sexes to come together in equality, and in fact the union made serious and consistent efforts between 1910 and 1922 to impose racial harmony within its ranks. Furthermore, it stood for industrial unionism as opposed to AFL-style craft unionism, and since most blacks were unskilled workers, affiliation with the IWW seemed only logical. The Wobblies were also praised for refusing to make time agreements with an employer—they would strike any time the rights of their members were in jeopardy, not just when a contract expired. This illustrated their philosophy of brotherhood: an injury to one was an injury to all. Finally, the IWW was a part of the worldwide trend toward an industrial commonwealth. Workers of the world would surely unite. The weapons, which the *Messenger* elevated into romantic symbols, were to be the "One Big Union," a perfect "counter-irritant" to a "one big capitalism," and the general strike, uniting industrial, agricultural, and even domestic workers in mass action.[4]

But by 1919 the IWW was rapidly weakening, primarily because of persecutions of leaders and locals by war-enthused superpatriots in and out of government. Some locals kept their strength, among them the Marine Transport Workers Industrial Union No. 8 of Philadelphia, which for several years controlled the waterfront in that city. The *Messenger* held that local up as an example both of interracial harmony and sub-stantive bread-and-butter economic gains. The Philadelphia dockers in return gave monetary support. Claims have been made that the *Messenger* gave the IWW "a great impetus" in recruiting black workers, but this assertion rests on little more than the journal's editorial defense of black organizer Ben Fletcher, its anti-AFL stance, and the fact that it was black-edited and primarily for black readers. Probably the most that the two editors did for the IWW was to form, in mid-1919, the National Association for the Promotion of Labor Unionism Among Negroes. Owen was its president and Randolph the secretary-treasurer, while the advisory board included prominent socialists, not all of an IWW stripe. The association's stated aims were to encourage black and white laborers to ally themselves, win higher wages and better conditions, and counter the exploitation of race differences by employers. It admitted that many blacks became scabs out of sheer economic necessity, but this was the fault largely of restrictive unions. Capitalists in turn exploited prejudice—the more prejudice, the greater the profits. The remedy was an organization

like the IWW that would draw no color line. The national association died
in late 1920 after futile efforts to organize black laundry and bakery
workers.[5]

It is doubtful whether the IWW had much chance of successfully appealing to a broad sector of black labor at this time. The Red Scare was
in full heat, the Wobblies had already been Red-baited and peace-baited
during the war, and blacks were no more immune to these distortions
than whites. The only way the IWW could gain significant black membership under such circumstances would be to secure strong control in a
particular locality and win real wage and hour improvements without
resorting to prolonged strikes or walkouts. Much depended on local circumstances. In neither Boston nor New York did the Marine Transport
Workers gain a foothold. But in Baltimore, Norfolk, and particularly
Philadelphia, the Wobblies established strong locals with blacks as the
hard-core membership and for a time supplanted the rival International
Longshoremen's Association. The Philadelphia unit was the only truly
successful, integrated IWW local in the postwar years, maintaining control
of the docks through 1922 despite government favoritism toward the
ILA. It was not revolutionary idealism or the dockers' conversion to
syndicalism that made for IWW success; rather, Local 8 was a practical
business union that got results, notably an eight-hour-day, forty-four-
hour work week.[6]

Despite the Philadelphia success, the Red Scare months and the early
twenties were not an auspicious time in which to organize black workers
into any union. With much of black labor on the defensive in the postwar
hard times, few were willing to take a chance on any organization. In only
one respect did the IWW stand a chance of attracting black workers; it
was an industrial, not a craft, union. But the obstacles to any unionism
among blacks were far greater: political conservatism, especially among
prominent leaders; workers' rural backgrounds; lack of class consciousness; ignorance of union ideals and goals; and fear of loss of jobs or of
white hostility. As Horace Cayton, then a young man wooed by the Wobblies, later recalled, one had liabilities enough being black without being
Red. That was reason enough for most blacks to steer clear not only of
the IWW, but of any radical union in the postwar months.[7]

On two counts the Wobblies earned the hearty support of the *Messen-*

ger. For one, they were doing the type of organizing that the black editors deemed important; second, they were implacably hostile to the AFL. During the war and the Red Scare years the magazine too was undeviating in its contempt for the AFL. Even as the twenties progressed and the views of the editors changed with the waning of the IWW, the periodical never ceased criticizing the craft union movement. And although Randolph finally came to seek AFL affiliation for his own fledgling union, he did so out of expediency and not because the AFL was the best of all possible unions. It was the only practical course. No warm or hearty feelings developed on either side.

Randolph and Owen had an intense dislike for Samuel Gompers at least from the first issue of the *Messenger* and probably before. Gompers was a vocal supporter of the war and took alarm when the People's Council of America for Democracy and Terms of Peace (which the *Messenger* supported) began to win converts among AFL locals in New York City. The People's Council, organized in mid-1917 by radical pacifists and socialists, endorsed Russia's peace proposals, called for an immediate and negotiated peace, demanded the restoration of civil liberties and abolition of conscription, and attempted to interfere with the war effort by urging workers in defense industries to strike. Not only did Gompers support the war personally, he had union motives as well: if labor could be kept firmly behind President Wilson, his support for future labor reforms might be bought. To counter the People's Council the AFL set up the American Alliance for Labor and Democracy to encourage labor patriotism and badger the People's Council. It is doubtful whether Randolph and Owen soon forgot Gompers's active prowar stand or his use of organized labor to support the war and muzzle dissent.[8]

Gompers's fervent patriotism was only part of the radicals' indictment; equally damning was his attitude toward colored labor and black people in general. In the words of a recent historian, Gompers "kept the Negroes out of the labor movement and then declared that they deserved no better because they had not made common cause with the white workingmen." He had also shown gross insensitivity to the aspirations and fears of the black masses in his response to the East St. Louis riots in mid-1917, implying that much blame for the riots should be placed on unscrupulous employers who lured blacks to the city to undermine white labor's position. After all, white workers in East St. Louis had been provoked by the importation of black (read "scab") labor. Black Americans could not easily forget which side Gompers was on.[9]

The AFL under Gompers had retreated a long way from its egalitarian beginnings, which did not endear it to either black workers or the *Messenger*. At its founding in 1881 the AFL made genuine efforts to implement racial harmony and to organize black workers. Unions asking to affiliate were required to pledge never to discriminate. But by 1895 the AFL plainly chose expansion over idealism. After 1900 it organized blacks in separate (subordinate) locals or in directly affiliated federal unions, neither of which guaranteed much security for their hapless members. Beginning about 1910 the AFL introduced what was to become for many years a convention ritual: passage of hollow resolutions urging blacks to join and welcoming them to the labor brotherhood. These charades reached a well-orchestrated perfection in the last years of the teens and the early twenties when the Federation's pious declarations led some black observers, not including Randolph and Owen, to conclude that white labor was finally sincere in opening its doors to its long-neglected black brothers.[10]

Organized labor continued to frustrate black ambitions through outright refusal, dissembling, and subterfuge, all the while giving optimists enough room to get themselves are out on a shaky limb. AFL conventions in 1916 and 1917 discussed the desirability of enrolling black labor, but set up no effective machinery. Despite the lack of substance, the New York *Age* headlined its report "Negro Is Now Recognized by Federation of Labor," and upon receipt of a noncommittal letter from Gompers on the subject, again insisted that a great leap forward had taken place. Nor was the *Age* the only one wearing tinted glasses; the Urban League and Emmett Scott as well saw sincerity in the Federation's vagueness and forecast a new day ahead. But the necessity for high-level conferences in 1918 between Gompers and a whole panoply of black figures and liberal whites belied the "progress" of the previous year. The Urban League formed an interracial blue-ribbon delegation that met with Gompers in February and April to urge that the AFL's internationals abolish all constitutional prohibitions against black members and appoint an AFL-wide black organizer. Gompers replied that the Federation was the unfortunate victim of bad publicity in the matter of race relations. Not enough attention had been paid to the wholesome relationships that generally prevailed between the races in the AFL. The delegation's proposals were subsequently referred to the AFL's Committee on Organization, which professed to find no fault with past or present Federation policy or behavior. This "unctuous self-exoneration" was of course heartily approved by the annual convention. For once the *Age* was silent; editor Fred Moore may have been too embarrassed to find an explanation.[11]

The AFL convention in June 1919 again paid lip service to the principle of organizing blacks, and again portions of the black Establishment waxed ecstatic. True, the Federation did condemn lynching and mob violence and proclaimed the brotherhood of all workers no matter their race. But teeth were absent. Yet the New York *Amsterdam News* could call this "one of the most far-reaching advantages that has come to Afro-Americans in recognition of their labors in essential industries during the world-war." Even William Monroe Trotter's Boston *Guardian,* usually more skeptical of white intentions, perceived the opening of "the gateway to real American life for the first time within the last half century." Other periodicals echoed the same. The Urban League, meanwhile, was so heartened that it tried to renew negotiations with the AFL; unfortunately, its inquiry received no response in 1919, and only a token one in 1920. The same dismal scenario was repeated in the 1920 AFL convention when a group of black delegates affiliated with federal locals presented a new set of resolutions, which were promptly discarded or emasculated. Again black optimists thought they saw the heavens open.[12]

Soon after the 1920 convention the NAACP asked the AFL to form a committee on Negro labor including representatives of the Federation, the "big four" independent railroad brotherhoods, and the NAACP. AFL Secretary Frank Morrison put off the suggestion with the disclaimer that the AFL was doing all it could to encourage the acceptance of blacks but could not and would not enforce any edict on the internationals. There the matter lay for that year, and the following year's convention made the issue clear by failing to pass a motion prohibiting color bars in union constitutions. The *Age* nonetheless discovered a silver lining: "Even this scant measure of consideration should be welcomed as a step gained, with the hope that organized labor may in the near future rise again to greater heights." Even on Gomper's death in 1924 that news-

paper continued to whistle in the dark, praising the labor leader's sincerity
in trying to bring blacks into the labor movement. But the record is plain:
the AFL underwent no fundamental change in policy from the prewar
segregationist orientation. Once a few all-black federal locals were established, complacency reigned. The AFL claimed that organizing blacks in
directly affiliated federal locals would give them all the protection they
would need. The obvious drawback here was that without the support of
a (white) international, isolated black workers in a particular craft had
no protection. If they struck, they might well find their places filled by
white union members. And the internationals, although they excluded
black workers, nonetheless claimed craft jurisdiction over the AFL-
chartered locals.[13]

There was no reason to be optimistic about the AFL's intentions
toward black labor, as the *Messenger* saw matters in 1919. The Federation's lip service to egalitarianism was calculated only to forestall the
march of radical unionism and prevent the few black locals from seced-
ing. Moreover, it was fatuous to believe, as did Gompers, that there could
be any partnership between capital and labor. In any case the adherence
to strict craft unionism and neglect of unskilled workers left most of
labor, black and white, out of the organized movement. Above all, the
AFL and its president were reactionary pure and simple, from their political attitudes to their countenancing of racial discrimination in union constitutions. Unwitting tools of capitalism, they had long before sold out
the rank and file, not to mention all of unorganized labor.[14]

It is no surprise, then, that the *Messenger* did not stake all its chips
on hopes for an affirmative, radical, interracial labor movement. Throughout the period 1917-1928 A. Philip Randolph and to a lesser extent Chandler Owen involved themselves in several all-black unionization efforts, concurrent with their encouragement of a broader interracial movement.
Their first labor ventures, in fact, involved racially exclusive unions, the
Headwaiters and Sidewaiters Society of Greater New York and the United
Brotherhood of Elevator and Switchboard Operators of New York. In
the employ of the former, Owen and Randolph edited the prophetic if
ill-starred *Hotel Messenger* until they were dismissed for being too candid
about who exploited whom in the pantry. The elevator and switchboard
operators union was formed in August 1917 and immediately sought
cooperation with the House Janitors' and Superintendents' Union so that

no union elevator runner would work with a nonunion janitor or super. Within a year, however, control of the union was lost to the AFL.

This setback did not sour the two radicals on union activity, however, for they were soon involved in promoting the IWW through the National Association for the Promotion of Labor Unionism Among Negroes. Around the same time they made another stab at a radical, all-black union by becoming affiliated with the infant National Brotherhood Workers of America (NBWA), founded by T. J. Pree and R. T. Sims in 1919. Using self-styled revolutionary methods, Pree and Sims hoped to emulate the United Hebrew Trades and provide racial solidarity for all black workers through a federation of black unions and a framework for organizing those who had no union affiliation. It is unclear who initiated the *Messenger*'s relationship with the NBWA, but the latter benefited, for a time at least, from getting a publishing mouthpiece. In exchange Randolph and Owen were put on the board of directors. Apparently, however, they were not greatly effective in increasing membership and were accused by Sims of being more interested in adding to their magazine's circulation. The editors' side of the story is not recorded. In any case, they parted ways and the NBWA c continued into 1921. What success it enjoyed ensured its downfall, however, for whenever a viable local was established, the AFL international dominating the craft moved in and convinced the newly organized workers that affiliation with a conservative, white-led, but immensely more powerful organization would bring them greater benefits. This was the dilemma and fate of several independent black unions of the day.[15]

Following disengagement from the NBWA, the two editors founded the Friends of Negro Freedom (FNF) in May of 1920. This was to be an all-black civil rights organization, more militant than the NAACP and eventually to supplant it. One of its goals was to provide popular education in union principles and where necessary to organize independent black unions. Before it could develop a full labor program, however, the FNF fastened onto the Garvey issue and neglected all others. Yet it kept alive the enthusiasm of Owen and Randolph for some sort of United Negro Trades to coordinate the activities of all black unionists and to organize all who were without organization. This type of umbrella group, they felt, was especially necessary in view of the continuing migrations; the new workers, if unorganized, could well become a hated part of the work force and provoke race riots. A United Negro Trades should encourage separate black unions only if white bodies refused to admit blacks on a basis of equality, but this was tantamount to admitting that such all-black unions *would* have to be formed, since few white-dominated unions guaranteed blacks anything approaching a square deal. Given the realities of craft union indifference to blacks, the United Negro Trades concept remained viable for years to come. Within two years Urban League branches were adopting the principle, and W. E. B. DuBois was for many years a proponent.[16]

Not only radicals conceived of independent, all-black unions in the teens and twenties. Particularly in the railroad industry, workers' self-preservation demanded some kind of organization, since the Big Four craft brotherhoods were adamantly opposed to black membership. The only alternative was a precarious existence between the hostility of white labor and the indifference, sometimes with a touch of paternalism, of white management. This tightrope characterized the history of small bodies like the Association of Colored Railway Trainmen and Locomotive Firemen and the Brotherhood of Dining Car Employees. The basic weakness of the all-black unions was that they were creatures of necessity, yet could not adequately defend themselves. The hostility of white organized labor could quickly snuff out almost any black union, either through agreement with white management, by absorption into a larger white body, or through violence. In theory the AFL could have granted black railroad workers an international charter; yet this idea was unthinkable. Not until the mid-thirties, after years of badgering, could Randolph wrest an international charter from the AFL for his Brotherhood of Sleeping Car Porters, and then only because there were no white workers in that craft. Small independent black unions simply had no economic or political clout. If they struck, they could easily be replaced. The wage agreements they negotiated were more the result of employer "generosity" than of union strength. There was precious little black and white proletarian class consciousness in the twenties, and this unhappy fact worked to the detriment of both radical unions like those the *Messenger* promoted and conservative organizations like those in the railroad industry.[17]

In mid-1925 Randolph and Owen charted a new tack: a liberal-labor coalition to promote inclusion of black workers in the white trade unions already existing. The Trade Union Committee for Organizing Negro Workers (TUCONW) was the result, and besides helping organize it, the two editors gave it a ready-made publication. The groundwork for the body came through efforts of the New York Urban League to bring together representatives of the more liberal New York unions, white radicals like Norman Thomas and Max Danish, and interested blacks. The aim of the TUCONW was "to reach the great mass of unorganized Negro workers in New York City with the message of trade unionism and eventually to enroll them in the unions of their trade." Once blacks gained union membership, the committee intended to stand behind them in the manner of a United Negro Trades and ensure that they received a square deal from their white fellow workers. Initial headquarters were established at the *Messenger* offices until a more permanent site could be found, while financing was provided by the Garland Fund.

The committee's initial efforts were auspicious, if not altogether successful. Applicants were sent to the ILGWU, Teamsters, Machinists, Bricklayers, Furriers, Bookkeepers, Stenographers and Accountants, and Printers unions, and a small number were accepted by several of them. The Machinists were well known for their lily-white policies, so the TUCONW was hardly shying away from a tough fight. After the TUCONW interceded with the motion picture projectionists' union, its Jim Crow local in New York was abolished. The most ambitious undertaking was the attempt to organize brutally exploited laundry workers, numbering nearly thirty thousand in New York City, two-thirds of whom were black women. This effort proved unsuccessful, partly because the TUCONW died out within a year, partly because the white unions did not come forth with their promised financial support. Randolph inadvertently contributed to the short life of the committee by inducing Frank R. Crosswaith, its executive secretary, to become an organizer for the Brotherhood of Sleeping Car Porters. Up to that time Crosswaith was the real sparkplug in the TUCONW. But in any case the TUCONW could only have achieved broad gains with the active support of the AFL leadership. The interest of needle trade liberals was not enough.[18]

The *Messenger*'s motives in joining with the TUCONW are not altogether clear. Certainly Randolph and Owen were sympathetic to the general purpose, but why did they so readily embrace a group that was not only interracial but seemed to show promise of being dominated, financially at least, by white unions? The editors had not despaired of all-black unionism, for the Brotherhood of Sleeping Car Porters was aborning. But so was another organization, the Communist-sponsored American Negro Labor Congress, and on this group Randolph pronounced anathema. It seems likely that the *Messenger* would not have so enthusiastically participated in the TUCONW had there been no Communist labor organization on the horizon. One method of scotching the Communist efforts would be to champion a moderate, interracial coalition.

In July 1925 Randolph began organizing the Brotherhood of Sleeping Car Porters. Despite reservations about any trade in which all workers came from one racial group—this might provide an excuse for racially exclusive unions or motivate white employers to hire only labor of their own race—he proceeded to draw the porters into a movement that was as much racial as it was economic. It was not an auspicious time to organize: the union movement was on the decline in the railroad industry, partly because of aggressive antilabor policies of major carriers, including the Pullman Company, which itself was suffering a decline in income. To free himself for his new duties Randolph put the day-to-day operation of the magazine in the capable hands of George S. Schuyler. The story of the long and frustrating fight for recognition of the porters, both by the Pullman Company and the AFL, has been told in detail elsewhere and will not be recounted here. But it should be noted that this effort was consistent with Randolph's view, expressed at various times in the twenties, that blacks would have to organize their own labor groups before they could compel recognition and a fair deal from the white union movement. White allies could never be completely dependable; blacks must keep overall leadership and determination of goals firmly in their own hands.[19]

Randolph's intense involvement with the Brotherhood after 1925 did not prevent him from organizing yet one more movement during the *Messenger*'s lifetime to encourage black unionism. In December 1927 Negro Labor Conferences were held in Washington, D.C., Boston, Chicago, St. Louis, Kansas City, and New York with the BSCP as an organizational base and with the assistance of the Urban League. Problems such as the failures of the AFL, workers' health, injunctions, and yellow dog contracts were discussed. A steering committee composed of prominent black friends of labor was to continue the work of the conferences and raise money for future gatherings, although there is no record that an ongoing organization was established.[20]

Long before the Negro Labor Conferences, even before the Trade Union Committee to Organize Negro Workers, A. Philip Randolph had come to believe that the pragmatic course for black workers was to seek entry into the American Federation of Labor. He was not shutting his eyes to the faults of that union, but it seemed clear in the twenties, when the company union and the open shop were being successfully imposed on many industries, that all labor must preserve and extend whatever collective strengths could be found. This did not mean that blacks should give up their own private battle to force organized labor to become more open-hearted in accepting colored workers. But Randolph had been forced to recognize, over the period 1919-1923, that industrial unionism, which held far greater prospect of real benefits for the working masses, showed few immediate prospects of becoming a reality. He became convinced that as many blacks as could do so must enter the craft-oriented AFL if the race was to join the mainstream of the American labor movement—despite that union's undeniably racist policies and troglodytic leader.

In what must have been a disillusioning admission, Randolph acknowledged that only rarely had workers in America embraced a labor organization that proposed radical economic changes and the abolition of the system of private property. It was a senseless diversion to throw revolutionary rhetoric at workers who as yet had little sense of class consciousness and no more sense of organization and union principles.[21] So out of practical necessity Randolph shelved his earlier radicalism in the hopes of being more successful in organizing black workers to gain entry into the mainstream labor movement. It would have been counterproductive to staff a union or movement with radical members and garb it with revolutionary doctrine, for there were enough obstacles of race to want to avoid the additional one of radicalism. The hope for an industrial union movement too had to be shelved for the time being. This does not mean that Randolph was "bought off" by the AFL; on the contrary, he chose his own course. Nor does it mean that he forsook his principles; again on the contrary, he remained a socialist at heart and dedicated to its fundamental vision.

The Red Scare was barely waning when the *Messenger* first began to tone down its attacks on the conventional white unions with the acknowledgment that while they had undoubtedly been less than faithful to black workers, it was still better to be with one's allies than with one's capitalist enemies. Beneath this lay the view that "white and black workers do not fight each other because they hate each other, but they hate each other because they fight each other, and the capitalists will spare no pains in seeing to it that the fight goes on." This view was to be oft repeated as the magazine urged interracial unionism.[22]

Despite justifiable hesitations about the sincerity of white workers toward their black fellow toilers, the *Messenger* early, and consistently, found much to commend in interracial labor cooperation. All workers had an interest in ending the World War—only capitalists and imperialists stood to gain. Labor solidarity would end the oppression of black people. Amicable race contact in labor unions was a good antidote to the Ku Klux Klan. Besides, what lurked under the white sheets was a body financed by Northern and Southern capital for strike-breaking and the suppression of labor in general. A united front of all the Klan's victims—Jews, blacks, Catholics, and labor—could counter this. In addition, the magazine's editors believed that black and white labor solidarity could stop lynching and compel enfranchisement of blacks in the South. This argument took on additional weight when it became evident that lynching was being used against white union activitists in the South in mid-decade. To forestall mob violence the *Messenger* proposed, beginning in 1921, that the AFL, as well as all independent unions, join with the federated (black) locals in establishing a race relations committee with the capability of instant action. Finally, while acknowledging that workers everywhere were divided by racial, philosophical, religious, and nationality differences, the *Messenger* quoted the memorable phrase of Mr. Dooley: "Workers of the world unite, you have nothing to lose but your liberty, and you haven't any."[23]

What the *Messenger* preached may have made good ideological sense, but did it speak to the actual facts of interracial labor cooperation? W. E. B. DuBois took a more cynical, and probably more realistic, perspective. He was willing to admit that the struggle for the emancipation of black workers and white workers was one and the same struggle, but he had more serious ambivalence about the innate goodness of white workers than did Randolph. The editor of the *Crisis* always held white workers at least partially responsible for the state of race prejudice, although he pinned more blame on the industrialist. And in contrast to the frequent examples of interracial hatred among members of the working class, DuBois professed to see much evidence of intraracial sympathy between the various black social classes.[24]

The past record of white labor's intentions toward blacks and the unskilled *was* hardly encouraging. Even large numbers of black members in a union provided no immunity. Although 76 percent of the strikers were blacks in the 1920-1921 bituminous coal strike, violence between the races was a common occurrence. In the Chicago stockyards unionization struggles of 1919, a recent historian comments, "it was conflict between the white rank and file and their black counterparts that retarded unionization. Labor historians have wasted much energy debating the AFL's attitudes toward black workers, when the truly bitter, and functional, racial animosities were not at the national but at the shop level." The same could be said for many other localities and industries.[25] It does not appear that the situation was as hopeful as Randolph often wished it to be. Yet there was no practical alternative but to seek cooperation with the white labor movement.

The *Messenger* frequently pointed out that some progressive unions attempted to give black workers an even break. Numerous editorials and articles praised the International Ladies Garment Workers' Union, the Amalgamated Clothing Workers of America, and the United Mine Workers. But not even the most progressive needle trade unions did as much as they could have, a fact that *Messenger* writers on a few occasions admitted. It took them many years to get around to employing black organizers, and too often their recruitment of blacks was unsystematic.[26] Despite these misgivings, it is understandable why Randolph respected the ILGWU and ACWA: during the World War they maintained ties with the peace movement and the Socialist party and in general mirrored the same radicalism as did the early *Messenger*. Besides, they were both industrial, not craft, unions.

The presence of black members in various garment locals does not prove, however, that egalitarianism was practiced. The unions accepted blacks in order to control their trades but in general restricted the race to the least skilled and least remunerative tasks. Chandler Owen's brother Toussaint was a master tailor in his hometown of Columbia, South Carolina, but when he came to New York City in 1922 he could not secure employment in the garment industry commensurate with his

skills. Spero and Harris found that there were practically no black cut-
ters or operators in New York, positions that paid $50 and $44 weekly,
although many black women were concentrated in the category of
finishers with a weekly union wage of $26. Blacks were more often given
the less remunerative piece-rate jobs than were whites. And all ILGWU
and ACWA locals in New York City were willing to admit black members.
Even in "good" unions real equality in pay, position, and social relations
was a goal not yet achieved in the twenties.[27]

It is not surprising, then, that the *Messenger* occasionally became
exasperated at the slow pace of liberalization in the white unions and
took an ambivalent attitude toward strikes. The magazine usually encouraged that they be respected, but some walkouts were harder to support than others, as, for example, the railroad strike in the South in late
1922. The magazine refused to shed tears over this scabbing: until the
unions learned to admit blacks this sort of development was bound to
happen. A year later Chandler Owen developed similar conclusions in a
searing article entitled "White Supremacy in Organized Labor." The
"closed shop," he said, meant just that—closed to black workers. Unions
were guilty of cooperating with management in defining certain "white
men's jobs." Where blacks enjoyed skilled positions in industry their
opportunities had been won through strike-breaking. By and large, the
white labor unions had accepted black members out of self-protection,
only because industry forced the unions to do so. Owen closed his indictment with the challenge that "it yet remains for organized labor to show
it is in practice fairer and more enlightened on the race question than
organized capital!"[28]

Given such treatment at the hands of white unions, one might reasonably expect that blacks would readily serve as scab labor. Indeed contemporary stereotypes viewed the black labor force as a vast pool of strike-
breakers. The *Messenger* refuted this notion by publishing some statistics
in 1925. It found that only about 5 out of the 30 million workers in the
country were organized, so there indeed existed a large number of potential scabs, the great majority of whom obviously would be white. Most
strikes that were broken by scabs, it was claimed, met defeat from white
strike-breakers for the simple reason that in many industries and geo-
graphic areas there were not sufficient numbers of blacks to be mobilized
as antiunion labor. Other evidence refutes the stereotype that blacks
made up the major group from which scabs were recruited. It has been

frequently charged that black scabs were responsible for the failure of
the steel strike of 1919. Certainly blacks crossed picket lines, but in
relation to the total strike-breaking force they only numbered around 10
percent. William Z. Foster, a leader of the strikers, wrote soon afterwards
that it was the lowest-paid, least-skilled workers of both races who led the
walkouts while the more skilled workers, nearly all white, lagged behind.
And in scurrying back to scab, it was the skilled workers who led the way.
The *Messenger* resolved that it was wisest to cooperate with organized
labor if at all possible. But the history of the twenties shows how shaky
a foundation this built: blacks' fidelity to unions did not materially
improve laboring conditions for the race.[29]

Not a few black observers sensed what is today more obvious: many
of the race's best opportunities in the late teens and twenties came either
through strike-breaking or in industries that solidly resisted unionization.
Not that scabbing always guaranteed one would keep one's new position
when the strike was settled. But in several instances important black labor
gains were made through strike-breaking. In the public utilities industry
blacks got linemen's positions in this manner in both the North and
South. Colored labor first entered the needle trades in New York, Chicago, and Philadelphia in appreciable numbers through strike-breaking.
Although blacks were never prominent in railroad shops, they were extensively used as mechanics' helpers and laborers and doubled their share
of such jobs from 1910 to 1930 primarily by crossing union lines. And
it is plain that in other areas, even where no permanent employment
gains were made, scabbing served the useful psychological function of
retaliation against working-class whites.

Some industries were known for their stubborn resistance to unionism
and this, too, could prove a boon to black labor. During the 1921 depression when many blacks in Detroit lost their new industrial jobs, the community leadership appealed to Henry Ford. He agreed to keep the percentage of black workers at his major plant (then Highland Park, but
soon to be River Rouge) roughly proportionate to the black population
ratio in the city. While blacks in other automobile factories worked
primarily in the hot and dirty foundries, Ford's workers at River Rouge
also labored with whites in mixed pairs on machines and assembly and
subassembly lines. Ford encouraged racial equality as a result of both
his authoritarianism-paternalism and his desire to prevent unionization.
If whites did not like working conditions, if they were uncomfortable

working alongside blacks, then they could leave. Ford had made up his mind not to heed the racial folklore of American industry. Black workers had two of their race on the payroll whose duties were to hear grievances and issue corrective orders in irksome situations. Put simply, Ford was offering blacks the best industrial jobs in the Detroit area, which gave him the choice of the best applicants as well as great community leverage, which would be extremely useful at a later date in resisting the United Auto Workers.

Two other major industries followed Ford's example, Homer Ferguson's Newport News Shipbuilding Company and Harvey Firestone's Firestone Tire and Rubber Company in Akron. The latter was a friend of Ford's and like him felt a sincere commitment, as well as self-interest, in giving employment to blacks. He did not, however, open as many higher occupational categories as did Ford; most blacks in the tire plants worked either as janitors and laborers or in the hot, unpleasant nonmechanized compounding departments. Ferguson was more willing to promote colored workers to the higher-skilled crafts, and he initiated apprenticeship programs to further this. By 1920 two-thirds of his five thousand employees were black, spread over nearly all occupational categories.[30]

Given these examples of employment progress through strike-breaking and the paternalism of antiunion capitalists, it was by no means clear that an alliance with organized white labor was the best means to improve the race's economic position. Not a few prominent spokesmen and organizations were promanagement. When Randolph began to organize the porters, he found most of the race's newspaper press solidly in Pullman's camp, believing that the company and its chairman of the board, Robert Todd Lincoln, had done almost as much for the race as had Lincoln's father. Opposition to the company's paternalism was thus rank ingratitude. In 1925 a widespread campaign of unsigned antilabor advertisements appeared in the country's largest black newspapers, and later a conference attended by fifty prominent race figures in Washington condemned the organized labor movement. The black Elks, in convention in 1925, took a stand against unionism, linking it to economic radicalism and Bolshevism. Instead, they declared, blacks should stand with capital and try to live up to the standards of the best class in the country, the large employers of labor.

Kelly Miller was the most prominent antiunion figure in the decade. Writing for the *American Mercury,* he admitted that by logic blacks should stand with labor, but common sense dictated an alliance with capital as "the issue of race is deeper than the question of wages." If labor should triumph over capital, race conflict would deepen, not end, for the white workers represented lynching. On the other hand, the captain of industry stood for law and order, and was inclined to be kindly and generous to colored workers, for he was neither of their class nor their race competitor. Hubert H. Harrison, certainly radical on other issues, agreed with Miller in the wisdom of social solidarity across race lines on the question of employment, rather than relying on class solidarity.[31] Unfortunately it was not easy to refute such arguments. There was ample evidence to support the antiunion position, and all Randolph could call upon was persistent hope and less than convincing evidence from a handful of liberal unions. Acting on this faith, he began to take more definite steps in 1923 to bring about the hoped-for rapprochement.

The first step in effecting such a reconciliation involved getting the white labor movement to make some gesture of welcome to black workers. Randolph engineered this by persuading Samuel Gompers and John L. Lewis, head of the United Mine Workers, to extend fraternal greetings to be printed in the Labor Day (September) issue. But a much more important step was his increasingly outspoken anti-Communism. An editorial in the August 1923 issue entitled "The Menace of Negro Communists" spelled out his objections: they were childish "disruptionists" bent on wrecking "all constructive, progressive, non-Communist programs," including the existing trade union movement. By seeking the ruin of the only present weapon labor had to work with—the AFL—the Communists were willing to risk destruction of all working-class solidarity for the sake of getting persons involved in what Randolph later called "mere political and social theory." Total opposition to the AFL would only be legitimate if the Communists in fact had something concrete to replace it with. They did not have anything in 1923, but two years later did set up the American Negro Labor Congress (ANLC).

Randolph's practical anti-Communism coincided with the mood of the AFL as it approached a zenith of Red-baiting. At its 1923 annual convention every progressive proposal was defeated under the guise of halting Communist incursions. The next year the AFL continued this line by attacking the Farmer-Labor party. While it is unlikely that Randolph became vocally anti-Communist because the AFL propaganda convinced him, or out of a deliberate calculation to curry favor with white labor, it was nonetheless propitious that this political stance came into focus at a time when the AFL was suffering from unusually severe spasms of reaction. Brazeal agrees that by 1925 the AFL found Randolph's "moderate" politics palatable and the newly organized BSCP a safe instrument for rallying black workers under the influence if not sponsorship of the AFL. When Randolph began to be attacked by the Communist party, this made him and the fledgling union all the safer. By 1926 Randolph was receiving frequent advice from AFL President Green and was an invited visitor to the 1926 convention.[32]

The opposition of the *Messenger* to the American Negro Labor Congress is somewhat difficult to reconcile with the fact that Randolph had by no means given up on the idea of interracial efforts to promote unionism among blacks. His deeper reasons had to do with skepticism about transplanting Russian Communist strategy and ideology intact to America. Ever since 1920 the *Messenger,* while preserving its socialist vision and continuing to admire the social advances of the Russian Revolution, nonetheless rejected an upheaval of that magnitude as a realistic solution in the United States. From the time of the postwar ideological schisms in the Left, this placed Randolph in the more moderate camp, to the right of the black Communists. The subsequent subservience of American Communism to foreign dictate only widened the gap. Aside from these philosophical differences, Randolph knew by 1925 that expedience, if nothing else, dictated that black labor throw in its lot with organized white workers; with Communist-led groups still targets for Red-baiting, efforts invested in them seemed futile. So his opposition to the ANLC was not unrealistic, but it marked a falling off from the radicalism and idealism of previous years.

President William Green of the AFL had attacked the ANLC even before its formal organization and warned workers of its Communist sponsorship. Lovett Fort-Whiteman, the head of the ANLC, countered by charging that Green had no right to speak for black labor. Randolph entered the fray by accusing Fort-Whiteman of being a puppet of Moscow and proceeded to detail why no Communist program then in existence was appropriate for American workers. It was false to assume, he said, that the United States was in a revolutionary age and that the tactics used to achieve the dictatorship of the proletariat and a soviet style of government in Russia were germane to this country. The reality of labor conditions in American was far different. Organized labor, albeit conservative, had managed to attain the highest standard of living for workers anywhere in the world. The black laborers' destiny was tied up with that of the white workers, so what injured one injured the other. To break up the AFL, or even supplant it, would be to destroy the strongest collective bargaining unit in the country, which included nearly all of those blacks who belonged to unions. Even nonunion labor derived benefit from the high wage standard gotten by organized workers. There was nothing wrong with having a Negro labor congress, but it must be American-controlled and have the financial and moral backing of the established American labor movement.[33]

Several of Randolph's points were valid, but he need not have reacted with such terror. Granted his unalterable opposition to Communist sponsorship of any organization proposing to remedy the black man's problems, the ANLC nonetheless had on its agenda important points for consideration and brought together a wide variety of both organized and unorganized workers to discuss them. Several years previously Randolph had called for united interracial efforts of farmers and industrial workers, and the ANLC was proposing just that. Other points in its platform included encouraging black and white workers to organize industrial unions; removal of all restrictions against blacks in the armed services; emancipation of agricultural peons; abolition of segregation, high rents, and related housing exploitation; equal school facilities for black and white children; an end to political and legal discrimination; and organization of the black masses against imperialism. This nine-point ANLC program concluded with the hope that "all Labor Unions shall affiliate with the American Federation of Labor whenever this is reasonably possible and create a large unity of labor."[34]

For several years the *Messenger* had belittled the minuscule size of the black contingent of the Communist party, intimating that its total membership could convene in one telephone booth or dark cellar, so Randolph's excessive concern is not easy to explain. In the abstract, at least, the ANLC program said all the right things. Labor unity under the umbrella of the AFL, while it is doubtful it could have been achieved, would have been a boon to all workers. Certainly the Communist party's power of "subversion" at this time is seriously to be questioned. While the sincerity of Randolph's anti-Communism need not be challenged, there was also the role of jealousy, which seemed to have played an important part in the opposition to Garvey under somewhat similar circumstances. The

Messenger had twice tried to form a militant, progressive coalition for black rights, through postwar radicalism and the Friends of Negro Freedom. Might the ANLC succeed where Randolph and Owen had failed? And there was a possibility that the uninitiated might confuse the BSCP and the ANLC. But more importantly, as Robert Minor pointed out, the ANLC threatened "professional class leadership" by bringing together a group of black industrial workers (farm laborers were regrettably absent) who elected their own delegates and moved the center of gravity toward themselves.[35] Randolph *was* a part of the "professional class leadership" and, compared to more conservative observers, it is plain that he overreacted.

Take, for example, George S. Schuyler, Randolph's managing editor, who noted:

> Even though I smell the Communist rat in this American Negro Labor Congress, I feel that it's a capital idea. If there are really representatives there of the Negro workers, their good common sense will prevent them from being carried away by Communist dialectic. It will, if only for propaganda purposes, be beneficial to the Negro workers, since it will arouse both capitalists and organized labor. Between the two, the Negro should be able to shake a few more plumbs [*sic*] off the economic tree.

No panic here. Nor was there any on the part of the New York *Age,* or even the conservative, Red-baiting New York *Times,* which gave extensive coverage to the convention.[36]

W. E. B. DuBois, writing in the *Crisis,* was inclined to view the ANLC with some sympathy because he had a great deal of admiration for the scope and audacity of Soviet Russia's social experiment although he did not consider himself a Communist. Besides, blacks had every right to learn what labor in England and Russia was doing and to sympathize with it if they wanted to do so. DuBois was under no illusions that the made-in-Russia Marxist interpretation of American conditions fit the reality, but he did not react as emotionally as did Randolph. Neither did *Opportunity,* the Urban League magazine, which chastised Green for overreacting and giving wide publicity to a group that probably would soon disappear. Anyway, the Communist menace had hardly been proved and the goals of the ANLC were not all subversive. Certainly the ANLC case against white unions was a valid one. But the *Messenger* could not take such a benign view, with some good reason. The ANLC was a plague on the BSCP over the next few years, alternately attacking it for "selling out" to the AFL and at other times seeking to mislead the unknowning into believing the two were one and the same organization.[37]

Unfortunately, the *Messenger*-AFL alliance in attacking the ANLC did not build concrete steps toward unionizing black workers. The reason had nothing to do with "radicalism"; rather, it boiled down to the un-willingness of white workers to consort with blacks on a level of equality. This was expressed with extraordinary baldness by AFL President William Green in an editorial in the *American Federationist* warning of the ANLC's designs. His statement reeked with the paternalism of Samuel Gompers. Blacks, he said, must improve themselves if they were to win an equal place in the American social order. Education was the key; other oppressed groups took up their bootstraps and improved themselves, and so, too, should blacks. Meanwhile the race must clean its own house of un-American elements like the Communistic ANLC. What was the reward for per-forming such cleansing? Blacks would earn the "moral right" to the AFL's "special care."[38] This concern had been hollow in the past; what was the expectation that it would be any less hollow in the future?

For the remaining years of the *Messenger*'s existence the AFL failed to begin to fulfill even this most minimal commitment. Green and Randolph became personal friends, but this made for little practical difference. Periodic conferences on black labor at the AFL's Brookwood Labor College made no difference in how the various internationals ac-cepted and rejected members. Even on the basis of jointly fighting Com-munist infiltration in the labor movement, precious little action was forth-coming. Randolph suggested that the AFL could forestall Communist advances among blacks by supporting the TUCONW, recognizing the various existing black unions, and appointing a member of the race to an executive position in the AFL. There is no record that the AFL even replied to this entreaty. The 1926 annual convention was especially dis-appointing to Randolph. No strong voice was raised for black workers, and not a word was uttered on their problems. Randolph was clearly disillusioned, but he had nowhere else to turn. The organization of the sleeping car porters had not produced a quick victory, and it was plain that a long and difficult siege lay ahead, making it all the more desirable to get AFL support. Randolph had committed himself to working with the AFL, had shelved economic radicalism; now if only he could get the AFL to work with him. But that was not to come within the lifetime of the *Messenger*. Although the AFL "endorsed" the BSCP, it was not until 1935 that an AFL charter was granted.[39]

Numerous commentaries of the day substantiate the record of the AFL's negligence. An Urban League report in 1930 was blunt: the official position of the AFL

comprises a number of resolutions urging organization of Negro workers; a protest here and vacuous decrees there against efforts of radicals at organization; segregated organization of Negro workers in certain occupations through local and federal labor unions; a few pleas for organization; the employment at various times of a few Negro organizers; and a total inability, if not unwillingness to compel International Unions to remove from their constitutions Negro exclusion clauses, or suffer expulsion from the Federation.

Spero and Harris echoed the same when they wrote that "the organization of the great body of Negroes, the unskilled, had never been seriously undertaken by the American Federation of Labor, its declarations of good intentions to the contrary, notwithstanding." In exasperation T. Arnold Hill of the Urban League wrote to President Green pointing out that the AFL's excuses and explanations, some in use for nearly forty years, no longer sufficed to hide white labor's culpability. Blacks had already made their sacrifices, walked their extra mile; it was time for the AFL to assume its share of the burden.[40]

But the AFL had already replied the year before in an article in the *American Federationist* entitled "Attempts to Organize Negro Workers." Its author was John P. Frey, and the burden of his message was not optimistic: with few exceptions the American trade union movement, he claimed, was more eager to unionize black workers than they were to be unionized. Booker Washington and his inheritors were blamed for obstructing the desired goal. Blacks simply had not cooperated, and to put the blame on the AFL was unfair. Not once did he concede that the AFL had been truly negligent. As for discrimination, while acknowledging that blacks were often victims, he nonetheless insisted that "there is no group in this country that I know of subject to more discrimination at the present time than the members of the American Federation of Labor."

Reaching the heart of the matter, Frey conceded that a major purpose of the AFL was to protect the job monopoly of certain persons so that the market would not be flooded. Could anyone blame workers who had worked hard to win that monopoly for not wanting to open the floodgates? If one goes to the wilderness and clears it and plants his gardens and fields, should he then be required to give it over or share it with newer pioneers? Let the later arrival take advantage of the plentitude of the land. Having so neatly solved the labor question, Frey quickly contradicted himself by noting with concern the rise in technological unemployment.[41] Where, then, was virgin land for the new generation of black workers to be found?

Perhaps Randolph approached an understanding of the futility of his attempted rapprochement with the AFL and hopes for interracial unionism at the very end of the *Messenger*'s life, which coincided with the lowest point in the fortunes of the BSCP. In an editorial in the last issue he peered into the future and sounded a tocsin for the thirties. Methods of production were changing. Many jobs that were in the skilled category a few years before were being taken over by machines or unskilled or semiskilled operatives. The craft unions had exhausted themselves in petty and injurious jurisdictional disputes and were no match for the power of capital. The time was at hand for labor to organize industrially because that was how the employers were organized. Industry was coming under one organization, from the production of raw materials all the way through to the finished product, while labor was still split into countless competing and jealous crafts. To keep pace, unions would have to organize on an industrial basis.[42] In other words, the AFL was no longer the answer. The problems of how to employ and unionize the 1.5 million blacks who left the South in the teens and twenties remained unsolved.

The migration of black folk from the South to Northern urban centers was another facet of the labor question. In the *Messenger*'s most militant period the South was represented as a hell-hole presided over by greedy capitalists and their political cohorts holding sway over hapless peasants. Migration northward was naturally welcomed: those fleeing the House of Bondage would find better industrial opportunities, more wealth, the chance for a decent education, the political power to help themselves as well as the brothers back home, and the opening of their life to a new consciousness of self and race. The population shift would also bring

relief to those still suffering Southern oppression by putting economic
pressure on the region's white rulers.[43]

But the magazine also recognized that serious problems would occur
unless Northern blacks undertook to aid and organize the migrants. The
newcomers could be easy prey to unscrupulous types and, most importantly, might serve to depress labor conditions by breaking strikes or accepting low wages. Self-interest and altruism both dictated that Northern-
ers, especially those working in the established service organizations and
writing in the press, take a hand in welcoming and orienting the migrants.
This the *Messenger* attempted in several ways. But it, like many in the
North, took a long time to see that one of the most crucial services to
perform was to help channel the migration and even at times discourage
it. Industrial opportunity for black workers was rarely at a consistently
high level in the twenties, and the unplanned and unpredictable flood of
labor out of the South could only mean instability for struggling black
communities in the North.

Owen and Randolph were not alone in the postwar months in popular-
izing the view that blacks should leave the hated South. W. E. B. DuBois
said the same thing in the *Crisis,* but where the two periodicals differed
was in analyzing why the North was hardly yet the Promised Land. The
elder editor ascribed this to the fact that over a million white Southerners had also recently removed to the North, where they both secretly
and openly fomented racial trouble. The *Messenger* addressed the question
from a socialist perspective and pinned the blame on a capitalist class
manipulating the fears of black and white workers. It is undoubtedly
true that when the high expectations of migrant blacks *and* whites came
up against the realities of discrimination and limited opportunity, racial
antagonism was bound to increase.[44]

The *Messenger,* at least through 1924, continued to encourage voluntary
migration in good times and bad, which reflected a genuine desire to help
the Southern brothers. This was not a superficial, unthinking invitation,
for the magazine proposed several steps that should be taken to help adjust
the newcomers. A continuous commentary in the boom year of 1923 centered on how the great influx of newcomers could most productively be
used and fit into the Northern way of life. This population movement
was not without dangers, for if blacks remained outside of unions, race
riots like that in East St. Louis would be the result. Unions must hire
black organizers, for most blacks were either ignorant of them or deeply

cynical of their intentions. Other obstacles came from Klan-infected white
labor and black leaders who taught respect for the rich and distrust of
white workers. College-educated blacks thought it fashionable to sneer
at the working class. Appealing to the Talented Tenth, Randolph and
Owen urged that those possessing educations cast their lot with the labor
movement and give vision, hope, and intelligence to the black masses;
white unions should employ them as organizers with the same pay and
authority as white organizers. But no significant numbers of the Talented
Tenth so embraced the black proletariat. Their goal was more often the
opposite, to put as much distance between themselves and the masses as
possible and seek identification with the culture of the white upper
classes.[45]

One of the major projects of the Friends of Negro Freedom, the civil
rights organization founded by the *Messenger* editors, was to help adjust
migrants to the North. Local councils were to help unionize the newcomers, aid in finding jobs and housing, and encourage better work and thrift
habits. This was not an emphasis on Bookerite bourgeois virtues so much
as a recognition of the difference in folkways between the North and the
South, between urban and rural areas. Too often the migrant accepted
discrimination and segregation on the rationale that he should not push
himself where he was not wanted; this could not be tolerated in the North.
The speed of industry and the need for new efficiency were also a problem;
persons who had been skilled workers in the South found the pace acceler-
ated in the North. The *Messenger* was not the only voice warning against
the all too frequent practice of quitting on payday and returning to work
only when one's earnings had been exhausted; the Urban League too
urged good work habits. Spero and Harris spoke of this ignorance of the
"discipline of industry" as the chief obstacle to steady black employment
in the North. And if negative stereotypes arose concerning black labor,
they would hardly discriminate between recent migrants and old-timers.[46]

The *Messenger* believed that the migrations would bring positive improvements to the South. Deprived of black labor, its rulers would have
to make concessions to the race. Capitalists would be forced to pressure
governments to improve social conditions and eliminate lynching. Besides,
if industry were paralyzed by a lack of black workers, there would be no
money to finance the campaigns of the likes of Cole Blease and James K.
Vardaman. A Georgia banker was quoted as saying that agriculture was
hurting as well. The magazine saw real effect in the migrations when the

newly inaugurated governor of Mississippi stated in early 1924 that the state and white citizens should treat blacks fairly, give them better educations, health services, and working conditions, and protect them in business dealings and the courts, all as matters of white self-interest. Even a decline in lynching was attributed by the *Messenger* to economic pressures caused by the egress of black workers.[47]

It was not until relatively late in the decade that the magazine came to the more realistic view that unplanned and indiscriminate migrations could do harm not only to the migrants but to those already in the North. Others had long held such apprehensions. Many "old settlers" in Northern cities feared that the influx would destroy the "amicable" race relations they believed they had won. Among many others, W. E. B. DuBois had long decried the "fact" that cultured black communities in Chicago, Philadelphia, and New York were being inundated by poor, uneducated migrants. These worries had as much to do with class insecurity and acceptance by white society as they did with pure economics, which was the more immediate concern of the *Messenger*.

In May 1927, Randolph proposed that the NAACP and Urban League direct and control migration in view of better absorbing the newcomers. When necessary, migration should be discouraged. The availability of industrial jobs must be the determinant, and Southern blacks could not know of opportunities unless some agency informed them.[48] Such a suggestion might have been helpful a decade earlier, although it is doubtful that any consortium of black organizations could have effectively regulated population movements. Undoubtedly most of the migration had been unplanned, which was not primarily the fault of the migrants themselves but of the varying push and pull factors involved. Certainly the burden on black communities in the North would have been lighter had migration been more attuned to actual available jobs, but to have tried actively to discourage one's brothers from leaving the land of the boll weevil, peonage, and lynching would have seemed traitorous to many. From the perspective of later years, it may seem shortsighted for the *Messenger* and others to have so eagerly encouraged migration in the twenties, but to race-conscious blacks in the North this was the only reasonable policy that an oppressed but proud race could follow. Those in the North knew that the Promised Land had not yet been found, but to many migrants the Mason-Dixon line must have seemed close to the River Jordan.

From its first issues the *Messenger* was anticapitalist in both tone
and content, but it could not long ignore or be totally antagonistic
toward business. Even in 1919 there was at least one alternative to capitalist marketing and distribution that was perfectly respectable from a radical viewpoint, and that was the cooperative ideal. From that date to the
end of the magazine's life, cooperation from the perspective of both producer and consumer was explored and largely approved. But even traditional capitalism eventually had to be given a more sympathetic look.
Events in the twenties impelled the magazine to shift farther to the Right
as socialism, or any other radical alternative, seemed to Randolph and
Owen to hold ever-decreasing chances for success. Just as the *Messenger*
turned to its once despised foe, the AFL, it also took a new look at
business. By 1924 the editors perceived the possibility of broadening
the magazine's appeal to the Talented Tenth and the Black Bourgeoisie
by publishing articles on business, society, culture, the home and family,
and sports. Black entrepreneurs were treated to sympathetic and often
uncritical acclaim. But neither journalistic boosterism nor more critical
commentary could solve the problems of the black economic sector, and
in the end what the *Messenger* and other observers had to say on the subject mattered little, for black folk simply had no effective way of control-
ling how and where their inadequate incomes were spent or their meager
savings, if they had any, were invested. Yet this probusiness tack is significant because it shows another facet of the magazine's continuing search
in the twenties to find a basis on which to build and demand racial
betterment.

The decade of the twenties, which saw impressive, if erratic, economic
and business expansion in the dominant white economy, was also an age
of business for the black community. World War I had given a tremendous
spur to black enterprise, and no longer was the black businessman the exception. Certainly many ventures begun during the war ceased soon after
it ended, and unsettled economic conditions in the first half of the decade
took their toll. But despite these risks, which, after all, were nothing new,
a mood of optimism was abroad. A wide spectrum of the bourgeoisie—
professionals, academics, businessmen—perceived new opportunities in
the expanding urban markets fueled by the migrations. These persons
urged their race to "buy black" and "support race business," although
this never did prove to be a viable platform on which to create an independent race economy. A new middle class was emerging, drawing to-

gether individuals from the Bookerite-National Negro Business League
camp with those oriented to the NAACP, smoothing over old antagonisms in the mutual quest for expansion and prosperity. It was this phenomenon of a solidifying bourgeoisie that the *Messenger* perceived and
to which it pinned hopes both for a more prosperous peridocal and for
a stronger race.[49]

By 1919 a wide spectrum, from DuBois to Garvey, from the *Messenger*
to the Chicago *Defender,* from the African Blood Brotherhood to George
Haynes's Division of Negro Economics, endorsed some form of coopera-
tivism in business; only middle- and upper-class conservatives did not add
their support. Cooperative stores and buying, in the *Messenger*'s view,
would ensure lower prices and better quality, for there would be no motive to adulterate merchandise or cheat, while savings could be used to
build meeting halls, schools, and libraries and to disseminate propaganda.
Joint action such as this would naturally give solidarity and strength to
the working-class movement. One of the major goals of the Friends of
Negro Freedom was to foster such mutualism. Producer cooperatives
and cooperative businesses were also approved so long as they were anti-
monopolistic. Granger socialism offered the black farmer a better life
through jointly owned banks, mills, gins, and storage facilities. By 1920,
as the magazine slowly tempered its hostility to capitalism, the small
independent businessman, black or white, was advised that he, too, would
have to practice some form of cooperation to fight the huge monopolies.
Only a purchasing trust guided by the best interests of the masses could
combat the big trusts. These themes were reiterated throughout the
twenties in article after article urging cooperation in consumption, business, and housing.[50]

The *Messenger*'s model of a cooperative system was not the only one
current in black America. Garvey's Negro Factories Corporation and
Black Star Line were cooperatives modeled primarily on nationalism
rather than socialism. The end result was to be a segregated economy
whereby black consumers could purchase all their goods and services
from within the race, with the resultant capital to be used for further
internal development (although stockholders were to be allowed a moderate profit). The various factories were to be staffed by UNIA members
under the responsibility of a Minister of Industries, who in turn reported
to the annual conventions, where broad policy was dictated and directors
were elected. One recent historian has remarked that "insofar as the UNIA

was a 'nation,' it was a nation with a collectivist economy." It was also
hostile to the black businessman on the outside. Garvey said of black
capitalists that their "only concern is to rob and exploit the unfortunate
of their own race." Non-Garveyite businessmen, who customarily urged
the masses to "buy black," reacted with almost universal hostility to the
UNIA competition.[51]

W. E. B. DuBois was long interested in cooperation and initiated a
Negro Co-operative Guild in 1918 to encourage the study of mutualism,
but without spadework the movement lay dormant. He did, however,
write occasional editorials commending the principle, but differed significantly from the *Messenger* perspective in encouraging a segregated economy based on race rather than class. By 1928 DuBois had worked out a
vast scheme of manufacturing and consumer cooperation among the
race's 12 million members, envisioning the raising of raw materials on
black-owned farms, transportation in black trucks, manufacturing in
black factories, distribution through black co-ops, and the patronage of
loyal black customers. From this "trust" would develop credit and cooperative banking with links to the rest of the black world. This perspective
was based on DuBois's increasing cynicism about interracial goodwill.[52]

The *Messenger* would have none of the group-economy argument, not
that there was anything wrong with black self-help. But a Jim Crow economy along capitalistic lines would never benefit blacks even if it were
possible, which it wasn't. Such a system would be self-defeating: why
should blacks cut themselves off from the other 90 percent of the population and the economy in which they all participated? One of the shortcomings of black business, large and small, was that it catered only to
black people; this was one of the reasons for the lamentable failure of
the Standard Life Insurance Company, one of the race's largest businesses.
Black firms should do what the white ones did—cater to anyone who was
a potential customer. Black insurance companies should write policies
for black and white, employing either white or mulatto agents who could
"pass" in selling to whites. After all, the magazine pointed out, Jews
were famous for their business acumen but did not limit themselves to
patrons of their own group. The *Messenger's* argument had its valid
points but ignored the fact that strictly "race" businesses were the
largest and most successful concerns owned by blacks (even though their
"success" was only moderate by the standards of the mainstream
economy).[53]

A segregated economy was objectionable from other perspectives. First, the *Messenger* editors believed, contrary to DuBois, that segregation in any form was odious. In the realm of business it tended to limit the market. And where a black businessman gained a monopoly on clients of his own race, he tended to exploit that clientele. The magazine also claimed that most persons who advocated a segregated economy were those who bought goods wholesale from whites, cheaply, and then sold retail to blacks, at expensive prices. In any case a segregated economy could not be protected, for nothing could prevent whites from entering a particular market. And how often, asked the *Messenger,* had it heard the cry "buy black" or "support race business"? Such appeals were not based on reality. One should buy where the goods were both cheapest and of best quality. "Buy black" frequently disguised the fact that the business was not efficient enough to compete with white ones. The emphasis should be on sound business practices, knowledge, and energy, not spurious racial appeals. If progressive methods were used, then there was nothing wrong in "buying black."[54]

Certainly DuBois and Randolph and Owen were serious in their arguments over the segregated economy and cooperation, but was either idea anything more than just another panacea? Harold Cruse suggests that it would have been far better for blacks in the twenties to be indoctrinated in economic cooperative lines than in trade unionism. The black community, he believes, constituted an ethnic minority ready-made for extensive cooperation along racial lines, especially since the white labor movement seemed adamantly unwilling to accept black workers as equals. True enough, if only some form of cooperation could have worked, but, with isolated exceptions, it never has in this country. Furthermore, the development of mass marketing and chain businesses effectively sabotaged cooperation by supplanting one of the chief aims of consumers' cooperatives—rationalization of retail trade and lower consumer costs. Whether any cooperative in its infancy could successfully compete with well-organized, highly capitalized, and monopolistic mass marketing is doubtful. The slim chances for success are illustrated by the Colored Merchant's Association (CMA), founded in 1929. Its aim was to "reduce operating costs of the Negro retail merchant through cooperative buying, the standardization of goods and equipment, and group advertising" using the CMA brand label. Even before the Depression set in, most business-

men found they could not afford the modest joining fee. Nor did the
public respond well to the new label, habituated as it was to the popular
brand names of the day. By 1934 the CMA was dead.[55]

   As for the prospects for a "buy black" chauvinism providing meaningful economic gains, again the prognosis was doubtful in the twenties, as
indeed it seems today. As Randolph put it in 1918, "a Negro consumer
does not buy the businessman's color. He cannot consume that." Abram
Harris feared that the segregated economy and its infant offspring, the
"Don't Buy Where You Can't Work" campaigns, would backfire by setting
a pattern for the dismissal of black workers where the majority of the
product's consumers were white. His training as an economist told him
that "nationalism, whether racial or otherside, has never found, nor has
it ever sought, validity in sheer economics." As for DuBois's scheme of
a totally insulated black world, the idea is appealing from a nationalist
perspective, but prospects for its successful implementation seem farther
removed today than they did in 1928. Nor have its dilemmas been resolved. Ralph Bunche noted a decade later that

   the apologists for the self-sufficiency ideology are in pursuit of a
   policy of pure expedience and opportunism through exploitation
   of the segregation incident to the racial dualism of America. They
   refuse to believe that it is impossible to wring more wealth out of
   the already poverty stricken Negro ghettoes of the nation. . . . In this
   sense, Negro business looms as a parasitical growth on the Negro society, in that it exploits the "race problem." It demands for itself
   special privilege and parades under the chauvinistic protection of
   "race loyalty," thus further exploiting an already downtrodden group.
   It represents the welfare only of the pitifully small Negro middle class
   group, though demanding support for its ideology from the race-
   conscious Negro masses.

Can a downtrodden group afford to allow a small segment of its whole
to exploit the rest, for dubious benefits? The answer for the black twenties must be negative.[56]

   The *Messenger*'s hostile attitude toward conventional black business
began to fade in 1920 and four years later was replaced by outright
boosterism. In 1924 and 1925 the magazine published nearly twenty

panegyrics to various black businessmen. Their content illustrated the
virtues (and the material possessions) of the new Black Bourgeoisie.
Featured in these portraits were a financier, several bankers, an architect,
insurance executives, realtors, theater entrepreneurs, and the singular
Mme. C. J. Walker. Twice the magazine devoted an entire issue to business
matters, and in February 1925 it began a monthly "Industry and Business" page. It seems not coincidental that several of the businessmen
praised were also those who advertised in the magazine. The two enterprises to which it devoted most attention were banking and insurance,
understandably, for many blacks hoped these heralded the salvation of
black business.

Boosterism has its place, but the *Messenger* compromised its standard,
so well upheld in other areas, of maintaining a critical perspective. Here
the magazine was no different from the pedestrian New York *Age,* which
covered the resolutions of every National Negro Business League convention as if they were prophecy. There were problems aplenty facing black
businesses and entrepreneurs that had serious reprecussions for the whole
race, but on these the magazine scarcely touched. For example, only a
small proportion of businesses in major black centers were Negro-owned
or provided white-collar jobs for members of the race. How should blacks
get employment from white concerns, or supplant such businesses? Other
major problems—a lack of capital, scarce credit, competition from better-
organized and better-financed white concerns—were similarly slighted.
The *Messenger* provided no searching analysis, even in the context of
insurance and banking. The magazine's standard advice was "efficiency"
—small comfort indeed to the struggling entrepreneur.

Much could have been said about banking and insurance, but about
all the magazine gave by way of constructive criticism was to advise that
sooner or later the insurance companies and banks would have to com-
bine into no more than two or three giants in order to maintain a competitive position vis-à-vis the white giants. Chandler Owen took the National Negro Business League apart in an article entitled "Toy Business
Men" and concluded that the pieces did not warrant putting back together. But criticism of the NNBL was easy and provided no solutions to
the real problems of black businessmen. The magazine might better have
addressed itself to more fundamental questions. Were black-owned banks
necessary, or could credit unions, building and loan associations, and

industrial loan societies bring as much benefit? Was it true, as Abram Harris posed it, that "like the Negro business man, the Negro banker is a marginal man whose opportunities for profit are few [and whose] success must depend in a large degree upon skillful exploitation of the Negro masses"? Could small black banks concentrate and gain viability in that fashion? Why did so many of them fail? A question posed by Myrdal had equal relevance in the twenties: Could a black financial institution, whether bank or insurance company, ever break out of the segregated community and become simply a bank, not a "black bank"? Myrdal saw no future for a segregated black financial system, and one wonders whether the *Messenger*'s editor did either.

Similar questions could apply to insurance. There were companies aplenty, almost all pitifully small compared to the white giants, and subject to absorption by any large institution that saw a profit in them. Yet the insurance industry provided a large segment of white-collar employment for the race, and a keen analyst might well have addressed the question of how this employment could be preserved and expanded. Both insurance and banking were highly speculative, growth fields in the twenties, and the most notable business advance in black Chicago in this period came in the former enterprise. When major institutions like the Standard Life Insurance Company or Brown and Stevens' Bank in Philadelphia went under, it was a blow to the race's expectations as well as to its investors' pocketbooks. Again, the *Messenger* might have pondered ways to preserve such important growth while minimizing the risks.[57]

By the time Randolph's periodical folded in mid-1928, it was no longer a radical magazine. It had championed black business, heaped praise upon praise, and accepted large commercial advertisements in return. On the labor front it still hoped for cooperation with the conservative, craft-unionist American Federation of Labor, although with the clear perception that such cooperation would be only grudgingly forthcoming. Randolph himself was enmeshed in day-to-day labor organization, with his socialist principles deemphasized. The magazine had come a long way from the heady days of 1919 and "scientific radicalism." In one respect this evolution is an accurate mirror of the problems and futilities of black militance in the twenties. With the demise of a viable form of evolutionary socialism, some movement away from the radical Left was inevitable, and with the failure of independent and radical black unionism there was nothing to do but form a dubious detente with the indifferent AFL. To have expected an inveterate young activist like Randolph to maintain a purist radicalism in a decade when it had no viable roots or foundations would be to expect the quixotic. In labor affairs some move toward the center had to be made in the twenties to keep touch with the reality of working conditions in the North and urban centers. The economy was soft, the black foothold on it was precarious, and there was no viable radical alternative in sight.

But it may be argued that this did not mean that, having rejected the suit of Communism, one had to accept the hand of business and the Black Bourgeoisie. The *Messenger* could have become a down-the-line labor journal, not radical necessarily, but exclusively oriented toward black workers. However, this would have meant, even in 1919, a fundamental alteration of the magazine's style and following, because from its earliest beginnings, despite its working-class emphasis, it also appealed to black and white radicals and even part of the Talented Tenth. Commentary on theater and books was not introduced to win new readers from among the toiling industrial masses. The black masses could not support a magazine that faithfully mirrored their interests alone. Thus the *Messenger* had to make some overtures to the bourgeoisie. Given Randolph's goals and aspirations, the evolution was inevitable. Once again, on the labor and business front, he found that there was no clear avenue out of the black twenties, out of the American dilemma. Solutions would have to wait for the next two decades.

NOTES

1. Both popular images and some scholarly work postulate that the twenties were indeed prosperous years for Northern blacks. But a hard look at census and related data confirms the view given here of serious economic difficulties. For a detailed examination of such statistics, see Theodore Kornweibel, Jr., "An Economic Profile of Black Life in the Twenties," *Journal of Black Studies* 6 in press.

2. *Messenger,* March 1919, Supplement.

3. U.S. Department of Labor, Division of Negro Economics, *The*

Negro at Work During the World War and During Reconstruction: Statistics, Problems, and Policies Relating to the Greater Inclusion of Negro Wage Earners in American Industry and Agriculture (Washington, D.C., 1921), pp. 20-21; Guichard Parris and Lester Brooks, *Blacks in the City: A History of the National Urban League* (Boston, 1971), p. 152; Jane Lang Scheiber and Harry N. Scheiber, "The Wilson Administration and the Wartime Mobilization of Black Americans, 1917-1918," in Milton Cantor, ed., *Black Labor in America* (Westport, Conn., 1970), p. 135. For the employment difficulties of black women, see Charles Lionel Franklin, *The Negro Labor Unionist of New York: Problems and Conditions among Negroes in the Labor Unions in Manhattan with Special Reference to the N.R.A. and Post-N.R.A. Situations* (New York, 1936), pp. 95-97; Joint Committee to Study the Employment of Colored Women, *A New Day for the Colored Woman Worker: A Study of Colored Women in New York City* (New York, 1919), pp. 23-25, 29-30.

4. *Messenger,* May-June 1919, pp. 8-9; July 1919, pp. 8, 14-15; August 1919, pp. 8-10; September 1919, pp. 6-7; Myland R. Brown, "The IWW and the Negro Worker" (Ed.D. dissertation, Ball State University, 1968), pp. 24ff.

5. *Messenger,* August 1919, pp. 11-12; August 1920, p. 22; July 1921, pp. 214-15; December 1923, p. 921; Philip S. Foner, "The IWW and the Black Worker," *Journal of Negro History* 55 (January 1970): 57-59; Sterling D. Spero and Abram L. Harris, *The Black Worker: The Negro and the Labor Movement* (New York, 1968), pp. 396-97.

6. Spero and Harris, *The Black Worker,* pp. 333-36; Brown, "IWW and the Negro Worker," pp. 60, 71, 73; Herbert R. Northrup, *Organized Labor and the Negro* (New York, 1944), pp. 137, 141-44; Franklin, *Negro Labor Unionist of New York,* pp. 189-91, 325ff.

7. Spero and Harris, *The Black Worker,* pp. 319-21, 413; Horace R. Cayton, *Long Old Road* (Seattle, 1964), pp. 117ff.

8. For details on these free-speech struggles, see Frank L. Grubbs, Jr., *The Struggle for Labor Loyalty: Gompers, the A. F. of L., and the Pacifists, 1917-1920* (Durham, N.C., 1968), pp. vii-viii; H. C. Peterson and Gilbert C. Fite, *Opponents of War: 1917-1918* (Madison, Wis., 1957), pp. 74-80; Charles Chatfield, "World War I and the Liberal Pacifist in the United States," *American Historical Review* 75 (December 1970): 1933-34.

9. Bernard Mandel, "Samuel Gompers and the Negro Workers, 1886-1914," *Journal of Negro History* 40 (January 1955): 276; Herman D. Bloch, *The Circle of Discrimination: An Economic and Social Study of*

the Black Man in New York (New York, 1969), p. 100; New York *Times,* July 7, 1917, pp. 1, 4.

10. Northrup, *Organized Labor and the Negro,* p. 8; Charles H. Wesly, *Negro Labor in the United States, 1850-1925: A Study in American Economic History* (New York, 1967), p. 264; John D. Finney, Jr., "A Study of Negro Labor During and After World War I" (Ph.D. dissertation, Georgetown University, 1967), pp. 31-36.

11. Finney, "Study of Negro Labor During World War I," pp. 276-83, 289, 293ff.; Franklin, *Negro Labor Unionist of New York,* pp. 91-93, 283-88; Wesley, *Negro Labor in the United States,* pp. 265-68; Parris and Brooks, *Blacks in the City,* pp. 135ff.; Abraham Epstein, *The Negro Migrant in Pittsburgh* (Pittsburgh, 1918), pp. 30-45; Spero and Harris, *The Black Worker,* pp. 107-11; New York *Age,* November 22, 1917, p. 1; November 29, 1917, p. 1; December 8, 1917, p. 4; February 9, 1918, p. 1; February 16, 1918, pp. 1, 4; May 4, 1918, p. 1.

12. "The Negro Enters the Labor-Union," *Literary Digest* 61 (June 28, 1919): 12; Finney, "Study of Negro Labor During World War I," pp. 296-97, 299ff.; Wesley, *Negro Labor in the United States,* pp. 269-73; New York *Age,* June 21, 1919, pp. 1, 4; March 27, 1920, p. 1; June 19, 1920, pp. 1, 4.

13. Frank Morrison to James Weldon Johnson, July 30, 1920, in Administrative File, Subject File Labor, General, NAACP Papers, Library of Congress; Spero and Harris, *The Black Worker,* pp. 110-11, 117; Wesley, *Negro Labor in the United States,* p. 274; Finney, "Study of Negro Labor During World War I," p. 333; New York *Age,* July 2, 1921, pp. 1, 4; May 13, 1922, p. 4; December 20, 1924, p. 4.

14. *Messenger,* May-June 1919, p. 7; July 1919, pp. 14-15; August 1919, pp. 10-12; October 1919, pp. 8-9.

15. Ibid., November 1917, pp. 13-14, 20; August 1919, p. 7; December 1919, pp. 16-19; *Crisis,* May 1918, p. 32; Jervis Anderson, "Early Voice," *New Yorker* 47 (December 2, 1972): 88-89; Spero and Harris, *The Black Worker,* pp. 117-19, 394-95.

16. Spero and Harris, *The Black Worker,* pp. 396-97; *Messenger,* April-May 1920, pp. 3-4; July 1923, p. 757; W. E. B. DuBois, *Dusk of Dawn: An Essay Toward an Autobiography of a Race Concept* (New York, 1968), p. 207; Franklin, *Negro Labor Unionist of New York,* pp. 98-101, 302-304.

17. Howard W. Risher, Jr., *The Negro in the Railroad Industry* (Philadelphia, 1971), pp. 36-37, 43-44; Northrup, *Organized Labor and the Negro,* pp. 71, 73-74; Franklin, *Negro Labor Unionist of New York,* pp. 97-98; Frank Morrison to John Fitzpatrick, January 2, 1919, in John

Fitzpatrick Papers, Chicago Historical Society; New York *Age,* June 13, 1925, p. 2; August 8, 1925, p. 10.

18. *Messenger,* August 1925, pp. 296-97; Brailsford R. Brazeal, *The Brotherhood of Sleeping Car Porters: Its Origin and Development* (New York, 1946), pp. 19-20; Franklin, *Negro Labor Unionist of New York,* pp. 101-10; Department of Research and Investigations, National Urban League, *Negro Membership in American Labor Unions* (New York, 1930), pp. 131-32; Roi Ottley, *"New World A-Coming": Inside Black America* (New York, 1968), p. 242; Gilbert Osofsky, *Harlem: The Making of a Ghetto: Negro New York, 1890-1930,* (New York, 1966), p. 154; Frank R. Crosswaith to James Weldon Johnson, July 25, 1925, November 9, 1925, Admin. File, Sub. File Labor, General, NAACP Papers; American Fund for Public Service, Inc., "Report for the Three Years 1925-1928" (New York, 1929), pp. 16, 22; Parris and Brooks, *Blacks in the City,* pp. 180-86.

19. John Henrik Clark, "A. Philip Randolph: Portrait of an Afro-American Radical," *Negro Digest* 16 (March 1967): 17-18; *Messenger,* August 1925, p. 303; "Officers of Pullman Porters Union Address Labor Conference," BSCP press release, May 2, 1927, Admin. File, Sub. File Unions, BSCP, NAACP Papers; *A. Philip Randolph at 80: Tributes and Recollections* (New York, 1969), p. 9. The early history of the BSCP is recounted in Brazeal, *Brotherhood of Sleeping Car Porters,* and Anderson, "Early Voice" (December 9, 1972).

20. New York *Age,* December 3, 1927, p. 1; December 10, 1927, p. 1; *Messenger,* January 1928, pp. 13, 21; March 1928, pp. 61, 71; Randolph to John Fitzpatrick, December 16, 1927, Randolph to Milton Webster, January 6, 1928, Webster to Randolph, December 17, 1927, January 4, 1928, in Brotherhood of Sleeping Car Porters Papers, Chicago Historical Society; Parris and Brooks, *Blacks in the City,* p. 186; Reverend A. Clayton Powell et al. to "Dear Friend," November 28, 1927, Admin. File, Sub. File Unions, BSCP, NAACP Papers.

21. Interview, A. Philip Randolph, July 13, 1972.

22. *Messenger,* March 1920, p. 6; August 1920, p. 66; September 1920, p. 82.

23. Ibid., February 1920, p. 5; March 1921, pp 194-95; July 1921, p. 209; February 1923, pp. 593-94; April 1923, p. 654; June 1923, pp. 735-36; July 1923, p. 758; December 1923, p. 919.

24. Elliot M. Rudwick, *W. E. B. DuBois: Propagandist of the Negro Protest* (New York, 1968), p. 252; Francis L. Broderick, *W. E. B. DuBois: Negro Leader in a Time of Crisis* (Stanford, Cal., 1959), p. 138; *Crisis,* March 1928, p. 98.

25. Darold T. Barnum, *The Negro in the Bituminous Coal Mining*

Industry (Philadelphia, 1970), p. 20; William M. Tuttle, Jr., "Labor Conflict and Racial Violence: The Black Worker in Chicago, 1894-1919," in Cantor, *Black Labor in America*, p. 107.

26. For favorable comments on various unions see the *Messenger,* November 1921, p. 274; December 1921, p. 296; June 1923, p. 736; July 1923, p. 758; June 1924, p. 178; September 1924, p. 279; April 1925, p. 157; for some misgivings see August 1920, p. 66; June 1925, p. 228.

27. Spero and Harris, *The Black Worker,* pp. 177-78, 337-47, 390-91; Scott Nearing, *Black America* (New York, 1969), p. 101; Anderson, "Early Voice" (December 2, 1972), pp. 115-16; Northrup, *Organized Labor and the Negro,* p. 124; Franklin, *Negro Labor Unionist of New York,* pp. 185, 200ff., 305ff.; Bloch, *Circle of Discrimination,* pp. 107-108; Joel Seidman, *The Needle Trades* (New York, 1942), pp. 37-38, 138, 140.

28. *Messenger,* March 1921, pp. 195-96; July 1921, pp. 215-16; August 1924, p. 247; February 1928, p. 37, show approval of strikes. Negative reactions are in November 1922, pp. 520-21; September 1923, pp. 810-11, 819.

29. Ibid, August 1925, p. 303; David Brody, *Labor in Crisis: The Steel Strike of 1919* (Philadelphia, 1965), pp. 162-63.

30. Northrup, *Organized Labor and the Negro,* pp. 78-79, 121, 154-55, 159, 174, 178; Bernard E. Anderson, *The Negro in the Public Utilities Industries* (Philadelphia, 1970), pp. 74-75; Risher, *Negro in the Railroad Industry,* pp. 45-46; Walter A. Fogel, *The Negro in the Meat Industry* (Philadelphia, 1970), pp. 34-36; Herbert R. Northrup, *The Negro in the Automobile Industry* (Philadelphia, 1968), pp. 11-15; Herbert R. Northrup, *The Negro in the Rubber Tire Industry* (Philadelphia, 1969), pp. 29-30; Lester Rubin, *The Negro in the Shipbuilding Industry* (Philadelphia, 1970), pp. 36-37.

31. Parris and Brooks, *Blacks in the City,* p. 184; Thomas L. Dabney, "Negro Workers at the Crossroads," *Labor Age* 16 (February 1927): 8-9; Kelly Miller, "The Negro as a Workingman," *American Mercury* 6 (November 1925): 310-13; "Labor Union Issue Divides Negro Leaders," Federated Press Eastern Bureau release, November 27, 1925, Admin. File, Sub. File Unions, BSCP, NAACP Papers.

32. *Messenger,* August 1923, p. 784; September 1923, p. 805; interview, A. Philip Randolph; Brazeal, *Brotherhood of Sleeping Car Porters,* pp. 129-32; James Weinstein, *The Decline of Socialism in America: 1912-1925* (New York, 1967), pp. 298, 310.

33. *Messenger,* July 1925, pp. 261, 275; August 1925, pp. 304-305; September 1925, pp. 324-25. Fort-Whiteman, ironically, had written fiction and literary criticism for the *Messenger*'s earliest issues.

34. National Urban League, *Negro Membership in American Labor Unions,* p. 129; Lovett Fort-Whiteman to Walter White, March 31, 1925, Fort-Whiteman to James Weldon Johnson, March 31, 1925, Admin. File, Sub. File Labor, General, NAACP Papers; ANLC, *A Call to Action* (Chicago: Daily Worker Publishing Co., n.d.); Robert Minor, "The First Negro Workers' Congress," *Workers Monthly* 5 (December 1925): 68-73.

35. Minor, "First Negro Workers' Congress," p. 72.

36. Schuyler to Pickens, April 6, 1925, Admin. File, Sub. File Labor, General, NAACP Papers; New York *Age,* September 5, 1925, p. 4; May 22, 1926, p. 4; New York *Times* (January 17, 1926): II, 1-2.

37. *Opportunity,* December 1925, p. 354; *Crisis,* December 1925, p. 60; Broderick, *W. E. B. DuBois: Negro Leader In a Time of Crisis,* p. 144. There are many examples of ANLC criticism and attacks on the Brotherhood in the BSCP papers, Chicago Historical Society. See, for example, Randolph to Milton Webster, June 14, 1928; Webster to Randolph, June 15, 1928; Randolph to Webster, June 27, 1928.

38. "Negro Wage Earners," *American Federationist* 32 (October 1925): 878-79.

39. A. Philip Randolph et al. to Hugh Frayne, February 1926, BSCP Papers, Chicago Hist. Soc.; "The Reminiscences of Benjamin F. McLaurin," Oral History Research Office, Columbia University, 1962, p. 206; Brazeal, *Brotherhood of Sleeping Car Porters,* pp. 22, 148-49; *Messenger,* November 1926, p. 336.

40. National Urban League, *Negro Membership in American Labor Unions,* p. 32; Spero and Harris, *The Black Worker,* p. 327; *Opportunity,* February 1930, pp. 56-57.

41. John P. Frey, "Attempts to Organize Negro Workers," *American Federationist* 36 (March 1929): 296-305.

42. *Messenger,* May-June 1928, pp. 108-109.

43. Ibid., July 1918, p. 9.

44. Ibid., March 1920, p. 2; *Crisis,* January 1920, pp. 105-106; Spero and Harris, *The Black Worker,* p. 385.

45. *Messenger,* January 1923, p. 562; June 1923, pp. 735-36; July 1923, p. 758; August 1923, p. 784; October 1923, p. 829; November 1924, p. 340; Nathan Irvin Huggins, *Harlem Renaissance* (New York, 1971), pp. 5, 49-50, 305-306; Abram Harris, "The Negro and Economic Radicalism," *Modern Quarterly* 2 (March 1925): 201.

46. *Messenger,* August 1922, p. 464; February 1923, p. 589; November 1923, pp. 859-60; January 1924, p. 5; November 1924, p. 40; May 1925, pp. 196-97; Spero and Harris, *The Black Worker,* pp. 163-64; Louise Venable Kennedy, *The Negro Peasant Turns Cityward: Effects of Recent Migrations to Northern Centers* (New York, 1930), pp. 118, 120ff.; Arvarh E. Strickland, *History of the Chicago Urban League* (Urbana, 1966), p. 48. Skilled black laborers in the South were also losing ground relative to white workers in the modernizing South, because of an inability to adjust themselves to new tempos; Lorenzo J. Greene and Carter G. Woodson, *The Negro Wage Earner* (Washington, D.C., 1930), p. 322.

47. *Messenger,* January 1923, p. 562; March 1923, p. 621; July 1923, p. 758; September 1923, p. 806; March 1924, p. 701; February 1925, p. 89.

48. Ibid., May 1927, p. 154; the comment on DuBois was suggested to me by Marilyn Leonard.

49. J. E. Harmon, Jr., Arnett G. Lindsay, and Carter G. Woodson, *The Negro as a Business Man* (College Park, Md., 1969), pp. 24-25; Theodore G. Vincent, *Black Power and the Garvey Movement* (Berkeley, Cal., n.d.), pp. 52-55; Carl S. Matthews, "After Booker T. Washington: The Search for a New Negro Leadership, 1915-1925" (Ph.D. dissertation, University of Virginia, 1971), pp. 216-18.

50. *Messenger,* March 1919, p. 8; May-June 1919, pp. 5, 8-9; August 1919, pp. 7-8; March 1920, pp. 6-7; December 1921, pp. 312-14; March 1922, pp. 371-74; August 1922, p. 464; November 1923, p. 856; July 1924, p. 234; April 1925, p. 157; April 1928, pp. 92, 95; May-June 1928, p. 108; Vincent *Black Power and the Garvey Movement,* pp. 47, 76-77; Department of Labor, *Negro at Work During the World War,* pp. 73-75.

51. Vincent, *Black Power and the Garvey Movement,* pp. 18, 25-26, 101, 103, 159, 166; Elton C. Fax, *Garvey: The Story of a Pioneer Black Nationalist* (New York, 1972), pp. 101-102, 107; Eric D. Walrond, "Imperator Africanus; Marcus Garvey: Menace or Promise?", *Independent* 114 (January 3, 1925): 9.

52. DuBois, *Dusk of Dawn,* pp. 280-81; *Crisis,* December 1919, pp. 48-50; February 1920, pp. 171-72; January 1922, p. 107; May 1928, pp. 169-70.

53. *Messenger,* September 1924, pp. 280-81; March 1925, p. 125; January 1928, p. 21; May-June 1928, p. 108.

54. Ibid., July 1922, pp. 443-45; August 1922, pp. 464-66; September 1924, pp. 280-81; March 1925, p. 125, October-November 1925, pp. 356-57.

55. Harold Cruse, *The Crisis of the Negro Intellectual* (New York, 1967), pp. 137-38; Gunnar Myrdal, *An American Dilemma: The Negro*

Problem and Modern Democracy (New York, 1944), 2: 802-803; Abram L. Harris, *The Negro as Capitalist: A Study of Banking and Business Among American Negroes* (Gloucester, Mass., 1968), p. 178.

56. *Messenger,* January 1918, pp. 13-14; Harris, *The Negro as Capitalist,* pp. 177-78, 180-81; Myrdal *An American Dilemma,* 2: 804.

57. *Messenger,* March 1925, pp. 125, 141; February 1927, p. 49; August 1927, pp. 247-48; New York *Age,* July 30, 1927, p. 4; Allan H. Spear, *Black Chicago: The Making of a Negro Ghetto, 1890-1920* (Chicago, 1967), pp. 181-82. Several analyses of the black economy depict the situation in the twenties and answer some of the questions the *Messenger* might have asked. For banking, see especially Harris, *Negro as Capitalist;* also Myrdal, *An American Dilemma;* Harmon, Lindsay, and Woodson, *Negro as a Business Man;* and Armand J. Thieblot, Jr., *The Negro in the Banking Industry* (Philadelphia, 1970). For insurance, see Linda Pickthorne Fletcher, *The Negro in the Insurance Industry* (Philadelphia, 1970). Harris, *Negro as Capitalist,* has comments on real estate and its relation to banking.

7 | Black Politicians and Race Leadership

Chandler Owen and A. Philip Randolph were compulsively political individuals. From first issue to last their magazine was filled with commentary on parties, leaders, and strategies. As they perceived it, the present and future of the race was a political question in the broadest sense: How should the race respond and make headway in the hostile or at best indifferent headwinds of the nation? What type of leadership, either in or outside of the formal party structure, was most likely to bring about constructive change, if indeed any could? How might the race organize itself to make a collective voice most effective? The two editors started with socialism, outlining its promise in the pages of the *Messenger* and running for office on the party ticket. But the Socialist party, whether in practical politics or on the level of ideology, did not prove to be a viable course for blacks as the twenties progressed. The magazine reflected this unwelcome conclusion, and its involvement in radical politics perforce declined after 1922. More attention was paid thereafter to the world of conventional politics.

Major party politics had little to offer in the twenties except to those few who stood to receive minor appointments. In condemning both Republicans and Democrats, the magazine spoke for vast numbers of disillusioned black Americans. The *Messenger* found only minute traces of liberalism on matters of race in either party and refused to delude itself, as many did, that the return of Republicanism in 1921 would bring racial improvement. The two editors were not surprised by Normalcy, by President Harding's renewal of Booker Washington's Atlanta Compromise, by the defeat at Republican hands of federal antilynching legislation. But an absence of viable radical alternatives forced them into a reluctant look at the bourgeois parties and eventual hopes for a left-labor third party in 1924. These expectations were dashed, however, not only in the defeat of LaFollette but also in the failure to forge a new liberal coalition.

If blacks were to gain anything through politics, the *Messenger* advised, they must learn to vote independently and eschew uncritical party loyalty. The theoretical possibility of successfully implementing this strategy existed. So indifferent was the Republican party to the black vote that almost any decent alternative might be attractive. Unfortunately neither the Democrats nor the Progressives offered an attractive choice. Black "participation" in national politics meant only an infestation of party hacks and patronage manipulators, neither of which had any real program for race advancement.

Race leadership was one of the most important aspects of the political question. Should blacks have "one great leader," as Booker Washington and Frederick Douglass had been? The *Messenger* opposed this concept, realizing that such a "leader" would be more the creation of white opinion than of black and that no individual likely to be so chosen was in fact fit to lead. (Besides, Randolph and Owen had ambitions to national leadership and feared more influential rivals, particularly W. E. B. DuBois.) On similar ideological grounds the *Messenger*'s editors opposed the NAACP and National Urban League and formed a new organization, the Friends of Negro Freedom, to accomplish what the others were unequipped to do. The FNF did not long survive, however, and the magazine finally settled on its most productive "political" venture, the unionization of the Pullman porters. It was political in the sense that successful economic organization would provide the base for broad political mobilization.

Politics, then, took the *Messenger* into Socialist propaganda and campaigning, political criticism and punditry, organization of an independent, black-led civil rights pressure group, and the porters' union. Throughout, it was trying to chart the most viable, opportune, and productive course for blacks to follow through the hostile seas of American racism. The magazine's ultimate failure to find a sure course is indicative of the obstacles black Americans in the postwar years found in the path to first-class citizenship.

The first three years of the *Messenger*'s life were closely connected to the fortunes of the Socialist party of America. This is not to say that the magazine was a party organ—there is no clear evidence that the party was underwriting it—but since the editors were themselves members and the party endorsed the magazine, it can justly be called the first Socialist magazine edited by and for blacks in America. Randolph and Owen had entered a well-established tradition of political journalism, for almost every black periodical of the day was partisan, and most were openly so.

By late 1917, Randolph and Owen were already waist-deep in Socialist politics as Morris Hillquit's campaign managers in Harlem. Their Independent Political Council was ostensibly to promote honest and progressive government and justice for the race, but was in reality an adjunct of the mayoral race. Little is known of the details of the two editors' campaigning, but the New York *Age,* which supported the Republican-Fusion candidate, reported that "organized cliques" of rowdies, alleged to be Socialists, made themselves obnoxious by interrupting and hissing Fusion speakers. Whether or not Randolph and Owen won many black votes for Hillquit, the results of the election proved encouraging to all radicals, since the Socialist party gained about a quarter of the votes in the splintered race.[1]

The magazine identified many good reasons why blacks should become Socialists. The party was the only one that condemned the war as useless bloodshed and of gain only to profiteers. Furthermore, 99 percent of blacks were workingmen and naturally had nothing in common with the two major parties. Both encouraged Jim Crow and lynching. Both supported rapacious capitalism's plutocracy, trusts, and monopolies. Capitalism, in fact, was at the root of all racial disorder, causing the South's backward economy and underlying that region's economic, political, and social arrangements. But socialism would eliminate all these evils. It would give the ballot to all, abolish vagrancy laws, child labor, peonage, and crop leins. A Socialist victory would lead to public ownership of utilities, lowered rents and cost of living, free schooling, clothing and doctors' care, and the nationalization of land through the single tax. As the *Messenger* described the party in article after article, every ill had its Socialist panacea.[2]

Randolph and Owen were not playing with words merely for the sake of appearing radical. American society in wartime and the postwar years had numerous social problems, problems for which the major parties offered cures as often harmful to the patient as they were helpful. Although the radical parties lacked the political leverage to implement their ideals, their proposals for labor and land reforms, health and educational improvements, and curbs on monopolistic capitalism, had more relevance to the travail of working people than did Democratic or Republican promises. It would be easy to dismiss the *Messenger*'s advocacy of socialism in 1918 and 1919 if one were to concentrate solely on electoral achievement or read the rhetoric in a historical vacuum; what must be done instead is to put its solutions alongside America's problems and only then weigh the party in the balance.

Oddly enough, the bitter ideological splits in 1919, which led to the formation of two new Communist parties and a weakened Socialist party, were hardly discussed in the *Messenger*; in fact, it seemed deliberately to avoid taking sides. Despite this it is clear that Randolph and Owen had no intention of supporting the left wing, although they probably decided not to dissipate the magazine's influence by becoming involved in factionalism. Airing the movement's soiled linen was not likely to encourage blacks to join, and in fact might bring about the opposite.

The most convincing evidence of where the *Messenger* stood is in two parts: its concurrence with the official Socialist party platform; and its participation in the 1920 elections. The convention in 1919 took pains to define differences with the left wing, acknowledging that it might become necessary at some time to throw off the oppressors by violence; but a more peaceful evolution, preserving civil order and rights, was preferable to a drastic Russian-style upheaval. The party did not see any immediate revolutionary potential in the United States and thus no need to break sharply with the methods of the prewar period. Workers would continue to be offered a new proletarian consciousness, would receive assistance as before in organizing politically and industrially along class lines.[3] The *Messenger* agreed with these sentiments and methods even though it continued to express admiration for Bolshevik Russia and advocated armed resistance to race violence.

The magazine's Socialist faith remained steadfast through the elections of 1920. It alleged that only the Socialist party systematically nominated blacks to public office, which was at least accurate for New York State. The party nominated five blacks, including Randolph, who ran for state Comptroller, and Owen, who sought to represent the twenty-first district in the Assembly. They acknowledged that most Socialist candidates had little chance of winning election, but their presence on the ballot might so frighten the other parties that they would begin to offer concessions to blacks to allay their discontent. Wall Street would force the South to stop lynching, once big capital realized that mob violence was driving blacks into the Socialist party.[4]

The results of the 1920 canvass have been interpreted by one historian of socialism as a sign of real strength for the party, considering the schisms of the previous year and the presence of another radical party, nearly identical in platform, on the ballot. The Socialist party fared well in several urban centers, including New York City. Randolph ran only slightly behind Debs; the presidential candidate polled 203,201 and Randolph gained 202,381 votes. Randolph, the only black on the statewide ticket, got more votes than any other Socialist candidate for statewide office. Owen did not fare as well, polling 1,032 out of 17,190 votes actually counted, but even this total is not inconsiderable considering the incessant propaganda of the *Age,* which solemnly declared that Socialist candidates were either stooges of the Democrats or the cat's-paws of murderous Bolsheviks.[5]

After the 1920 elections the *Messenger's* interest in socialism began to decline, paralleling the fortunes of the party, and comparatively little comment was to be found in the magazine's pages in the following year. The editors still maintained some party activities and in 1921 spoke to a packed crowd in Richmond's St. Luke's Hall, with police lining the building inside and out. But they took little part in New York City's municipal elections in that year, commenting afterward that the diminished Socialist vote was not unexpected. Hard times, they said, were inauspicious for radicalism. Only in times of improvement would discontent rise. And in addition the party suffered from internal dissension, few funds, and after-

shocks of the persecutions of Palmer and Lusk. Randolph again found
a place on the ballot in 1922, this time running for Secretary of State on
the combined Socialist and Farmer-Labor line, a coalition including some
of the more progressive labor unions. The *Messenger* predicted that the
ticket would garner about 150,000 votes in the state, but Randolph collected only 129,461 votes, 5 percent of the total for that office, a decline
from the 7 percent that he had received two years before.[6]

Following the disappointing 1922 returns, the *Messenger* could not
delude itself: the prospects for a popular radical alternative were rapidly
receding. Talk of a third-party candidacy of Robert LaFollette was not
inspiring. He was no socialist, and many of his backers represented reactionary labor. Eugene Debs remained no more than a sentimental favorite. To make matters worse, both the Communist and capitalist press
charged that the Socialist party had gone soft on the Klan. By the time
of the 1924 elections the editors were confused and disheartened. No
party stood foursquare on principles. The *Messenger* had always before
told its readers to vote for the party, not the man, and to mark the straight
Socialist ticket. This was contrary to the advice of W. E. B. DuBois to pick
good men and disregard party labels, but by late 1924 the magazine had
adopted the DuBoisian view as a matter of expediency.[7]

After 1924 faith in a successful Socialist party was largely gone. And
neither the more radical Communist party nor its black adjunct, the
African Blood Brotherhood, was to be trusted. Owen had already left
for Chicago, divorcing himself from radical politics, and Randolph had
given up active involvement in the Socialist party both from disillusion-
ment and the need for respectability while organizing the sleeping car
porters. W. E. B. DuBois was going through a similar evolution, admitting
that prospects for both a viable socialist movement and enlightened
white labor were for the moment dead.[8]

Socialism failed to become a viable avenue for racial improvement in
the late teens and twenties, and the reasons illuminate the collective mind
of the black community. One major factor was the antiradicalism that
infected persons of all races. New York was clearly the exception so far
as socialist inroads were concerned: in Chicago, the next largest urban
concentration of blacks in the country, votes for the Communist and
Socialist parties in the Black Belt were almost nonexistent up to 1930.
Persecution of unorthodoxy during the war and Red Scare had taught

the "dangers" of any form of collectivism, making it all too easy for
most individuals to confuse socialism with Bolshevism. The New York
Age was guilty of such a faulty equation. Frequent attacks on socialism,
whether well or ill informed, undoubtedly disinclined many blacks from
any sympathetic consideration at the very time when the movement
should have been most appealing to the race. As Randolph expressed it,
the radical movements were destroyed in large-measure by the legacy
of Burleson, Palmer, Daugherty, and others of their ilk.[9]

There was little class consciousness in the black community, and this
too was an important reason for the rejection of socialism. Blacks scorned
poor whites in general and distrusted association with them. Young James
W. Ivy discovered that "Negroes were not interested in *Das Kapital*, dialec-
tics, or the class struggle, but in how to get the white man off their backs,
and they didn't see how Socialism or Communism could do that, since
they were white ideologies." Ivy remembered a skeptic asking A. Philip
Randolph whether the advent of socialism would assure that even Socialist whites would no longer act like racists. Randolph answered in metaphor,
describing a canoe with two paddlers, black and white, both being forced
to cooperate to keep the craft afloat whether or not they liked one another personally. The questioner remained skeptical. Rather than being
convinced by socialism that white workers were their best friends, many
blacks were persuaded only that socialism intended to abolish organized
religion and dispossess the white employing class, the latter an alleged
source of racial improvement. Significant numbers of the race, both
leaders and commoners, agreed not only that the uprooting of capitalism
would mean the uprooting of the existing social order, but also that it
would unjustly dispossess the only benefactors the race could claim. Why
should blacks by sympathetic to radicals who sneered at the very things
the race was trying to attain: material prosperity, possessions, the affluent life? Radical solutions may have promised long-range achievement
of such goals, but capitalism seemed, to many, to promise it a good deal
sooner. Blacks wanted *their* piece of the action, and action in America
meant Horatio Alger, participation in mainstream economics, and individual salvation through individual economic mobility.[10]

The Socialist party itself contributed to the failure to convert blacks
by often appearing to give little support to their aspirations. At base
the party could not admit and then construct a program to deal with
the reality that racism was separate from economic exploitation. Social-

ists, even those who were foreign born, had been shaped by the American environment and creed, and they consequently dealt with the issue of race, when they bothered seriously to recognize it, with little discernment of how a more equitable social system could be established. Like Americans at the opposite end of the political spectrum, they were captives of the Social Darwinist pessimism. Although the party did not reject black membership, it nonetheless doubted, with few exceptions, real black equality. Its right wing, closely tied to conservative trade unionism, believed blacks could not be successfully organized, and viewed them as essentially irrelevant to the movement. Victor Berger's Milwaukee *Social Democratic Herald* once declared that "there can be no doubt that the Negroes and mulattoes constitute a lower race." This may have been acceptable sociology for the day, but it was hardly politic for the Socialist party's efforts, feeble as they were, among blacks.

Individual Socialist locals, some even in the South, made occasional efforts to organize blacks, but the national organization failed to foster such a spirit. Annual conventions temporized on this question as well as other issues of importance to the race. Both Eugene Debs and Morris Hillquit, the two Socialists Randolph most admired, believed that the party did not need any resolutions on the "Negro question" because the black man was a worker and nothing special should be offered to one class of workers and not to others. Given this lack of initiative by the party's center and Left, the right wing, composed of persons like Berger, usually dominated the committees that drew up resolutions on immigration and race. And in a day when overt racism was popular and respectable, even those Socialists who did not side with the likes of Berger nonetheless were in agreement that the party should not encourage social equality. Most wanted to believe that socialism would not bring any significant increase in contacts between the races. What divided white Socialists was not the question of blacks' allegedly degraded position—there was near unanimity on this point—but only the question of whether the gap could ever be narrowed.[11]

Party activity increased among blacks in the postwar months, but this did not mean that its longstanding views had changed. One writer has observed that encouragement of the *Messenger* was the only serious bid organized socialism ever made for black support, and there is considerable truth to the assertion. The case of Eugene V. Debs illustrates this. Debs was the white figure most revered by black workers and was a real inspiration to Randolph. He stood for both a purity of brotherhood and a hard-nosed sense of the plight of downtrodden workers, a rare combination of loving compassion and ideological sagacity. But despite his undoubted humanity and sincerity, Debs could not accurately perceive the caste nature of the American racial system. Writing in 1918, he declared that "the negro is my brother. . . . I refuse any advantage over him and I spurn any right denied him, and this must be the attitude of the Socialist movement if it is to win the negro to its standard." Noble sentiments indeed. But Debs also believed that blacks must make their own solution, unite themselves industrially and politically "in behalf of their class," as a working class. He did not conceive of the necessity for racial consciousness, racial unity, racial organization. This view dominated the party into the twenties. Race was not the issue; after all, whites exploited whites, England exploited Ireland. Blacks' problems were class problems.[12]

By the early twenties, black as well as white members of the Socialist party began to defect leftward toward the Communist party. This was due in part to anti-Sovietism in the Socialist party, but also to the fact that the Communist party abandoned the Debsian view that socialism could offer nothing special to any particular racial or ethnic group. The old Socialist party thus lost the image of a genuinely radical movement by ignoring the cultural, political, and economic implications of the black caste position. The Communist party itself eventually fell into the same trap, although after a different series of strategies. Ultimately neither communism nor socialism proved able to retain black converts because both dealt superficially or not at all with the real problems of black life. The *Messenger* abandoned the Socialist party for this reason, as well as for more practical political reasons. Randolph, if not Owen, retained an active interest until about 1924, when the party no longer spoke to black realities. Support faded because there was no sense in hitching the ever-struggling periodical to a movement that no longer had an active and viable program for black and white workers.[13]

It was a rare black publication that did not take sides in partisan politics, and the *Messenger* was no exception. Being the creation solely of its editors it was under no constraints to limit political comment. Owen and Randolph, like their rival on the *Crisis*, saw themselves bringing keen political analysis and direction to intelligent members of their race, without regard to party sensibility or Establishment disapproval. The *Messen-*

ger's function was to criticize all that needed criticism, to subject to with-
ering analysis all issues and questions, to spare no group or person. In
political commentary it slowly drifted away from the radicalism of the
late teens, into a more sedate and less strident cynicism and disillusion-
ment by the late twenties. It was a long distance to travel for the magazine to end its life on the point of supporting Al Smith for President, but
by then no radical alternatives existed and blacks could only vote for the
man, not the party.

The steps the *Messenger* took to reach such conclusions are instructive
of the dilemma facing the race. Prior to 1917 the majority of blacks,
out of cynicism and resignation if nothing else, probably agreed with
most Caucasians that it was in fact a white man's country. The World
War changed that drastically by convincing the majority of blacks that
they were integral members of the body politic.[14]

But the political structure did not respond to this new outlook after
the war. No major party wanted black participation, only black votes.
No major party, including the remnant Progressive coalition in 1924,
considered meaningful concessions or programs for the race. But blacks
nonetheless had to attempt to strike bargains, gain whatever they could,
even if it were only a few patronage plums.

The early *Messenger* took a dim view of conventional party politics.
Arrayed against war and reaction in the late teens, it came naturally to
the view that the major parties were essentially alike and not to be trusted.
The Republican party, the race's traditional haven, took the hardest
knocks. The *Messenger* saw correctly that where Republicans controlled
city governments, as in Washington, D.C., and Chicago, these governments
had failed to protect the lives and property of blacks both before and
during the race riots. Blacks had supported the Republican party for
over half a century, and what had they gotten in return? The party had
not even freed the slaves out of altruism, but only to gain their services
in putting down the rebellion. So the race owed the Grand Old Party
nothing. Censuring New York's first black assemblyman, the magazine
announced that "he does not know that his being a member of the Republican party makes him an enemy of the Negro." Socialism, not Republicanism, was the answer.[15]

By late 1920, while the *Messenger* recognized that the Socialist party
stood no real chance of winning the election, it believed that a significant
number of votes for a radical party would so scare the capitalist parties

that they would make concessions to blacks in order to remain in power. Black discontent funneled through Socialist ballots would win racial reforms. This less than apocalyptic role for the Socialist party, although realistic, would hardly be effective in recruiting new black members, and its enunciation marks an important step away from the political fringes for Randolph and Owen. While proclaiming that "Debs is the *Heart* of the campaign," the two devoted much the greater amount of space to attacking the "Demo-Publicans" in 1920. Harding and the Republicans were to be especially distrusted; campaign promises of federal action to stop lynching and protect civil rights only betrayed a "cynical interest" in the race. Why had the party, in power so long, done nothing about these issues before? How many Republicans voted against the Jim Crow car in the last session of Congress?[16]

W. E. B. DuBois also concluded that there was no essential difference between Republican and Democrat; both stood for lily-whitism and reaction. But since neither third party could win, despite the fact that they both were of high principles, and since it would be disastrous for either the Democrats or the Republicans to win without the aid of black votes— this might encourage the victor to initiate new aggression against blacks— DuBois urged that blacks split their ticket in the traditional manner so as to make as few enemies as possible. The *Messenger* was not slow in exposing the contradictions in the elder editor's logic.[17]

There was much truth in what both monthlies had to say about the sincerity of the parties. Neither the Republican platform nor Harding's campaign promises were seriously meant to be fulfilled. Despite this, most black voters supported the Republican party nationally in 1920. Those who did so out of rational decision and not habit hoped that the victorious party would reverse the discriminations of the previous Democratic administration. But in general the campaign did not create much excitement, and the socialist agitation of the *Messenger* probably did little to change black voters' thinking about the major parties. Yet Randolph and Owen should be given credit for an accurate prediction of the coming decade of Normalcy. The public had voted *against* rather than *for* issues, against the League of Nations, against labor unions, against enforcement of civil rights for blacks. White voters throughout the twenties in fact showed no inclination to support these issues. The *Messenger* clearly saw that the election ratified a trend in American life away from reform and radicalism.[18]

The return of the presidency to the Republican party proved a disappointment to most blacks. The most immediate issue was the suspicion, gaining credence daily, that the new administration had no intention of perpetuating the traditional black-and-tan state organizations in the South but was instead bent on breaking the Solid South by creating an all-white Republican party there. When a group of black leaders interviewed the President in late 1921 and was told that none of their race would be appointed in the South, consternation rifled the black community. The *Messenger,* however, refused to be shocked.[19]

If Harding had been indiscreet at this interview, he was doubly so in a widely publicized address at Birmingham, Alabama. Quoting from Lothrop Stoddard, he proclaimed that social equality was desired by neither race, although blacks should be guaranteed political and economic equality. Chandler Owen saw the speech as a restatement of Booker Washington's Atlanta Compromise. He pointed out that it was impossible to eschew social equality and at the same time encourage economic equality. If a person paid the regular fare but then had to ride a Jim Crow car, this was a denial of economic opportunity. And once again the specter of intermarriage was close to the white man's statements. Owen charged that Harding and his white Southern listeners were really in favor of amalgamation so long as it involved only white men and black women. The *Messenger*'s longstanding position was reemphasized: "Unconditional, unequivocal, absolute social equality."[20]

The Birmingham speech was merely one part of a growing mountain of evidence that Normalcy meant a return to the days of neglect for the concerns of the race. Warren G. Harding himself must share much of the blame for this. While not a man of overt ill will toward blacks, the President had only a superficial understanding of racial matters and lacked any sense of moral urgency or even strong political necessity in pushing for the reforms desired by the race. Harding's only positive actions were to issue one appeal for antilynching legislation and cautiously to approve the idea of an interracial commission. But he made no real effort to gain passage of either; had he really desired the latter, he could have created it by executive order. The *Messenger* had long before spotted Harding's "interest" in blacks: he had done nothing on their behalf while a Senator.[21]

The most stinging disappointment for blacks during the Harding years was the treachery of the Republican party in helping defeat the Dyer Anti-lynching Bill. The *Messenger* and most blacks realized that no fed-

eral law would immediately put an end to the gruesome practice, but a
start could be made through legislation that would penalize officials who
failed adequately to protect the lives of mob victims. Long before the
crucial Senate vote, the magazine saw that the bill had no chance with
both parties maneuvering to kill it. It did pass the House but was defeated
in the Senate when the Republican majority refused to give it support.
The President himself failed to assert any influence at the crucial moment.
While DuBois condemned both parties, he stressed that the Democrats
had lynched the antilynching bill. But in fact the party of Lincoln, and
its president, was more responsible for the defeat.[22]

The defeat of the Dyer Bill in December 1922, added to the results
of the midterm elections the previous month, led the *Messenger* again
to thoughts of a left-labor third party movement. Organized capitalism
seemed to be driving toward one monolithic party to oppose labor and
radicalism, and the masses must soon decide whether they were capitalists or workers. The Farmer-Labor and Socialist movements still had the
best programs—taxes on property and big income, not on labor; levies
for schools, not battleships. Randolph saw hope in the Midwestern
progressive-liberal-radical movement coalescing around Robert LaFollette.
DuBois also perceived a trend toward a national third party, although he
still held to the theory of voting for individuals, not parties, in local
elections. In such elections one did not need a third party—one should
merely vote for friends and against enemies, be they Socialists, Democrats,
or Republicans. In presidential and senatorial elections, on the other hand,
DuBois questioned whether "any Negro voter in the future [could] support the Democratic or Republican party in national elections without
writing himself down as an ass." The *Messenger* was soon to adopt the
advice of voting for a third party nationally and for good individuals
locally.[23]

The national elections of 1924 were the most disappointing ones for
the *Messenger*'s editors during the magazine's lifetime, for here all hopes
for a viable third-party movement were dashed. At first they invested
their faith in progressive insurgency. On the surface the Conference for
Progressive Political Action seemed appealing because it drew together
farmers, workers, and middle-class business interests. The CPPA would
never win the election, the magazine conceded, but it would encourage
a European-style plural party system and might eventually evolve into

an American labor party. It is significant that Randolph and Owen did not assume that such a labor party would be the natural or inevitable home of black voters. Rather, this new party would give them a more strategic position since there would be increased competition for their votes and better political bargains to be made.[24]

Yet even the Conference for Progressive Political Action failed to take a militant stand, neither condemning the Klan nor making any definite pronouncement on black-related issues. William Pickens, attending its convention as an NAACP observer, found no black delegates. In desperation he himself tried to introduce resolutions of interest to the race, but was rebuffed. Owen and Randolph separately tried their hands at making sense out of the campaigns, and both failed to find easy, clear-cut choices. Owen, implicitly rejecting the *Messenger*'s past philosophy, concluded that voting for a third party might well ensure the victory of the worst of the two major parties. There seemed little likelihood that the LaFollette coalition would sponsor fundamental changes, as one of its chief props was the lily-white Machinists' Union. Randolph first advised blacks to split their votes equally among the three parties but eventually reversed field and half-heartedly advised a vote for LaFollette, not because he was necessarily the best candidate, but to show that blacks were intelligent and independent. It was a confusing and disheartening campaign for the erstwhile radicals, as it was for W. E. B. DuBois as well.[25]

The history of left-liberal internecine warfare shows that there was indeed much to disillusion the by-then anti-Communist editors. The Farmer-Labor contingent had done its best to bring together all radical elements but it could not gain the cooperation of the Socialist party, which felt the times inopportune for a new third party. When the Farmer-Laborites persisted and called a convention, they invited the attendance of the Workers party (Communists), which proceeded to dominate the meeting, form a Federated Farmer Labor party, and quickly alienate both the labor base of the parent group and the Socialist party. By 1924 open hostilities broke out between the Federated Farmer Laborites and the more bourgeois Conference for Progressive Political Action, the latter supporting the independent candidacy of LaFollette but not desiring a formal third party for fear of alienating Samuel Gompers. The CPPA and Gompers Red-baited the Federated Farmer Laborites and persuaded LaFollette to repudiate them. No wonder the *Messenger* con-

cluded that LaFollette's position was little advanced from that of Coolidge
and Davis.[26]

Most of the country's eligible black voters cast their ballots for
Coolidge in 1924, unconvinced that the Democrats really wanted them
and believing that LaFollette, whatever his virtures, had no chance of
winning. W. E. B. DuBois and Randolph offered differing postmortems.
The elder editor was once again entrapped in the need, felt by so many
blacks, to believe that progress was possible through politics. Two members of the race had put up creditable, though losing, battles for Congress;
blacks everywhere had voted against Klan candidates; blacks had been
prominent in the councils of the major parties; the Progressives were a
force to be reckoned with in the future. Randolph's view of the political
realities was more accurate. LaFollette had in fact made a poor showing
and won few black votes, in part because he never spoke to a black
audience. There was little prospect for a permanent third party because
the most hard-working and cohesive element of the progressive coalition,
the Socialists, were pitifully weak. Labor was not yet independent enough
for a third party, while liberals continued to vacillate. Blacks still voted
Republican nationally. It was plain to Randolph, and he was not wrong,
that the country was upon conservative times. This judgment signaled the
end of the *Messenger's* espousal of third-party politics. After the 1924
election the magazine lost interest in political commentary and carried
little mention of the partisan world until the 1928 election came into
focus. What was there to say except that the major parties were totally
uninterested in the needs of the race and Calvin Coolidge hopelessly
ignorant?[27]

By the time the 1928 presidential campaign began, the *Messenger*
had long before concluded that prospects for a third party were nil. But
this was not belabored, for the magazine was by then guardedly impressed
with the candidacy of New York's Governor Al Smith, a progressive
on taxation, government reorganization, public power, and housing. Besides, the election of a Catholic might just teach the country a lesson in
pluralism and tolerance. DuBois, too, welcomed the prospect of Smith's
candidacy, hoping it might break the Solid South since there was little
chance Dixie would vote for a man both wet and Catholic. As the conventions neared, the *Messenger* took a somewhat more practical view
of the New Yorker, perceiving more accurately the limits of his liberal-

ism and the dangers of a campaign focused on religious prejudice. Nonetheless the risk was worth taking; blacks could strike a blow for themselves by helping to send a Catholic to the White House.[28]

The *Messenger* did not live to witness and comment on the conventions. Whether it would have sustained the enthusiasm for Smith can only be conjectured, but it should be noted that black voters developed serious qualms about him as well as about Hoover.[29] Whatever the case, it is doubtful that editors like Randolph and DuBois swayed many voters in 1928. The *Crisis*'s circulation was lethargic, and the *Messenger*'s, never truly vigorous, was far from its peak. The political commentary of these journals is important not so much for the immediate impact they had on the black population but as a barometer of the hopes, aspirations, delusions, and disappointments inherent in seeking racial improvement through politics. It did not come to pass in the twenties, and this helps explain the *Messenger*'s shift from party-line Socialism to political expediency.

Black voters in the twenties began for the first time to desert the Republican party in significant numbers and vote independent or support more attractive Democratic candidates. Such a course of action was not easy to take, because black leadership remained staunchly Republican. Although the *Messenger* started from the opposite pole, it eventually accepted this strategy too. That independent voting was a reasonable alternative is evidence of the miserable record compiled by the party of Lincoln. But switching party allegiance did not appeal to enough black voters in the twenties for real political leverage to develop, which indicates that the Democratic party did not perceive the opportunity and take steps to make itself more attractive to the colored electorate.

Advice to vote independent was not novel in the twenties. William Monroe Trotter advocated it as early as 1904, claiming that in close contests Northern black voters could determine the outcome of even presidential elections. DuBois had the same elusive dream of a black balance of power. The *Messenger* never took quite so wishful a stance, but it did believe that if neither party presented a decent alternative, the most sound advice was to sell one's vote, as Chandler Owen put it, to whichever party would offer the most. Above all, the black vote must not be taken for granted by either party. A situation in which vote-splitting could be successful was made possible by the same social forces that created the

Messenger itself: the migrations and the booming Northern urban black
population. Here were concentrated votes that might be bartered for
antilynching legislation or enforcement of the War Amendments.

But these same social forces also made for meager results. White politicians, realizing the potential influence of highly populated black wards,
gerrymandered districts to deny them representation, especially in New
York and to a lesser extent in Chicago. Another obstacle to effective
independent voting was the "parasitic swarm of petty Negro politicians
which overran every Negro ward. Almost always devoid of loyalty to
the race, these men often conducted an open market in black ballots."
So long as "leaders" were concerned more with personal advancement
and a few flashy jobs than with substantive racial issues, independent
voting would fail in the purposes that Randolph, Owen, Trotter, and
DuBois outlined. Nonetheless there were some gains in black political
consciousness during the twenties, and it would be inaccurate not to
assign some of the credit to the *Messenger*. Increasingly, Republican statements of goodwill and a few token appointments did not deceive the
new generation of black voters. Particularly in New York City, but also
true elsewhere, black voters began to turn to the Democratic party, a
move that signifies a more acute sense of the use of politics for group
ends. It was this urban trend that paved the way for massive political
realignments in the thirties.[30]

Republican blunders contributed to the degree of success in independent voting and changing party allegiances in the twenties. Not since
Theodore Roosevelt's presidency had the race received anything approaching favorable treatment from the party in power. Republican platforms
from 1916 through 1928 mirror this indifference. Never during the
twenties did official party campaign materials call for enforcement of
the Fourteenth or Fifteenth Amendments, let alone deal with other civil
rights. On the local level, white Republicans did not seek out black voters
so much as blacks vainly sought out the party. In cities controlled by
Republican machines and administrations, willing black voters were
courted only to the extent they were needed to bolster the party's power.
With the exception of Chicago, black Republicans were not seen as an
integral element of the urban coalition. In New York City, where both
parties had strong organizations, the black masses got essentially nothing
from either. Even the unswervingly Republican New York *Age* was forced

to admit that the party acted as if it believed it could dispense entirely with black votes and still win elections.[31]

The Republican party also declined in the eyes of black voters because of the ignorance and indifference of its Presidents. Black America had overwhelmingly supported Harding and gotten nothing in return. Despite comments in his Birmingham speech favoring political equality, neither the President nor other party leaders gave support to attacks on disfranchisement. Congress, with Republican majorities, similarly failed to deal with the voting problem. Only four Senators seriously fought for passage of the Dyer Anti-lynching Bill while Harding sat on his hands. The party also failed its black constituents on the Klan issue, mustering no interest in investigations proposed by the NAACP and the Commission on Interracial Cooperation. During the 1924 campaign Coolidge's running mate virtually endorsed the Hooded Knights despite the fact that LaFollette and Davis denounced them. On top of all this, continuing Republican flirtations with lily-whitism and segregation in federal offices added immeasurably to black distress. In short, the party relegated blacks to the "Republican rumble seat" despite the fact that they constituted the largest ethnic group in the party and the minority least eager to leave it. But that was part of the problem. While some blacks were ready to desert the party, many more were begging for the chance to remain. The threat of black defections simply was not immediate enough for party leadership to have to take it seriously.[32]

The case of Calvin Coolidge reveals the stumbling blocks to moving the racial status quo off dead center. His were not sins of commission, but of omission. Personally he may have favored many of the changes blacks wanted, but could not bring himself to issue an executive order to abolish discrimination in the bureaucracy or do more than speak unforceful words against mob practices. Coolidge undoubtedly feared increased government intervention, as did many other Republicans, but the larger reason for his inaction was, paradoxically, idealism. A believer in appeals to reason and the efficacy of tolerance, he was naïvely confident that the Golden Rule would work. His duty, as he saw it, was to issue sermons, moral injunctions, not to initiate practical action. Coolidge was not antiblack, and in fact had a cordial relationship with Robert Russa Moton, but was nonetheless more ignorant even than Harding of the stirring in black America.[33]

One may well ask whether the Republican party in the twenties could afford to take a stance on behalf of blacks and their ill-protected rights. The question of Southern resistance is crucial here; one hardly expects a party to commit suicide by championing an unpopular cause. But it is probably true that the GOP was so strong in the twenties that a mildly pro-Negro policy would not have been even partially disastrous. If so, the neglect of blacks is harder to justify. Furthermore, it was shortsighted to concentrate on building up a shaky lily-white party in the South while ignoring the political value in the North of a more liberal policy that would attract the urban masses, native white, black, and immigrant. The weak stand on the Klan did not only hurt the party in black wards. It was caught in a paradox of its own making: to crack the Solid South meant to champion lily-whitism, and to court black votes in the North meant some emphasis on civil rights. In the end the party could not give a wholeheartedly positive commitment to either, although preferring the former, and in so doing prepared the ground for the black revolt of the thirties. The only thing that prevented wholesale defections during the twenties was the fact that the Democrats managed to construct a record that was, with few exceptions, even worse, while third parties offered somewhat more in principles but nothing in viability.[34]

From its beginnings the *Messenger* distrusted black politicians, nearly all of whom happened to be Republicans, and this distrust remained to the end of its publishing life, the harshest criticism coinciding with the magazine's most radical period, 1917-1920. In these years the editors' self-appointed duty was to expose the politicians' servility to the corrupt major parties as well as the dubiousness of their ideas for racial improvement. As Randolph and Owen saw it, the major parties were the political expressions of the capitalist ruling class and black politicians its lackeys, mere "hirelings of white bosses." Being a Republican automatically made one an enemy of the race. He who accepted a political job allowed his mind and mouth to be silenced. The politicians made no militant demands during the war in exchange for black America's support; had they been truly race-conscious, they would instead have bargained for work at decent wages, freedom from social discrimination, protection from mob violence, and voting rights and educational opportunities. To trust such individuals, in the *Messenger*'s view, was futile: "Fleas don't protect

dogs, nor will big Negro leaders or white politicians protect the defenseless Negro." Such views represent the extreme of black reaction against
Establishment politics in the late teens.[35]

The politicians most frequently disparaged by the *Messenger* were
Charles W. Anderson, Benjamin Davis, Sr., Perry Howard, Henry Lincoln
Johnson, W. H. Lewis, Roscoe Conkling Simmons, and Robert Terrell.
All these men were Republicans. What many of them also had in common
was ties to Booker Washington and the Tuskegee Machine. Washington
had at one time or another helped obtain federal appointments for most
of them, and since the *Messenger* from its conception was anti-Bookerite
in philosophy and language, anyone with ties to Tuskegee, past or present,
was more than a little suspect. Washington's political clout—which frequently boiled down to influence-peddling—was a source of deep resentment for many in the opposite camp, from W. E. B. DuBois on down. The
Messenger was not inclined on any grounds to favor Washington's legacy
or his successor. Of the black politicians Charles W. Anderson was particularly objectionable, probably because he was the Tuskegee Machine's
right-hand man in New York City. He believed that more and better-
paying political jobs were efficacious in advancing the race, a course of
which the *Messenger* heartily disapproved. Anderson was well known as
a loyal party man, which was reason enough for the magazine to dislike
him. Finally, he had been prominent in bolstering black patriotism during
the war and was made an honorary colonel by the 367th Infantry. But
the only black colonel the *Messenger* had kind words for was the victimized
Charles Young.[36]

The *Messenger* objected to Judge Robert Terrell on several grounds,
one being his agility in serving both North and South, black and white,
Democrat and Republican, Hoke Smith, Woodrow Wilson, and Henry
Cabot Lodge. Obviously something was suspect about such adroitness.
Terrell was also a prominent supporter of the World War, which earned
him no laurels from Randolph and Owen, but worst of all they accused
him of having adopted a cringing posture during the Washington race
riots, "deploring" the retaliation of black folk against their white persecutors. And the fact that he was a Bookerite appointee did nothing to
improve his standing with the magazine. The same held true for Assistant
Attorney General William H. Lewis, who consciously allied himself with
Booker Washington in order to gain advancement. In common with other

politicians he was a patriotic speaker on Emmett Scott's circuit during the war. To the *Messenger* Lewis was simply a political hack, although he won applause when he bolted the GOP in 1924.[37]

Howard, Johnson, Simmons, and Davis were manipulators without public office, products of Southern Republican rotten boroughs. To succeed in that world one had to be a wheeler-dealer, and maintaining Tuskegee ties was essential. Neither ability endeared them to the *Messenger,* nor did their patriotic efforts during the war. The magazine was not alone in criticizing them for wire-pulling and patronage-selling, and even the *Age* was moved to admit, on the passing of Henry "Linc" Johnson, that "the game still consists in electing delegates to the national convention and manipulating their votes so as to have a claim upon the successful candidate, when the time comes for parcelling out the patronage." Did such men play a valuable role in purchasing significant recognition for the race's political claims, as some have alleged?[38] Obviously the Republican hierarchy did not interpret a few plums to political small-fry as "recognition of the race." The unfortunate conclusion is that these figures were fooling their race, if not themselves, when they attached great importance to a Registrar of the Treasury and a Collector of Internal Revenue. The *Messenger,* ever alert to political motives, knew better. Writing in its first issue what could as well have been repeated in its last, the magazine noted that "it is a true saying that half loaves given to the common people prevent their taking measures to get the whole loaf." Black officeholders, in other words, had been paid off to keep silent, not to protest. Blacks had not chosen their own leaders, so obviously they could not control them. Fully committed black leadership would have to develop independently of the major parties. "Negro political leaders are bought and bossed and the rank and file are ruled and robbed."[39]

Until about 1924 the attitude of the magazine toward black politicians and officeholders changed little. Between 1921 and 1924, however, the emphasis was increasingly on the trials and disappointments of black office-seekers who did not receive the political plums they so keenly desired from the new Republican administration. When the President named a white man as Registrar of the Treasury, the black press rose in protest, but the *Messenger* instead applauded: "We congratulate Mr. Harding on his wallop to the jaw of the old crowd Negro politician.

This will pull more Negroes from the GOP than tons of arguments made by the *Messenger* ever could." If blacks deserved political jobs, make them meaningful ones, like a cabinet post. A year later Owen and Randolph again rejoiced when another seeker was denied Senate confirmation; such appointments only hurt the race by lulling the masses into thinking they had gotten something when they really had not. "Better that there be no Negro job holders at all than that the interests of the masses be ignored as a consequence." This view still put the *Messenger* far beyond most other critics of the period—even W. E. B. DuBois, who, while discouraged by the caliber of black Republican leadership, nevertheless believed it was helpful for the race to be "represented" by them. Nor did the elder editor lambaste the Republican aspirants as did the *Messenger,* which called Anderson, Terrell, Johnson, Howard, and Lewis "political hogs . . .at the trough," "sleek, fat, pot-bellied Negro politicians [who] have been trafficking for a half century in the sweat and blood and tears of toiling Negro washer women, cotton pickers, miners, mill and factory hands."[40]

Many blacks entertained the vain hope that once Coolidge won a popular mandate in 1924, he would open up the appointments floodgate, but this wish was not to be granted. Neither, for that matter, did the President relax federal segregation as had been hoped; instead it reached new heights between 1924 and 1928. Although the *Messenger* adopted an I-told-you-so attitude toward disappointments in Coolidge, it had by 1925 ceased blanket attacks on black politicians for the practical purpose of winning support for unionization of the sleeping car porters. Thereafter it was black politicians and leaders who were in the Pullman camp that received the magazine's criticism, and chief among these adversaries was an old target, Perry Howard.[41]

Howard represented the Republican rotten borough of Mississippi and was that state's national committeeman as well as a special assistant to the Attorney General. So thoroughly acceptable was he to white Southerners that in his first (and successful) political contest the Klan burned a cross to warn voters away from his white opponent. From that time on, Howard assembled a record that can only be called venal. He and "Linc" Johnson proved willing to sacrifice the good of the race for their own political advancement in the Tuskegee Veterans Hospital affair, making it all the more difficult to guarantee a black staff for the facility. Howard's

Machiavellian plotting to help defeat the Dyer Anti-lynching Bill was
even more unconscionable. Consistent in his own self-interest, a year
later he advised blacks not to oppose the Ku Klux Klan, for "we have
many friends among Klansmen."[42]

Not long after the Brotherhood of Sleeping Car Porters was organized,
stories reached the press of how an agent of the federal government had
joined the Pullman Company to help stymie the new union. Howard
claimed only that he was checking on a group of "wild-eyed, long haired,
leather-lung starving bolshevists and communists" directed by Moscow.
The Department of Justice, caught in an embarrassing position, denied
responsibility for Howard's statements, while Howard, at the same time,
denied that he was in the employ of the Pullman Company; in fact
he received some four thousand dollars from Pullman. Randolph's radical
past was his Achilles heel and Howard made the most of it, but in the
end Red-baiting was not a particularly effective weapon against the BSCP.

The fight quickly degenerated into personal attacks in which Randolph
had as good a store of ammunition as did his opponent. Howard brashly
challenged Randolph to a debate in Chicago, where the young editor un-
mercifully trounced him, in the process gaining for the porters a strong
Chicago local. Randolph also exposed the fact that his opponent was in
the pay both of the government and of the Pullman Company, thus involved in a conflict of interest, since his ostensible duties in the Justice
Department were in regard to railroad regulation. The New York *Age,*
officially neutral on the porters' struggle, could not ignore this dual
allegiance: "The spectacle of a special assistant to the U.S. Attorney
General rushing about the country making speeches officiating for the
Pullman Company and resorting to questionable methods to thwart the
efforts of members of a race to which he professes to be a leader is not
relished nor approved by self-respecting Negroes." The *Messenger* also
accused Howard of selling government offices in his role of patronage
referee for the state of Mississippi, but when he was brought to trial a
(white) federal jury in his home state refused to convict him; Howard
had always been careful to see to it that most of the patronage jobs he
dispensed went to Democrats. Bounding back with great durability, he
was still serving on the Republican National Committee in 1958 as its
senior member.[43]

It is odd that the *Messenger,* in commentary and involvement in
political controversy, focused overwhelmingly on national figures and

did not concern itself more with local partisan politics, particularly in New York City. This was where the real political action was in the twenties, where changing voting patterns and a new electorate were becoming visible and viable. Here, too, were well-known politicians, many as venal as those put in the spotlight by the *Messenger*. But aside from occasional brief comments on the Thompson machine and its black allies in Chicago and a few remarks on New York City's black Democratic boss Ferdinand Q. Morton, the magazine all but ignored the active two-party systems that prevailed in several cities. Randolph and Owen were more concerned with the effect of national politicians as leadership images, for both white and black Americans, than with the practical results that some local politicians were reaping. For that matter, few Harlem intellectuals addressed themselves, in practical terms at least, to issues like tenements, urban violence, crime, and poverty.[44] The editors recognized these problems in the abstract but thought it more important that prominent black Republicans, either through actual venality or participation in a political charade, threw the race up for ridicule and hurt the chances for effective national legislation. The *Messenger* was not shortsighted in calling for more enlightened, more independent leadership at the national level, but in the process it slighted the vital building of local power bases that were important, at the very least, if a black man was ever to deliberate again in the national Congress. The lessons of other ethnic groups had not yet been learned; the utility of local machine organization was not yet recognized.

The twenties were, indeed, a difficult time for black politicians at the national level. The Republican dream of lily-whitism and a two-party South took its toll on the older generation of officeholders who had hoped that the party's return to power would have broad enough coattails for them all. By mid-1928 there were only seventy-seven more blacks in all categories of federal service than in mid-1920, and most black government employees, in any case, held low-paying positions. The number of blacks holding presidential appointments was smaller at the end of the Coolidge years than during the Roosevelt-Taft era. In the South a dog-eat-dog fight ensued over the remaining, and fast diminishing, Republican patronage allotted to the race. The worst in black politics became identified with Negro Republicanism, and by 1930 it would be easy to term most black Republican leaders Uncle Toms; some were quite frankly associates of the underworld. City bosses like "Mushmouth"

Johnson and "Teenan" Jones of Chicago and "Bob" Church of Memphis displayed little of the idealism that had characterized Reconstruction-era politicians. Yet the public gave them an importance greater than their actual worth because blacks associated such bosses with the race's struggle for civic and political rights.[45]

E. Franklin Frazier and Horace Mann Bond, both writing in the mid-twenties, verified the *Messenger*'s analysis of the corruption and worthlessness of black Republican politics in the South, but they realized more clearly that the migrations had shifted political power to the cities and away from the South in general. Perry Howard might be keeping his position warm for years to come, but the real action was no longer in dispensing patronage. Independence from the Republican party was being forged in Northern cities. Republican shadow machines would remain for years in the South as a symbol of the party's "concern" for the race, but the hopes of the old wheeler-dealers had already been dealt a mortal blow in 1921 when Harding did not hand back all the positions lost during Woodrow Wilson's tenure. Men like Howard represented no real influence in the South, and yet, in the twenties, bloc power was only beginning to be forged in the cities. The *Messenger* sensed this change, but not clearly enough to lead the new urban forces. The magazine's commentary on politics and politicians in the twenties was not hope for the future, but anathema on the present.[46]

Republican warhorses were a bane on black life because their positions in the party made them "representative Negroes" and thus leaders of a sort, at least to the unknowing white public. There was also another group that the *Messenger* thought equally dangerous, the so-called race leaders. The magazine sensed what is today more plainly seen, that too often such "leaders" were the creations of white public opinion. Any nationally known black person in whatever field was liable to be trumpeted as *the* racial spokesman. This phenomenon was particularly common after the death of Booker Washington as no one individual rose to preeminence to fill his shoes. It had suited the white Establishment to have in Washington one spokesman for black America, and another such accommodating individual to take his place would have been equally welcomed.[47] The *Messenger* sensed this and distrusted all of the individuals who might be considered the race's new spokesman—W. E. B. DuBois,

Kelly Miller, Robert Russa Moton, Emmett Scott, and James Weldon
Johnson, not to mention Marcus Garvey.

All of these figures with the exception of Garvey were dismissed by
the *Messenger* as "Old Crowd Negroes," with DuBois the archetype.
From the beginning he was the magazine's favorite whipping boy. There
seems to have been an almost compulsive need on the part of the young
editors to attack their rival at every turn, and their disclaimer of personal
ill feeling cannot be taken at face value. The attacks on DuBois, not
declining in intensity until after 1925, were motivated by personal considerations as well as differences over racial strategy. On a liberal-to-
conservative scale there are obvious distinctions between the prominent
black figures in the postwar years, but the *Messenger* insisted that DuBois
was as reactionary as Robert Russa Moton. One of the magazine's more
vulgar attacks was a cartoon depicting DuBois, Moton, and James Weldon
Johnson giving encouragement to white rioters and lynchers.[48] The implication was that all "leaders" save the radical crowd were duping the race
into an ambush of white violence.

Randolph and Owen's bill of particulars against DuBois will be given
in some detail because it serves as the stereotype whereby all other leaders were condemned. As they saw him in the years 1918-1920, DuBois
was a "white folks' nigger," quieting angry blacks and placating the
majority race. He did not believe in revolution, it was charged, and made
matters worse by insisting that revolution meant violence and bloodshed
and organized murder. This was understandable, for DuBois was said to
possess no philosophy of the class struggle or conception of blacks as
part of the proletariat. His labor views were likewise baleful. He vilified
the only fair union, the IWW, by tarring it with the brush of pro-Germanism and failed to see that the One Big Union principle was the wave of
the future. On the contrary, he took pleasure in the defeat of striking
white workers and exulted in strike-breaking by blacks.

DuBois's politics were similarly reactionary, so the magazine charged.
He was an opportunist, swinging to the party most likely to win in order
to curry its favor. His advice to readers was to vote for "good men"
even though they represented a reactionary party, rather than for a good
party. A vote for the Socialist party, he thought, was a vote thrown away.
Where the *Crisis* editor erred was in putting faith in the alleged decency
of America and possible reformation of the Republican party. In the

meantime his view of political progress was the hopelessly corrupt one of measuring improvement by the number of black officeholders. As for DuBois's actions during the war, the *Messenger* found them inexcusable; he linked the IWW to the Germans, advised blacks to "Close Ranks" and put aside their grievances, and approved of Jim Crow officer training camps and YMCAs, all of which betrayed good socialist principles. Underlying this was the vain belief that loyal participation of blacks in the war effort would win them an end to discrimination. DuBois's personal maneuverings to win an army commission did not go unnoticed. Finally, he was charged with suppressing radical news or news about rival leaders by ignoring them in the *Crisis;* there had been nothing in that journal about black Socialist candidates, including Randolph.

What explanations did the *Messenger* have for DuBois's shortcomings? He was, first of all, a man of the previous generation. His role had been to provide a bridge from the era of Booker Washington to the modern age. Before the war he was "radical" insofar as he opposed the Bookerite political and economic program, but was hopelessly out of touch with the realities of the postwar world. He was ignorant of modern political science, his knowledge of economics was no more current that Adam Smith, and in sociology he only knew Comte. In addition to these defects in background, Chandler Owen charged that DuBois had a "much overrated mentality." Finally, it was alleged, DuBois lacked the courage to prevent being controlled in mind and speech by the NAACP board. In short, he was "a discredit to Negroes and the laughing stock among whites."[49]

There are more than a few grains of truth in many of the charges against DuBois, but they prove neither venality, treachery, nor dishonesty. Rather they show that the editor of the *Crisis* was a transitional figure. One recent author identifies two intellectual revolts in the period 1890-1933. The first, of which DuBois was the leader, was directed against Uncle Tom and the slave psychology that preached submissiveness to things as they were, against Bookerite "accommodationism." The second revolt, or second phase in a process of self-emancipation, came about when blacks no longer needed myths about themselves, when they could identify with blackness and come to terms with their race without needing to idealize it as did sociologist-philosophers like DuBois and Kelly Miller. Thus the end of World War I marked a new period in black thought.[50] The *Messenger* stood at the beginning of this second phase, not fully attuned to the Renaissance and racial national-ism, but sensing that the idealizations and faith of the DuBoisians were an unsure foundation. Where the *Messenger* failed was in not carrying the revolution far enough; it eventually retreated toward a safe but intel-lectually dead-ended embourgeoisement. It too was transitional.

Many of the *Messenger's* shafts at DuBois, while poisoned, nonethe-less reflect reality, for he was a man struggling to deal with a world far different from that pictured in his own lofty, self-oriented idealism. In-consistency, self-aggrandizement, heights of unreal optimism and depths of despair, disdain for the views of others and extreme confidence in his own, all were present. His stand on the war presents such a paradox. Many young intellectuals, not just those associated with the *Messenger,* criticized DuBois for temporizing on the war issues; some of them called him "Der Kapitän" in honor of his having so avidly sought a commission. How could one explain DuBois's early opposition to the war and partic-ularly to the War Department and Civil Service Commission, and then understand his approval of segregated officer training camps and partici-pation in George Creel's CPI propagandizing? How explain the "Close Ranks" editorial? There seemed to be no consistency, no principle, no dependable leadership.[51]

DuBois's militancy represents another difficulty. He liked to give the impression of radicalism, considering himself the race's foremost radical for his longtime emphasis on civil rights and opposition to accommoda-tion, but by 1918 he was hardly "radical" when measured by the actions of others. His socialism was closer to the humanitarian-reformism of Jane Addams than to the political activism of Debs. Suspicious of radical cant about the brotherhood of all workers, he knew, as Owen and Ran-dolph later came to admit, that white workers themselves saw little kin-ship to black laborers. Regarding the charge that he high-handedly sup-pressed news of rival, more militant race leaders, throughout his life he assumed the role of censor of black thought to ensure that only the best examples be put forward.[52]

By 1923 the *Messenger* had moderated itself enough to concede that DuBois was a prominent, if not preeminent, race leader. No longer was it necessary to harp on his lack of a modern education, and on one occa-sion the younger editors even became so charitable as to recommend him for a Nobel Prize and a 100 percent raise in salary. But the antagon-ism was still there, not far below the surface. In mid-1925 there occurred

over the space of three months a stream of vicious insults consisting of
a largely irrelevant editorial dredging up "Close Ranks," another ridicul-
ing the failures of the Pan African Congress, and a funny but cruel piece
questioning why DuBois should have been awarded the Spingarn Medal
in 1920. While the reason for this outburst is unclear, it again shows, as
was seen in the Garvey episode, that dislike, distrust, and envy for a more
famous rival could lead the *Messenger* into an intemperance that did it
no credit and undoubtedly lost it friends and readership. After this incident the magazine rarely mentioned the name of the *Crisis* editor. Randolph probably realized, as the Pullman porters' bitter fight started, that
he needed every ally he could find in the black press, and since DuBois
was favorably disposed toward the porters it was important that his support not be jeopardized. One thing, at least, is clear in this episode.
Throughout the twenties the *Messenger* feared that DuBois might become the race's preeminent leader, whether by his own election, selection by whites, or some consensus in the black community. There
was no way the magazine could feel good about such a possibility.[53]

Randolph, Owen, and Schuyler were not the only ones sniping at
DuBois—internecine warfare among so-called leaders and aspirants to
leadership was considerable in the late teens and early twenties—but
DuBois reacted to aspersions on his intelligence, character, and ideas by
maintaining an unperturbed Olympian exterior, ignoring the *Messenger*
not only in the *Crisis* but in his personal correspondence as well. Yet he
was a sensitive man, and his rivals' censure did not fail to wound. DuBois
was on close terms with the Grimké family in Washington, and so too
were the young *Messenger* editors. When the elder figure visited the
Grimkés he made sure that the two young "whippersnappers" were not
to be there also; he had no desire to meet them, much less debate with
them, believing, rightly, that they had little respect for either his opinion, his age, or his position. It should be added that while the *Messenger*'s
style of criticism was too often ignoble, the ideological differences were
not. DuBois in many respects was not cut out for race leadership. Eric
Walrond wrote that he was "undoubtedly the most brilliant negro in
the United States. . . . Poet, scholar, editor, and author, he is the man to
whom the country turns with any question bearing on the intellectual
life and progress of the negroes. Proud, haughty, an incurable snob, he is
probably the most unfit man temperamentally for the craft of leadership."

One could not neatly divorce DuBois's personality from his ideas; both were important aspects of his leadership.[54]

DuBois was not the only "Old Crowd Negro" to be attacked by the *Messenger;* nearly every other prominent spokesman for one or more segments of the black community was defective in goals and strategy. Those who had favored the war had obviously not understood the implications of international conflict on the lives and resources of the colored world, nor the priority of defeating the Huns of Georgia before the Huns of Germany. The Tuskegee Machine, never having had an appropriate strategy for the Northern black community, believed that the postwar period was not the time to push for new rights, but to sit quietly while white America rewarded the race for its devoted war service. DuBois at least wanted to push forward to new struggles, but had neither the clearness of perception nor the executive talents to lead. So to the *Messenger*'s eye the old leadership was either bankrupt or, at best, unable to take advantage of the new possibilities of the postwar world. It was as simple yet as complex as that. A new world demanded new leaders. In the end the two editors found only themselves truly qualified.[55]

William Monroe Trotter was a "radical" of the previous era, having opposed both Washington and DuBois, but this was no automatic passport to grace as far as the *Messenger* was concerned. It was true that Trotter was the only figure who had the magnanimity and courage to preside at one of the editors' antiwar meetings in Boston even though he personally was a lukewarm supporter of the war. A believer in New Negro militance, he again displayed courage in frankly telling the Senate Foreign Relations Committee that blacks, at home and abroad, might have to resort to insurrection if a lasting and just peace was not ensured. And he had made personal sacrifice in surreptitiously traveling to Paris to try to present the cause of the black race to the Peace Conference. But his domestic political views could not be forgiven. Trotter was criticized for putting faith in the goodness of the Republican party and believing that political progress for the race could be measured by the number of black officeholders. Urging blacks to vote for Harding was seen as tantamount to voting for slavery. Beside this, Trotter regarded himself as an elder statesman and demanded deference for past service. The *Messenger,* however, was the last journal to be charitable on those grounds.[56]

Another person frequently called a radical was Kelly Miller, although that label could hardly have been more inappropriately applied. The

Messenger had a full bill of particulars against him. Like DuBois, Miller
was a discredit to the race and an object of ridicule among whites. The
magazine called him the most reactionary black academic in the country
because he opposed unionism, women's suffrage, and socialism. Politically, said the magazine with accuracy, he stood somewhere between DuBois
and Washington. His use of logic left much to be desired, as his usual
mode of discourse was to argue from biblical quotation. "Untrained and
poorly informed on modern economic, political and social problems,
Miller is not prepared to lead." During the war he had been, predictably,
a vocal advocate of 100 percent Americanism. Occasionally Randolph
or Owen found something for which to compliment him—the former
wrote in 1926 that Miller was a tireless fighter for civil rights—but even
this was tempered with damaging criticism: Miller "fawns before the
altar of big business and glorifies the so-called capitalists' benefactions to
the race." The magazine's overall assessment was that he was a hopeless
conservative of little value to the race.[57]

Miller was one of the best-known black figures, primarily because of
his long tenure at Howard University, and one whose great disappointment in life was in failing to become a national race leader. In the early
part of the century he had been an associate of Washington, and by the
teens was at home both with the NAACP and the Hampton-Tuskegee
circle. Less sympathetic critics called him a straddler, and to many younger
blacks he was simply passé. Like DuBois, he could never become a popular figure with the masses because he was simply too distant. And even
moderates of the Urban League stripe censured his unabashed partiality
for capitalism. Blacks should steer clear of unions because their best hope
lay with the kindness and generosity of the captains of industry. When
Randolph began to organize the Pullman porters, Miller was among the
most prominent figures opposing this move. As a conciliator and media-
tor between conservative and radical he was out of place in the twenties,
and lacking a strong race consciousness, he was ill-equipped to understand
the new generation.[58]

The post-1915 crop of Bookerites received no quarter from ex-Southerners Owen and Randolph. Robert Russa Moton, former Hampton
Institute official and new principal of Tuskegee, was particularly offensive because he was "set up and considered by the white ruling class as a
leader of the Negro." In such circumstances he must obey those who
paid his salary. He was hindered as well by personal defects: "Moton has

neither the courage, [modern] education nor the opportunity to do anything fundamental in the interest of the Negro." On other counts the
magazine found cause for censure. Moton, it was charged, used Tuskegee
as a scab factory and joined with Samuel Gompers in organizing strike-
breaking. During the war he urged blacks to patriotically shelve their
grievances and told returning soldiers, in his words, to "be modest and
unassuming," advice that seemed to Owen and Randolph an open invitation for white rioters and lynchers to prey on blacks without fear of
retaliation. Finally, Moton was a Republican, and the magazine went so
far as to allege that President Harding cleared his Birmingham speech
with the Tuskegee principal before it was delivered. The *Messenger*'s two
young editors, expatriates from the South, knew that accommodation
meant impaired self-esteem, as well as the danger that white acceptance
of Bookerite leadership could jeopardize or erode Northern privileges
and rights.[59]

Moton had been born into plantation society and from an early age
believed that Southern whites were basically friendly and well-disposed
toward black people. Yet during the great migrations he had kept silent
as violence and intimidation increased against Southern blacks, afraid to
jeopardize Tuskegee with brave but suicidal statements. Does this make
him an Uncle Tom, or was he merely an astute politician when he wrote
Woodrow Wilson to assure him that most blacks did not approve when
William Monroe Trotter disputed the President's good intentions? He undoubtedly played the political game with Harding and Coolidge, agreeing
that "good" whites should be appointed to the exclusion of blacks in
the South so as to build up a viable Republican party there. And the
general labor philosophy of Moton's Hampton-Tuskegee circle was antiunion and favored welfare capitalism.

Then there was the matter of his controversial advice to black doughboys in France.

In war you have met the test and won, but a far greater test and a
much more doubtful victory awaits you now than you faced during
the past year and a half. . . . This is a battle not against Germans, but
this time against Americans, not against white Americans, but against
black Americans. . . .
    It is a battle of self-control, the passions and desires, the battle
against laziness, shiftlessness, wilfulness.

To many commentators Moton simply depicted social realities and urged his race to quietly go about its business, but others, including W. E. B. DuBois and the *Messenger*'s editors, viewed him as a race traitor. Certainly Moton was no venal, servile creature, but his advice was clearly out of step with the mood of the New Negro, out of step with the very expectations raised by the war of which he so heartily approved.

There were some in the postwar years who hoped Moton would don the mantle of Booker Washington and become the race's preeminent leader, although he plainly did not want this role. But from the Northern perspective, at least, he was out of step with the changing mood of black America. Moton believed in accepting a half loaf on the dubious theory that this would give the race a moral claim to the other half at some future time. Such a strategy of small, incremental gains was simply reactionary, not only to Randolph and Owen, but to many others in the late teens and twenties who advocated great leaps, fundamental change.[60]

Another Tuskegean who felt the sting of the *Messenger*'s attacks was Emmett Scott, Booker Washington's personal secretary and later Howard University's registrar. The same charges brought against Moton were leveled at Scott: collusion in Harding's Birmingham address; support of the Republican party; antiunion activities with Samuel Gompers. In addition, he was coauthor with Judge Robert Terrell of the appeal to Washington, D.C., blacks not to fight back against white rioters. During the war, the magazine charged, he had been silent on the Houston riot executions in his capacity of special assistant to Secretary of War Newton Baker and had done nothing to try to save the soldiers' lives.

There was truth to more than a few of these charges. Scott was, in one blunt assessment, " an old hand at dampening Negro dissent [who] could not mistake his function in the War Department," and in fact he was advised by his chief that unrest among blacks must be discouraged. It was clear that the government envisioned no tampering with racial folkways. In fairness it should be noted that Scott managed to rectify a few cases of draft board discrimination and helped open the field artillery to members of the race, even though he was not given sufficient authority to function as an ombudsman for black troops. But his most notable achievements were in propaganda, working closely with George Creel's Committee on Public Information. Scott had obvious aspirations to preeminent race leadership; yet he never reached such a position, in large part because of the jealousy and fear of rivals, not chiefly Randolph and Owen.[61]

George E. Haynes was another well-known black criticized by the *Messenger* as just another "me-too-boss, hat-in-hand leader" who, in the employ of the ruling capitalist class, issued palliatives and placebos to the poor suffering black masses. As Director of Negro Economics in the Department of Labor, it was charged, Haynes failed to propose viable plans for postwar readjustments. He placed too much emphasis on common labor, had no solution for farm tenantry, did not favor the only nondiscriminatory union (the IWW), was vague on education and unrealistic on housing. His major shortcoming was a belief in the efficacy of capitalism in solving social problems. Furthermore, the *Messenger* could not forgive Haynes and the Urban League—he was one of its founders— for the conferences with Samuel Gompers, which only served to further disillusion black workers.[62]

Haynes's task in the Division of Negro Economics was to remove all obstacles to efficient mobilization and advise the Secretary of Labor on any matter of concern to black workers. Unfortunately his authority was severely limited. The Division had no enforcement powers and was forced to rely solely on education and persuasion. In the end he could do little about discrimination by the U.S. Railroad Administration and white unionists, nor could he rectify Southern compulsory labor laws. Haynes's only true success was, as in the case of Emmett Scott, in the field of propaganda, allaying discontent by acquainting black labor with its crucial role in the war effort. He certainly entertained no radical reforms; it was not within his personal makeup, much less within his powers, to use the wartime labor shortage as a lever to extract concessions from government and unions. Another reason for the *Messenger*'s enmity was Haynes's philosophy of racial pacifism, which was closely akin to that of Booker Washington. He envisioned a solution to the race's problems based on black patience and humility. Randolph and Owen, on the contrary, believed neither in the Christian spirituality Haynes talked of nor in humility.[63]

What lay behind the *Messenger*'s opposition to the likes of Moton, Miller, Haynes, Scott, and DuBois—what made it fear these men even more than the black Republican bosses—was its concern that another "One Great Leader" might arise, one who, like Booker Washington, would be the creation of white folks, the single voice on what blacks thought and wanted. Scott most clearly aspired to this eminence; DuBois did not, although Randolph and Owen saw him as the most probable candidate.

Neither did Robert Russa Moton have appetite for such a role, although
his staff and admirers urged him to become the second Booker Washington.
As for Garvey, who threatened the *Messenger* at least as much as did DuBois,
he simply assured everyone that he was the One Great Leader. Kelly Miller
saw himself as the Great Conciliator. None of these individuals in fact
came close to filling Washington's shoes, but this was not so apparent
to observers in 1920. From hindsight we can note that the *Messenger*'s
apprehensions about a reactionary, captive "leader" for all the race were
unfounded, but in its time such fears were not baseless. What it could not
perceive was that the day of unitary leadership was fading fast; never
again would there be a Frederick Douglass or a Booker Washington.[64]

The most important factor militating against one preeminent leader
after Washington had to do with changes in the black community itself.
Black America was becoming less homogeneous, more stratified. Contemporary observers agreed that this new diversity was fostering a new
type of leader, a person recognized for accomplishments in his particular
field without reference to race. An influential person in the twenties
might well be a "leading writer" or a "leading politician" or a person of
note in any number of fields, often like Owen and Randolph, young,
educated, of impressive intellectual gifts, and divorced from Bookerite
perspectives. This new leadership class was itself far from homogeneous,
and part of the *Messenger*'s task was to differentiate between them. Not
only was there an old crowd and a new one, there were important distinctions as well among New Crowd Negroes.[65]

A. Philip Randolph represented that segment of the New Crowd that
had a distinctly economic viewpoint to add to the civil libertarianism of
others, both in the new and old crowds. Figures as diverse as DuBois,
Miller, Trotter, T. Thomas Fortune, James Weldon Johnson, even Frederick Douglass, in Randolph's analysis, had "struck out against the race's
detractors," against the likes of Thomas Dixon and James K. Vardaman
and Cole Blease, "instead of against the race's exploiters, the pawnbrokers,
loan sharks, turpentine still and plantation owners, . . . lumber mill and
railroad barons who overwork and underpay the black proletariat." The
personal fight of these older figures against discrimination was not un-
merited, but they were unable to see that there were factors to the so-
called race problem other than race. They had damned the detractors
of the race but had then either blessed its exploiters (who subsidized black

industrial schools and colleges, black social work, even black protest) or else failed vigorously to condemn them.

Here was a line on which Randolph separated himself from nearly the whole of the black leadership Establishment. If he had been consistent in nothing else, he was consistent in advocating programs focused on economic gains for the masses of the race. The *Messenger* had always insisted that one could not divorce the economic from political and legal problems, that behind the Republican and Democratic parties stood organized capitalism and antiunionism. But the Old Crowd leadership, and some of the New, did not have this clear perspective. Thus it was futile to establish an umbrella organization or "Sanhedrin" comprising both crowds, as Kelly Miller attempted. Just as no "One Great Leader" could speak for the entire race anymore, no one "United Negro Front" could either.[66]

Randolph's *Messenger* was distinctive in form and content from the views of the rest of black leadership, yet care should be taken not to overstate the differences. Certainly no race leader, no philosophy of change, was able to wrest meaningful concessions from white America in the twenties; it was all the race could accomplish simply to preserve what had been won in the previous decade. Black progressives, including Randolph and Owen and DuBois, failed as practical political leaders insofar as winning a significant number of whites to the cause of racial justice went. But Randolph and DuBois, at least, came to discard the emphasis on cultivating white alliances, perceiving, with Garvey, that strictly racial organization was the most important emphasis. Randolph, at least, put no faith in the "black vote," for he knew whites did not need black votes. He resolved in mid-1928 to rededicate the Brotherhood of Sleeping Car Porters as a racial organization first, not simply a labor union. Build strength internally, within the black community—this was the lesson of the teens and twenties.

The group of radicals, mostly young, who made up the *Messenger* circle made one stab at racial organization along traditional civil rights-protest lines. The impulse for this step drew on their distrust of the race politicians and race leaders whose organizations—the Republican party, NAACP, National Urban League, and National Negro Business League— were all, in one way or another, either corrupt or compromised. So the

New Crowd Negroes' response to the deficiencies of the existing groups was to form one along more militant lines. The result was the Friends of Negro Freedom, which lived a bare three years. The failure of the FNF to reach maturity, the failure to create a broad civil rights coalition, may have been seminal in turning Randolph back to more specific economic organization and eventually the Brotherhood of Sleeping Car Porters.

During the first four years of the *Messenger*'s life a steady stream of invective against the two large interracial organizations found voice in the magazine. If the Urban League was more often mentioned, it was only because the NAACP was already being attacked in the person of DuBois. The magazine's fundamental objection was that both were adjuncts of a white ruling Establishment whose backbone included corporation executives, "charitable" foundations, and a sprinkling of liberal do-gooders. Their interest in blacks, the magazine claimed with some justification, was more patronizing than sincere, and not without ulterior motive. The NAACP's program was too narrowly defined, in the opinion of the magazine. It concerned itself only with legal rights and was limited to hopelessly bourgeois and usually futile tactics of genteel protest. The Urban League was if anything worse, the Northern-Western adjunct of Bookerism, an instrument of Wall Street, in the business of saying nice things to employers, providing scabs for industry, and preventing unionization and social equality. All this was perfectly explicable when one realized who paid the League's bills. Neither organization had a "consistent and reliable program on any one of the important questions of the Negro. . . . there is little or no scientific work being done by them because there is no scientific thought being applied to the problem. In a word, there is no philosophy of the Negro problem."[67]

The New Crowd Negro's philosophy needed articulation in an untainted national organization. The Friends of Negro Freedom was deliberately constructed to avoid some of the prominent features of the other two groups. It was most similar to William Monroe Trotter's by-then moribund National Equal Rights League in that it was to be entirely black-led. Trotter recognized that whites invariably played a moderating function and watered down militant programs. And philosophically he thought it only proper for blacks to finance and lead a movement for their own emancipation. Similar considerations motivated Randolph and Owen. They perceived that the NAACP was top-heavy with whites at the national leadership level and had no program for racial economic improvement or, for that matter, fundamental reorganization of American society apart from race relations. The Association did not think in terms of class struggle and proletariat, nor did it carve out a mass base, partly because, in attempting to become respectable, its branches had been put under the guidance of upper-class blacks. Whether the FNF could avoid this Talented Tenth orientation remained to be seen.[68]

The Urban League was an even worse model for a militant black organization because of its white leadership and financing and its conservative social philosophy. Influential local branches, taking their cues from the industries and capitalists who sponsored them and paid their bills, adopted an antiunion line and provided scabs or nonunion labor when needed. The League saw its social work mission as rectifying individual failings, not societal ills. Much emphasis was thus put on making recent migrants middle-class in mien and habit. Blacks must make themselves better equipped to meet their new responsibilities in the Northern cities if whites were ever to welcome them there. Besides all this Owen and Randolph knew that in at least one city they had been barred from churches at the instigation of the local League branch.[69]

The March 1920 issue of the *Messenger* announced the formation of the Friends of Negro Freedom to take up where the NAACP left off and to begin where it had never started. A national "call" was signed by an impressive range of the race's more militant members. Included were Cyril V. Briggs, Grace Campbell, and W. A. Domingo, three Communists or Communists-to-be who would soon leave for the more radical programs of the African Blood Brotherhood. Domingo was at this time still on the *Messenger* staff, as were signers William N. Colson and George Frazier Miller, the latter also an NAACP branch officer. Several other influential NAACP members also joined the call: the Reverend Robert W. Bagnall, Association director of branches and soon to be a *Messenger* staffer; Archibald Grimké, schoolteacher Neval H. Thomas, and historian Carter G. Woodson, all from Washington. T. J. Pree, Randolph and Owen's old associate from the National Brotherhood Workers of America, was also a founder. Finally, from Chicago, C. Francis Stradford, attorney for unpopular causes, participated in the call. On the whole the initial leadership included several NAACP members who found that organization too slow-moving, too hampered by constraining white leadership. In structure the body nonetheless mirrored some NAACP characteristics. Chapters would be organized around cities and towns, were to be nonpartisan, but not apolitical. Other races could secure membership, but only blacks could lead. International as well as local and national issues would come within the FNF's purview.[70]

The founding convention was held in Washington, and Bagnall was named chairman of the executive committee. Resolutions were adopted after being written by a committee whose secretary was Chandler Owen. They expressed what the magazine had been saying for the previous three years. There was no such thing as a Negro problem, for no oppressed race could make itself a problem; the issue of the races was an economic one. The document noted the high proportion of blacks in the industrial labor force, high cost of living, scarce housing, and inflated dollar. Rent strikes and boycotts of high-priced and unfair merchants were urged. Unflattering stereotypes in motion pictures were to be fought. A major educational goal was to free black colleges from the white hands that controlled them and molded their students. A national black holiday was to be celebrated on, of all days, John Brown's birthday. Unquestioning obedience to the major parties was decried, and the Socialist party was recommended without being mentioned by name. Finally, the document averred that "destruction preceeds [sic] construction, and that the country needs some destruction of lynching, peonage, and other practices." All in all, the convention may have been exciting to newcomers but could not have proved startling to faithful readers of the *Messenger*.[71]

The FNF undertook several enterprises, the most ambitious of which, of course, was trying to establish a nationwide organization. The chief instrument of this was the *Messenger*. Organizing was to be stimulated by Chandler Owen's cross-country speaking tours. Owen was tiring of day-to-day activities of the magazine anyway and seems to have welcomed the chance to escape. His travels were to accomplish four related purposes: organize FNF locals; present the philosophy of the New Crowd Negro to a wider public; describe the race-economic problem to organized labor groups; and increase the circulation of the *Messenger*.[72]

Another major FNF goal was to rid the country of the Garvey menace. It is uncertain how successful the locals outside New York were in this campaign, but the New York FNF, spearheaded by Owen, Randolph, Bagnall, and William Pickens, played a major role in crystallizing sentiment against the West Indian. Its four forums on the "Garvey menace," coinciding with the 1922 UNIA convention, drew large, uproarious audiences. Although he was not the sole focus of the New York local, George S.

Schuyler remembers that Garvey was the principal one and the most frequent topic of discussion.[73]

The FNF proposed to act on questions of nationwide implication. One executive committee meeting considered the lack of insurance coverage for blacks whose property had been destroyed in the recent Tulsa race riot; this was of concern because most insurance policies had disclaimers for riot damage. The executive committee decided, on another issue, to attempt negotiations with several employers to open up new jobs in theaters (for actors), railroads (for engineers, conductors, and switchmen), and organized baseball. A Friends of Negro Freedom union label was adopted that would signify to black consumers that a particular union offered good employment opportunities to the race. On the touchy issue of scabbing it was agreed that all efforts should be made to get blacks in unions, and if the unions adamantly refused, then scabbing would only be encouraged if the new workers got guarantees of permanent employment. The FNF also recognized the need to aid the ever-arriving migrants from the South, urging locals to help unionize the newcomers, protect them from the pitfalls of the new urban life, and in general help them adjust as easily as possible to the different folkways and faster pace of the North.[74]

The new organization had good ideas aplenty, which makes its short life doubly tragic. It hoped to stimulate consumer cooperation in housing, food, clothing, and fuel, not just in urban areas, but the rural South as well. A business committee was to provide constructive criticism to race entrepreneurs and educate them to rely on good commercial practices, not race pride on the part of customers. A comprehensive program was outlined to deal with one of the most pressing urban problems for blacks— housing congestion and exploitation. Lower rents, proper services from landlords and municipalities, and reform legislation were all stressed. Tenants leagues were to be organized that would investigate the assessed valuation of the properties they occupied from city records, determine what a reasonable rental should be, and then negotiate with the landlord on that basis. Compromise was hoped for, but rent strikes were not ruled out. Pressure would be placed on city governments to enact rent controls and ensure that ghetto streets were kept as clean and well lighted as in affluent white neighborhoods and similarly free from protected gambling and prostitution. A separate committee of each local was to investigate merchants who overcharged black customers or were discourteous and to

preview movies and plays that displayed derogatory stereotypes, negotiate with the management for redress, and if this proved unsuccessful,
organize a boycott. Finally, each branch was responsible for its own self-
preservation, which included maintaining its racial integrity. Every appli-
cant would be investigated by a membership committee to "keep out dis-
reputable and corrupt politicians, fanatics, cranks, business crooks, chronic
disturbers, notorious nuts."[75] It was an ambitious program, and a good
one. If only it could discover the key to a large and eager membership.

The most successful programs of the FNF were the educational forums,
although results varied from city to city. The Philadelphia chapter sched-
uled such speakers as Congressman Dyer and Senators LaFollette and
Penrose. The New York Forum was probably the most active, meeting
every Sunday afternoon in a vacant store in the Lafayette Theater building. Speakers included Jean Longuet, French socialist leader and grand-
son of Karl Marx; Walter White; Norman Thomas; Algernon Lee, director
of the Rand School; and James O'Neal, editor of the socialist New York
Call. This lineup reveals the continuing interest of Owen and Randolph in
socialism, even by late 1922, and also shows how much the New York
FNF was the creation of the two. George Schuyler remembers that he
attended Forum sessions where "some of the sharpest minds in Harlem
assembled to make irreverent comments on subjects sacred and profane."
The discussions were invariably lively, and topics other than those on the
"Negro question" were discussed.[76]

The FNF did not enjoy a long life. It is hard to pinpoint the date of
its demise, but mention of it in the *Messenger* ceased after November
1923. It is probable that after the first burst of enthusiasm, several chapters disintegrated and only the strong survived. Which locals were particularly active, aside from those in New York and Philadelphia, is not known.
Certainly the FNF failed in one major goal—it had no more of a mass
base than did the NAACP. The tone and language of its appeals and resolutions were still geared toward the Talented Tenth. The Forum, or Chatau-
qua, idea was something appealing more to the new black middle class
than to the mass of workers; the latter may have benefited from forums
on Garvey, but it is likely that a lecture on Othello held much less interest
for them. The times simply were working against the FNF. The early twenties were not auspicious for starting a new protest and action organization
with either a mass base or a Talented Tenth constituency. Maintaining

all-black leadership and largely black membership also presented obstacles.
In addition a group like the FNF could too easily be called radical or
"Red," although the Communist party had no influence in it. Militancy
in general was on the defensive, whether in third-party politics, in labor,
or in racial protest. Even the established groups like the NAACP and
Urban League were on the decline.[77]

It is little wonder that the FNF did not survive beyond its infancy.
It possessed a ready-made mouthpiece, but only a comparatively small
number of black people read the *Messenger,* much less agreed entirely
with its point of view. In politics and race advancement its position, even
in 1922, was more militant than could be accepted by most Negroes. So
a period of flux ensued from the end of the FNF to the beginning of the
Brotherhood of Sleeping Car Porters. The magazine temporarily lost its
bearings and took an unprofitable tack toward black business, but then
righted itself, trimmed its sails of the outward taint of radicalism, and
embarked on its most purely racial venture. The BSCP became its final
and most productive cause, even though the magazine did not live to see
the triumph. The new porters' union represented the best possibility for
a solution to the race's problems in the twenties, not because it could
mobilize the entire race, but because it would concentrate on a small group
and enable it to first gain economic emancipation and then move on to
more political solutions.

The experience of the twenties had taught Randolph that economic
and political issues were inextricably intertwined, but that no political
solution was likely until the race, primarily through its own efforts,
gained a measure of economic security and power. This was the thrust
of the Brotherhood, a grassroots organization depending solely on black
support, black idealism, a black will to struggle. What the porters could do
for themselves, the whole race might accomplish. None of this came to
pass in the twenties, but the *Messenger*, in rejecting purely political solutions, pointed the way to the thirties and forties. Without the BSCP the
National Negro Congress would have been a different body, and without
the BSCP there would have been no March on Washington Movement. So
the rejection of Old Crowd racial and political leadership and the abandon-
ment of purely civil-libertarian goals were the first steps in what was to
become mass action militancy, the key to black self-emancipation in
the present time.

NOTES

1. *Messenger,* November 1917, pp. 16-20, 28, 33; January 1918, p. 12; New York *Age,* November 1, 1917, pp. 1, 4.

2. *Messenger,* January 1918, p. 12; July 1918, pp. 8-9; March 1919, pp. 9-12; August 1919, pp. 13-16; October 1919, pp. 15-16; December 1919, pp. 10-11, 13-15.

3. James Weinstein, *The Decline of Socialism in America: 1912-1925* (New York, 1967), p. 218.

4. Sterling D. Spero and Abram L. Harris, *The Black Worker: The Negro and the Labor Movement* (New York, 1968), p. 411; *Messenger,* February 1920, pp. 6-7; May-June 1920, pp. 6-8; August 1920, p. 64; October 1920, pp. 100, 106-107; November 1920, pp. 127, 133-34, 138-39.

5. James Malcolm, ed., *The New York Red Book: An Illustrated State Manual* (Albany, 1921), pp. 530, 534-40, 560, 570-71; Weinstein, *Decline of Socialism,* pp. 73n, 236-38; New York *Age,* September 18, 1920, p. 4.

6. Thomas L. Dabney to the author, September 11, 1972; *Messenger,* October 1921, pp. 259-60; November 1921, p. 273; December 1921, p. 298; July 1922, pp. 447-48; October 1922, p. 497; December 1922, p. 539; James Malcolm, ed., *The New York Red Book: An Illustrated State Manual* (Albany, 1923), p. 522.

7. *Messenger,* August 1923, pp. 792-93; October 1924, pp. 312, 313, 325-28, 330; November 1924, p. 339; December 1924, pp. 369-71, 390.

8. Ibid., August 1923, p. 749; Francis L. Broderick, *W. E. B. DuBois: Negro Leader in a Time of Crisis* (Stanford, Cal., 1959), p. 148; *Crisis,* June 1925, pp. 61-62.

9. Harold F. Gosnell, *Negro Politicians: The Rise of Negro Politics in Chicago* (Chicago, 1967), p. 320; A. Philip Randolph, "The Negro and Economic Radicalism," *Opportunity,* February 1926, p. 63; New York *Age,* June 28, 1919, p. 4; August 9, 1919, p. 4; September 18, 1920, p. 4. It is likely that the stridency and iconoclasm of the *Messenger* itself alienated some who might otherwise have been receptive to socialism; see William Pickens's letter to the New York *Age,* December 13, 1919, p. 4.

10. James W. Ivy to the author, January 15, 1971; Abram L. Harris, Jr., "The Negro and Economic Radicalism," *Modern Quarterly* 2 (1925): 207; Thomas L. Dabney to the author, September 11, 1972; New York *Age,* June 28, 1919, p. 4; August 9, 1919, p. 4; Sally M. Miller, "The Socialist Party and the Negro, 1901-20," *Journal of Negro History* 56 (July 1971): 229.

11. Henry Lee Moon, *Balance of Power: The Negro Vote* (Garden City, N.Y., 1949), p. 122; Wilson Record, *The Negro and the Communist Party* (Chapel Hill, N.C., 1951), pp. 17, 19; Weinstein, *Decline of Socialism,* p. 73; Berger is quoted in James P. Cannon, *The First Ten Years of American Communism: Report of a Participant* (New York, 1962), pp. 230-31; Miller, "Socialist Party and the Negro," pp. 220-29; R. Laurence Moore, "Flawed Fraternity—American Socialist Response to the Negro, 1901-1912," *Historian* 32 (November 1969): 1-18.

12. Interview, A. Philip Randolph, July 13, 1972; Baltimore *Afro-American,* January 6, 1922, p. 1; Eugene V. Debs, "The Negro: His Status and Outlook," *Intercollegiate Socialist* 6 (April-May 1918): 11-14; Miller "Socialist Party and the Negro," pp. 228-29.

13. Weinstein, *Decline of Socialism,* pp. 243-47; Record, *Negro and the Communist Party,* p. 45; Harold Cruse, *The Crisis of the Negro Intellectual* (New York, 1967), p. 42. Randolph personally remained a socialist in philosophy, but he plainly despaired of electoral success after 1924.

14. William M. Tuttle, Jr., "Views of a Negro During 'The Red Summer' of 1919—A Document," *Journal of Negro History* 51 (July 1966): 215.

15. *Messenger,* January 1918, p. 12; July 1918, pp. 8-9, 30-31; September 1919, pp. 8-10; December 1919, pp. 13-15; November 1920, pp. 140-42.

16. Ibid., February 1920, pp. 2-3; April-May 1920, pp. 6-8; August 1920, pp. 64, 66; September 1920, pp. 82-83; October 1920, p. 100; November 1920, pp. 131, 133-34, 147.

17. *Crisis,* August 1920, pp. 174-76; September 1920, pp. 213-14; *Messenger,* November 1920, pp. 140-42.

18. Robert K. Murray, *The Harding Era: Warren G. Harding and His Administration* (Minneapolis, 1969), p. 54; Richard Sherman, "The Harding Administration and the Negro: An Opportunity Lost," *Journal of Negro History* 49 (1964), 151-53; Elbert Lee Tatum, *The Changed Political Thought of the Negro 1915-1940* (New York, 1951), pp. 94-95; *Messenger,* December 1920, p. 165.

19. *Messenger,* March 1921, p. 194; November 1921, pp. 275-76.

20. Ibid., December 1921, pp. 301-306.

21. Sherman, "Harding Administration and the Negro," pp. 156-58, 160. Murray, *Harding Era,* pp. 398-400, attempts to rehabilitate the President's record. While Harding could not risk alienating more powerful groups in the party, he nonetheless "tried to placate the Negro as much as possible." This explanation, however, is unconvincing.

22. Richard Sherman, "Republicans and Negroes: The Lessons of Normalcy," *Phylon* 27 (1966): 70n; *Messenger,* January 1922, p. 327;

January 1923, pp. 562-63; *Crisis,* January 1923, pp. 104-105; Robert H. Brisbane, *The Black Vanguard: Origins of the Negro Social Revolution, 1900-1960* (Valley Forge, Pa., 1970), pp. 62, 120; Sherman "Harding Administration and the Negro," p. 161; James Weldon Johnson, *Along This Way* (New York, 1933), p. 371.

23. *Messenger,* February 1923, pp. 595-98; *Crisis,* January 1923, p. 105.

24. *Messenger,* July 1924, pp. 210-11.

25. Ibid., August 1924, p. 247; September 1924, pp. 290-91, 293-94, 296, 298-99; October 1924, pp. 325-28, 330; November 1924, pp. 340, 345-47; Sheldon B. Avery, "Up From Washington: William Pickens and the Negro Struggle for Equality, 1900-54" (Ph.D. dissertation, University of Oregon, 1970), pp. 113ff.; Eugene Levy, *James Weldon Johnson: Black Leader, Black Voice* (Chicago, 1973), pp. 276-78; *Crisis,* July 1924, p. 104; August 1924, p. 154; September 1924, pp. 199-200; October 1924, p. 247; November 1924, p. 13.

26. Weinstein, *Decline of Socialism,* pp. 272ff., 282, Chapter 8.

27. *Crisis,* December 1924, pp. 55-56; *Messenger,* December 1924, pp. 369-71, 390.

28. *Messenger,* February 1926, p. 46; May 1927, pp. 154-55; June 1927, p. 191; January 1928, p. 13; March 1928, p. 60; May-June 1928, p. 109; *Crisis,* November 1927, pp. 311-12.

29. Walter White, *A Man Called White* (Bloomington, Ind., 1970), pp. 99-101; Tatum, *Changed Political Thought,* pp. 99-103.

30. Stephen R. Fox, *The Guardian of Boston: William Monroe Trotter* (New York, 1970), pp. 36-37, 147; Brisbane, *Black Vanguard,* pp. 113-14; *Messenger,* December 1921, p. 298; Sherman, "Republicans and Negroes," pp. 67, 77.

31. Tatum, *Changed Political Thought,* pp. 110-11; Sherman, "Republicans and Negroes," pp. 66-67; Brisbane, *Black Vanguard,* pp. 115, 117; John L. Blair, "A Time for Parting: The Negro During the Coolidge Years," *Journal of American Studies* 3 (1969): 178; New York *Age,* October 2, 1926, p. 4.

32. Sherman, "Harding Administration and the Negro," p. 163; Sherman, "Republicans and Negroes," pp. 69-74; Blair, "A Time for Parting," pp. 177, 185-86, 197.

33. Blair, "A Time for Parting," 183-84, 186, 192-96, 198-99.

34. Murray, *Harding Era,* pp. 402-403; Sherman, "Republicans and Negroes," pp. 63-66, 77; Gosnell, *Negro Politicians,* pp. 31-32.

35. *Messenger,* November 1917, pp. 14-16; January 1918, pp. 23-24; July 1918, pp. 15-19, 30-31; May-June 1919, pp. 9-10; August 1920, p. 66; November 1920, pp. 131-32, 147.

36. August Meier, *Negro Thought in America: 1880-1915* (Ann Arbor, Mich., 1963), pp. 254, 309; Gilbert Osofsky, *Harlem: The Making of A Ghetto: Negro New York, 1890-1930* (New York, 1966), pp. 161ff.; New York *Age,* May 25, 1918, p. 2; July 15, 1918, p. 1; *Messenger,* November 1917, p. 32; January 1918, pp. 23-24; July 1918, p. 17; May-June 1919, pp. 9-10; July 1919, p. 17; November 1920, p. 132; July 1921, pp. 216-17; April 1923, p. 657; March 1924, p. 72; July 1924, p. 211; December 1924, p. 374.

37. Meier, *Negro Thought in America,* pp. 239-41, 244-45; Richard Bardolph, *The Negro Vanguard* (New York, 1959), p. 199; *Messenger,* January 1918, p. 23; July 1918, p. 17; May-June 1919, p. 9; July 1919, p. 17; September 1919, pp. 7-8; October 1919, p. 28; November 1920, p. 132; July 1921, pp. 216-17; October 1924, p. 313; New York *Age,* May 4, 1918, p. 2; May 25, 1918, p. 2; December 26, 1925, p. 1; Robert T. Kerlin, *The Voice of the Negro: 1919* (New York, 1920), pp. 76-77.

38. Bardolph, *Negro Vanguard,* p. 200; Meier, *Negro Thought in America,* pp. 230, 234-35, 252, 309; *Messenger,* May-June 1919, pp. 9-10; December 1919, pp. 25-26; November 1920, p. 132; July 1921, pp. 216-17; October 1921, p. 258; March 1924, p. 72; July 1924, p. 211; August 1924, p. 238; December 1924, p. 374; December 1925, pp. 378-79; New York *Age,* September 19, 1925, pp. 1, 7; Paul Lewinson, *Race, Class and Party: A History of Negro Suffrage and White Politics in the South* (New York, 1932), p. 129.

39. Bardolph, *Negro Vanguard,* p. 200; *Messenger,* November 1917, pp. 14-16.

40. *Messenger,* July 1921, pp. 216-17; October 1921, p. 258; February 1922, p. 351; April 1923, pp. 657, 671; *Crisis,* May 1921, pp. 7-8; July 1921, pp. 101-102; January 1922, pp. 106-107.

41. August Meier and Elliott Rudwick, "The Rise of Segregation in the Federal Bureaucracy, 1900-1930," *Phylon* 28 (1967): 184; *Messenger,* December 1924, p. 374; May 1925, p. 196.

42. New York *Age,* May 25, 1918, p. 2; December 16 1922, p. 4; January 6, 1923, p. 4; December 8, 1923, p. 4; Avery, "Up From Washington," p. 121; Peter Daniel, "Black Power in the 1920's: The Case of Tuskegee Veterans Hospital," *Journal of Southern History* 36 (August 1970): 368-88; Bernard Eisenberg, "James Weldon Johnson and the

National Association for the Advancement of Colored People, 1916-1934"
(Ph.D. dissertation, Columbia University, 1968), pp. 162-63; *Messenger,*
January 1923, pp. 562-63; *Crisis,* January 1923, p. 104; Brisbane, *Black
Vanguard,* pp. 201-202; Levy, *James Weldon Johnson,* p. 263.

43. Spero and Harris, *The Black Worker,* pp. 437-38; Brailsford R.
Brazeal, *The Brotherhood of Sleeping Car Porters* (New York, 1946), pp.
33-36; *Messenger,* October-November 1925, p. 352; January 1926, pp.
30-31; February 1926, pp. 52-53; April 1926, p. 111; July 1927, p. 242;
Gosnell, *Negro Politicians,* p. 31; Lewinson, *Race, Class and Party,* pp.
172, 181-82; New York *Age,* November 7, 1925, p. 1; V. O. Key, *Southern
Politics in State and Nation* (New York, 1950), pp. 286-88; Jervis Anderson,
"Early Voice," *New Yorker* 47 (December 9, 1972): 55-56.

44. Nathan I. Huggins, *Harlem Renaissance* (New York, 1971), pp. 4,
26-27.

45. Roi Ottley, *"New World A-Coming": Inside Black America* (New
York, 1969), pp. 211-12; Brisbane, *Black Vanguard,* p. 121; Sherman,
"Republicans and Negroes," pp. 74-76; Laurence J. W. Hayes, *The Negro
Federal Government Worker: A Study of His Classification Status in the
District of Columbia, 1883-1938* (Washington, D.C., 1941), pp. 37, 63-64.

46. E. Franklin Frazier, "The American Negro's New Leaders," *Current
History* 28 (April 1928): 59; Horace Mann Bond, "Negro Leadership
Since Washington," *South Atlantic Quarterly* 24 (1925): 124-25; Key,
Southern Politics in State and Nation, p. 286; Carl S. Matthews, "After
Booker T. Washington: The Search for a New Negro Leadership, 1915-
1925" (Ph.D. dissertation, University of Virginia, 1971), pp. 213-14.

47. The "one great leader" syndrome is defined and analyzed in
Matthews, "After Booker T. Washington."

48. *Messenger,* September 1919, pp. 9-10, 16-17.

49. Ibid., January 1918, pp. 23-24; July 1918, pp. 15-19, 27-28;
May-June 1919, pp. 9-10; July 1919, pp. 10-12; September 1919, pp.
9-10; October 1919, pp. 8, 17-18, 20; December 1919, pp. 7-8; September 1920, pp. 84-85; November 1920, pp. 140-42; September 1921, pp. 246-48;
October 1921, p. 257; Chandler Owen to Mary White Ovington, April 11,
1919, Ovington to Owen, April 10, 1919, John Haynes Holmes to Ovington, July 21, 1919, in Administrative File, General Correspondence,
NAACP Papers, Library of Congress.

50. S. P. Fullinwider, *The Mind and Mood of Black America: 20th
Century Thought* (Homewood, Ill., 1969), pp. 65-67, 72, 123.

51. "The Reminiscences of George S. Schuyler," Oral History Research
Office, Columbia University, 1962, pp. 79-80; W. E. B. DuBois, *Dusk of*

Dawn: An Essay Toward an Autobiography of a Race Concept (New York, 1968), p. 310; interview, A. Philip Randolph, July 13, 1972; Elliott M. Rudwick, "W. E. B. DuBois in the Role of *Crisis* Editor," *Journal of Negro History* 43 (July 1958): 225ff.

52. *Crisis,* October 1921, pp. 245-47; June 1925, pp. 61-62; DuBois, *Dusk of Dawn,* pp. 282-84, 288-90; Broderick, *W. E. B. DuBois: Negro Leader,* p. 137; Elliott M. Rudwick, *W. E. B. DuBois: Propagandist of the Negro Protest* (New York, 1968), p. 251.

53. For praise or well-mannered criticism, see *Messenger,* February 1923, p. 593; August 1923, pp. 781-83, 792-93; July 1924, p. 210; December 1924, p. 374; May 1925, pp. 197, 209; the spiteful articles are in May 1925, pp. 209-10; June 1925, p. 228; July 1925, pp. 259,262.

54. Interview, George S. Schuyler, October 16, 1970; Herbert Aptheker to author, January 20, 1971; interview, A. Philip Randolph; Eric D. Walrond, "Imperator Africanus; Marcus Garvey: Menace or Promise?", *Independent* 114 (January 3, 1925):10.

55. *Messenger,* November 1917, p. 31; Matthews, "After Booker T. Washington," pp. 150-61, 195-214.

56. *Messenger,* July 1918, pp. 15-19; December 1919, pp. 20-21; November 1920, pp. 131-32; A. Philip Randolph to Stephen R. Fox, June 19, 1969, kindly lent by Stephen R. Fox; Fox, *Guardian of Boston,* pp. 219, 223-30, 232-33, 236-37, 249-50, 252-53, 279; New York *Age,* October 4, 1919, p. 2; *Treaty of Peace With Germany. Hearings Before the Committee on Foreign Relations, United States Senate* (66th Cong. 1st Sess., Sen. Doc. 106) (Washington, D.C., 1919), pp. 680-81, 693.

57. *Messenger,* January 1918, pp. 23-24; March 1919, pp. 22-23; May-June 1919, pp. 9-10; October 1919, pp. 17-18, 20; June 1922, pp. 422-24; July 1922, pp. 443-45; February 1923, p. 593; August 1923, p. 782; January 1924, p. 8; March 1924, pp. 72-73; December 1924, p. 374; July 1925, p. 260; February 1926, pp. 42-43, 60; *Opportunity,* February 1926, p. 62.

58. *Opportunity,* January 1926, pp. 4-5; Brisbane, *Black Vanguard,* p. 179; Meier, *Negro Thought in America,* pp. 183, 213-18; Fullinwider, *Mind and Mood of Black America,* pp. 72, 97-100; Carter G. Woodson, "Kelly Miller," *Journal of Negro History* 25 (January 1940): 137-38; Matthews, "After Booker T. Washington," pp. 31-36; Kelly Miller, "The Negro as a Workingman," *American Mercury* 6 (November 1925): 310-13; Anderson, "Early Voice," (December 9, 1972), p. 66; Bernard Eisenberg, "Kelly Miller: The Negro Leader As a Marginal Man," *Journal of Negro History* 45 (July 1960): 182-97.

59. *Messenger,* July 1918, pp. 21-22, 28; July 1919, pp. 31-32; August 1919, p. 10; September 1919, pp. 16-17; September 1920, pp. 90-91; November 1920, pp. 131-32; December 1921, p. 301.

60. Robert R. Moton, "The American Negro and the World War," *World's Work* 36 (May 1918): 74; Robert R. Moton, "An Inter-Racial Commission at Work," *Outlook* 129 (September 14, 1921): 59; Robert Russa Moton, *What the Negro Thinks* (Garden City, N.Y., 1929), pp. 134-40; New York *Age,* April 12, 1919, p. 4; Matthews, "After Booker T. Washington," pp. 45, 187-88, 194-95; Eric D. Walrond, "The New Negro Faces America," *Current History* 17 (February 1923): 786-87; William Hardin Hughes and Frederick D. Patterson, eds., *Robert Russa Moton of Hampton and Tuskeegee* (Chapel Hill, N.C., 1956), pp. 149, 152, 192-200.

61. *Messenger,* January 1918, p. 33; July 1918, pp. 8, 21-22; August 1919, p. 10; September 1919, pp. 7-8; September 1920, pp. 90-91; November 1920, pp. 131-32; December 1921, p. 301; Meier, *Negro Thought in America,* p. 254; Fox, *Guardian of Boston,* pp. 219-20; Claude McKay, *Harlem: Negro Metropolis* (New York, 1940), pp. 152-53; Matthews, "After Booker T. Washington," pp. 45-53, 97-111, 124-27, 158-60, 242-43, 262; New York *Age,* October 25, 1917, p. 2; July 6, 1918, pp. 1,7; May 24, 1919, p.2; Jane Lang Scheiber and Harry N. Scheiber, "The Wilson Administration and the Wartime Mobilization of Black Americans," in Milton Cantor, ed., *Black Labor in America* (Westport, Conn., 1970), pp. 124-25.

62. *Messenger,* July 1918, pp. 8, 21-22; May-June 1919, pp. 12-13; July 1919, p. 7; August 1919, p. 10; September 1920, pp. 90-91.

63. Brisbane, *Black Vanguard,* p. 64; Fullinwider, *Mind and Mood of Black America,* pp. 95-96; Abram L. Harris, "The Negro Problem as Viewed by Negro Leaders," *Current History* 18 (June 1923): 414; Arvarh E. Strickland, *History of the Chicago Urban League* (Urbana, Ill., 1966), pp. 50-51; Scheiber and Scheiber, "Wilson Administration and Mobilization," p. 127; Emmett J. Scott, *Scott's Official History of the American Negro in the World War* (New York, 1969), pp. 367-68; Guichard Parris and Lester Brooks, *Blacks in the City: A History of the National Urban League* (Boston, 1971), p. 105; George E. Haynes, "What Negroes Think of Race Riots," *Public* 22 (August 9, 1919): 848-49; John D. Finney, Jr., "A Study of Negro Labor During and After World War I" (Ph.D. dissertation, Georgetown University, 1967), pp. 160, 183, 193ff., 209, 245ff.

64. Matthews, "After Booker T. Washington," pp. 245-46.

65. Brisbane, *Black Vanguard,* p. 133; Frazier, "American Negro's New Leaders," pp. 57-59; Harris, "Negro Problem as Viewed by Negro

Leaders," p. 418; Bond, "Negro Leadership Since Washington," pp. 120-21, 129; Herbert J. Seligmann, *The Negro Faces America* (New York, 1924), p. 294.

66. Randolph, "Negro and Economic Radicalism," pp. 62-63.

67. *Messenger,* July 1918, pp. 21-22; December 1919, p. 4; March 1920, p. 3; September 1920, pp. 90-91; December 1920, pp. 174-77; July 1921, pp. 209-10.

68. Brisbane, *Black Vanguard,* pp. 62-63; Wilson Record, *Race and Radicalism: The NAACP and the Communist Party in Conflict* (Ithaca, N.Y., 1964), p. 6; Charles Flint Kellogg, *NAACP: A History of the National Association for the Advancement of Colored People. Vol. I, 1909-1920* (Baltimore, 1967), p. 291; Fox, *Guardian of Boston,* p. 140; *Crisis,* August 1921, pp. 151-52; *Messenger,* October-November 1925, p. 346; Eisenberg, "James Weldon Johnson," pp. 112, 114-20, 131-32.

69. Brisbane, *Black Vanguard,* p. 67; Strickland, *History of the Chicago Urban League,* pp. 14, 32-34, 59, 73; *Messenger,* March 1920, p. 3; Parris and Brooks, *Blacks in the City,* pp. 95-96, 152, 180-86.

70. *Messenger,* March 1920, pp. 12-13; April-May 1920, pp. 3-4; Chandler Owen to John Fitzpatrick, April 7, 1922, John Fitzpatrick Papers, Chicago Historical Society.

71. *Messenger,* September 1920, pp. 88-90.

72. Ibid., March 1922, p. 379; May 1922, pp. 407-10; June 1922, pp. 424-26; March 1923, pp. 632-33.

73. George S. Schuyler, *Black and Conservative: The Autobiography of George S. Schuyler* (New Rochelle, N.Y., 1966), p. 124.

74. *Messenger,* June 1922, pp. 429-30; February 1923, p. 589.

75. Ibid., August 1922, pp. 464-66.

76. Ibid., November 1921, p. 274; March 1923, p. 624; Schuyler, *Black and Conservative,* pp. 124, 133-34; interview, George S. Schuyler.

77. Brisbane, *Black Vanguard,* p. 62; Strickland, *History of the Chicago Urban League,* p. 78; interview, George S. Schuyler; Nancy J. Weiss, "From Black Separatism to Inter-racial Cooperation: The Origins of Organized Efforts for Racial Advancement, 1890-1920," in Barton Bernstein and Allen Matusow, eds., *Twentieth-Century America: Recent Interpretations,* 2nd. ed. (New York, 1969), pp. 66-84.

Epilogue

By 1928 the patience and morale of the Brotherhood of Sleeping Car Porters and the *Messenger* were very much strained. The AFL continued to refuse an international charter to the young union and would not grant one until 1936. Internal dissension among BSCP officers was nasty and enervating. The various ploys to force the Pullman Company to the negotiating table had all failed. The only weapon left, seemingly, was to threaten a strike, which presumably would force compulsory arbitration under the Railway Labor Act. The union gained its membership's wary endorsement and a strike date was set for early June, but the chairman of the Federal Board of Mediation, convinced that the BSCP could not bring out all the porters, would not order the desired arbitration. With all its chips gone there was nothing for the Brotherhood to do but leave the game to try to raise a new stake. The strike was called off and the BSCP soon hit rock bottom. There was almost nothing to show for three years of effort. The Pullman Company was firing right and left any who had voted to strike, while the Communist American Negro Labor Congress sniped from the sidelines that Randolph had sold out to the bourgeois AFL. The *Messenger* was one of the first casualties.

The beleaguered magazine, heavily in debt and losing money with every issue, having lost most of its readership among white liberals and much of the black middle class, having now only frightened porters to support it, managed to publish one final issue early in June before expiring. Not even the faithful could buy it—any porter seen possessing a copy was soon an ex-porter. Randolph wanted to keep the magazine going somehow, not only out of sentiment but knowing that the BSCP needed a mouthpiece to hold together the broken pieces. For two months he and Chicago organizer Milton Webster searched for the means to save it, but how could a monthly magazine be published when the BSCP headquarters had to give up its telephone and default on the electric bill? There was a source of money, a check for ten thousand dollars, signed by someone Randolph scarcely knew, with the note that he deserved a trip to Europe. The check went back by registered mail, for no sum was large enough to buy off the Brotherhood's organizer. And so the *Messenger* died of starvation. George S. Schuyler, the only paid editor at the end, found new employment in Chicago while Randolph picked up the union's pieces. For the magazine there was not even a decent funeral—there was hardly anyone left to mourn.[1]

There were two lessons from this defeat, lessons that the *Messenger* had been studying for the previous eleven years. Both had to do with strategy, and the first concerned allies. The events the magazine had viewed and interpreted made nothing clear if not the painful reality that no one could be depended on but oneself. No one of power and responsibility in American life, no organized group, took responsibility for the flaws in the economic structure. Business, which benefited immensely from the black population shift to the cities, did not concern itself with the resultant social consequences, except for an occasional paternalistic gesture by a Ford, Carnegie, Rockefeller, or Rosenwald. Business saw no value in the rational organization of labor in unions, and instead used race differences to fight unionism. Government too was uncaring. During the twenties the federal government was presumed to have no obligation, moral or legal, to do anything about unemployment relief—the prevailing constitutional interpretation on this issue dated from a veto by President Franklin Pierce in 1854!

Nor did government via the political process take one significant step toward redressing the grievances of lynching, civil discrimination, peonage, and segregation. Only from the Supreme Court did any amelioration come, and that was a pitifully slow process. Black politicians had absolutely no practical influence, and race leaders like DuBois and Moton had scarcely more. What little access to the councils of the nation blacks had did them no good. And organized labor was as uninterested in the black worker as it had been twenty years previously. In picking up the shattered pieces of the Brotherhood, Randolph perceived this more and more clearly. The movement would have to be rebuilt, but by black hands alone. Support from white organizations would be declined. Writing to Milton Webster, Randolph announced barely two months after the aborted strike that "the Brotherhood is going to rest upon its power solely. The Pullman Company is coming around, but not on account of anything else but the porters and the Brotherhood." Responding to the claim of critics that the Pullman Company would rectify porter grievances if only Randolph resigned, he told Webster that "never again will Negroes permit white people to select their leaders for them. I would make it very emphatic that upon that principle we shall not compromise, not only with respect to the Pullman porters but with any Negro movement . . . [which] stands for the self-expression and interest of Negroes by Negroes for Negroes."[2]

The second lesson was a related one, an economic lesson. Simply stated, jobs and decent incomes were prerequisites to human rights. Blacks' political and social privileges would not be secure until a firm economic floor had been laid. Randolph had come to see, in his travels ever since the first reading of Marx and Ward, that "a good weekly pay check had to be won first. Then, after the children were fed, a better fight could be waged for dignity and self-pride." Socialism taught him that the race-color question had an economic foundation, yet he knew too well that the race's leadership class scarcely grasped this crucial point. And so he knew that struggling for entry into the Republican party was not only fruitless but a reversal of priorities. So, too, was an outward-looking black nationalism as Marcus Garvey proposed. Bread-and-butter organization, starting with small groups like the Pullman porters, was the necessary first step of the climb out of the abyss. Randolph knew it would be no easy accomplishment when he willingly devoted the rest of his life to that ascent; nothing had come easy except frustration in the *Messenger* years, and the next decades brought nothing different. All he had for psychic ammunition was a belief in the ultimate success of struggle, that if he and

his compatriots worked at something long and hard enough it would
eventually bear fruit. Always the optimist, always a battler—this was the
leadership and the ideal he had to offer.[3]

What meaning is there in the *Messenger*'s decline and demise? Its cause
and crusades had not been in vain, only too soon or too visionary. Abram
Harris wrote at the dawning of the thirties that there had been all too
many obstacles to economic radicalism in the post-World War period.
The black population still clung fast to orthodoxy, conservative religious
traditions and leaders. The bourgeois, Horatio Alger mentality had articulate spokesmen and was as strong as in the days of Booker Washington.
Racial antagonisms between black and white labor contradicted at every
turn the doctrine of class consciousness and solidarity of the proletariat.
Not sparing the editorship of Owen and Randolph, Harris pointed out
tactical errors the magazine had made. Both racial journalism and practical economic reform had too often been smothered by the heavy cloak of
socialist cant. Valid criticism on occasion was negated by the vituperation
of the argument. Movements were initiated when the magazine and its
editors lacked the power to sustain them. Propaganda too frequently took
the place of constructive planning and management. But beyond these
failings Harris knew that the cultural background of the black working
class predisposed it against radical solutions or perspectives.[4]

What Harris failed to appreciate was that Randolph and Owen came
to realize most of these obstacles and shortcomings by about 1923 and
consequently attempted to change tack. They tried various methods—
intraracial solidarity between black worker and black bourgeois, interracial coalitions of white liberal and black intellectual—to make racial
journalism and practical economic reform compatible and possible. But
if there was no fertile soil for economic radicalism, there was scarcely
more in which even middle-class reform could take root. Witness the decline and hard times of the Urban League and NAACP in the twenties.
The *Messenger*'s instincts of 1917 were right: if there was ever to be a
time for the success of fundamental economic reform, that time was
during and immediately after the war. To wait until several years later
would be to throw away the race's best opportunity since Reconstruction.
If the *Messenger* had begun bourgeois in 1917, its chances would not

have been even as good as those of the NAACP for successful enactment
of basic racial reforms. Furthermore, an unsuccessful bourgeois-centered
group could hardly have turned, in 1923, to economic radicalism. Certainly the magazine made mistakes, but they were mistakes of tactics,
by and large, not of strategy. American racism, conformity and indifference, Republican Normalcy, business boom and labor depression—these
were simply overwhelming foes. That such an uncompromising periodical
lasted even eleven years is extraordinary.

From its earliest issues the magazine was characterized by flamboyance,
adventurousness, and courage, and these qualities never left it. If at times
it sank to pettiness and envy, this only proves the human fallibility of
its editors. But such blots are overshadowed by achievements, the most
significant of which was providing a forum for testing ideas and strategies
of potential value to the black community, of exploring every possible
avenue for racial advancement, every ideology, no matter how unpopular.
This was a function that no newspaper dared to perform and which no
magazine tied to an interracial protest organization would be allowed to
do. The *Messenger*'s modest readership is not a mark of insignificance.
What was discussed in its pages is an accurate tabulation of nearly every
issue of importance to black America at that time: government repression of racial militancy; civil rights; cultural pluralism and nationalism;
Africa and internationalism; unemployment and labor unions; Establishment politics; race leadership. The magazine analyzed these questions,
espoused points of view, and drew to it individuals who wished to discuss and act further. These persons were some of the brightest young
(and a few old) minds of the teens and twenties, men like Randolph
and Owen, Theophilus Lewis, George S. Schuyler, Wallace Thurman, Abram
Harris, W. A. Domingo, William N. Colson, George Frazier Miller, James
W. Ivy, Joel A. Rogers. That the magazine was important to them and
others in that day makes it important fifty years later—important both
as a cultural artifact and as a key to the trials of black life in the twentieth
century. And we might note its importance to white life as well. In the
words of Randolph: "I think that the *Messenger* magazine was a contribution, not only to Negroes, but to America. Because America needed to
really know that Negroes had the capacity and the will and the spirit
to develop an organ such as this."[5] Whites did not believe blacks possessed

this spirit, but a long line of them, from A. Mitchell Palmer and Clayton Lusk and James Byrnes to Samuel Gompers, William Green, and Robert Todd Lincoln, learned differently.

It is a rare man that can sum up his life's meaning in the space of four short sentences, but A. Philip Randolph did just that on the morning of his eightieth year.

We are creatures of history, for every historical epoch has its roots in a preceding epoch. The black militants of today are standing upon the shoulders of the 'new Negro radicals' of my day—the '20s, '30s and '40s. We stood upon the shoulders of the civil rights fighters of the Reconstruction era and they stood upon the shoulders of the black abolitionists. These are the interconnections of history.[6]

And this is the place of the *Messenger,* at a unique historical juncture, a window through which we may better see the black teens and twenties. That there was no way out for black people in those years was hardly the fault of the magazine or its chief editors. The fault lay, and still lies, elsewhere.

NOTES

1. George S. Schuyler, *Black and Conservative: The Autobiography of George S. Schuyler* (New Rochelle, N.Y., 1966), p. 165; Brailsford R. Brazeal, *The Brotherhood of Sleeping Car Porters: Its Origin and Development* (New York, 1946), pp. 56-57, 84-85, 85n; frequent correspondence between Randolph and Milton Webster, May-July 1928, Brotherhood of Sleeping Car Porters Papers, Chicago Historical Society; Saunders Redding, *The Lonesome Road: The Story of the Negro's Part in America* (Garden City, N.Y., 1958), p. 260; Jervis Anderson, "Early Voice," *New Yorker* 47 (December 9, 1972): 80-82, 87, 89, 94.

2. Walter A. Fogel, *The Negro in the Meat Industry* (Philadelphia, 1970), pp. 42-43; Anderson, "Early Voice" (December 9, 1972): 87-88; Randolph to Webster, August 27, 1928, BSCP Papers; Irving Bernstein, *The Lean Years: A History of the American Worker, 1920-33* (Baltimore, 1966), p. 241.

3. Anderson, "Early Voice" (December 16, 1972), p. 79; *A. Philip Randolph at 80: Tributes and Recollections* (New York: A. Philip Randolph Institute, 1969), p. 5; "Homage to A. Philip Randolph on his 80th Birthday," *The United Teacher* (May 4, 1969); "The Reminiscences of Benjamin F. McLaurin," Oral History Research Office, Columbia University 1962, pp. 41-42.

4. Sterling D. Spero and Abram L. Harris, *The Black Worker: The Negro and the Labor Movement* (New York, 1968), pp. 398-401.

5. Interview, A. Philip Randolph, July 13, 1972.

6. Phyl Garland, "A. Philip Randolph: Labor's Grand Old Man," *Ebony* 24 (May 1969): 31.

Bibliographic Essay

A complete bibliography would run to many pages and would be a needless repetition of the notes. Hence no attempt will be made to list all the sources consulted in this study. What I have attempted here is to list those works of an analytic character, or which provide large chunks of important evidence and detail. These are items that one might profitably consult first; should the reader wish additional depth, works cited in the footnotes can then be perused. For convenience this essay is divided into primary and secondary sources, although I am well aware of the arbitrariness of these divisions.

PRIMARY SOURCES

Interviews and Oral Histories

This study profited enormously from the reminiscences and memoirs of individuals who worked for the *Messenger* or viewed its career first-hand. The late Arna Bontemps and James W. Ivy both granted me extensive interviews and in addition provided leads on others to consult. Theophilus Lewis, Ernest Rice McKinney, A. Philip Randolph, and George S. Schuyler also gave generously of their time. The oral histories of Schuyler, McKinney, and Benjamin F. McLaurin, taped by the Oral History Research Office of Columbia University (1962, 1961, and 1962, respectively) may be consulted for details on the period of the teens and twenties. Correspondence with Roger Baldwin, Thomas L. Dabney, Miriam Allen De Ford, and Scott Nearing provided additional incidents and insights.

Manuscript Collections

The Manuscript Division of the Library of Congress houses the Brotherhood of Sleeping Car Porters Papers and the National Association for the Advancement of Colored People Papers. The NAACP Papers do not deal in particular with the *Messenger,* but they provide information on countless events of these years. The Brotherhood of Sleeping Car Porters Papers at the Chicago Historical Society have more material on the *Messenger* than those in the Library of Congress. Also in Chicago are the John Fitzpatrick Papers, which, again, shed background light. The James Weldon Johnson Collection at Yale University includes the papers of Wallace Thurman, Langston Hughes, and Carl Van Vechten, all of which provided occasional details to illuminate the *Messenger*'s role in the Harlem Renaissance. William Pickens's papers, in the Schomburg Collection (New York Public Library, 135th Street Branch) were also of some use, although the Schomburg was most important to this study as the primary reference library. The Tamiment Institute in New York City possesses copies of three pamphlets authored by Chandler Owen and A. Philip Randolph in 1917. Correspondence between the two editors, reflecting chiefly the last years of Owen's life, is in the possession of the A. Philip Randolph Institute in New York.

Documents

The Red Scare concern over black radicalism can be seen clearly in various federal documents: U.S. Department of Justice, *Annual Report of the Attorney General of the United States for the Year 1920* (Washington, D.C., 1920); U.S. Senate, *Investigation Activities of the Department of Justice,* 66th Cong., 1st Sess., Sen. Doc. 153 (Washington, D.C., 1919); U.S. House of Representatives, *Attorney General A. Mitchell Palmer on*

Charges Made Against Department of Justice by Louis F. Post and Others. Hearings Before the Committee on Rules, House of Representatives, 66th Cong., 2nd Sess., Pt. 1 (Washington, D.C., 1920); and in the *Congressional Record,* 66th Cong., 1st and 2nd Sess. (Washington, D.C., 1919). The most prominent of the state investigations of radicalism is detailed in New York Legislature, Joint Legislative Committee Investigating Seditious Activities, *Revolutionary Radicalism: Its History, Purpose and Tactics, with an Exposition and Discussion of the Steps Being Taken and Required to Curb It,* 4 vols. (Albany, 1920). The race riots of 1919 should be viewed in part as an offshoot of the Red Scare, and the best analysis of one of these conflicts is the report of the Chicago Commission on Race Relations, *The Negro in Chicago: A Study of Race Relations and a Race Riot* (Chicago, 1922).

Official concern over the loyalty, or lack of loyalty, of the black population during World War I is mirrored in U.S. Senate, *Brewing and Liquor Interests and German and Bolshevik Propaganda. Report and Hearings of the Sub-Committee on the Judiciary,* 3 vols., 66th Cong., 1st Sess., Sen. Doc. 62 (Washington, D.C., 1919); and U.S. Senate, *Treaty of Peace With Germany. Hearings Before the Committee on Foreign Relations, United States Senate,* 66th Cong., 1st Sess., Sen. Doc. 106 (Washington, D.C., 1919).

Economic conditions impinging on the rapidly urbanizing black population in the teens and twenties can be gauged from the following: Alba M. Edwards, *A Social-Economic Grouping of the Gainful Workers of the United States* (Washington, D.C., 1938); U.S. Department of Labor, Division of Negro Economics, *The Negro at Work During the World War and During Reconstruction: Statistics, Problems, and Policies Relating to the Greater Inclusion of Negro Wage Earners in American Industry and Agriculture* (Washington, D.C., 1921); U.S. Department of Commerce, Bureau of the Census, *Fifteenth Census of the United States: 1930, Unemployment,* Vol. 2 (Washington, D.C., 1935); and U.S. Department of Commerce, Bureau of the Census, *Negroes in the United States: 1920-32* (Washington, D.C., 1935).

Newspapers and Periodicals

Three periodicals cover nearly the entire period from the beginning of World War I to the onset of the Depression: the *Messenger,* the *Crisis,* and *Opportunity.* Taken together they present a more easily accessible

picture of the political, economic, cultural, and nationalist concerns of
the race than can be gotten from the weekly newspapers. These weekly
newspapers, however, provide a wealth of detail not found in the magazines and cannot therefore be overlooked. In addition they provide a
fuller picture of the social life of the black community. For this study
the New York *Age* was indispensable, and the Chicago *Defender,* Baltimore *Afro-American,* and Washington *Bee* were important sources for
certain topics. The New York *Times* was surveyed for the entire period
and yielded considerable material on white reactions to black militancy,
white fears over black disloyalty, and the inability of whites to accept
with equanimity the New Negro spirit. The ambivalent response of whites
to a black role in World War I can also be gauged by using the clipping
file on that subject in the NAACP Papers in the Library of Congress.

The white periodicals of the day yield a rich harvest of commentary
on the new mood, cultural developments, and nationalist tendencies in
black life, from the perspectives of both white and black commentators.
A careful perusal of the *Reader's Guide to Periodical Literature* will un-
cover many articles useful in researching practically any topic in this
period. Nearly every major magazine probed the meaning of the race
riots and postwar militancy, many foreseeing the approach of race warfare; notes in Chapter 3 should be consulted for citations too numerous to list here. The *New Republic* and *Nation* wrote frequently during
the war and Red Scare on threats to free speech and civil liberties that
both black and white radicals faced. The AFL's magazine is a convenient
source for that union's self-satisfied view of its "attempts" to bring black
workers into the ranks of organized labor; see particularly "Negro Wage
Earners," *American Federationist* 32 (October 1925); and John P. Frey,
"Attempts to Organize Negro Workers," *American Federationist* 36
(March 1929). Dissenting views are provided in Thomas L. Dabney,
"Negro Workers at the Crossroads," *Labor Age* 16 (February 1927);
Dabney, "Organized Labor's Attitude Toward Negro Workers," *South-
ern Workman* 57 (August 1928); and Abram L. Harris, "Negro Labor's
Quarrel with White Workingmen," *Current History* 24 (September 1926).

Literary Digest is a useful tool for assessing public opinion as expressed
in newspapers countrywide and helps to prevent the distortion possible
from concentrating solely on Eastern organs of news and opinion. *Current
History* maintained an interest in developments in black life and occasional-

ly provided white America with badly needed information on important black figures besides Marcus Garvey, Robert R. Moton, and W. E. B. DuBois. See particularly E. Franklin Frazier, "The American Negro's New Leaders," *Current History* 28 (April 1928); Abram L. Harris, "The Negro Problem as Viewed by Negro Leaders," *Current History* 18 (June 1923); and Eric D. Walrond, "The New Negro Faces America," *Current History* 17 (February 1923); as well as Kelly Miller, "After Marcus Garvey-- What of the Negro?", *Contemporary Review* 131 (April 1927); Alain Locke, "The Negro Speaks for Himself," *Survey* 52 (April 15, 1924); and Horace Mann Bond, "Negro Leadership Since Washington," *South Atlantic Quarterly* 24 (April 1925). White America seemed especially curious about Marcus Garvey, and many national magazines provided varying views, depending on whether the author was black or white, although none was entirely sympathetic to the West Indian. Whites were also apprised of the fact that the black press had found a new voice and was not simply an important source of Negro opinion, but a major community institution. See Eugene Gordon, "The Negro Press," *American Mercury* 8 (June 1926); Gordon, "The Negro Press," *Annals of the American Academy of Political and Social Science* 140 (November 1928); and Charles S. Johnson, "Rise of the Negro Magazine," *Journal of Negro History* 13 (January 1928).

Books

There are several important works of an autobiographical nature that describe and analyze the years in which the *Messenger* published—but unfortunately none from the pen of Chandler Owen or A. Philip Randolph, although the latter is at work on his memoirs. One does get, however, considerable detail on the magazine and its day-to-day life from George S. Schuyler, *Black and Conservative: The Autobiography of George S. Schuyler* (New Rochelle, N.Y., 1966), which amplifies on many of the themes introduced in his oral history taped by Columbia University. Horace R. Cayton, *Long Old Road* (Seattle, 1964), describes a youth spent in the years of flux under discussion here, as does William L. Patterson, *The Man Who Cried Genocide: An Autobiography* (New York, 1971). The three autobiographical or quasi-autobiographical works of W. E. B. DuBois describe events parallel to those the *Messenger* participated in; see *Dark-*

water: Voices From Within the Veil (New York, 1920); *Dusk of Dawn:
An Essay Toward an Autobiography of a Race Concept* (New York, 1968
[1940]); and *The Autobiography of W. E. B. DuBois: A Soliloquy on
Viewing My Life from the Last Decade of Its First Century* (New York,
1969). Other perspectives on the NAACP and the postwar struggle for
civil rights may be found in James Weldon Johnson, *Along This Way*
(New York, 1933), and Walter White, *A Man Called White* (Bloomington,
Ind., 1970 [1948]). Langston Hughes, *The Big Sea* (New York, 1940),
and Claude McKay, *A Long Way From Home* (New York, 1937), view
events largely from the cultural perspective, although the latter also
describes its author's radical experiences in this period.

Several white commentators wrote perceptive volumes detailing various
aspects of black life in the late teens and the twenties; most were in one
way or another personally involved in either radicalism or efforts to improve racial conditions. Mary White Ovington, *The Walls Came Tumbling
Down* (New York, 1970 [1947]), and Herbert J. Seligmann, *The Negro
Faces America,* 2nd ed. (New York, 1924), both wrote from the perspective of NAACP service. Scott Nearing, *Black America* (New York, 1969
[1929]), wrote from a radical stance. Robert T. Kerlin, *The Voice of
the Negro: 1919* (New York, 1920), is about the best introduction to
New Negro militancy through a wide variety of primary sources that
can be found; its author was a sympathetic professor of English who lost
his position in a Southern college for obvious reasons. Frederick G.
Detweiler, *The Negro Press in the United States* (Chicago, 1922), admirably supplements Kerlin's volume and again focuses on the more militant
aspects of black expression.

The National Urban League concerned itself extensively with the
problems of black labor in the period between World War I and the
Depression, and two of its publications in particular should be consulted:
Department of Research and Investigations, National Urban League,
Negro Membership in American Labor Unions (New York, 1930); and
Charles Lionel Franklin, *The Negro Labor Unionist of New York: Prob-
lems and Conditions Among Negroes in the Labor Unions in Manhattan
with Special Reference to the N.R.A. and Post-N.R.A. Situations* (New
York, 1936). The best overview of labor conditions in this period remains
the splendid work of Sterling D. Spero and Abram L. Harris, *The Black
Worker: The Negro and the Labor Movement* (New York, 1968 [1931]).

One should also consult Lorenzo J. Greene and Carter G. Woodson, *The Negro Wage Earner* (Washington, 1930), and Charles H. Wesley, *Negro Labor in the United States, 1850-1925: A Study in American Economic History* (New York, 1967 [1927]). For the problems and plight of black businessmen, two primary sources are Abram L. Harris, *The Negro as Capitalist: A Study of Banking and Business Among American Negroes* (Gloucester, Mass., 1968 [1936]), and J. H. Harmon, Jr., Arnett G. Lindsay, and Carter G. Woodson, *The Negro as a Business Man* (College Park, Md., 1969 [1929]).

Primary sources on World War I of importance to this study came mostly from newspapers. However, three war histories written soon after the conclusion of hostilities have some value: Kelly Miller, *Kelly Miller's History of the World War for Human Rights* (Washington, D.C., 1919); Emmett J. Scott, *Scott's Official History of the American Negro in the World War* (New York, 1969 [1919]); and W. Allison Sweeney, *History of the American Negro in the Great World War* (New York, 1969 [1919]); for additional homefront details, see James Weldon Johnson, *Black Manhattan* (New York, 1969 [1930]).

In an analysis of Marcus Garvey, three volumes are particularly important (in addition to the *Messenger,* the *Crisis,* and Garvey's own weekly *Negro World,* of which only scattered copies of pre-1923 issues have survived). See Amy Jacques Garvey, *Garvey and Garveyism* (Kingston, Jamaica, 1963), and the same individual's *Philosophy and Opinions of Marcus Garvey,* 2 vols. (New York, 1969 [1923, 1925]). Valuable background on West Indians in the United States is provided by Ira De Augustine Reid, *The Negro Immigrant: His Background, Characteristics and Social Adjustment, 1899-1937* (New York, 1969 [1939]).

To supplement the account of NAACP activities given in the *Crisis,* one may consult the Association's *Annual Reports* (New York).

SECONDARY SOURCES

Periodicals

Biographical data about persons connected with the *Messenger* have until the very recent past been sketchy and incomplete. A major gap was filled, and admirably, by a series of articles by Jervis Anderson, "Early Voice," *New Yorker* 47 (December 2, 9, 16, 1972); these articles were later published in book form: Jervis Anderson, *A. Philip Randolph: A Biographical Portrait* (New York, 1973). Several *Messenger* staff members are the subject of short articles. See the present author's biographies of Chandler Owen and Robert W. Bagnall in Rayford Logan, ed., *Dictionary of American Negro Biography* (New York, 1977), and "Theophilus Lewis and the Theater of the Harlem Renaissance," in Arna Bontemps, ed., *The Harlem Renaissance Remembered* (New York, 1972); the Bontemps volume also includes Mae G. Henderson, "Portrait of Wallace Thurman." W. Burghardt Turner, "Joel Augustus Rogers: An Afro-American Historian," *Negro History Bulletin* 35 (February 1973), describes one of the long-time *Messenger* columnists. For a useful comparison between the journalism of the *Messenger* and *Crisis,* see Elliott M. Rudwick, "W. E. B. DuBois in the Role of *Crisis* Editor," *Journal of Negro History* 25 (July 1940).

Several articles help illuminate radical activities during and immediately after the World War. See Sally M. Miller, "The Socialist Party and the Negro, 1901-20," *Journal of Negro History* 56 (July 1971); R. Laurence Moore, "Flawed Fraternity—American Socialist Response to the Negro, 1909-12," *Historian* 32 (November 1969); J. M. Pawa, "Black Radicals and White Spies: Harlem, 1919," *Negro History Bulletin* 35 (October 1972); and Jane Lang Scheiber and Harry N. Scheiber, "The Wilson Administration and the Wartime Mobilization of Black Americans, 1917-1918," in Milton Cantor, ed., *Black Labor in America* (Westport, Conn., 1970). For an interesting comparison, see W. F. Elkins, " 'Unrest among the Negroes': A British Document of 1919," *Science and Society* 32 (Winter 1968). A provocative study, although not totally applicable to the white response to the New Negro, is Richard Hofstadter, "The Paranoid Style in American Politics," in David Brion Davis, ed., *The Fear of Conspiracy: Images of Un-American Subversion from the Revolution to the Present* (Ithaca, N.Y., 1971).

The political options open to black Americans in the postwar years, and the responses of established black leadership, are examined in several articles. John L. Blair, "A Time for Parting: The Negro during the Coolidge Years," *Journal of American Studies* 3 (1969); August Meier and Elliott

Rudwick, "The Rise of Segregation in the Federal Bureaucracy, 1900-1930," *Phylon* 28 (Summer 1967); Richard Sherman, "The Harding Administration and the Negro: An Opportunity Lost," *Journal of Negro History* 49 (July 1964); Sherman, "Republicans and Negroes: The Lessons of Normalcy," *Phylon* 27 (Spring 1966); and Nancy J. Weiss, "From Black Separatism to Interracial Cooperation: The Origins of Organized Efforts for Racial Advancement, 1890-1920," in Barton J. Bernstein and Allen J. Matusow, eds., *Twentieth-Century America: Recent Interpretations* (New York, 1969), all describe various political options. The responses of members of the black Establishment to some of these options are discussed in Pete Daniel, "Black Power in the 1920's: The Case of Tuskegee Veterans Hospital," *Journal of Southern History* 36 (August 1970), and Bernard Eisenberg, "Kelly Miller: The Negro Leader As a Marginal Man," *Journal of Negro History* 45 (July 1960).

Black-white labor relations are examined in Melvin Dubofsky, "Organized Labor in New York City and the First World War, 1914-1918," *New York History* 42 (October 1961); Philip S. Foner, "The IWW and the Black Worker," *Journal of Negro History* 55 (January 1970); and William M. Tuttle, Jr., "Labor Conflict and Racial Violence: The Black Worker in Chicago, 1894-1919," in Cantor, *Black Labor in America.* Two articles analyzing the Talented Tenth's response to Marcus Garvey are Wilson Record, "The Negro Intellectual and Negro Nationalism," *Social Forces* 33 (October 1954), and Charles W. Simmons, "The Negro Intellectual's Criticism of Garveyism," *Negro History Bulletin* 25 (November 1961).

Books

Several overviews provide convenient introductions to black life in the first third of the present century. Still indispensable is Gunnar Myrdal, *An American Dilemma: The Negro Problem and Modern Democracy,* 2 vols. (New York, 1944); two recent interpretations are Robert H. Brisbane, *The Black Vanguard: Origins of the Negro Social Revolution 1900-1960* (Valley Forge, Pa., 1970), and S.P. Fullinwider, *The Mind and Mood of Black America: 20th Century Thought* (Homewood, Ill., 1969). The standard work on black thought and intellectual life of the pre-World War I period remains August Meier, *Negro Thought in America: 1880-*

1915 (Ann Arbor, Mich., 1963). Political currents may be assayed in
Harold F. Gosnell, *Negro Politicians: The Rise of Negro Politics in Chicago*
(Chicago, 1967 [1935]); Henry Lee Moon, *Balance of Power: The Negro
Vote* (Garden City, N.Y., 1949); Roi Ottley, *"New World A-Coming":
Inside Black America* (New York, 1968 [1943]); and Elbert Lee Tatum,
The Changed Political Thought of the Negro, 1915-1940 (New York,
1951). Descriptions of the social conditions and consequences of the
never-ceasing northward migrations can be found in two excellent his-
tories, Gilbert Osofsky, *Harlem: The Making of a Ghetto; Negro New
York, 1890-1930* (New York, 1966), and Allan H. Spear, *Black Chicago:
The Making of a Negro Ghetto, 1890-1920* (Chicago, 1967), as well as
in the older work of St. Clair Drake and Horace R. Cayton, *Black Metropolis: A Study of Negro Life in a Northern City,* 2 vols. (New York, 1962
[1945]); for pre-World War I New York, see Seth M. Scheiner, *Negro
Mecca: A History of the Negro in New York City, 1865-1920* (New York,
1965). Three histories of civil rights organizations help round out the
picture of black life and thought in this period. Charles Flint Kellogg,
*NAACP: A History of the National Association for the Advancement
of Colored People. Vol. 1, 1909-1920* (Baltimore, 1967), is comprehensive for the Association's first decade, but a full history of its activities
in the twenties is still to be written. For the National Urban League, see
Arvarh E. Strickland, *History of the Chicago Urban League* (Urbana,
Ill., 1966), and Guichard Parris and Lester Brooks, *Blacks in the City:
A History of the National Urban League* (Boston, 1971).

None of the standard histories of antiwar activity during World War
I deal satisfactorily, if at all, with black objections, although Frank L.
Grubbs, Jr., *The Struggle for Labor Loyalty: Gompers, the A.F.L. and
the Pacifists, 1917-1920* (Durham, N.C., 1968), does provide some helpful background. A recent volume, Arthur E. Barbeau and Florette Henri,
The Unknown Soldiers: Black American Troops in World War I (Philadelphia, 1974), is a competent survey of the race's military role although
it, too, slights antiwar activities. There is a wealth of books on the Red
Scare and the attendant erosion of civil liberties, and the following were
particularly useful: Lawrence H. Chamberlain, *Loyalty and Legislative
Action: A Survey of Activity by the New York State Legislature, 1919-
1949* (Ithaca, N.Y., 1951); Stanley Coben, *A. Mitchell Palmer: Politician*

(New York, 1963); Julian F. Jaffe, *Crusade Against Radicalism: New York During the Red Scare, 1914-1924* (Port Washington, N.Y., 1972); Paul L. Murphy, *The Meaning of Freedom of Speech: First Amendment Freedoms from Wilson to FDR* (Westport, Conn., 1972); and Harry N. Scheiber, *The Wilson Administration and Civil Liberties, 1917-1921* (Ithaca, N.Y., 1960).

Socialist, Communist, and other left-wing activities among the black population in the World War and postwar period are treated in works covering several points on the spectrum. Wilson Record's two books, *The Negro and the Communist Party* (Chapel Hill, N.C., 1951) and *Race and Radicalism: The NAACP and the Communist Party in Conflict* (Ithaca, N.Y., 1964), are written from a position unsympathetic to Communism, as is, in greater extreme, William A. Nolan, *Communism versus the Negro* (Chicago, 1951). Theodore Draper, *American Communism and Soviet Russia* (New York, 1960), gives a good account of the African Blood Brotherhood and black converts to Communism in the early twenties. James W. Ford, *The Negro and the Democratic Front* (New York, 1938), sketches black-Communist relations from the perspective of the latter. The best analysis of the Socialist party's relations with the black population in the wartime period is James Weinstein, *The Decline of Socialism in America: 1912-1925* (New York, 1967).

Biographical studies of important black figures are increasing in number with pleasing results, although the lives of several others are yet unrecorded. For DuBois, see Francis L. Broderick, *W. E. B. DuBois: Negro Leader in a Time of Crisis* (Stanford, Cal., 1959), and Elliott M. Rudwick, *W. E. B. DuBois: Propagandist of the Negro Protest* (New York, 1968). Of three full biographies of Garvey, Edmund David Cronon, *Black Moses: The Story of Marcus Garvey and the Universal Negro Improvement Association* (Madison, Wis., 1955), is still useful, but should be supplemented with the excellent work of Theodore Vincent, *Black Power and the Garvey Movement* (Berkeley, Cal., n.d. [1972]); Elton C. Fax, *Garvey: The Story of a Pioneer Black Nationalist* (New York, 1972), adds little that is new in either detail or interpretation. The impact of Garveyism on blacks can also be gauged from Theodore Draper, *The Rediscovery of Black Nationalism* (New York, 1970), and Harold R. Isaacs, *The New World of Negro Americans* (New York, 1967). Other biographies of value include Jervis

Anderson, *A. Philip Randolph: A Biographical Portrait* (New York, 1973); Stephen R. Fox, *The Guardian of Boston: William Monroe Trotter* (New York, 1970); William Hardin Hughes and Frederick D. Patterson, eds., *Robert Russa Moton of Hampton and Tuskegee* (Chapel Hill, N.C., 1956); Eugene Levy, *James Weldon Johnson: Black Leader, Black Voice* (Chicago, 1973); Emma Lou Thornbrough, *T. Thomas Fortune: Militant Journalist* (Chicago, 1972); and several dissertations to be noted below. For biographical sketches of a vast number of individuals, Richard Bardolph, *The Negro Vanguard* (New York, 1959), is a valuable tool. Biographies of persons figuring prominently in the Harlem Renaissance can be found in Arna Bontemps, *The Harlem Renaissance Remembered* (New York, 1972), and to a lesser extent in Robert A. Bone, *The Negro Novel in America,* rev. ed. (New Haven, Conn., 1965). The best introduction to the Renaissance is the splendid work of Nathan Huggins, *Harlem Renaissance* (New York, 1971); provocative opinions on black cultural developments in the twenties, not always valid, can be found in Harold Cruse, *The Crisis of the Negro Intellectual* (New York, 1967).

A good place to begin to assay the economic life of the race, including the prospects for both the laboring man and the capitalist, are the "Racial Policies of American Industry Report Series" and the "Studies of Negro Employment" series, both sponsored by the Wharton School and published by the University of Pennsylvania Press, now numbering nearly forty volumes total. See the notes to Chapter 6 for specific citations. Background on the labor situation in the postwar years can be gotten from Irving Bernstein, *The Lean Years: A History of the American Worker, 1920-1933* (Baltimore, 1963), and John H. M. Laslett, *Labor and the Left: A Study of Socialist and Radical Influences in the American Labor Movement, 1881-1924* (New York, 1970). More specific commentary on black labor will be found in Brailsford R. Brazeal, *The Brotherhood of Sleeping Car Porters: Its Origin and Development* (New York, 1946); Horace R. Cayton and George S. Mitchell, *Black Workers and the New Unions* (Chapel Hill, N.C., 1939); and Herbert R. Northrup, *Organized Labor and the Negro* (New York, 1944). Richard Sterner, *The Negro's Share: A Study of Income, Consumption, Housing and Public Assistance* (New York, 1943), and Gunnar Myrdal, *An American Dilemma,* should also be consulted for this topic.

Dissertations

Of the several dissertations used in this study, six were of particular value. Three deal with various aspects of black labor: Myland R. Brown, "The IWW and the Negro Worker" (Ed.D. dissertation, Ball State University, 1968); John D. Finney, Jr., "A Study of Negro Labor During and After World War I" (Ph.D. dissertation, Georgetown University, 1967); and J. A. Gross, "The NAACP, the AFL-CIO and the Negro Worker" (Ph.D. dissertation, University of Wisconsin, 1962). Three studies deal with black leadership: Sheldon Bernard Avery, "Up from Washington: William Pickens and the Negro Struggle for Equality, 1900-1954" (Ph.D. dissertation, University of Oregon, 1970); Bernard Eisenberg, "James Weldon Johnson and the National Association for the Advancement of Colored People, 1916-1934" (Ph.D. dissertation, Columbia University, 1968); and especially Carl S. Matthews, "After Booker T. Washington: The Search for a New Negro Leadership, 1915-1925" (Ph.D. dissertation, University of Virginia, 1971), which has a good analysis of the white role in the creation of black "leadership." While not of great value to the present work, Dorothy Deloris Boone, "A Historical Review and a Bibliography of Selected Negro Magazines, 1910-1969" (Ed.D. dissertation, University of Michigan, 1970), is of use in the study of black journalism.

Index

International Ladies Garment
Workers Union, 187, 191-92
International League of Darker
Peoples, 135
International Longshoremens
Association, 180
Interracial labor cooperation,
prospects for, 190-91
Ivy, James W., 25, 226; on *Mes-
senger* staff, 28-29, 274

Jamaica, Marcus Garvey's pros-
pects for success in, 155
Jim Crow legislation, 88
Johnson, Charles S., 25, 92, 106,
128
Johnson, Georgia Douglass, 118,
122, 126, 127; *An Autumn
Love Cycle*, 127
Johnson, Helene, 118, 122, 126
Johnson, Henry Lincoln, 239,
240, 241
Johnson, James Weldon, xv, 24,
254; on black attitudes in the Red
Scare, 93-94; caricatured by the
Messenger, 73; on Marcus Garvey,
142, 163; on musical revues, 111;
on World War I, 9, 14-15
Johnson, "Mushmouth," 243-44
Jones, Eugene Kinkle, 25; quoted, 60
Jones, "Teenan," 244
Justice Department: anti-radical
propaganda, 78; anti-radical
raids, 78-79; on black dissent
and anti-war expression, 23;
compared to the Lusk Committee, 84-85; view of Garvey
movement, 95-96; view of native
communists, 75-76. *See also*
Palmer, A. Mitchell

Kempton, Murray, 35
Kerlin, Robert T., 43, 47; *Voice
of the Negro: 1919*, 43
King, Martin Luther, Jr., 99
Krigwa little theater group, 126
Ku Klux Klan, 83, 94, 95, 155,
166, 190, 225, 233, 234; aids
Perry Howard, 241, 242;
Garvey's relations with, 136-37,
157-58, 174; and human hand
threat, 140; as a political issue
in the twenties, 237
Kuusinen, Otto, 96

Lafayette Players, 116
Lafayette Theater, 108, 109, 260
LaFollette, Robert, 225, 232,
260; candidacy in 1924, 233-34;
on the Klan, 237
Laundry workers, New York
City, 187
Lee, Algernon, 260
Lester, George B., 8
Lewis, John L., 195
Lewis, Theophilus, 120, 125, 274;
early life, 108; on the dignity of
black actors, 113; on black playwrights, 112; on little theater
groups, 114-15; on black revues
and comedies, 109-111; on prospects for a national black theater,
115; on the black theater's relation to Broadway, 116; on
Harlem's white-owned theaters,
114; on the tastes of black
audiences, 113, 116; on white-
authored plays on black themes,
112; as literary critic, 117-19;
on black poetry, 118, 130n;
praised by contemporaries, 109,

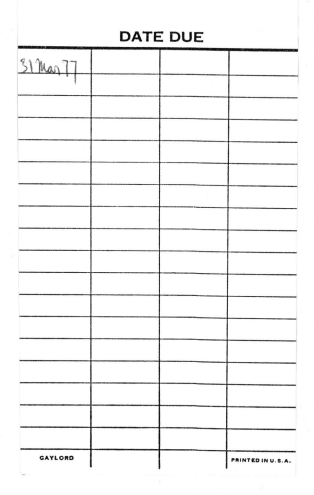

DATE DUE

31 Mar 77			
GAYLORD			PRINTED IN U.S.A.